GREAT BRITAIN
1900–1965

Great Britain
1900–1965

ANTHONY WOOD

LONGMAN

LONGMAN GROUP LIMITED
*Longman House, Burnt Mill, Harlow, Essex CM20 2JE, England
and Associated Companies throughout the World.*

First published 1978
Fourth impression 1984

ISBN 0 582 35145 (Cased)
ISBN 0 582 35146 4 (Limp)

Printed in Malaysia
by Art Printing Works Sdn. Bhd., Kuala Lumpur.

CONTENTS

Part IV

THE PURSUIT OF RECOVERY 1922–1929

Part V

DEPRESSION AND THE DICTATORS
1929–1939

Part VI

THE SECOND WORLD WAR 1939–1945

Part VII

THE EMERGENCE OF CONTEMPORARY BRITAIN

MAPS

PREFACE

The purpose of this book is to provide the student with an outline of the history of Great Britain during the first sixty-five years of the twentieth century. In itself the date 1900 is of no particular significance, but it is numerically neat and does allow some elaboration of the period immediately before the First World War. This seemed an essential starting-point, since it contains the antecedents of most of the issues that were later to arise; it also supplies the background against which one can gauge the full extent of the remarkable changes that have taken place in the course of the century.

The choice of the closing date is rather more debatable. I felt that the 1950s and 1960s positively demanded inclusion within the span of the story, but the study of the immediate past naturally presents certain problems. Original sources are not fully available and, as Lord Acton said, the living do not give up their secrets with the candour of the dead. Still, they are perhaps less reticent than they used to be and there is no lack of material on which to draw. A greater complication is that the closeness in time makes it difficult to achieve a sense of perspective and there is consequently a danger of drifting into an undifferentiated list of legislation and social statistics. The years after 1951, however, do have their own distinctive features in relation to the first half of the twentieth century, and I believe that it should be possible to sketch a fairly broad survey of this period, even at the risk of succumbing to contemporary prejudice. This is what I have attempted in the last two chapters.

I would like to take this opportunity of thanking the Master and Fellows of Churchill College, Cambridge, for all their kindness and hospitality during my term there as a Schoolmaster Fellow Commoner, when I was able to begin work on this book. I also wish to thank Mrs Stella E. Batt, who typed the entire manuscript. Lastly, I am most grateful for all the help that I received from my daughter Liisa in drawing the maps and from my wife in preparing the index. They have had to live with this book rather longer than usual and accordingly I dedicate it to both of them.

Winchester, 1977   A.C.W.

I

The Roots of the
Twentieth Century

I

The Edwardian Scene

There was very nearly no Edwardian era at all. When King Edward VII succeeded his mother, Queen Victoria, in January 1901, he was already fifty-nine and could easily have died from an operation for appendicitis shortly before his coronation. As it was, he only reigned for nine and a half years, and it is perhaps strange that his name should lend itself to so brief a period, not particularly distinct from the years that had immediately preceded it. The old Queen, however, had spent the last part of her life in the seclusion of widowhood, whereas Edward appeared openly to relish the trappings of monarchy. The throne came once more into the public eye and the contrast to his mother was sufficiently sharp to give Edward's reign its own personal flavour. Indeed, the corpulent figure of an elderly *bon viveur* was not an inappropriate symbol of the final flowering of Victorian opulence.

In 1901 the population of the United Kingdom stood at approximately 41·5 million, of whom three-quarters were resident in England and Wales. Their numbers were still rising. The drop in the death rate after 1900, markedly in infant mortality, outweighed the effects of a birth rate in decline since 1870, and despite the departure of 3 million emigrants in the first decade of the twentieth century, the population had reached 45 million by 1911.

Rather less than a quarter of these still lived in rural conditions. In 1900 London had 6·5 million inhabitants; Glasgow, Liverpool, Manchester and Birmingham were each well over 500,000, and altogether some seventy-four cities could claim more than 50,000. Towns had become encased in dormitory suburbs, and the development of public transport had ushered in the age of the commuter. In London, whose first underground railway dated back to 1863, there were 3,000 motor-buses by 1913, but elsewhere the electric tramcar and the horse-drawn bus were the mainstay of Edwardian civic life.

This urban concentration had done little to create a general homogeneity. The principal feature of Edwardian England was a profound social inequality, emphasized by a strong sense of class distinction. It was like some great iceberg, a tip of affluence protruding above the submerged mass. This was nothing new. Early commentators, such as Disraeli and Matthew Arnold, had already remarked on the wide gulf between rich and poor. In 1905, however, a Liberal MP, L. Chiozza Money, attempted a more precise definition of the situation in financial terms, calculating that a third of the national income was in the possession of 1·25 million people; even a half of it was held by no more than 5 million, while the other half was shared between the remaining 38 million.

It is the richest section of society which is most commonly associated with the Edwardian period. Landed families and industrial and financial magnates could enjoy the magnificence of their country houses, staffed by armies of domestics who fostered their own sense of hierarchy in the servants' hall. The loosening of Victorian restraints now allowed the vast entertainments and gargantuan meals described in V. Sackville-West's novel *The Edwardians*. Their wealth lay scattered across the country in the rent rolls of great estates and investments in the City; in 1873 some 4,000 people possessed approximately half the land of England and Wales, and one-third of that belonged to 400 members of the peerage; nine families owned the five square miles of inner London.

The general nature of this upper class was aristocratic, but it was not a totally exclusive caste. At this level English society had for a long time been relatively mobile. The last years of the nineteenth century had seen a considerable *entrée* by the new rich, and of the 246 titles created between 1886 and 1914 some seventy were gained by representatives of recent wealth. 'Was he born in what the radical papers call the purple of commerce,' asked Lady Bracknell in Oscar Wilde's *The Importance of Being Earnest*, 'or did he rise from the ranks of the aristocracy?' Some of the older families put it more bluntly. 'Well,' said the Duke of Devonshire on hearing that his daughter wished to marry a young publisher, Harold Macmillan, 'books is better than beer,' but the gibes about the 'beerage' were a little unfair, since brewers were hardly numerous in the House of Lords, and in all no more than one-sixth of the peers were first generation from a non-landed background.

Below this élite were the gentry and the wealthier salaried classes. Of the successful professional men some 47,000 earned over £2,000 a year, while a slightly larger group lay in the region of £1,000. From there the social ladder ran down through the gradations of the lower middle classes whose income above £160 put them within the reach of income tax at eightpence (3½p) in the pound. This was the world of Mr Pooter in *The Diary of a Nobody* and of the young men in Jerome K. Jerome's

Three Men in a Boat. They were the occupants of the small suburban villas that now surrounded the big towns, many with their own resident maid—the accepted hallmark of a modest gentility. This section of society was made up predominantly of many types of clerk, since recent years had brought an enormous increase in the number of white-collar workers. It included, as well, shopkeepers, some senior shop assistants and highly skilled workers, such as engineers; and despite a salary of only £75, 190,000 elementary schoolteachers were also reckoned to come within this bracket.

Below all these lay the 38 million who shared the other half of the national income: again, not an amorphous mass, but a spectrum as variegated as the classes above them. One of the greatest divides of the time, which had recently become even wider, was that between skilled and unskilled workers. The skilled worker earned on average £2 a week and had the protection of the various contributory schemes organized by his trade union; the unskilled averaged £1 a week. The distinctions were keenly observed and one writer, Robert Roberts, describing his upbringing in a Salford slum at this time, mentions the 'public houses, where workers other than craftsmen could be frozen or flatly ordered out of those rooms in which journeymen foregathered. Each part of a tavern had its status rating; indeed, "he's only a taproom man" stood as a common slur'.[1]

In a famous survey of living conditions in York, published in 1901, Seebohm Rowntree attempted to define a poverty line—an income which, in relation to the size of the family, would just provide the rent and a bare minimum of food and fuel. Rowntree's dietary, which included no meat, vegetables or fruit, was devised before any firm knowledge of vitamins had been established and his poverty line was hardly adequate to sustain human life. Nevertheless, according to his findings 15 per cent of the wage-earners of York were living below it and a further 28 per cent could not manage to organize their family budget to cover the basic requirements he had specified. Throughout the country roughly a quarter of all male wage-earners lay below this line, and it was small wonder that 11 per cent of the children attending elementary schools in London were reckoned to be suffering from malnutrition; in 1900 the requisite height for Army recruits had to be lowered to five feet—and even then, half of those who volunteered were rejected as physically unfit. For many of the poor, drink offered the simplest escape and the public house, it was said, was the shortest way out of Manchester.

The higher wage-earners lived mostly in tiny four-roomed houses, simply furnished, but with most of the attributes of a reasonable home. The lower paid were victims of a situation in which towns had been unable to keep pace with the influx from the countryside. In England and Wales 7·5 per cent and in Scotland 50 per cent of the population lived more than two to a room. 'In among the respectable rows of "two up and two down" houses', runs Roberts's description of Salford, 'we had the same blocks of hovels sharing a single tap, earth closet and open midden; each house with a candle for light, an oil lamp or a bare gas jet.'[2] Even with these relative differences the slums in which the poor lived had a depressing squalid uniformity. D. H. Lawrence, writing of the coal-mining district outside Nottingham where he grew up, described the 'little four-roomed houses with the "front" looking outward into the grim blank street, and the "back" with a tiny square brick yard, a low wall and a w.c. and ash pit, looking into the desert of the square. . .[3]

Below these classes there remained the destitute. In 1903 an American writer (see p. 25) living for a time in the East End of London described the endless march from dosshouse to dosshouse. Men aged quickly through undernourishment and hard manual labour, but there was no retirement for the elderly and if they could not live with their families, the workhouse was the only resort. These institutions were designed to offer a lower level of life than that which any work outside could provide, and in the early years of the century several prison governors were reporting that many of their inmates had chosen to go to gaol as a preferable alternative.

In the countryside squire and parson presided over a world of small farmers. In 1901 these numbered more than 224,000 in England and Wales, the majority of them tenants of estate owners and mostly with holdings of less than 50 acres. Agriculture had been seriously affected by a continuing depression in the last decades of the nineteenth century (see p. 21) and by 1900 annual rents had fallen to an average of £1 an acre, but amid the prevailing sense of economic insecurity farmers had generally opted to remain tenants-at-will rather than to accept the liability of a long lease.

Farmers at least continued to farm, but this could not be said of agricultural labourers; the impact of depression and the lure of the town had brought about a reduction in their numbers in England and Wales from almost a million in 1871 to 665,000 in 1911. On the whole this drop was beneficial for those who stayed on the land, because a shortage of labour caused wages to rise. In the North and the Midlands these had reached 18 shillings (90p) a week by 1900, although in East Anglia, which was worst hit by the depression, they were as low as 12 shillings (60p). This comes well below Rowntree's poverty line, but the conditions in the countryside do not apply in the same way; farm workers had the advantage of a cottage and cheap sources of food, and in a letter written to Rider Haggard in 1902 Thomas Hardy reckoned that their position had greatly improved since the days of his boyhood. Even so, in his survey of rural England Haggard found a deep sense of discontent among agricultural labourers. 'In many instances his cottage accommodation is very bad; indeed, I have found wretched and insufficient dwellings to be a great factor in the hastening of the rural exodus; and he forgets that in the town it will probably be worse. So he goes, leaving behind him half-tilled fields and shrinking hamlets.'[14]

The social pattern in Great Britain at the beginning of the twentieth century had its parallel in the organization of the educational system. The wealthy classes sent their children to boarding public schools; for them the university meant Oxford or Cambridge. The less affluent resorted to fee-paying day schools and grammar schools, and sometimes to the new universities which by now numbered about ten in England and Wales. For all other children there was only the elementary school, compulsory until the age of thirteen. In 1900 these were dealing with nearly 5 million pupils at Anglican or nonconformist foundations, or at those run by the local school boards in accordance with the Education Act of 1870. State secondary education was sparse and by 1906 only 689 secondary schools had been established, mostly attended by children who came from the lower levels of the middle class.

A more liberal system of further education was to be found in Scotland, where the universities had long been geared to receiving students from the local schools and where it was quite normal for a boy of humble background to work his way through college. Outside Scotland opportunities were considerably less, but there was a great range of mechanics' institutes and polytechnics, and since 1869 local authorities had been encouraged to provide the means for technical education. A Department of Science and Art had been established at South Kensington and a scholarship of a guinea a week enabled the young H. G. Wells to study there under Professor Thomas Huxley. The authorities certainly meant well; before the First World War expenditure on education by local governments and the treasury rose greatly. It was not impossible for the poor student to get through, but he needed the stamina and sense of dedication that Wells was later to describe in his novel *Love and Mr Lewisham*, and the gulf between the options open to the rich and the poor remained enormous.

The elementary schools did at least help the spread of literacy, as could be seen from the rapid development of a popular press. Throughout the Edwardian period over 2,500 papers, mostly weekly, were published every year. Alfred Harmsworth, later Lord Northcliffe, was one of the first to realize that news must be presented in a striking and personal way with an emphasis on the sensational in order to appeal to the man in the street, and among his many ventures the *Daily Mail*, which he started in 1896, was selling nearly a million copies a day by 1901.

Indeed, reading habits seemed to be on the increase everywhere. The use of public libraries expanded considerably; publishers embarked upon the issue of uniform editions, such as Oxford's World's Classics and Dent's Everyman's Library. Many of the best-selling novelists are now no longer read, but this was also the period of Joseph Conrad, E. M. Forster, Arnold Bennett, Henry James, John Galsworthy and the early social novels of H. G. Wells. There was a remarkable output of children's literature: Kipling's *Just So Stories*, Barrie's *Peter Pan*, Grahame's *Wind in the Willows* and, at a younger level, the work of Beatrix Potter. Boys' magazines flourished too and many working-class children caught their only glimpse of a fantasy public-school world in the adventures of Billy Bunter at Greyfriars.

Despite the drab circumstances of the poor, Edwardians of every class were certainly capable of enjoying themselves. Football, cricket and the Oxford and Cambridge boat race attracted enormous crowds. Lawn tennis at Wimbledon and the Test Matches with Australia had both started in 1877, and horse racing was the sport of more than kings. Bicycling was the new craze within the reach of many who were unlikely to afford one of the 15,000 motor-cars on the roads by 1900. Silent films could be seen at the local picture palaces, and the music hall has become almost a symbol of the age. In London and some of the larger provincial cities permanent orchestras were now established, and Henry Wood had started his Promenade Concerts at the Queen's Hall in 1894, as a means of bringing music to a wider audience.

This was a society increasingly secular in its outlook. Bicycling, railway excursions and the weekend house-parties of the rich, all made their inroads into Sundays, and although the young continued to be sent off to Sunday school, church-going was slightly in decline. Religious feeling was still strong enough, however, to make the school boards a scene of contention between Anglicans and nonconformists; the chapel played a great part in the background of the leading trade unionists, and churchmen were prominent in the struggle to bring help to the poor in the slums. In the main, religious belief was not challenged; it was still the acknowledged convention and in the working-class districts, where church-going was rare, it was sufficiently Protestant for all Roman Catholics to be regarded with suspicion.

The sepia photographs of the time have captured many of these facets of the Edwardian scene. They certainly form a more satisfactory record than the clichés of nostalgia recalling the pageantry of a great empire and the sense of world power, a memory that can no more escape the strains of 'Pomp and Circumstance' than its composer Edward Elgar could himself. Yet not even the photograph is adequate to establish the character of a period so rich in contradictory images. Many aspects of Victorianism were fading long before the death of the Queen; many others were to survive until after the First World War. They varied from region to region and from family to family. It is almost impossible to give a precise definition of the term 'Edwardian', but it has usually been associated with the more pleasant features of these years and that at least is a tribute to King Edward himself whose reign, contrary to his mother's earlier misgivings, lent an air of benign dignity to this closing phase of the long Victorian calm.

2

Aspects of Government

1. The system of government

The British constitution has never been a clearly defined system, merely a historical concept, always in a state of evolution as one modification has been laid upon another. The Restoration Settlement of 1660 and the Revolution of 1688 had confirmed the role of Parliament as an indispensable element in the law-making process, but it would be impossible to give an exact date to the decline of the sovereign's effective participation in government. The royal veto on legislation had not officially been used since 1707; the Parliamentary Reform Act of 1832 had deprived the King of most of his influence at the time of general elections; subsequent Reform Acts had finally destroyed what remained of this, and in 1867 Walter Bagehot in his treatise *The English Constitution* could refer to Queen Victoria and Edward, Prince of Wales, as a retired widow and an unemployed youth whose principal functions were to act in a dignified capacity.

Nevertheless, some vestiges of royal power survived. Behind the scenes the Queen could advise, and frequently did so. Only she could create peers, and as a last resort this could be used to alter the balance of voting in the House of Lords. Most important of all, she retained the right to choose her own Prime Minister. In fact, the emergence of the Conservative and Liberal party organizations in the second half of the nineteenth century had meant that the leader of the party with a majority in the House of Commons normally assumed office and, unless this was in serious doubt, the Queen had little part to play; there had been no escape from Mr Gladstone for Victoria. And when the change took place during the lifetime of a government, she was expected to act on the advice of the retiring Prime Minister. There was, however, one line of escape open to her; she did not have to ask for that advice, and in 1894 she carefully avoided doing so, selecting Lord Rosebery, when Gladstone, his predecessor, would have preferred Lord Spencer.

Once in office, the Prime Minister was unquestionably the head of the government. He chose all ministers of state at every level. There was a statutory limitation on the number of those who could be appointed from the House of Commons, and in 1892 the Queen had refused to accept two of Gladstone's nominees on personal grounds, but apart from this he had a completely free rein; he was not even restricted to those who were members of either House of Parliament at that moment. The precise composition of the cabinet, the inner circle of government, also rested with him, although it normally included the ministers who headed the major departments of state. During the course of an administration some degree of cabinet solidarity was expected and a minister positively at variance with his colleagues would resign. But this was a fairly flexible convention; until 1916 no formal minutes were taken and, as Lord Curzon once remarked, 'the cabinet often had the haziest notion as to what its decisions were'.

The political life of the government depended on the balance of forces in the Houses of Parliament, which sat from February until August, although pressure of business would sometimes call for longer sessions. Legislation could be initiated in either House and a Bill did not become law until it had been passed by both of them. Thus any measure put forward by the House of Commons could be rejected by the Lords who, in 1901, had a membership of 591, including 26 bishops, and 16 Scottish and 28 Irish peers. The retention of this highly significant negative function by the hereditary peers had led recently to radical demands for a change in their power or composition. In the main, however, the Lords had used their constitutional right with some caution; it was generally agreed that they should not tamper with any finance Bill, and it had only been in the Liberal administration of 1892–95 that they had seriously interfered with the government's programme of legislation.

The crucial area was the House of Commons. Here the distribution of seats had gradually been rationalized by the successive Reform Acts of the nineteenth century and, except for a few two-member boroughs, the United Kingdom was divided into single-member constituencies. Of the 670 seats there were 465 for England, 30 for Wales and 72 for Scotland. Ireland, still governed from Westminster after two unsuccessful attempts by Gladstone to establish Irish Home Rule (see p. 15), was represented by 103.

A general election had to be held at least once every seven years, although a prime minister could ask the sovereign for a dissolution at any time before that. The underlying purpose of the Reform Acts had been greatly to increase the size of the electorate, while still weighting the system in the interest of the propertied class, and the right to vote consequently rested upon a complex series of qualifications rather than any general principle of universal manhood suffrage. In the boroughs rate-paying householders, lodgers paying £10 a year and occupiers of premises worth £10 could all vote; in 1884 this qualification had been extended to the counties, while there remained the older franchises for the forty-shilling freeholder, the £5 copyholder and various types of leasehold. This was far from a system of 'one man, one vote', and in 1900 the registered electorate of 6,730,935 for the whole of the United Kingdom amounted to only 58 per cent of the adult male population. Furthermore, although the introduction of the secret ballot in 1872 had deprived the richer class of direct influence over the votes of their tenants or employees, the varied nature of the franchise gave to some 500,000 of the electorate, who held property in different parts of the country, a plural vote which they could exercise during the two or three weeks that the polling lasted.

Nevertheless, it could be said that the nineteenth century had seen the extension of the franchise to a good many levels of society. The composition of the House of Commons itself had altered rather less. It was true that all religious and property qualifications had by now been removed, and in theory it was open to any man to gain a seat as a member, even if he was not qualified to belong to the electorate. In practice there remained one great obstacle: MPs were not paid. As a consequence the Commons tended to be a gathering of gentlemen of means, whether Liberal or Conservative, and the principal change had been the growth in the numbers of those whose wealth lay in commerce or industry.

There was thus no great social gulf between the majority of MPs and the House of Lords, and, allowing for the vagaries of political life, the holders of ministerial office selected from either House came mostly from the uppermost stratum of society. There seemed nothing strange about this. 'At certain political houses I frequented,' wrote Somerset Maugham in his autobiography, 'they still talked as though to run the British empire was their private business. It gave me a peculiar sensation to hear it discussed, when a general election was in the air, whether Tom should have the Home Office and whether Dick would be satisfied with Ireland.'[1]

This preponderance of the richer class was also reflected in the various branches of the executive and the judiciary and in the hierarchy of the Church of England. The Victorians had dealt great blows at the earlier system of patronage, but had been careful not to damage the fabric of society. Purchase of Army commissions had been abolished in

1871, but regiments still chose their young officers from the better-known public schools; and in the Navy Sir John Fisher, the First Sea Lord, calculated in 1906 that the cost of a naval officer's training restricted the possibility of such a career to some 300,000 families. The Civil Service, numbering 106,000 in 1901 and organized in three grades—administrative, executive and clerical—was by now largely recruited by competitive examination, but there were still many areas where the well-connected candidate had little to fear, and in any case only university graduates were eligible to compete for the administrative grade. Social cachet was not necessarily incompatible with excellence of quality and the higher posts of the British Civil Service were for the most part occupied by men of the greatest ability; they were, however, almost exclusively the preserve of the public school and Oxford or Cambridge.

At the same time Victorian reform had also been concerned with the reshaping of local government, devising new representative institutions with a fairly uniform franchise. Since 1835 the councils of the municipal boroughs had been elected by all resident rate-payers. In the country-side day-to-day government had remained in the hands of the justices of the peace who, as there was a property qualification, were drawn mostly from land-owning families. In 1888, however, their administrative functions were taken over by county councils, elected by rate-payers and based on the borough system of aldermen and councillors, but headed by a chairman instead of a mayor. And in 1894 the smaller units were tidied up by a further Act which reconstituted the parish councils and turned the local sanitary authorities into urban and rural district councils, also elected on a rate-payer franchise.

The impact of all these new processes varied greatly. As in the House of Commons, the members of the bodies thus elected were unpaid, but in the boroughs this had not seriously affected the composition of their councils. Councillors could easily combine their duties with their every-day work and in the last part of the nineteenth century many cities, such as Birmingham, had come under radical control and had carried through a programme of public services with an energy that earned it the name of 'municipal Socialism'. In the counties non-payment mattered more and in any case the natural conservatism of the countryside ensured that the membership of the new councils was drawn largely from the classes that had always been predominant there.

In all, at local as well as national level, there was a striking uniformity throughout the country in the blending of social and political power.

'The country is still ruled by a legislature, a judicature, an armed force and an executive drawn from an upper class of which the territorial interest supplies the main element and direction' wrote Hilaire Belloc in an essay in 1897. .... 'And this assertion is in proportion truer as we regard the higher and more powerful positions; for, while it would be easy to discover a second-rate consul or curate, or an urban magistrate who has no link with the country houses, to find a series of ambassadors, judges or bishops in this position would amount to a stupendous miracle.'[2]

2. Ireland

'My boy, when you have been in public life as long as I,' said an elder statesman to young Winston Churchill, 'you will know that nothing ever really happens in this country.' His remark summed up the leisurely confidence that characterized the general atmosphere of Victorian government, but it glossed over one aspect of the United Kingdom that few politicians had been able to ignore. In Ireland it seemed that something was always happening. The situation here was the outcome of earlier centuries when Ireland had been subjected to a gradual process of conquest, prompted by England's need to check infiltration by any foreign power. Throughout the country English landlords, the heirs of settlers whose estates had been granted to them by the crown, represented an Anglo-Irish Protestant ascendancy over an Irish Catholic peasantry. Thus the upper class in Ireland were separated from the rest of the population not merely by the social distinctions that were common to the whole of the United Kingdom, but also by religion and origin. The only region of Ireland that differed from this was to be found in the north-east in a part of the old province of Ulster, where there had been a much more concentrated process of settlement by English and Scots, mostly in the course of the seventeenth century. Here in at least four of the counties all classes were predominantly of Protestant stock, regarding themselves as Irish, but utterly apart from the Catholic population of Ireland.

By the Act of Union in 1801 the old Dublin parliament, which had been a Protestant preserve, had been abolished and Irish representation at Westminster had been established with a hundred seats in the House of Commons, and twenty-eight peers in the House of Lords. After Catholic emancipation in 1829 a genuinely Irish party could be formed, and from then on the British parliamentary scene was to be spasmodically harassed by demands for economic relief and political autonomy for Ireland. The Irish nationalist party could reckon to hold some eighty-five seats, a factor which no political leader could ignore, and in the last decades of the nineteenth century a series of reasonably constructive governmental measures had slowly transformed the face of Ireland.

The Liberal party under Gladstone took the first radical steps, but although his disestablishment of the Anglican church in Ireland in 1869 did help to diminish one obvious instance of unfairness, the crux of the matter lay in the land. Two further Acts by the Liberals in 1870 and 1881 aimed to improve the lot of the tenant, but it was the Conservatives who first embarked on a positive effort to assist tenants in purchasing their own holdings. Two Acts in 1885 and 1891 enabled Irish farmers to raise loans through the British government, and the most striking instance of this policy was to be seen in an Act of 1903, whereby the government itself paid part of the price of an estate and allowed the purchaser to repay the rest over a period of $68\frac{1}{2}$ years.

By the beginning of the twentieth century, when Ireland's population had fallen to the more economic level of less than 4·5 million, the growth of peasant proprietorship had done something to reduce the poverty and insecurity of the Irish farmer. This could not, however, wipe out the thought of centuries of subjection. In an age when national movements were active everywhere on the Continent, Home Rule with an Irish parliament at Dublin was the consistent demand of the Irish nationalist party. This was to prove far more intractable than the question of land purchase. Whatever concessions they might make to Irish farmers, the Conservatives were adamant that Ireland must continue to be governed from Westminster. Gladstone, on the other hand, was eventually won round to Home Rule and did his best to bring it about with two Bills in 1886 and 1893, but the first of these failed to pass the House of Commons, when a section of Liberals seceded from the party, and the second was rejected by the Lords (see p. 30).

The objections to Home Rule did not merely arise from the mistrust with which the English regarded Ireland. They were to become increasingly centred on its implications for Ulster. Here the Protestant Irish stated positively that they would never submit to government from Catholic Dublin, and the Conservatives had taken up their cause in defence of the Union. 'Ulster will fight,' declared Lord Randolph Churchill in 1886, 'and Ulster will be right.' This was an internal tension which seemed insoluble, and after Gladstone's retirement the Liberals wanted only to be allowed to forget an issue which had already wrought such havoc within their party.

They were soon relieved of any immediate responsibility, as the Conservatives returned to office in 1895. John Redmond, the leader of the Irish nationalist party, could consequently make little headway in the House of Commons, and this in turn was to have its own repercussions. Home Rule had always been conceived as a limited form of autonomy operating within the framework of British government. Now, as impatience over the impasse at Westminster mounted, more extreme views began to develop, and at the beginning of the twentieth century Arthur Griffith, an Irish journalist, formed Sinn Fein—Ourselves Alone—a body which demanded that Ireland should declare her own independence unilaterally, only maintaining a link with the United Kingdom through allegiance to the crown. Thus, despite all previous legislation, the Irish question remained unresolved and Ulster and Sinn Fein were increasingly to see themselves as the final arbiters.

3. Imperialism and the Empire

The rule of Westminster and Whitehall was not restricted to the boundaries of the United Kingdom. It extended over the possessions that the British had been picking up all round the world for more than two centuries; this had been the incidental outcome of commercial and military struggles with their European opponents, a process so haphazard that it has been said that the British Empire was largely acquired in a fit of absence of mind.

Some of these gains had been no more than isolated points or islands acting as trading-posts or naval stations. Those along the coast of West Africa had been important in the days of the slave trade; in the Mediterranean Gibraltar (captured in the war of the Spanish Succession) and Malta (taken from the French in 1800), served as naval bases, and Cyprus was ceded by Turkey in 1878. In the Atlantic St Helena was an important port of call on the route to India, and Ascension Island and Tristan da Cunha had been occupied in 1816 to keep an eye on the exiled Emperor Napoleon. Mauritius (taken from the French in 1810) and Aden (occupied in 1839 to serve as a coaling station) were further stages on the way to the Far East, where Singapore in 1819 and Hong Kong in 1840, founded on uninhabited islands, had become great commercial centres.

Other more extensive possessions were open to a fuller economic development. The West Indies were a rich source of sugar; and in addition, the British, like several other western European countries, had established scattered settlements along the edges of vast continental land masses. The American colonies had declared their independence in 1776, but there remained Canada, taken from the French in 1763. Australia, first used for the deportation of convicts, was to grow into a series of separate settlements during the early nineteenth century, and New Zealand was annexed in 1840 to forestall French ambitions in the Pacific.

The native inhabitants of these territories were relatively small in numbers—American Indians and Eskimos in Canada, Aborigines in Australia, Maoris in New Zealand—and a process of emigration from the United Kingdom gradually built up a population predominantly of British stock. With them went conceptions of British government, and the individual colonies had soon organized their own elective assemblies. For a time direct control rested with the Colonial Office, but in the course of the century there had emerged the notion of dominion status, whereby central parliamentary governments established in Canada, Australia and New Zealand could exercise virtual autonomy in their domestic affairs, the link with the crown being represented by a governor-general. In Australia the geographical distances between the colonies, and in Canada the problem of the French province of Quebec made a federal constitution more appropriate, whereas New Zealand eventually set up a unitary system on the English model

India presented a very different aspect. This really was an empire, acquired in the course of the eighteenth-century struggle with France. The many different peoples of this vast subcontinent were divided primarily by religion (300 million Hindus and 70 million Muslims), but there were many other complications, including some 200 languages and dialects, immense regional variations, and the caste system which created the different classes of Hindu ranging from the Brahmins to the untouchables. Over much of this area Great Britain maintained a direct rule through the viceroy with 60,000 British troops and 150,000 Indian troops commanded by British officers. There was, too, a large population of British civilians, administrators and businessmen. British India, however, only included parts of the continent—Bengal and the valleys of the Ganges and the Indus, the eastern coastal region, the central provinces and the area around Bombay. This was divided into seventeen provinces—eleven principal ones, two border regions in Baluchistan and the North-West Frontier, and four smaller districts. The rest, comprising nearly half the territory of India and a quarter of its population, remained under the rule of Indian princes who, after surrendering control of their foreign policy, continued to run their own domestic affairs.

It would have been understandable if in this situation the British had concentrated merely on administration, but before the end of the century a few very cautious steps had been taken towards including Indians in the processes of government. In 1885 an Indian national congress, almost entirely Hindu, had been formed to press for this; Indian rural and municipal councils, partly elective, were set up to work alongside British district officers, and in 1892 the viceroy was to be assisted by an advisory council including a minority of nominated Indian members. It was only a beginning, and not a particularly successful one, but from it much was later to emerge.

At the time when these acquisitions were being made, the idea of empire had aroused little emotional response, and it was only in the last years of the nineteenth century that imperialism began to exercise a fascination of its own. A fever of nationalism among many European countries found expression in annexing large areas of the earth's surface, and although economic and strategic considerations played their part in this, the principal motive now was prestige. Great Britain, too, was caught up in this new mood which seemed to affect all classes. The masses awoke to the realization that they had a great empire. It had little bearing on their everyday lives, but they found that they liked the idea and in the elementary schools their children were left in no doubt over their great inheritance. 'Empire Day of course had special significance,' wrote Robert Roberts of his elementary school in Salford. 'We drew union jacks, hung classrooms with flags of the dominions and gazed with pride as they pointed out those massed areas of red on the world map. "This and this and this," they said, "belong to us!" '[3] The popular press took up the same theme, and the golden and diamond jubilees of Queen Victoria in 1887 and 1897 were vast pageants advertising the worldwide extent of the British Empire.

In recent years it has become fashionable to mock the attitudes that accompanied this period of imperialism. Yet it was not all flag-waving and a search for an outlet for investment. It had, too, a genuine sense of idealism, the belief in a civilizing mission to which generations of young men devoted their lives as district officers in remote regions with little thought of personal gain. This was the underlying theme of Rudyard Kipling's writings, the first instance of an imperial literature, which, contrary to their later image, stressed the obligations of service and the need for humility before the responsibilities of colonial rule; and in government circles the constructive conception of empire took the form of schemes for an imperial federation which would establish a great *pax Britannica* across the world.

It so happened that all this fervour coincided with the exploration of the interior of tropical Africa. In the past the flag had followed trade; now it followed the missionaries as well, and between 1880 and 1890 the map of Africa was carved up among the European Powers, each striving to establish frontiers which would hinder the colonial development of the others. In the west, Great Britain gained the Gold Coast and Nigeria; in the east, Kenya, Uganda and Zanzibar. Initially these territories were mostly run by trading companies, but eventually their control was taken over by the Colonial Office. Concern over Egypt was governed largely by strategic considerations, since it was the key point on the overland route to India and acquired a heightened significance once the Suez Canal had been completed in 1869. Great Britain and France, who had long struggled for influence in this area, eventually joined forces in 1882 in a combined operation, from which the French withdrew, leaving Egypt under British administration, although not strictly a part of the empire. This, in turn, led in 1898 to the conquest of the Sudan, the territory to the south controlling the upper waters of the Nile on which the simple economy of Egypt depended.

In all these regions the acquisition of empire had only involved the occasional clash with native peoples, and the Europeans themselves had avoided coming to blows. In the south of Africa the situation was complicated by the presence of the Boers, the descendants of the Dutch who had originally colonized the Cape. The British had taken over these settlements during the Napoleonic war, and the Boers had eventually moved north to establish two republics of their own, the Transvaal and the Orange Free State. British settlement at the Cape and in Natal had continued to develop, and when the ambition of Cecil Rhodes resulted in the annexation of Bechuanaland and, later, Rhodesia to the north of the Boer republics, this process of encirclement naturally alarmed the Boers. Almost at the same time their hopes of preserving their pastoral way of life were shattered by the discovery of gold on the Rand just to the south of Pretoria, the capital of the Transvaal; this brought an influx of speculators and mining engineers of all nationalities, predominantly British. The growing antagonism between these so-called Uitlanders and the Transvaal government was not likely to be resolved by the uncompromising personalities of the British High Commissioner, Sir Alfred Milner, and the President of the Transvaal, Paul Kruger, and the struggle finally came to a head with the outbreak of the Boer War in October 1899.

The war was fought out in three phases. During the first few months the Boers, who outnumbered the few British forces in South Africa, held the initiative and used it to lay siege to Ladysmith in Natal, and

Kimberley and Mafeking on the western border of the republics. Then, as reinforcements arrived, Lord Roberts was able to relieve the besieged towns and by June 1900 had overrun the two Boer republics. A third phase followed when the Boers refused to admit defeat and carried on a long guerrilla resistance, which led General Sir Herbert Kitchener, now in command, to clear the territory systematically, removing the civilian population into large internment camps. Peace did not come until May 1902, when the Boers finally agreed to surrender their independence with the signing of the Treaty of Vereeniging.

The Boer War had many emotional repercussions. It aroused a storm of anger among the European Powers against Great Britain. It created a moral furore at home, when the conditions in the internment camps were revealed, and it played havoc within the Liberal party, which became hopelessly divided over its attitude towards the war. Its most wounding aspect for the British public was the shock of the early Boer victories. For several months the armed might of Great Britain, on whose Empire the sun never set, had been rudely challenged by a small community of farmers. The self-confidence, which the record of imperial success had built up, was now suddenly shaken. There was a touch of hysteria in the wild excitement that greeted the eventual relief of Mafeking, and the pomp and circumstance that attended the accession of Kind Edward VII could not disguise the fact that the reign had opened on a note of doubt.

3

New Challenges at Home

1. The threat to the Edwardian economy

At first sight the economy of Great Britain at the beginning of the twentieth century still seemed to enjoy the great margins of security that she derived from her early industrial revolution. It was true that her vast imports, principally of food and raw materials, outweighed her exports to the extent of about £150 million a year, but this gap was almost closed by her earnings from services such as shipping, banking and insurance. In addition, her income from her growing investments overseas gave her a surplus of £100 million a year, rising by 1913 to £200 million, most of this being invested abroad, where her total assets on the eve of the First World War amounted to £4,000 million.

Nevertheless, the assumptions on which Great Britain's place in the world economy was based were now becoming more precarious. Free trade had been an article of faith throughout the years of her prosperity, but it was open to question whether this absence of protective tariffs was not by now a liability. The most striking instance of this was to be seen in agriculture. The development of farming machinery and of the new railway systems in North America had made it possible to cultivate the great prairies whose corn could now flood into Europe at prices that undermined the position of the British wheat farmer. The resultant depressed state of English agriculture was to run on into the 1930s and the landed classes gradually sold off their large tenant farms, so that the proportion of land farmed by owner-occupiers rose from 10 per cent in 1870 to 36 per cent in 1927. This change, however, took place mostly after the First World War. A more immediate consequence was that livestock became more profitable than corn, and between 1870 and 1914 the total acreage of arable land under cultivation dropped from about 15 to 11 million acres, while pasture rose correspondingly from 11 to 16 million acres.

Originally the industrialist had welcomed the importation of agricultural goods, because this enabled foreign countries to purchase his manufactures, but here too the long-term prospect now seemed less healthy. The more recent industrialization of western European countries and of the United States had created a new element in the competition for markets, and although Great Britain's export trade was still increasing between 1880 and 1913, her share in the world export figures is calculated to have dropped from 19·6 to 14·1 per cent.

The general growth of industrialization need not in itself have been disastrous; the real danger to the Edwardian economy lay in more detailed aspects of these changes. First, British management chose to continue with industrial methods that had served them well in the past, but did not promise as much for the future. In engineering, for example, although reliance on skilled craftsmen had ensured work of a very high quality, this was by now being outdated by new American methods of mass production and the development of interchangeable spare parts. Specialization of labour along a production line allowed the American industrialist to mobilize large numbers of semi-skilled workers and by 1913 the United States was responsible for half of the world's engineering output in contrast to Great Britain's 11·8 per cent. Again, only a very small percentage of coal was mechanically cut in British coalmines. This did not prevent output from rising from 110 million tons in 1870 to 290 million tons in 1913, but the greater use of machinery and more modern equipment had enabled the German mines almost to equal the British figure by the latter date, while American output had reached 500 million tons. Similarly, although British output of pig-iron and steel increased in the years before the war, Germany's output of pig-iron was almost 50 per cent greater than Great Britain's by 1914, and her industry exploited far more wholeheartedly a new technique devised in 1879 by a Welsh chemist, Gilchrist-Thomas, whereby phosphoric ore could be used for the cheaper production of steel.

Second, British commerce remained centred upon the old types of commodity; coal, iron, steel, ships, machinery and textiles represented two-thirds of British exports in the period 1911–13. In some fields this was still viable; in shipbuilding, for example, Great Britain was responsible for 60 per cent of the world's tonnage between 1900 and 1914. Yet the stress on finished manufactured articles ignored the need that many countries felt to develop their own industries, and it was the Germans and the Americans who captured much of the market for production goods. This was bound eventually to bring added competition from new foreign producers who were protected by walls of tariffs, and British textiles, particularly vulnerable to this, fell back increasingly on sales within the Empire.

Third, the last decades of the nineteenth century had seen the beginning of a second phase of the industrial revolution: the use of electric power, the development of a wide range of chemical products and the invention of the internal-combustion engine with the consequent demand for rubber and petroleum. Many of the initial discoveries relevant to all this had been made by British scientists, yet British industry was so tied to older processes and so lacking in a body of trained technologists that it was again Germany and the United States who at once took the lead in these new fields. By 1913 the output of the German electrical industry was three times as great as the British, and Great Britain's share of the world output of chemical products was only 11 per cent in contrast to the United States' 34 per cent and Germany's 24 per cent. Stuttgart even supplied the khaki dye for British army uniforms.

Many reasons have been suggested for this retardation of British industry. It is tempting to put the blame on a society whose upper classes despised too close a connection with trade or technology. Thus, the second and third generations of a successful industrialist family would pass through a public school on to the City or one of the professions in preference to the grittier aspects of industrial enterprise. But this is hardly adequate as an explanation of a national phenomenon. More telling was the almost total absence of scientific training in Great Britain. As early as 1867 Lyon Playfair, a professor of chemistry at Edinburgh University, commenting on this problem in a letter to *The Times*, had written: '... the one cause upon which there was most unanimity of conviction is that France, Austria, Prussia, Belgium and Switzerland possess good systems of industrial education for the masters and managers of factories and workshops ....'[1] In 1913 Great Britain's university population numbered 33,000 as against Germany's 60,000, and whereas Germany produced 3,000 graduate engineers every year, there were in England and Wales only some 500 to emerge with a degree in any branch of mathematics or science.

Fundamentally the problem was economic. Great Britain's early start in the industrial revolution meant that any radical change would mean an entire restructuring of the extensive plant and the training of a new work force. All this would entail a considerable dislocation as well as resistance from trade unions of skilled workers, fearful of finding themselves displaced. So, while output could be increased with present methods and markets could still be found, the British industrialist preferred to repair and maintain his existing machinery, and the continuing profits, which otherwise would have been largely absorbed by any major transformation, were instead re-exported in more immediately lucrative foreign and imperial investments. In this way the British failed to keep their lead and were condemned to the harder task of trying to catch up later on. When that time came in the second half of the twentieth century and they were genuinely striving to rectify the situation, they often accused themselves of living on their past. It was a salutary thought, but the charge would have been more applicable some seventy years earlier.

2. The pressure for social change

The enjoyment of a continuing prosperity which masked a threatened economy did not mean that complacency was universal, and at the turn of the century there were many who felt a passionate need to jolt their society out of its easy assumptions. In 1902 H. G. Wells published a fascinating blueprint for the twentieth century entitled *Anticipations*.

> The nation that produces in the near future the largest proportional development of educated and intelligent engineers and agriculturists, of doctors, schoolmasters, professional soldiers and intellectually active people of all sorts ... will certainly be the nation that will be the most powerful in warfare or in peace, will certainly be the ascendant or dominant nation before the year 2000.[2]

And Bernard Shaw preached the same doctrine, practising his usual tactics of shock, when in *Man and Superman* in 1903 he depicted Henry Straker, the chauffeur-mechanic, as the New Man on whom all would eventually depend.

The New Man might seem to many Edwardians a rather remote personality. The New Woman was determined to make a more immediate appearance. In the last decades of the nineteenth century there had gradually developed among many young ladies a desire to defy the masculine Victorian world which liked to keep its womenfolk in a state of decorous subordination. This had mainly been a social movement— an assertion of a woman's right to own property, to smoke, to wear bloomers, to ride a bicycle, to take a job or to enjoy a greater sexual freedom—and it made its principal impact among the upper and middle classes. As yet it had brought little economic relief; before 1914 the average wage of a working-class woman was one-third of a man's. Nor had it gone far in the political field; it was only in 1897 that Mrs Fawcett founded the National Union of Women's Suffrage Societies to agitate for the extension of the vote to women, and Mrs Pankhurst's suffragettes, as they were called, did not turn to militancy until after the Liberal victory in 1906 (see p. 74).

Technology and feminine emancipation were active causes, but they lacked the dramatic sense of urgency excited by the appalling living conditions of the poor in the large cities. Individual response to this had taken two forms. Some concentrated their efforts on providing institutions of education which might enable a younger generation to find a means of escape. Since the 1870s the University Extension Movement had been establishing colleges for working men; Ruskin College was founded at Oxford in 1899, and from 1903 the Workers' Educational Association offered classes to every age group. Others attempted a more direct alleviation of poverty through many types of mission in the slums: Dr Barnado's home for destitute children, founded in 1870, William Booth's Salvation Army in 1878, and Toynbee Hall, which in 1882 became a model for other social settlements.

These and many similar charitable organizations could only offer a feeble palliative, but they did at least bring to light a social evil which was to be the subject of a growing number of publications. The poor were too inarticulate and too harried by the circumstances of their existence to be able to draw attention themselves to their plight. Only one, Robert Tressell, a house decorator, succeeded in describing his own class in his novel *The Ragged Trousered Philanthropists*, and this was not published until 1914, three years after he had died of tuberculosis. Other writers inevitably viewed the problem from the outside, but their work was none the less compelling. In 1883 a missionary group, the London Congregational Union, produced a grim picture in *The Bitter Cry of Outcast London*, and this was followed in 1890 by William Booth's *In Darkest England and The Way Out*. Soon others were adding their own impressions of human degradation in slumland. An American, Jack London, in *People of the Abyss* (1903), described his investigations when living as one of the poor in the East End, and in the same year a future Liberal MP, C. F. G. Masterman, published a collection of essays about similar scenes in south London.

All these were types of personal reportage, but there were also two publications that attempted to study the facts of poverty on a scientific basis. In 1901 Seebohm Rowntree's statistical analysis of living conditions in York (see p. 5) was so horrifying that after reading it Winston Churchill declared: 'I see little glory in an empire which can rule the waves, but is unable to flush its sewers.' The second was the work of Charles Booth, a Liverpool shipping magnate, who had long been intrigued by the nature of life in the East End of London. He was well aware of the squalor of the slums, but he had little use for sporadic philanthropic efforts to relieve it. 'The admixture of Gospel and giving,' he said, 'produces an atmosphere of meanness and hypocrisy and brings discredit on both charity and religion.'[3] Equally, he was opposed to doctrinaire political solutions and objected strongly to a Socialist claim that 25 per cent of the population of London lived below the poverty line. Convinced that this was an exaggeration, he set out in 1886 on a vast study of *Life and Labour of the People of London*, which ultimately filled seventeen volumes and took as many years to complete. Ironically his researches eventually disclosed a situation even worse than had been suggested; 35 per cent lay below the poverty line and he calculated that the vast majority of these did not owe their position to any innate failings, but were simply the victims of unemployment, illness, low pay or the size of their families.

None of those who participated in these activities had any doubt about the seriousness of the problem. 'The origin of the ferment,' wrote Beatrice Potter, one of Charles Booth's assistants, 'is to be discovered in a new consciousness of sin among men of intellect and men of property.'[4] Yet probably very few of them would have agreed with Oscar Wilde, when he said that 'the proper aim is to try and reconstruct society on such a basis that poverty will be impossible'. Edwardian social work still rested on the Victorian ideal of charity designed to direct a man towards self-help. 'The law should not do for the individual that which he might do for himself without undue delay or an undue expenditure of energy,' wrote Herbert Samuel in 1902; 'for otherwise self-reliance would be weakened.'[5]

This was no solution. The problem was too huge for the average individual to be able to do much for himself. The working class, however, remained for years indifferent to any radical alternative, despite the fact that such an alternative already existed. The philosophy of Marxism was by now firmly established on the Continent and provided a hard dogmatic edge to what had previously been shapeless movements of social protest. In 1877 the German Social Democratic party had won half a million votes and thirteen seats in the German Reichstag, and according to Marx's thesis Great Britain's industrial development should have meant that she too was ripe for the appearance of some similar political movement.

None came. Those who attempted to foster one found themselves frustrated by what Masterman called 'the invincible .patience of the English workman'. It was perhaps characteristic of England that the leader of one such organization, Henry Hyndman, should be a man of considerable wealth who had been educated at Cambridge and played cricket for Sussex. The Social Democratic Federation—the SDF—was undoubtedly Marxist in inspiration, being committed to a policy of nationalizing 'all means of production, distribution and exchange'; yet even at the height of its influence in the 1890s its membership was probably never more than two or three thousand.

Many other small socialist groups were less attracted to the doctrinaire aspects of Marxism, preferring the vaguer thought of a spiritual regeneration of society. In 1885, after breaking with Hyndman, William Morris established the Socialist League. Morris's Socialism was essentially emotional, a personal revolt against the material and moral ugliness of capitalism; he dreamed of a return to what he imagined was the simple purity of a medieval society, and in 1890 he described in *News from Nowhere* a Utopian glimpse of some future state of England, where there would apparently be no need for money at all. Other movements came close to a revival of earlier forms of Christian Socialism, but although many individual clergymen, Anglican and nonconformist, were deeply concerned with the need for social reform, religion was never to play the part in political radicalism that it had done at the beginning of the nineteenth century.

In contrast to these missionary movements the Fabian Society, established in 1884, was a small intimate gathering of middle-class intellectuals meeting from time to time in each other's houses, mostly in London, reading and debating papers and arranging for the publication of tracts which might help to explain the message of Socialism in the context of English society. Unlike the other groups they were not concerned with developing a great mass following; their methods were based on a belief in gradualism—the Micawber club, Hyndman called them—trusting that through their propaganda and through the election of Fabians to various bodies of local government they might eventually exercise an influence out of all proportion to their size.

The Fabians proved to be much more than a drawing-room debating society, largely owing to the distinguished quality of their early members. Bernard Shaw, at the beginning of his literary career in London, was one of the first to join them. This tall young red-headed Irishman with his fluent wit in debate and his gift for making polemical pamphlets actually readable was an enormous asset for the Fabians, but the bulk of the hard writing which is associated with the Society was the work of the Webbs.

This was a remarkable couple. Sidney Webb, short, rotund, bespectacled, was a clerk at the Colonial Office, a man of great mental precision, ideally suited to the analysis of complex material—'the ablest man in England' Shaw called him.[6] Beatrice Potter, an attractive young woman from a moneyed middle-class background, had become deeply involved in the study of social conditions while working with Charles Booth. She and Sidney Webb met in 1890 and there was some consternation in Beatrice's family two years later when their engagement was announced. In fact, this was to be a marriage of true minds. The Webbs spent their honeymoon in the study of trade-union records in Dublin and Glasgow, and from then on their lives were dedicated to the joint production of long solid tomes on the history of trade unionism, industrial democracy, English local government and the English Poor Law, surveys which were to provide the basic information for future social reform.

There were many others: Annie Besant, an advocate of atheism and birth control, and a leader in the organization of women's labour; Hubert Bland, the husband of Edith Nesbit, a writer of children's books; and Graham Wallas, later a professor at the London School of Economics, which was founded by Sidney Webb in 1898 out of a bequest to the Fabians. Some years afterwards H. G. Wells was for a short time a member, but left after failing to turn the Society into a vehicle for his own plans; the occasion was always described somewhat tartly in Fabian circles as 'the episode of Mr Wells', to which Wells replied by including an unattractive picture of the Webbs in his novel *The New Machiavelli*.

Thus the Edwardian scene was not merely one of prosperous complacency and imperial pride. In many quarters there was a sense of disquiet. Angry young women were caught up in a crusade to establish their rights; philanthropists were outspoken in their criticism of a society that remained blind to the conditions in the slums, and for years tiny ginger groups had skirmished around the great bulk of the British working class attempting to goad it into political action. In the main, few of these movements envisaged a revolution in the style of the continental upheavals during the nineteenth century; for them social change meant legislation along constitutional lines, and the realization of their aspirations was to depend on the impact which they could make upon the attitudes of the political parties at Westminster.

4

The Fortunes of the Parties

1. Conservatives v. *Liberals*

Ever since the passing of the Reform Act of 1867 the two major parties, the Conservatives and the Liberals, had been aware of a possible discrepancy between the emotions of a mass electorate and the comfortable establishment of wealthy families who saw themselves as the governing class. As a consequence, there had developed in the latter half of the nineteenth century far more elaborate party organizations attempting to bridge the gulf between the leadership and the prospective voter. Both parties set up their own central agencies, but the most significant feature was to be seen in a variety of associations at a constituency level, which eventually created their own national framework—the Conservative National Union in 1867 and the National Liberal Federation in 1877—each acting as instruments of liaison for their party, working on the detail of local support and the selection of future candidates.

It was not long before these associations were beginning to conceive a more ambitious function for themselves as centres of control dictating the party's legislative programme. This was abhorrent to Conservative and Liberal leaders alike. Indeed, the new claim raised a profoundly important constitutional issue, since it implied that MPs were to become the puppets of two national associations operating outside Parliament, and the politicians had consequently become engaged in a struggle with their own supporters to retain their independence of action. The outcome was the same for each party. By the 1890s it had been made clear that although the decisions of the association conferences might be a useful sounding-board, they were not absolutely binding on MPs, whose prime loyalty was to their parliamentary leaders. The requirements of tactics in the House of Commons predominated, and for Conservatives and Liberals respectively the armchairs of the Carlton Club and the Reform Club remained the real seats of power.

It was not only in their organization that the two parties were changing. Their composition, too, has been greatly affected by events of recent years. The Conservatives, at one time the stronghold of the landed classes, were by now being joined by the industrial and commercial interest which predominated among Conservative MPs after the general election of 1885. The new allegiance went a good way down the social scale, attracting the lower middle-class inhabitants of the new suburbs and the more affluent sections of the enfranchised working class. The record of the Conservative party had shown that it was not opposed to reform, but its principal concern lay in the protection of property, the defence of the Church of England, the maintenance of the Empire and a determination to preserve the union with Ireland; and the long run of Conservative governments from 1886 until 1905, with only one short Liberal administration from 1892 to 1895, showed that these aims were not unrealistic in terms of electoral appeal.

The position of the Liberals was fundamentally different. Although the Conservatives had been badly shaken by their leader Robert Peel's decision to abandon the Corn Laws in 1845, they had at least had a solid core on which to base a recovery. The Liberals, from the time of their emergence in the 1860s, had always been somewhat hybrid. The loose-knit coalition of Whigs, Peelites and radicals had brought together landed magnates, nonconformist businessmen and mid-Victorian trade unionists, whom the moral fervour of Gladstone's leadership had carried into power in 1868. Peace, retrenchment and reform had stood for a defence of free trade, a restructuring of domestic institutions to allow a greater efficiency in government, and a determination to avoid foreign or imperial adventures, thus keeping armaments to a minimum. By 1874 much of this had been achieved and henceforward the Liberals were threatened with open disunity over their future policy. Gladstone him-self was consumed with his personal moral aims—horror at Turkish atrocities and a passion to establish Home Rule for Ireland—while the rank and file were torn between the Whig establishment, fearful of Gladstone's increasing extremism, and the radicals headed by Joseph Chamberlain who wished for more daring social programmes with which to capture the working-class vote.

It was the Irish issue that brought the crisis to a head. In 1886 Gladstone's first Home Rule Bill was unacceptable to many Liberal MPs who seceded from the party. These Liberal Unionists, as they styled themselves, were as ill-assorted a group as their parent body—an amalgam of the two wings, Lord Hartington's Whigs and Chamberlain's radicals—but for a time they did try to preserve some collective iden-tity, holding some seventy-eight seats in the Commons. Eventually, however, Chamberlain, whose interests had by now shifted towards the development of the Empire, took them formally into the Conservative party.

This split had robbed the Liberals of the money and local influence of many county families and of the electoral appeal of Joseph Chamberlain. And still it did not enable them to close their ranks. After the failure of the second Home Rule Bill in 1893, Gladstone's final retirement left the Liberal party shot through with dissension and personal intrigue, as they passed once more into Opposition after their electoral defeat in 1895. The original Liberal aspirations had been largely the product of a time that was already passing, and the older Gladstonian Liberals such as Sir William Harcourt and John Morley, were confronted by a new generation: Sir Edward Grey, from a Northumberland landed family, Herbert Asquith, the son of a Yorkshire woollen manufacturer, and R. B. Haldane, a Scottish barrister. The younger men wished to discard the question of Home Rule and looked for greater participation in imperial affairs. In the party as a whole there were divided views over an approach to the working class, and the consequent anarchy of political aim, coupled with the need to husband nonconformist support, was to give an undue prominence to sectional issues such as the disestablishment of the Welsh Church.

Over this discordant scene Gladstone's successors tried in vain to achieve an effective leadership—first Lord Rosebery, then Harcourt, until in 1899 the task fell to Sir Henry Campbell-Bannerman, a wealthy Scot with a long experience of political life. 'If Sir Henry Campbell-Bannerman has a defect,' commented *The Times*, 'it is that he is not prone to excess of activity.'[1] He was, however, a man of immense tact and patience and he was to need all this when the outbreak of the Boer War provided the Liberals with a further opportunity for tearing themselves apart.

Predictably the older Gladstonians opposed the war as a manifestation of imperialism, and these so-called pro-Boers were joined by some of the radicals, of whom David Lloyd George, a young Welsh lawyer, was the most virulent opponent of the government. On the other hand, the Liberal imperialists—Asquith, Grey and Haldane—maintained that the war had been forced on Great Britain by the Boers, and they set up their own organization in support of it. This divide within the Liberal party was epitomized by a vote in October 1899 on an Opposition amendment criticizing the negotiations on the eve of the war. Only 92 out of 186 Liberals supported it; seventy-seven, including Campbell-Bannerman, abstained, while fifteen voted with the government.

Amid the fury of a party apparently in a state of dissolution

Campbell-Bannerman tried desperately to find some common ground on which the Liberals could take their stand as a credible alternative government. He kept the line open on domestic questions. He turned his mind to the more remote problems of the ultimate settlement in South Africa, and he was careful to restrict any comment on the conduct of the war to extreme issues, as when he castigated the government for its 'methods of barbarism' in the internment camps (see p. 20), where thousands of Boer civilians had already died. There was little hope of ousting the Conservatives in the election of 1900, fought out amid the fever of the war, although the government's majority was reduced to 134 seats from the 152 that had given them power in 1895. This might be a straw in the wind, but when the war ended in 1902, the Liberal party was still in no position to challenge the long supremacy of the Conservatives, and it would have been hard to imagine that they were approaching the greatest electoral triumph of their history.

2. The trade unions and the beginnings of the Labour party

For many years the struggle between Conservatives and Liberals had been the principal feature of the parliamentary scene, while the Irish Nationalist party had pursued its objectives by playing one off against the other. Soon, however, this pattern was to be upset, when a section of the working class embarked on a new political venture of their own.

This had been long in coming. After the last echoes of Chartism had died away in 1848, the leaders of the working class had chosen to concentrate on creating more powerful trade unions out of amalgamations of small craft societies. Engineers, iron-founders, boiler-makers, shipbuilders, carpenters and joiners, cotton-spinners and two large groups of miners had all achieved a considerable degree of central organization in the middle decades of the nineteenth century and the total trade union membership by 1888 has been calculated at about 750,000.

These unions were essentially non-political. They were highly exclusive, consisting only of skilled workers, rather less than 10 per cent of the total adult male working population. The character of the secretariats at the head of each illustrates perfectly the way in which the upper sections of the working-class population had come to terms with the existing framework of society; they were all imbued with Victorian ideals, highly responsible in their sparing use of the strike weapon, husbanding their considerable financial resources and determined to emphasize the respectability of their organizations. The Trades Union Congress (the TUC) first met in 1868, but this was to be no more than a common meeting ground for discussion of current problems, and the jealousy with which each union guarded its independence made it extremely improbable that the Congress would become a weapon for united working-class action.

Thus any political aspirations had been fairly dormant during the period of trade-union growth, and even when the Parliamentary Reform Acts of 1867 and 1884 had seemed a good step towards the political emancipation that had been the aim of the Chartists, their attitude remained highly cautious. They had little sympathy with the idea of forming a separate parliamentary party. MPs were unpaid, and the financial support of a number sufficiently large to make some impact on the House of Commons would be a considerable drain on their funds. In any case, they saw little future for such a party, even supposing that it could achieve a strong negotiating position in the Commons, as its legislation could always be blocked by the House of Lords. Most of all, they suspected that it might easily become a vehicle for Socialist ideas, and to the trade unions of that time Socialism was anathema on account of its doctrinaire basis and its foreign origin.

Instead, they placed their faith in a policy of liaison through the parliamentary committee of the TUC. They could argue that the Conservative and Liberal parties were both aware of the importance of the working-class vote, and this strategy of bargaining behind the scenes proved to be highly effective. In 1871 Gladstone's Criminal Law Amendment Act had widened the boundaries of the unions' legitimate activity and had given legal protection to their funds; in 1875 Disraeli's Conspiracy and Protection of Property Act had extended their rights to include 'peaceful picketing' in pursuance of a trade dispute, and by 1880 they had gained two Factory Acts, two Merchant Shipping Acts and an Employer's Liability Act.

Such a record, at a time when only two working-class MPs had been elected to the House of Commons in 1874, seemed adequate testimony to the efficacy of the parliamentary committee of the TUC. To the trade unions the creation of an independent working-class party consequently appeared utterly unnecessary, and it was not until the 1890s that two new factors suggested that this situation might eventually change.

The first of these was a startling expansion of the trade-union movement itself. Aided by the revival in trade at the end of the 1880s and a widespread sympathy that the recent publicizing of the condition of the poor had inspired, radicals turned their attention to the great mass of unskilled labour which until now had lacked any effective trade-union system. In 1888 the girls employed by Bryant and May in

London were encouraged to carry out a successful strike in order to gain an improvement in their working conditions. In 1889 Will Thorne organized the London gas workers in a National Union with some sixty branches and gained almost at once a change from a twelve-hour to an eight-hour working day. In August of that year there broke out a far more devastating strike among the London dockers in protest against the pay and conditions of casual labour. Few of these workers had any organization at all, and the task might have proved too much for their leader, Ben Tillett, if he had not received assistance from Tom Mann and John Burns. These two members of the Amalgamated Society of Engineers, both of whom belonged to the Social Democratic Federation (SDF), set about a major campaign at the end of which the dockers won their sixpence an hour; and a new docker's union with Mann as president and Tillett as secretary had acquired 30,000 members before the end of the year. In the north other vast national amalgamated unions soon followed this initiative, and at the same time a General Railway Workers Union was established to cater for those who had no place in the more exclusive Amalgamated Society of Railway Servants.

The beginning of the organization of unskilled labour had a twofold effect on the trade-union world. By 1892 the new unions had added about 140,000 members to those already represented by the TUC; at the same time many of the older unions, conscious of a need to strengthen their internal position against these newcomers, lowered their entrance qualifications within their own trades: the engineers, for example, increased their membership from 53,000 to 71,000 between 1888 and 1891. The combined effect was to bring the total trade-union membership close to 1·5 million. The older unionists viewed this sudden influx with mixed feelings, since they had always regarded themselves as the aristocracy of labour. 'A great number of them,' wrote John Burns, 'looked like respectable city gentlemen; wore very good coats, large watch chains and high hats.'[2] The same could hardly be said of the more recent recruits who brought with them a greater extremism and a sense of social grievance which was bound to run counter to the older unionists' desire for a respectable place in the pattern of Victorian society; and from 1890 the TUC was to become a battleground between these two attitudes.

The second factor in the emergence of a working-class political party was a sense of disillusionment among many of them over their parliamentary tactics. After Gladstone's first attempt to establish Home Rule for Ireland in 1886 (see p. 30) had led to the secession of the right-wing element from his party, the Liberals looked as if they might offer the main hope for social reform. This so-called Lib-Lab philosophy was greatly encouraged by the sweeping measures listed in the Newcastle programme on which the Liberals under Fabian persuasion fought the election of 1892. In the event, however, the Liberals gained only a minute majority; Gladstone was entirely concentrated on one last effort to achieve Irish Home Rule before his retirement, and the House of Lords was particularly intractable in rejecting a large number of Liberal measures, including Home Rule itself.

Thus the Lib-Lab philosophy appeared to be fruitless, and this realization, coupled with the recent expansion of the trade-union movement, was now to awaken a new sense of political ambition. The first manifestation of this was the founding of the Independent Labour Party (the ILP). In the summer of 1892 a campaign launched by the weekly *Workman's Times* had made it clear that there was plenty of support for the forming of local branches to establish an organization for returning working-class MPs to Parliament, and in January 1893 120 delegates, mostly from the north and including some Fabians and members of the SDF, met at Bradford to give shape to the new project.

The principal figure behind this was one of the three working-class candidates returned in the 1892 election. Born in Lanarkshire, the illegitimate son of a servant girl, Keir Hardie had worked in the mines since the age of ten. By the time he was thirty he had built up two miners' unions, and the publications of the SDF had converted him to Socialism, although he never actually joined the federation; the Bible rather than Karl Marx was the mainspring of Keir Hardie's political philosophy. It was consequently hardly surprising that the central object of the ILP programme devised at the Bradford meeting should be 'to secure the collective ownership of the means of production, distribution and exchange'. The delegates, however, were aware of the need for caution. As one of them remarked, 'the new party has to appeal to an electorate which has as yet no full understanding of Socialism',[3] and the title selected for the organization carefully avoided the word in order not to frighten off potential supporters.

The aspirations behind the founding of the ILP were significant, but they could not resolve one crucial difficulty. There was a lack of funds. In the working-class world only one source could overcome that deficiency, and in January 1894 a Fabian tract entitled *A Plan of Campaign for Labour*, derived from an article by Sidney Webb and Bernard Shaw, made a plain statement of the matter. They declared that the clear need for the future was a political party financed by the trade unions, and that

£30,000 must be raised for the support of fifty Labour candidates at the next election.

For the moment this, too, remained only an aspiration. The trade-union leaders did not warm to the invitation to make free with their funds. They were not to be drawn, and in 1895 as a measure of reinsurance the conservative element in the TUC carried through a change in the standing orders that might check the growth of Socialist influences within the Congress. They established the system of the card vote, whereby a delegate's vote was related to the numerical strength of his union, a move which gave a preponderance to the vast cotton and mining unions who were known to be opposed to the forming of a political party. The more radical trades councils, local federal bodies, were excluded altogether, and no delegate could take his place unless he was a trade-union officer or working at his trade—a ruling which operated against John Burns and Keir Hardie. Thus, at this point any working-class political organization seemed hopelessly cut off from the only available means of obtaining financial backing.

Within five years this prospect had entirely altered. The reason for the change was that in the later part of the 1890s the trade unions suddenly found that the established position on which they had been content to rely was now being seriously challenged. Employers were increasingly strengthening their position by forming employers' associations in particular crafts and by organizing pools of free, that is non-union, labour as a strike-breaking force. In 1897 the Amalgamated Society of Engineers and in 1898 the miners of the South Wales coal-fields embarked on long strikes and in both instances the employers won the struggle. The issues had included the old disputes over pay and the length of the working day, but there was now a new one, far more disconcerting for the unions. Technological advance was making it possible for firms to employ unskilled men, where previously they had needed skilled workers—a process known as 'dilution'. This threatened to cut the ground from beneath the older unions, but their demand that the new machines should still be operated by skilled workers was rejected by the employers as an intolerable intrusion into the sphere of management at a time when the industry of the nation was seriously feeling the effects of German and American competition.

At the same time the employers were advancing on another front. There were many areas of vagueness in existing legislation concerning the rights of trade unions. These had remained largely unexplored during the economic recession of the 1880s, when the unions had been on the defensive, but with the revival of trade and the growth of the new unions at the end of that decade employers began to test their position in a number of court cases, where everything rested on the personal interpretation of the law by the judges. Some decisions favoured the unions, but a great many went the other way. It was declared that unions had not the right to boycott an employer who had supplied materials to another faced with a strike; they were not to issue black lists of non-union firms and workers; even their powers of picketing could in certain circumstances be defined as malicious conspiracy.

Behind all these setbacks lay one dread. Until now it had been assumed that if a firm sued for the losses which it had suffered from a strike, the resultant damages could only be imposed on the officials of the union who as private individuals could afford to pay very little. 'When it comes to the question of framing a writ against them,' declared *The Times* in 1897, 'these officers of a well drilled army, acting on a common plan and disposing of a common purse, sink at once into individual artisans with no greater and no less responsibilities than other private citizens.'[4] How long would it be before a judge would take the plunge and impose far heavier damages on a trade union as a corporate entity? That moment came in September 1900 with the Taff Vale decision, but before then the accumulation of all these dangers had at last convinced the trade unions that they dare no longer dispense with a political party which might enable them to reinforce their position with new legislation in the House of Commons.

At the Trades Union Congress of 1899 a proposal was put forward by James Holmes of the Amalgamated Society of Railway Servants, whereby the parliamentary committee should be instructed to summon a meeting of 'all the cooperative, socialistic, trade union and other working organizations' for the election of a special congress to find ways of increasing the number of working-class MPs in the next Parliament, and after a three-hour debate the motion was carried by 546,000 card votes against 434,000.

On the strength of this relatively narrow majority a meeting of 129 delegates was held in London in February 1900, and out of its discussions the political organization later known as the Labour party was born. The principal achievement of the meeting was to establish a Labour Representation Committee (the LRC) of twelve members, consisting of seven trade unionists, one Fabian, two SDF and two ILP members. An essential aim was to create an atmosphere of cooperation to quieten the fears of the unions that were still holding back. Thus, despite the number of Socialists on the committee, the delegates were careful to avoid giving the impression that the new party would run on purely Socialist lines. Future parliamentary candidates were only required to belong to the working class and policy was to be left to the tactical demands of the situation in the House of Commons. Trade unions who wished to support a candidate would do so by contributing 10 shillings (50p) per annum for every thousand members—a figure which was purposely kept very low—and the secretary of the committee was to be J. Ramsay MacDonald who, although a member of the ILP, was generally acceptable to the trade unions because of his earlier efforts to remain on good terms with the Liberals.

The meeting of the delegates had excited little interest at the time; to many it seemed just one more piece of working-class bureaucracy, and the immediate efforts of the LRC may have confirmed that view. They were confronted almost at once by a general election in October 1900— too soon for their preparations to be complete and at a time when the emotional fervour of the Boer war created an extraneous factor. The LRC endorsed fifteen candidates in the campaign, but only two, Keir Hardie and Richard Bell, were able to win their seats.

It was the law courts that entirely changed the situation. In 1900 a strike in the Taff Vale Railway Company in South Wales had led to an application by the manager of the Company for an injunction against the secretary of the Amalgamated Society of Railway Servants after the picketing of stations in Cardiff. In September 1900 Mr Justice Farwell not merely granted the injunction, but also stated that the union itself was liable. The court of appeal reversed this finding, but when the case was taken to the House of Lords, Farwell's original decision was upheld. Inevitably the union now found itself sued and in December 1902 was faced with damages and total costs amounting to £42,000. The Taff Vale dispute had finally produced the blow which the unions had feared for some time. From now on none of them would be secure; a strike which caused financial loss to a firm might be followed by action in the courts which would very soon drain any union's funds, and the series of court decisions that quickly followed showed that this was no empty fear. The immunity which they had believed the Acts of 1871 and 1875 gave them had proved an illusion.

There was only one hope—fresh legislation—and only one means available. Between 1901 and 1903 the membership of the LRC rose from 375,000 to 861,000. The unions' subscription rate was increased from ten shillings to £5 for every thousand members. In 1902 Sir Henry Campbell-Bannerman, leader of the Liberal Opposition, agreed to support a resolution in the Commons that 'legislation is necessary to prevent workmen being placed by judge-made law in a position inferior to

that intended by Parliament in 1875'; and in 1903 a working arrangement was made between Ramsay MacDonald and Herbert Gladstone,
the chief Liberal whip, whereby Liberal associations would be
encouraged not to compete with LRC candidates in about thirty constituencies at the next general election. In this way the opponents of the
trade unions had at last broken down the innate conservatism that had
stood so long in the way of the creation of a Labour party, and the
working class now turned to organizing their discordant and confused
elements into a political striking force that could act on their behalf at
Westminster.

5
Conservative Decline 1902–1905

S hortly before the turn of the century an observer in the House of Commons described the First Lord of the Treasury taking his place on the front bench. 'Up go two square-toed spatted feet on the table opposite. The legs are arched and suggest a switchback railway. The soft brown meditative eyes, denoting the man of thought rather than the man of action, are now peering upwards through glasses into the amber glow of the fanlight in the ceiling. As he gazes, he yawns.'[1]

This was Arthur James Balfour who succeeded his uncle, Lord Salisbury, as Conservative Prime Minister in July 1902. At fifty-four he was one of the foremost debaters in the House, a master of parliamentary repartee and of political tactics. 'Had his life been cast amid the labyrinthine intrigues of Renaissance Italy,' Winston Churchill wrote of him later, 'he would not have required to study the works of Machiavelli.'[2] Balfour's conservatism was governed by a sense of caution and quiet scepticism, the philosophic doubt on which he had once written a treatise. 'Of the two evils it is better, perhaps, that our ship shall go nowhere than it shall go wrong,' he had said, 'that it should stand still than it should run upon the rocks.'[3] The problem facing Balfour during his premiership, however, was that nothing would stand still. For the next three and a half years he was to be beset by a series of provocative issues which threatened to bring the Liberals back into harmony and which, but for his finesse, might well have split the Conservatives.

The first of these was the Education Act of 1902. This established that all elementary and secondary schools outside the fee-paying sector were to be financed from local rates and to be brought under the administration of the county councils and county borough councils. It was a sensible attempt to rationalize the expanding field of education, but it was bound to arouse the old sectarian dispute. The Act of 1870 had created sufficient indignation among the nonconformists who objected to the voluntary Anglican and Roman Catholic schools receiving support from the tax-payer, but at least the financing of these had until now come directly from the Treasury; only the non-sectarian elementary schools had been able to draw on support from local rates and they were controlled by school boards which had become a battleground for Anglican and nonconformist. Now, by the Act of 1902, the school boards were abolished and the Anglican church schools could rely on rates paid by all religious denominations in the district, while retaining a majority of Anglicans on their managerial committees. The difference between local and national financial support might seem subtle, but the heat that it engendered was intense. Thousands of nonconformists refused to pay their rates; in his autobiography Kingsley Martin described how every year household goods would be confiscated by the authorities from his father, a nonconformist minister, and then, after being auctioned in the market-place, would be brought back to him by his congregation. In Wales whole towns and counties defied the Act.

Among the Conservatives the Act put Joseph Chamberlain in a somewhat embarrassing situation in view of his nonconformist support in Birmingham, but almost at the same time he was to make his own devastating contribution to the difficulties of the party. Ever since he had taken over the Colonial Office in 1895 he had become increasingly preoccupied with ideas for transforming Great Britain and her Empire into a more closely knit unit of mutual support. A colonial conference in July 1902 had suggested that the chances of creating any political or military union were as yet remote; for the dominions this would seem like a surrender of the independence which they had only just gained. In the economic sphere, however, Canada had expressed a desire for a system of imperial preference, whereby existing duties on goods exchanged between the mother country and the Empire would be reciprocally lowered, while duties on foreign imports would be raised.

This proposal was certainly in the spirit of Chamberlain's aims, but he knew perfectly well that it was also tantamount to a return to protection. For the previous half century the sanctity of free trade had been unquestioned by either party. Despite the strain that it was now imposing on agriculture (see p. 21), it had an emotional hold as the supposed basis of British prosperity. Furthermore, the principal imports from the Empire were foodstuffs, and imperial preference was bound to mean higher duties, and hence higher prices, for food imported from foreign countries.

This could be political dynamite. The Liberals would certainly rally to the defence of free trade; the Conservatives, torn between a belief in the Empire and doubts about protection, might easily become divided and Chamberlain could hardly relish the prospect of endangering the party which he had only just joined ten years after his secession from the Liberals. Consequently he hesitated at first. Eventually, however, he decided to press the matter with his colleagues and Balfour now found himself confronted with an issue of far greater danger to the Conservatives than the passing of the Education Act.

For the moment the debate in the cabinet remained centred on a single technical point. In his budget of 1902 Sir Michael Hicks Beach, the Chancellor of the Exchequer, had revived a small registration duty on imported corn and flour. This had been a temporary measure to cover a large deficit and C. T. Ritchie, a convinced free trader, who succeeded Hicks Beach in July, had every intention of removing it in the budget of 1903. It was here that Chamberlain saw an opportunity to insert unobtrusively the thin end of a wedge for the initiating of his scheme, and in November 1902 he persuaded the cabinet that the duty should only be remitted on colonial produce, while still being charged on foreign imports. The decision, however, was merely provisional and in March 1903, on Chamberlain's return from a long tour of South Africa during which his thoughts on imperial preference had crystallized, he found that Balfour and the cabinet, moved by Ritchie's threat of resignation, had agreed that the duties should be remitted in their entirety.

Chamberlain's response to this was to turn the question over to public debate. On 15 May 1903, in a speech at Birmingham, he issued the challenge.

> I say it is the business of British statesmen to do everything they can, even at some present sacrifice, to keep the trade of the colonies with Great Britain, to increase that trade, to promote it, even if in doing so we lessen somewhat the trade with our foreign competitors.
> ... You want an empire. Do you think it is better to cultivate the trade with your own people or to let that go in order that you may keep the trade with those who are your competitors and rivals?[4]

There now seemed no escape from a major controversy in which the question of the Empire was almost at once smothered by the political implications of protection. For the Liberals, the watchdogs of free trade, it seemed to offer a splendid opportunity. 'Wonderful news today,' said Asquith to his wife, when he read the report of Chamberlain's speech, 'and it is only a question of time when we shall sweep this country.'[5] From now on the Conservatives faced disintegration, as young Conservative imperialists flocked to Chamberlain, while cabinet ministers, such as the Duke of Devonshire and Ritchie, clung fervently to free trade. In the midst of this Arthur Balfour, not personally opposed to the gist of Chamberlain's ideas, struggled to keep his government in existence. He was to need all his dexterity to cope with the situation, but for the moment he succeeded. By the autumn of 1903 he had managed to engineer a series of resignations by which the government shed its extremist free traders and protectionists. Joseph Chamberlain gave up the Colonial Office so that he might be free to stump the country in support of his policy, while his son Austen retained the essential link with the government through taking over from Ritchie as Chancellor of the Exchequer.

But this reshuffle could not solve the problem and although Balfour's government had regained a superficial homogeneity, its attitude appeared equivocal. However much Joseph Chamberlain might seek to conceal the issue of protection under the guise of tariff reform in the interest of the Empire, it was difficult for him to maintain the distinction. Indeed by October 1903 he was elaborating a general indictment of free trade. 'Agriculture, as the greatest of all trades and industries of this country, has been practically destroyed,' he announced at Greenock, 'Sugar has gone: silk has gone: iron is threatened: cotton will go!'[6] The arguments of the Tariff Reform League, supported by *The Times*, the *Daily Telegraph* and the *Daily Express*, echoed throughout the country for the next two years, and in city after city tariff reformers were pursued by Liberal free traders who expostulated on the iniquities of the 'dear loaf' which food taxes would create. Almost twenty years before, Joseph Chamberlain had split the Liberals over the question of Home Rule for Ireland, and now that same voice seemed destined to revive their political fortunes.

Against the background of this general storm a series of smaller upsets continued to undermine the Conservative ascendancy. In 1904 a Licensing Act allowed the liquor trade to set up a fund to provide compensation for publicans whose licences had been withdrawn on grounds of redundancy in accordance with an earlier Act. The temperance element of the population, strongly represented among nonconformist Liberals, naturally took offence, but this at least was a calculated risk for the Conservatives who drew powerful support from the brewers and distillers.

So, too, it could be said that their policy in dealing with the conquered Boer republics was consistent with their attitude towards empire. After the peace, Balfour's government aimed at establishing a fairly close control from London so as to ensure a British preponderance throughout the whole of South Africa. 'You must give us time thoroughly to anglicize the Transvaal,' wrote Lord Milner, the High Commissioner, to the Colonial Office. 'We must increase the British population first. We cannot afford to risk the experiment of self-government.' The former Boer republics were first administered as Crown Colonies; then in 1905 a move was made by Alfred Lyttleton, the Colonial Secretary, towards establishing local constitutions, but the scheme for the Transvaal found little favour with the Boers, since the proposed property qualifications and the shaping of the constituency boundaries weighted the franchise strongly in the interest of British residents; and in any case the powers of the legislature were to be fairly restricted.

This was all too colonialist in the eyes of the Liberals, but the constitution of the Transvaal was not likely to be a vote-catching issue of any great significance. It was another feature of Milner's work that awoke a more effective protest. In his determination to foster the general economic development of South Africa he had overcome the shortage of kaffir labour on the Rand gold fields by importing thousands of indentured Chinese who were kept herded together in great compounds in appalling living conditions. The Liberals raised an outcry on humanitarian grounds. The working class saw the matter from a different angle and the annual report of the TUC in 1904 condemned a situation in which 'white labour in the Transvaal should be ousted and replaced by yellow slave labour'.

The trade unions at this time were generally rather sensitive about the security of the market for their labour and had already expressed alarm at the great number of foreign workers who had been migrating into Great Britain. In 1905 the government attempted to mollify them with an Aliens Act which restricted the means of entry, but as this did not include workmen brought in under contract, it did little good. Indeed, the Conservatives had paid only mild attention to the working-class element in the electorate. They had parried Labour's efforts to gain legislation that would end the threat to trade-union finances implicit in the Taff Vale decision. They had allowed the prospect of tariff reform to raise the spectre of dearer food, and although an Unemployed Workmen's Act in 1905 had empowered the Local Government Board to set up labour exchanges, this had left unemployment assistance dependent on charitable funds.

Thus it seemed that in these years the Conservatives were set on a disaster course. The Liberals had regained their sense of unity and the

Labour movement looked increasingly to them for a working arrangement at the next election. Only Balfour's skill had kept the Conservatives together during the tariff reform controversy and it was beyond his philosophy to do more than that in the present situation. The ship would not stand still and the rocks were clearly in sight.

6

New Challenges Abroad

1. The making of the Anglo-French entente

It was not only in the domestic sphere that forces of change were at work in Great Britain; her foreign policy, too, was having to respond to a diversity of new circumstances. Throughout the nineteenth century it had been enough for her to regard France and Russia as her most likely opponents. Russian interests in the Straits, Persia and Afghanistan, French ambitions in Belgium, north Italy and the Mediterranean, the occasional colonial dispute—these had sometimes given rise to minor alarms, but while her naval supremacy remained unchallenged, she could afford to stand aside from any serious continental entanglement.

By the end of the century the relative simplicity of this situation had changed. In Europe unification of Italy in 1860 had added a new factor on the naval scene in the Mediterranean. Still more significant was Bismarck's creation of a German federal empire after Prussia's defeat of France in 1871; where previously there had been a patchwork of duchies and kingdoms supplying the small change of diplomatic transactions, the presence of Imperial Germany with a greater population, a more powerful industry and a more effective military machine than either France or Austria, upset the old balance of the European Powers on which the long peace of the nineteenth century had rested.

For the moment a new balance of a sort was fairly soon achieved. The Dual Alliance of 1879 was a treaty between Germany and Austria for mutual defence against Russia, and in 1882 Italy joined them in a Triple Alliance which extended the terms to include similar arrangements against France. Bismarck worked hard to prevent any counter-alliance which these treaties were only too likely to provoke, but by 1894, shortly after his resignation, France and Russia had finally come together with a pact for mutual defence against the Central Powers. The two systems thus formed were not aggressive in intent; they did not preclude the making of individual agreements between members of the rival blocs, and since their existence gave all the states concerned a greater sense of security, they may even have contributed to the peace of Europe until the final breakdown in 1914.

Nevertheless the situation that they created was explosive. They placed too much emphasis on the distinction between a defensive and an aggressive war—never easy to establish; they involved, too, plans for automatic mobilization in certain contingencies. This was particularly dangerous, since all general staffs of the time were convinced that victory was most likely to be gained by the launching of a sudden knock-out blow, and in the race to strike first mobilization could mean war. Furthermore, the existence of the Franco-Russian alliance after 1894 meant that the German general staff were faced with the probability of having to fight on two fronts; and it was in response to this that General von Schlieffen devised a plan whereby France should be defeated first with a great advance wheeling through Belgium and swinging down to the west of Paris, after which the German Army would be free to deal with the eastern front. The existence of the Schlieffen plan consequently suggested that if war should ever break out between Germany and Russia, the initial stage would be a German invasion of Belgium and France. At the same time the rivalry between Russia and Austria* over the decaying power of Turkey-in-Europe was now exacerbated by the growth of an intense nationalism among the small states of Serbia, Bulgaria and Greece. Any change in the situation in the Balkans could easily draw Russia and Austria into conflict, and in that event the two networks of alliance made it far more likely that this would lead to a general European war.

The division of Europe into two armed diplomatic blocs was not in itself a source of immediate anxiety for Great Britain; a greater cause for concern was the occasions when continental powers seemed prepared to combine against her. When, for example, in 1897 Austria and Russia came to an agreement to accept the *status quo* in the Balkans, Russia could turn her full attention to the Far East, probably to the detriment of British interests there. And three years later the entire Continent, looking in anger at Great Britain's war with the Boers, appeared ready to form a league against her.

The real force behind such fears was the realization by the British government that their naval predominance could now no longer be safely assumed. In the 1880s French, Italian and Russian naval building had created a challenge that in 1889 stimulated the British to pass the Naval Defence Act providing for ten new battleships and thirty-eight large and small cruisers. 'Our Fleet should be equal to the combination

*Since 1867 the Habsburg empire had assumed the official title of Austria-Hungary.

of the two next strongest navies in Europe,' declared Lord George Hamilton in 1893.[1] Yet this reiterating of the two-power principle was no more than a desperate yearning for the circumstances of the mid-nineteenth century; it bore little relation to reality.

In 1898 the German government, too, embarked upon the building of a navy which German industry might eventually make the greatest challenge of all. This was later to become a factor of enormous emotional and political force, but at the time it was the prospect of the combined French and Russian fleets that worried the British government most. In 1901 an Intelligence assessment of 'the military requirements of the Empire in a war with France and Russia' drew the gloomiest conclusions, and in the same year Lord Selborne's cabinet memorandum declared that the growth of the American, Japanese and German navies, in addition to the existing threat from France and Russia, made the two-power principle already a thing of the past.

The naval issue was only one facet of a much wider development. What really threatened to undermine the assumptions on which earlier British foreign policy had been based was a proliferation of rivals from whom she could no longer stand aloof. The sheer variety of ambitions now at work was more than one Power alone could hope to contain. In the Mediterranean France and Italy looked longingly at areas on the North African coast. Overseas the United States and Japan were emerging as new Powers. The development of great railway projects was to open up an intensified struggle in Asia; the concession which Germany had gained from Turkey in 1899 for the building of a railway from Constantinople to Baghdad might ultimately affect British interests in the Persian Gulf; a Russian railway already extended to the frontier of Afghanistan and the construction of the Trans-Siberian railway seemed to herald new Russian activity on the northern borders of China.

It was the fear of Russian encroachment on her position in China that first suggested a new direction for British foreign policy. This took the form of two unsuccessful attempts to reach some kind of agreement with Germany. The first of these, in 1898, was an unauthorized approach by Joseph Chamberlain, who dreamed of incorporating the United States as well in some great Anglo-Saxon Teutonic union; the second, in 1901, was the result of an official negotiation undertaken by Lord Lansdowne, the Foreign Secretary, in which Germany demanded as her price that Great Britain should join the Triple Alliance. Both schemes were ruled out by the Prime Minister, Lord Salisbury, who rightly recognized that neither country had anything to offer the other. The British would not think of committing themselves firmly to the Central Powers; what they were seeking was an ally to help them resist Russia in China, and the Germans had not the slightest intention of antagonizing Russia for the sake of promoting British interests in the Far East.

In fact, as had been strongly stated in Foreign Office memoranda, the natural ally for Great Britain at this moment was Japan, whose own designs on the mainland of China had been seriously threatened by a recent Russian occupation of Manchuria. Indeed, unless Japan could now find an ally against Russia, she might be driven to make a bargain with her instead. Thus the collapse of the German negotiations was followed almost at once by the signing, in January 1902, of an Anglo-Japanese treaty whereby each promised strict neutrality in the event of either of them being at war with one Power, and mutual assistance in the event of war with more than one.

A great deal of academic discussion has ensued over whether the Anglo-Japanese treaty marks the end of British isolation. The British could argue that the treaty was a non-European arrangement purely designed for one particular purpose. Nevertheless, the implications were enormous. They had committed themselves to going to war, if certain conditions were fulfilled at some unspecified date in the future, thus ignoring the constitutional objection that Lord Salisbury had made to joining the Triple Alliance six months before: that no British government could bind its successors with such a promise which a later House of Commons might not allow them to keep.

The treaty was published on signature and had a great impact on the European Powers and, in particular, on relations between Great Britain and France. The general assumption was that its terms now made a Russo-Japanese war highly probable. To Germany the treaty seemed a natural expression of Anglo-Russian hostility and the German Emperor William II was hopeful that it might eventually allow Germany to draw Russia over to her side. For the French the new situation was extremely alarming. A Russo-Japanese war would throw a new strain upon the maintenance of the Franco-Russian alliance, and if they were forced to join Russia against Japan, they might find themselves involved in a purposeless war with Great Britain.

It was these considerations, as much as his desire for British agreement to France's acquisition of Morocco, that led Delcassé, the French foreign minister, to open conversations with the British government in the hope of resolving outstanding differences between them. The negotiations went slowly at first, but French objections fell away after the Russo-Japanese war had begun with a Japanese attack on Port Arthur in February 1904, and the settlement between Great Britain and France was concluded in April 1904.

In the light of later events the Anglo-French *entente* must seem a most startling reversal of British foreign policy, the first step towards an alignment that was to make Great Britain and France allies in two great wars against Germany. The *entente*, however, was not a treaty of alliance; it was merely a series of agreements ending a variety of disputes over the frontiers of Senegambia in west Africa, spheres of influence in Siam, and the fisheries off Newfoundland, as well as a mutual recognition of British interests in Egypt and of French interests in Morocco. Such a reconciliation after centuries of hostility was striking enough, but the British were still far from seeing it as a move against Germany, although their nervousness over the growth of the German fleet had contributed to their desire to come to terms with at least one of their potential opponents.

It was the German reaction that really gave substance to the Anglo-French *entente*. William II had been pressing on with his hopes of winning over Russia and in July 1905 at a private meeting with Tsar Nicholas II at Björkö, the two sovereigns agreed to a defensive alliance. Neither of their governments would accept this, however; the Germans reckoned that it meant too great a liability; the Russians knew that the war against Japan was lost when the Baltic fleet had been sunk in the straits of Tshushima after an epic voyage round the world, and now clung desperately to their alliance with France which any agreement with Germany would certainly undo.

Bülow, the German chancellor, and Holstein, the head of the German foreign office, were more interested in weakening the new Anglo-French *entente*, and to them, Morocco seemed to be the issue on which to stage a confrontation. Accordingly, in March 1905, William II was persuaded to land at Tangier and to announce that he regarded Morocco as an independent country where he could not allow any interference with German economic interests. His demand for an international conference was not merely a direct challenge to France's colonial ambitions; it was designed to show the French that the British would do little to support them despite their improved relations.

As usual, the German government had miscalculated. British public opinion turned heavily against Germany; King Edward described his nephew's action as 'the most mischievous and uncalled-for event which the German emperor had ever been engaged in since he came to the throne'.[2] The British government suspected that Germany was aiming at a port on the Atlantic coast. It was thus vital to dissuade France from yielding to this pressure, and in June Lord Lansdowne warned the German ambassador that Great Britain would stand by France in the event of war. In the outcome Delcassé was forced to resign. The Germans did get their conference at Algeciras in January 1906, but this only revealed a new solidarity between Great Britain and France and the position that the French had earmarked for themselves in Morocco was largely confirmed by its findings.

Thus the Moroccan crisis had gained the Germans nothing. The events of these months had revealed that the *entente* was much more than a settlement of colonial disputes; they had produced a moment of truth in which it was clear that Great Britain dared not let France turn to Germany, and although the military conversations which were opened between British and French generals in December 1905 remained purely informal, they symbolized the revolution that British foreign policy had undergone, an involvement as effective as any actual alliance.

2. The new sense of insecurity and the debate over strategy

It was not only the politicians and the professionals at the Foreign Office who had become uneasily aware of the precariousness of British power. The same theme had captured the imagination of a number of writers exploring the idea of the possible invasion and occupation of Great Britain by an enemy force. As early as May 1871 'The Battle of Dorking', published in *Blackwood's Magazine*, described a landing in the south of England, culminating in the collapse of the last line of defence on the North Downs. Many similar stories followed, the enemy being conceived first as France, then significantly, by the turn of the century, as Germany. In 1903 Erskine Childers, a dedicated yachtsman, depicted in *The Riddle of the Sands* two Englishmen on a sailing trip off the north German coast discovering a rehearsal for the assembling of a vast German invasion force; and in 1906 William Le Queux's *The Invasion of 1910*, serialized in the *Daily Mail*, was advertised by sand-wich-boardmen dressed in German uniform.

The purpose of most of these works was seriously propagandist, their message the material and psychological unreadiness of the British to face an imminent danger. The writers were the spokesmen of those who wanted compulsory military service and who feared national decadence. 'Is it not becoming patent,' wrote Childers in a postscript to his novel, 'that the time has come for training all Englishmen systematically either for the sea or for the rifle?'[3] Le Queux was more damning. 'In the hour of trial amidst smoking ruins among the holocausts of dead which marked the prolonged, bloody and terrible battles on land and sea, the spirit of the nation quailed and there was really no great leader to recall it to ways of honour and duty.'[4] These warnings of approaching disaster certainly did not go unnoticed. In 1871 'The Battle of Dorking' had provoked Gladstone to make a reply—'be on your guard against alarmism'; and Le Queux's *Invasion of 1910* also led to questions in the House of Commons. In fact, Le Queux had been greatly assisted over the military detail in his story by Field-Marshal Lord Roberts, who as President of the National Service League was constantly demanding the creation of a large standing army, and when one of the characters commented: 'they should have listened to Lord Roberts',[5] it was clear that the collaboration had been close.

At the time the introduction of conscription was hardly a viable political cause, but Balfour's government did at least respond sufficiently to the new sense of insecurity to undertake certain fundamental reforms in the organization of the existing forces. Among many deficiencies the Boer War had revealed an almost total absence of any central planning and coordinating mechanism for the services. The Defence Committee, set up in 1895, had been too much at the mercy of personal and departmental jealousies to serve any useful function, and in 1903 Balfour himself took over as chairman of what was now to be the Committee of Imperial Defence (CID). The First Lord of the Admiralty, the First Sea Lord, the Director of Naval Intelligence, the Secretary of State for War, the Commander-in-Chief and the Director of Military Intelligence were all to be standing members, and the Prime Minister was to have the right to co-opt any other temporary members. The CID, however, remained a purely advisory body; there were vast areas in the military, naval and imperial field that it failed to coordinate, and its activity in 1914 shows that it was still a far cry from the degree of central planning that was needed. Yet in the context of its time, when viewed against the vacuum that had existed before, its creation does suggest that an earlier complacency had been shaken.

At the same time efforts were being made to reorganize the Army command. A War Office (Reconstitution) Committee, set up by Balfour under the chairmanship of Lord Esher, succeeded in establishing an Army Council of officers and civil servants, which superseded the post of Commander-in-Chief. Among the units the infantry were re-equipped with the Lee–Enfield rifle and the artillery were to receive new thirteen-pounder and eighteen-pounder guns. Apart from this there was little change; the Esher committee's proposal for the forming of a general staff along the lines of all the other European Powers was turned down and the Army remained largely in its Victorian mould, an instrument for short colonial excursions rather than for any effective intervention on the Continent.

The reason for this lack of interest in creating a large modern army lay in the general belief that the Navy was still the principal guardian of British security. Public confidence in Britannia's divine right to rule the waves remained firm throughout the Victorian era, and as national and imperial rivalries grew more intense, had tended to become more outspoken. The Navy League, designed to foster general support, was created in 1894 and in the following year there took place the first official ceremony in Trafalgar Square in commemoration of Nelson's victory.

Nevertheless, it is a sad fact that by the end of the century that confidence was utterly unfounded. Quite apart from the shipbuilding programmes of other Powers, the British Navy was to a large extent living in the past; there was no system of training for higher officers, no general staff and no study of naval strategy which might now be seriously affected by the development of the mine, the submarine and the torpedo. The fleets were distributed in the Mediterranean and across the world, leaving the protection of British home waters for much of the year in the care of a few outdated ships described by one authority as 'an absolute disgrace to a naval Power'.[6]

Fortunately the Navy did find a champion who was capable of imposing swift revolutionary change. Sir John Fisher became First Sea Lord in 1904. He was a man of ruthless energy, heedless of convention, splattering his letters with biblical references and heavy underlinings, and until his retirement in 1910 he dedicated himself to the reform of the Navy. Already by 1902 the Admiralty had become convinced that the type of naval force that Germany was building pointed unmistakably to a desire to challenge Great Britain in particular, and once the Anglo-French *entente* had been formed, the distribution of British ships could be redevised on the assumption of German rather than French hostility. Accordingly Fisher reduced the Mediterranean fleet and established instead a greatly strengthened Channel fleet based on Dover, and an Atlantic fleet at Gibraltar. He called home many of the ships scattered around the world, scrapped more than 150 that were obsolete, and embarked on a campaign for the building of dreadnoughts. These were to be battleships faster than any other, carrying ten twelve-inch guns whose range would enable the ship to remain clear of the menace of torpedo attack, and were to be supported by a new Invincible class of battle-cruiser.

These changes in the services reflect some awareness of Great Britain's new relationship to the Continent, and they went a little way towards meeting the demands of those who felt alarm at her vulnerability. They did not, however, resolve the fundamental question of the role that these forces should play if Great Britain became involved in a major continental war. The debate, which had gone on since the 1880s, was essentially one between the generals and the admirals, each seeing their own service as the key to any future strategy. The military insisted that the Navy should remain in home waters to protect the country from invasion—'the bolt from the blue' envisaged by the author of 'The Battle of Dorking'. With that safeguard the Army would then be free to be ferried across the Channel for a major land campaign on the Continent. The Admiralty, however, regarded the invasion scare as a plot to reduce the Navy to a subordinate role by tying it to home waters. They maintained that the defence of British soil would still be possible if the Navy put out to blockade enemy ports—the 'blue water' school of thought— and they had their own proposals for the Army, part of which should remain at home to deal with any enemy invasion forces that did escape the Navy, while the rest could provide small expeditionary forces to be landed on the coasts of the Continent.

The argument became more heated in the early years of the century, and towards the end of the Conservative administration the government seemed on the whole to favour the naval view. 'Invasion of these islands is not an eventuality that we need seriously consider,' said Balfour in May 1905,[7] to the fury of Lord Roberts, and when Haldane took over as Secretary of State for War in the new Liberal government, he declared the need for 'a highly organized and well equipped striking force which can be transported with the least possible delay to any part of the world where it is required'.

All this might sound like a victory for the Navy, but the question was not settled yet. If the British Army was to be a striking force, where was it to strike? The military conversations between the British and the French which had started in December 1905 pointed increasingly to the likelihood that this would be at the side of the French, and it seemed that if war were to break out, the Navy would not have escaped the role of running a ferry service across the Channel after all.

7
Liberal Heyday 1906–1911

By the autumn of 1905 Balfour and most of his colleagues had little doubt that a Conservative electoral defeat was purely a matter of time. The only issue was the moment and the manner of their going. To linger on while the present Parliament ran its full term seemed likely to do more damage to the party and many in the cabinet favoured an immediate dissolution. Balfour, however, considered that this would give the Liberals an advantage in the subsequent general election, since as the principal party of Opposition they would be able to concentrate on all the current discontents. He preferred resignation. This would bring the Liberals into office and confront them with the task of fighting an election as the government in power at a time when their internal divisions might still be too recent to stand the strain of formulating a common policy. The cabinet saw the wisdom of this and on 4 December 1905 Balfour resigned.

As it turned out, Balfour's tactics did not save the Conservatives; they merely rescued Campbell-Bannerman from a factional attack within his own party. In September 1905 Asquith, Grey and Haldane had met at Grey's fishing lodge in Relugas in the north-east of Scotland and had agreed that, in the event of a Liberal administration being formed, they would only consent to serve in it if Campbell-Bannerman went to the House of Lords with a peerage and left the leadership in the House of Commons to Asquith. A conversation in November with Campbell-Bannerman suggested that he might be harder to shift than they had imagined and Balfour's eventual decision to resign finally undermined the hopes of the Relugas compact. The Asquith group had always envisaged presenting their ultimatum after a Liberal victory at the polls, but now victory had still to be achieved and it was vital that the party should present a united front to the electorate. The day after Balfour's resignation, Campbell-Bannerman kissed hands at Buckingham Palace; fortified by his wife's resolute advice, he was determined to remain in the Commons and within three days any indications of a refusal to serve under him had vanished.

As a result, Campbell-Bannerman was able to put together a government of highly talented individuals. Asquith became Chancellor of the Exchequer, Grey Foreign Secretary and Haldane Secretary of State for War—not Lord Chancellor as he had hoped. Herbert Gladstone went to the Home Office, Lloyd George to the Board of Trade, and John Morley to the India Office. John Burns was the first member of the working class to enter the cabinet, taking over the Local Government Board, while of the junior ministers young Winston Churchill, who had left the Conservatives in 1904 in order to defend free trade, became Under-Secretary of State for the Colonies.

The defeat of the Relugas compact was followed within a few weeks by the end of any hopes that Balfour might have had that his resignation would place the Liberals at a disadvantage. The general election of January 1906 proved to be a massive vote of no confidence in the Conservative record and the Liberals were returned with an overwhelming majority—'floated into Parliament on the river of free trade', as John Burns put it. Conservative strongholds fell everywhere; not a single Conservative was elected in the whole of Wales and Balfour lost his own seat for East Manchester. By the end of the polling the Liberals held 377 seats and the Conservatives had been reduced to 157. The Irish Nationalists had been unlikely to change very much and came back with eighty-three members, while the LRC returned thirty officially sponsored candidates.

This outright majority for the Liberals meant that they would not have to rely on either of the two minor parties, and for the Irish there was consequently little likelihood of a new attempt at Home Rule. Labour at least could expect a rather greater hearing from the radical wing of the Liberals and in any case could reflect upon an auspicious beginning to their political life—the outcome of the 1903 agreement with Herbert Gladstone, whereby Labour and Liberals had fought their constituency campaigns in cooperation with each other (see p. 39).

The awareness of his new position of strength had a marked effect on Campbell-Bannerman. He spoke with an air of decision which the Commons had not known when he had been leading a weakened Opposition. Early in the first session he dealt tartly with some debating point from Balfour who had by now managed to find a seat. 'I say: "enough of this tomfoolery". It might have answered very well in the last Parliament, but is altogether out of place in this Parliament. The tone and temper of this Parliament will not permit it. . . . Move your amendments and let us get to business.'[1]

The business to which Campbell-Bannerman wished first to attend was the settlement of South Africa. However divided the Liberals might have been over the Boer War, they were certainly sympathetic to a more wholehearted form of self-government than that suggested by the Lyttleton constitution (see p. 44) for the Transvaal. This was withdrawn, to the delight of Jan Christian Smuts who had come immediately to London in the hope of effecting a change. Smuts, a young Boer commander in the recent war, had represented a more moderate attitude towards the British, and the policy of cooperation which he and his associate Louis Botha now advocated was to be a highly significant factor in the future history of South Africa. A new constitution devised by the Liberals late in 1906 granted the Transvaal universal white manhood suffrage with a six months residential qualification. Constituencies were organized more fairly, and Dutch and English were both to be official languages. Presenting this to the House of Commons, Winston Churchill appealed to the Opposition to join with the Liberals in ratifying the settlement. 'With all our majority we can only make it the gift of a party; they can make it the gift of England.' The Conservatives, however, saw the gift as nothing less than the surrender of the fruits of a hard-won victory and objected strongly. Fortunately for the Liberals the new constitution did not have to be passed by the House of Lords and was merely promulgated by Letters Patent in November 1906. In the subsequent elections in the Transvaal the Boer nationalist party was successful and Botha became prime minister; in June 1907 a similar constitution was established for the Orange River Colony, the new title of the Orange Free State.

Self-government in the former Boer republics was soon followed by a move towards unification, greatly encouraged by Lord Selborne, High Commissioner since 1905. This time it was not to be imposed from above, but was worked out in 1908 by a national convention of representatives from the four colonial parliaments. The scheme that was eventually drawn up was unitary rather than federal. Southern Rhodesia opted out, and Basutoland, Swaziland and Bechuanaland remained British protectorates. Otherwise, the four governments of the Transvaal, the Orange River Colony, Natal and Cape Colony surrendered their sovereignty to a single legislature at Cape Town consisting of two chambers, the Senate representing the provinces, and the House of Assembly elected according to existing franchises. For local internal affairs each colony retained an elective council, but their powers were specifically delegated to them by the central government. In 1909 this constitution was approved without amendment at Westminster and in 1910 Botha became the first prime minister of the new Union of South Africa.

The treatment of the Boers in these years was a remarkable instance of a truly liberal attitude towards empire. In 1906 Churchill had asked Smuts whether he had ever known a conquered people being allowed to govern themselves. Yet this is what the Transvaal constitution had granted and the centralized system of the subsequent Union, which ended any independence for the largely British colony of Natal, made an eventual Boer preponderance much more likely over the whole of South Africa. This was a long way from the policies of Lord Milner, but Liberal idealism was ultimately to gain its reward with South Africa's voluntary support of Great Britain in the two world wars under the premierships of Botha and Smuts.

The Liberal administration was also to set its mark on affairs in India. Here the somewhat autocratic temperament of Lord Curzon, Viceroy from 1898 to 1905, had stirred up powerful ambitions. The National Congress was demanding self-government similar to that enjoyed by British dominions, and extremists had embarked on a campaign of sporadic violence. Lord Minto, who took over from Curzon in 1905, was constantly urged by John Morley at the India Office to hasten the extension of Indian participation in existing organs of government, and in 1909 the Morley–Minto reforms were accepted by Parliament in the Indian Councils Act. There was to be one seat for an Indian on the Viceroy's executive council and two in London on the Secretary of State's council. Provincial councils were to be enlarged and to be allowed to vote on financial matters. The Act also tried to cope with the antagonism between Muslim and Hindu; the Muslims had complained that existing organs of local government were dominated by Hindus, and so a specific number of seats were set aside to be filled by separate Muslim elections. This last seemed only a small step; yet with its assumption of an irreconcilable divide it could be said to have implied the ultimate solution of partition in 1947. As in South Africa, the Liberal administration of the Empire was to have consequences that reached far into the twentieth century.

Meanwhile at home the government had had to make good its pledge to Labour. This must mean some kind of protection for trade-union funds against the dangers opened up by the Taff Vale decision, but the formulation of this legislation soon gave rise to second thoughts among the Liberals. They were uneasy at the prospect of granting the unions unconditional immunity from actions for damages, since this would give them an unprecedented position in an industrial society. 'Do not let us create a privilege for the proletariat,' said Sir John Walton, the Attorney-General, 'and give a sort of benefit of clergy to trade unions.'[2]

The original draft of the Trade Disputes Bill, launched in 1906, made it clear that the Liberals did not intend to do so. This went no further than allowing a trade union freedom from liability for any action taken by one of its branches, provided it disowned that action immediately; thus the Bill left untouched the central problem of the consequences of strike action by the trade union itself. The Labour groups in the Commons now combined to draw up their own Bill which would provide the immunity that they needed, and Campbell-Bannerman eventually cut through the debate by declaring his preference for the Labour Bill, despite the misgivings of the lawyers. Its terms were then incorporated in the government's proposals which became law in December 1906.

The same year saw another sop to Labour from the Liberals. In 1897 and 1900 the Conservatives had already passed Acts which made an employer liable to pay compensation for any injury sustained in the course of work. This, however, had only referred to a limited number of specified trades and there had been considerable working-class pressure for a much wider application of the principle. In 1906 the Liberals' Workmen's Compensation Act extended the system to most categories of workers and added liability for the contracting of industrial diseases, of which a committee at the Home Office ultimately compiled a list of twenty-four.

These Acts were really no more than the settlement of a political debt; they were not seen as a prelude to the creation of the twentieth-century welfare state of which this Liberal administration has sometimes been regarded as the founder. Indeed, there was nothing very radical about the Liberals' early years in office. They believed in reform, but the attitude of most of the cabinet was essentially Gladstonian, aiming merely to modernize and to create a fairer framework within which the individual would be free to improve his lot by his own personal endeavour.

Even Lloyd George at the Board of Trade was initially concerned with establishing a greater efficiency. In 1906 the Merchant Shipping Act did improve seamen's living conditions, but its principal effect was to impose on foreign ships in British ports the regulations concerning cargo and life-saving apparatus which British shipowners already had to observe. In 1907 the Patents and Designs Act gave greater protection to the inventor, but it was also aimed at foreigners who often took out patents in Great Britain to withhold the use of new methods or machinery from British industry. In future the government would have the right to cancel a patent if it had not been put into use within three years in Great Britain. Similarly the establishment of the Port of London Authority in 1908 was devised chiefly to rationalize a confused situation in order to make London more efficient in the competition with continental ports.

Social legislation at first ran along the lines of earlier decades; in 1907 laundry workers were brought within the provisions of existing Factory Acts, and an Act of 1908 limited the working day in the coalmines to eight hours, although an amendment in the House of Lords established that this was not to include the winding time going down or coming out of the pit. There were other more positive measures, but they did not appear to spring from governmental initiative. It was due to Labour pressure that a School Meals Act in 1906 permitted local education authorities to provide free lunches for schoolchildren, despite arguments that this would undermine a sense of responsibility in the family; and it was Liberal backbenchers who insisted on another Act in 1907 requiring schools to carry out medical inspections.

In 1908 the introduction of a non-contributory old age pension did mark a new departure. It was designed to relieve the elderly of dependence on the Poor Law and provided 5 shillings (25p) a week for single people and 7 shillings and 6 pence (37½p) for married couples. Even here twinges of the Gladstonian conscience made some of the stipulations appear grudging and parsimonious. Recipients had to be seventy years of age, although Labour had campaigned for sixty; they must not be in receipt of any other income exceeding £31 a year, and anyone who had 'habitually failed to work according to his ability, opportunity and need', or who had served a prison sentence during the previous ten years was not eligible. Not even these provisions satisfied a former Liberal Prime Minister, Lord Rosebery, who declared that the scheme was 'so prodigal of expenditure as likely to undermine the whole fabric of the Empire'.

In this atmosphere it was hardly surprising that the alliance between the LRC and the Liberals should wear thin. Labour was pressing for an official recognition of every man's right to work, and in 1907 Ramsay MacDonald introduced a Bill which would have made local authorities responsible for providing either work or financial maintenance for the unemployed, but this did not get as far as a second reading. Labour had other worries, too, at this time. Among some branches of the trade unions there had been objections to the enforcing of the political levy on their funds in support of what many of them regarded as a Socialist organization. Among these W. V. Osborne, the secretary of the Walthamstow branch of the Amalgamated Society of Railway Servants, decided in 1906 to take the matter to court, and when the case finally reached the House of Lords in December 1909, judgment was given in favour of Osborne. From now on it seemed that the finances of the LRC would have to depend upon purely voluntary contributions from individual trade unionists, and with this threat to their funds it was natural that Labour should look for some relief by pressing for the payment of MPs.

In April 1908 Sir Henry Campbell-Bannerman, who had been incapacitated by a series of heart-attacks, was forced to resign and died less than three weeks later. Asquith, who had long been regarded as his natural successor, returned from Biarritz to receive from Edward VII the premiership which he was to hold until December 1916. Under his rule the cautious pace of Liberal legislation seemed unlikely to change. Asquith had not been devoid of ambition—the Relugas compact was evidence of that—but for him political life was far from being a consuming passion. It had to leave time for bridge, a copious private correspondence, a wide range of reading and the company of a large family of children. Once committed to a course of action, he could be quietly ruthless, as in 1911, when he broke the power of the House of Lords, but in the main Asquith preferred non-commitment. His reactions were governed by what his wife Margot called 'the steadiness of the Asquith temper', and his leadership was principally confined to unravelling the disputes that might arise between his ministers, an intellectual exercise which, as a successful barrister, he rather enjoyed. This detachment meant at least that ministers had a free rein to run their departments, and it was because Asquith was not prepared to interfere with the radicalism of others that the pace did now begin to quicken.

In 1908 Lloyd George took over as Chancellor of the Exchequer, handing on the Board of Trade to Winston Churchill. These two very remarkable men were both convinced of the need for far-reaching changes. Neither of them sat very easily to the requirements of party discipline and consequently neither was ever entirely trusted by his colleagues. Each was a man of energetic ebullient mind, each destined to lead the nation in war. There were, however, enormous differences between them in background and assumptions. Lloyd George was the product of a relatively humble upbringing in Wales; Churchill, born in Blenheim Palace, was a scion of the ducal house of Marlborough. Lloyd George had opposed the government's policy during the Boer War; Churchill had been trained as a cavalry officer, had taken part in the battle of Omdurman in the Sudan in 1898, and had served as a war correspondent in South Africa, where he had escaped from captivity after becoming a prisoner of the Boers. Of the two, Lloyd George's radicalism was of a deeper dye. 'I believe there is a new order coming from the people of this country,' he had said during the election campaign of 1906. 'It is a quiet but certain revolution, as revolutions come in constitutional countries.' In contrast, Churchill's attitude was paternalist, coloured by the memory of his father Lord Randolph's cry of Tory Democracy. 'He desired in England,' wrote C. F. G. Masterman, 'a state of things where a benign upper class dispensed benefits to an industrious, *bien pensant* and grateful working class.'

Despite these differences their partnership was established almost as soon as they had occupied their new posts. Lloyd George had just spent a holiday in Germany, where he was deeply impressed by the system that existed there for insurance against sickness, accidents and old age; at the same time, Churchill was convinced of the need for some similar arrangement to deal with unemployment which was mounting sharply in 1908 and 1909. To them the answer seemed to lie in a comprehensive national scheme, but since it would take their departments some time to elaborate the precise details of this, Churchill decided to press ahead in the interval with another aspect of unemployment.

He had to hand a study of the subject by William Beveridge, a young social investigator who had been particularly concerned with the problems of casual labour. Churchill's plan was to establish a national network of labour exchanges, incorporating the few that already existed, all to be brought under the control of the Board of Trade. This would ease the search for work and in addition the exchanges would eventually become an integral part of the administration of a system of national insurance. The Act was passed in 1909 and began to take effect early in the next year under Beveridge's direction.

Labour's response to this was lukewarm. They complained that it made no absolute statement of the right to work and they were inclined to regard the new exchanges as a potential source of blackleg labour during a strike. Churchill came rather closer to satisfying them with the Trade Boards Act of 1909. In an effort to deal with the evils of sweated labour this set up boards of representatives of workers, employers and the Civil Service, who were to establish minimum wage rates in four trades: tailors, and box, lace and chain makers—in all, some 200,000 workers.

The full scheme for national insurance against unemployment and ill health was not ready for presentation to the House of Commons until 1911. One section of the Bill established compulsory insurance against unemployment for more than two million workers in a limited number of occupations—engineering, building and shipbuilding—whereby the employer, the worker and the Treasury each made a contribution of 2½d (1p) a week, so that when unemployed the worker could receive 7 shillings (35p) a week for a total period of fifteen weeks in a year. This part of the scheme was based almost entirely on Churchill's work, although by 1911 he had departed from the Board of Trade to the Home Office and thence to the Admiralty and consequently did not get all the credit that was his due.

Health insurance proved more intricate. It was to be far wider than the arrangements for unemployment—compulsory for all manual workers and voluntary for anyone else earning less than £160 a year, although it did not include the self-employed or the non-employed. Free medical treatment and a payment of 10 shillings (50p) a week during sickness for a maximum period of six months were the main benefits. It was to be financed by weekly contributions—4 pence (2p) from the worker, 3 pence (1½p) from the employer and 2 pence (1p) from the state—this payment being registered by a stamp on an insurance card. These terms were more advantageous than those offered by many independent schemes already organized by private companies. Lloyd George recognized, however, that it could be politically dangerous if these companies were put out of business and accordingly insisted that they should all be incorporated within his scheme as approved societies.

There were many forms of protest. Among Labour MPs Philip Snowden led a group of dissidents who maintained that insurance should be financed by general taxation and not by contributions from those whom it was designed to benefit, but Ramsay MacDonald, who had become chairman of the parliamentary party in 1910, accepted the government's principle, which Labour itself adopted in the Attlee administration after the Second World War (see p. 391). Conservative anger was rather noisier; the press led a furious campaign; employers of domestic servants spoke bitterly of the tyranny of stamp-licking and at a great meeting at the Albert Hall denounced the Chancellor of the Exchequer to the strains of 'Taffy was a Welshman, Taffy was a thief'.

Lloyd George could afford to ignore most of this. What was more serious was the objections of the British Medical Association, who feared that free medical attention under the state would mean the loss of doctors' professional independence. In 1912, before the Act took effect, they fought a long resistance similar to that which Aneurin Bevan had to face in devising the National Health Service in 1946 (see p. 392). Lloyd George eventually overcame this by almost doubling the payment to doctors who were already working in private insurance schemes, and when a large number of the poorer paid of these agreed to cooperate, the BMA finally gave way.

All these measures suggested that the state had a responsibility to make a positive contribution to human welfare, and although they went far beyond anything conceived by Gladstone, they could in some sense be regarded as a logical extension of earlier Liberal views rather than a flat contradiction of them. The same could not be said of the government's concern with the armed forces. Here the growing tensions abroad left them little option and they were compelled towards a programme whose purpose and expense were entirely at odds with the fundamentals of Liberalism.

The changes in the Army were largely organizational and involved no extra cost. They were nevertheless momentous. Within a few months of his arrival at the War Office Haldane had created a general staff of seventy-five officers. The system of army corps was abandoned and in 1907 the regular military forces were regrouped in six infantry divisions and four brigades of cavalry. Behind this a new formation of part-time soldiers, a Territorial Army of fourteen divisions, was to act as a secondary reserve for the regular Army, providing training units and manning coastal fortresses in time of war. And in 1908 the existing cadet corps at the public schools were merged in a single organization, the Officers Training Corps (OTC). With these measures, Haldane created the military establishment with which Great Britain was to go to war in 1914—a remarkable transformation, providing at least a nucleus from which there could be developed the mammoth army that he was far from envisaging at the time.

It was the expansion of the Navy that created the real expense. At first the Liberal government, true to its earlier ideals, had attempted reductions and in 1906 and 1907 the annual building programme of dreadnoughts (see p. 53) dropped from four to two. Assuming that Germany maintained her published programme of four battleships a year, this would still give the British Navy a reasonable superiority in 1911. To the Admiralty, however, there seemed good reason to believe that the German building programme was going well ahead of schedule and after the excitement of the Bosnian crisis in 1908 (see p. 85) R. McKenna, the First Lord of the Admiralty, placed before the Commons in March 1909 naval estimates that demanded that six new dreadnoughts should be laid down. The admirals would have liked eight and public opinion supported them with a popular music-hall song: 'We want eight and we won't wait'. Other members of the cabinet, however—Lloyd George, Churchill, Burns and Morley—were determined to wait and the ensuing wrangle only ended with a compromise propounded by Asquith, which settled for four dreadnoughts straight away, to be followed by four more if the need arose.

The building of these dreadnoughts meant an increase of £3·5 million on the naval estimates, but this was not the only new expenditure that faced Lloyd George in devising the budget of 1909. The old age pension had cost more than had been anticipated; so might the system of national insurance against sickness and unemployment which was still under preparation. There were plans for establishing experimental farms, and the development of the motor-car was demanding an improvement in roads. Thus since Lloyd George was determined that none of this domestic programme should be sacrificed, he had the task of finding an extra £16 million in all.

He was undaunted by the prospect. 'This is a war budget,' he announced in the Commons at the end of April 1909. 'It is for raising money to wage implacable war against poverty and squalidness.' Income tax was put up to 1 shilling and 2 pence (6p) in the pound with tax allowances for earned income and children. Supertax was introduced at 2 pence (1p) in the pound on incomes over £5,000. Death duties and taxes on tobacco and whisky were raised, and new ones introduced on cars and petrol. The most striking innovation centred on land: a type of capital gains tax of 20 per cent at the time of transfer, a capital tax of a halfpenny ($\frac{1}{4}$p) in the pound on the value of undeveloped land and minerals, and a 10 per cent duty on the increased value of property at the end of a lease.

By modern standards the rich were not being asked to pay very much; indeed, when the land taxes were finally established, they yielded so little that they did not even cover the costs of collection. By Edwardian standards, however, the new charges were startling. The upper class considered that land, the mainstay of hereditary wealth, had been singled out for attack and that the nationwide process of valuation which the taxes must entail would provide the information for higher taxation in the future. They were convinced that the whole direction of the budget, including the proposed forms of expenditure, was openly Socialist and their minds were hardly put at rest when Winston Churchill declared: 'We do not only ask today, "How much have you got?"; we also ask, "How did you get it? Did you earn it by yourself or has it just been left you by others?" '

Inevitably the debate in the Commons was ferocious. The House continued to sit throughout the summer and it was not until 4

November after 554 divisions that the budget was passed and then sent up to the House of Lords. It was at this point that the Lords took the step which was to goad the Liberals into forcing the surrender of a major bulwark of Conservative power. On 28 November, after five days of debate, they rejected the budget by 350 votes to 75.

This action was the supreme instance of a policy which the Lords had adopted ever since the Liberals had taken office. They had shown that they intended to come to the rescue of the heavily outnumbered Conservative Opposition by rejecting or virtually redrafting Bills sent up to them from the Commons—tactics with which they had already experimented during the previous Liberal administration of 1892–95. In 1906 an Education Bill which could have deprived the Anglican voluntary schools of most of their independence was so altered by amendments that it had to be withdrawn. In the same year a Bill to restrict the rights of plural voters in parliamentary elections was openly rejected. In 1907 two Scottish Land Bills were wrecked and in 1908 a Licensing Bill which would have greatly reduced the number of public houses was thrown out.

It did not escape notice that they were careful not to interfere with legislation that was popular with the working classes, and the Liberals, taking their stand on an undeniable mandate from the country, reckoned that the Lords were going far beyond the bounds of constitutional propriety in using their position to play party politics. Campbell-Bannerman was so incensed that he at first contemplated another general election on this issue, but eventually contented himself with the passing of a resolution in the Commons in 1907 that the powers of the House of Lords should be reduced to a suspensory veto, whereby they would only be able to delay the enactment of a Bill during two sessions. The fate of the Licensing Bill showed that the Lords were not prepared to take the hint and now the rejection of Lloyd George's budget in 1909 seemed a final gesture of defiance.

For Asquith there was only one possible course: dissolution and a new appeal to the electorate. Strictly speaking the Lords could claim that they were within their rights in forcing the government to refer back to the country over what they regarded as a highly questionable budget, but for many Liberals this most recent example of obstruction was the last straw. They meant to take up the challenge and to give legal effect to Campbell-Bannerman's resolutions, which would end for ever the power of the House of Lords to reject legislation acceptable to the Commons.

Asquith realized perfectly well that the struggle over this would be lengthy. The first step must be a government Bill, but the Lords were certain to reject this and in the last analysis their resistance could only be overcome by a vast creation of peers. King Edward, however, regarded the whole situation with extreme distaste and let Asquith know through his secretary, Lord Knollys, that he would only consent to such a course after a second general election had put the precise terms of the constitutional revision squarely before the electorate. Asquith thus had to fight the campaign of January 1910 with the knowledge that he had not yet any guarantee that victory would give him the power that he needed.

The outcome of the election was a considerable setback for the Liberals. They won 275 seats, a figure almost exactly matched by the Conservatives' 273. There were forty Labour MPs. Of the Irish, twelve had broken away from John Redmond, whom they regarded as subservient to the Liberals, but the seventy who remained under Redmond's leadership now held the balance. This new situation only added to the frenzy over the struggle with the Lords, since the removal of their veto could open the road to the successful passage of a third Home Rule Bill—the price of Irish support which was now indispensable to the government.

Asquith's approach to the new situation was cautious. He had to admit to the House that he had as yet no guarantee from the King for the creation of peers. There were, too, members of the cabinet, particularly Grey, who were doubtful about the wisdom of depriving the Lords of their veto and would have preferred to reform the composition of the chamber without touching its political power. Asquith was clear in his own mind that this would be inadequate and eventually in April 1910 three resolutions were passed in the Commons adumbrating his proposed legislation. The Lords were to have no right to reject any Bill defined by the Speaker as a money Bill; any other Bill which was passed three times in three successive sessions in the Commons in the space of two years would become law regardless of the Lords' opposition; and since all power would now be vested in the Commons, a general election must be held at least once every five years. In the same month the Lords hastily passed the original budget, but it was too late to escape the retribution that its earlier rejection was about to bring upon them.

King Edward did not live to see the end of the crisis. He died on 6 May 1910 and Asquith, who had been away on a short cruise to Portugal, returned at once to continue the negotiation with his son who succeeded as George V. The new King hoped passionately to avoid beginning his reign with a creation of peers and both sides agreed to try to find some form of agreement at a series of constitutional conferences in July and October. There were many issues. Could the Lords be sure that a finance Bill might not have certain social implications that went beyond the strict terms of a budget? Would it be possible to arrange a joint session of a limited number of Lords and Commons after the second rejection of a Bill? Should there be a national referendum on any constitutional measure—which of course would include the question of Irish Home Rule? Throughout the summer the argument raged to and fro and at one point Lloyd George was even canvassing the possibility of a coalition government, but Balfour refused, believing that this would only split the Conservatives.

Asquith held quietly to his original objective. In November, when no agreement had been reached, King George was informed that the cabinet requested an immediate dissolution together with a guarantee that after the election he would create the number of peers needed to overcome the resistance of the House of Lords to the Bill. The King now found himself at the very centre of the dispute and at the mercy of the conflicting views of two court officials. His own secretary, Sir Arthur Bigge, believed that George must reject Asquith's advice even though this would mean the resignation of the government; to consent to a creation would bring the monarchy undesirably into the political arena. Equally, his father's secretary, Lord Knollys, believed that it would be fatal not to consent. If he refused, the King might incur the charge of attempting to come to the aid of the House of Lords. Knollys went on to assure the King that in the event of Asquith's resignation Balfour would not be prepared to form an administration and the King would then be in the humiliating position of having to return to Asquith. In fact, Knollys had every reason to believe that Balfour would have formed an administration, as became clear some years later, but he was determined to deflect the King from making a move which might fatally compromise the monarchy. At any rate, the stratagem worked and George consented to give Asquith a secret undertaking for a creation of peers, if this should prove necessary.

Armed with this guarantee Asquith now went to the country. The election of December 1910 produced almost no change at all—Liberals and Conservatives with 272 seats each, forty-two Labour and eighty-four Irish. The Parliament Bill, based on the three resolutions, passed its third reading in the Commons on 15 May 1911. Inevitably it was totally transformed by amendments in the Lords and on its return to the Commons Asquith wrote to the King to remind him of his promise. George asked merely that the Lords should have time to consider the

Commons' rejection of their amendments and Asquith decided to bring the matter to a head by informing the Conservative leaders in the Commons and the Lords, Balfour and Lord Lansdowne, that the King had agreed to create the requisite number of peers.

The last hope of the Conservatives had now gone and on 24 July there followed a scene of uproar in the House of Commons. In the heat of a blazing summer the Opposition screamed and shouted at Asquith as he stood at the dispatch box—'a squalid frigid organized attempt to insult the prime minister' as Winston Churchill described it. After half an hour Asquith, unable to make himself heard, sat down and a little later the Speaker was forced to suspend the proceedings. It did not matter. Asquith already had a list of 249 Liberal candidates for ennoblement and the only question now was whether the Lords would fight to the end, thus necessitating a creation of peers which would leave them with a permanent Liberal majority in their own chamber.

For a time it seemed as if they might do this. The supporters of the eighty-eight-year-old Lord Halsbury were determined 'to die in the last ditch'. Then Lord Curzon, horrified at the idea of the consequent dilution of the peerage, rallied an opposing faction and on 10 August 1911 the House of Lords voted by a narrow majority in favour of the Parliament Bill in its original form. Thus under duress the Lords had consented to the extinction of their absolute veto on any future legislation and the British governmental system had moved sharply in the direction of a modern democracy. From now on, within the first three years of a Parliament that ran its full five years, a government would only need a firm majority in the House of Commons for any of its measures to reach the statute book.

It was not only the Liberals who viewed the prospect with satisfaction. The Irish party could reckon on a decisive attempt at Home Rule. For Labour the situation was still more exciting. By an appropriate coincidence, on the same day that the Lords admitted defeat, a resolution in the House of Commons established a salary of £400 for each MP. A majority in the House of Commons would now mean real power, and the large number of MPs that this would require would no longer be a drain on Labour's funds, previously embarrassed by the Osborne decision. The circumstances that had inhibited their parliamentary ambitions had been removed and the Liberals had opened the way to the party by whom they were eventually to be ousted.

8
Liberal Tribulations 1911–1914

With the passing of the Parliament Act and the National Insurance Act in 1911 the Liberals might well feel that they had earned the gratitude of a large part of the nation. Yet it did not seem that the nation was grateful at all. At the very moment when the government had concentrated all legislative power on the elective House, they were to be harassed by a series of movements furiously attempting to gain their ends by direct action outside Parliament. For two years the country was torn by vast strikes in which there were clashes with the police and the military; at the same time the suffragettes turned to a policy of violence, and in Ulster, after the government had put through the third Home Rule Bill, the resistance of the Protestants, strongly supported by the Conservative party, brought the country to the brink of civil war, only averted by the outbreak of the far greater conflict on the Continent.

1. Industrial strife and suffragettes

The period of industrial unrest that now faced the Liberal government had very little connection with their legislative programme. It was mainly the consequence of an economic pattern that had been unfolding during the previous two decades. The years between the mid-1870s and the mid-1890s, allowing for minor fluctuations, had generally been a period of depression, but wages had fallen less sharply than prices and the position of the worker, reinforced by the rapid growth of trade unionism at the end of the 1880s (see p. 33), had improved somewhat. After the middle of the 1890s this pattern began to change. The increase in the supply of gold from the South African mines, the material demands of the armaments race and the greater purchasing power abroad consequent on the expansion of overseas investments, all contributed to take the country into a period of boom, reaching a series of peaks in 1896–1900, 1905–07 and 1910–13. This naturally brought about an increase in the cost of living; average wage levels, however, did not everywhere rise to the same extent and many workers were likely to find themselves worse off at a time when the personal expenditure of the rich was becoming ostentatiously lavish.

This was the general background to a number of issues that had already created anxiety and indignation in the minds of labour leaders. The fiercer resistance of employers in the 1890s had stimulated the forming of the Labour Representation Committee, but the subsequent Osborne judgment (see p. 61) had seemed to put this new political organization at risk. Industry itself was entering a significant phase of readjustment as modern types of machinery threatened to make old skilled trades redundant. There were, too, particular problems likely to hamper improvement in wages; in the mines the seams easiest to reach had been worked out and the greater cost of deeper shafts and more remote coal-faces was not matched by any equivalent rise in sales; on the railways goods rates were kept down by an Act of Parliament at a time when running costs were mounting. Thus, in both these industries the managements were determined to economize just when the trade unions were urging the establishment of a fair wage based on the cost of living in place of the sliding scale whereby wages were related to the state of the market. Another demand was the right to work, but the labour exchanges of 1909 and the limited system of insurance benefits created in 1911 seemed hardly likely to abolish unemployment; they merely made it more tolerable. Indeed, it was unfortunate for the Liberal government that their National Insurance Act, which was a great social measure, should come at a moment when the worker's contribution of 4 pence (2p) a week was most certain to be resented.

The first few years of the twentieth century had been a time of reasonable industrial calm. The Taff Vale judgment was a deterrent against serious strike action, and in any case unemployment, which was always a curb on trade-union resistance, almost doubled between 1901 and the beginning of 1905. In 1906 the Trade Disputes Act ended the immediate threat to union funds and a new boom reduced the fear of unemployment. The combination of these factors might have introduced a period of strife and in 1907 Lloyd George at the Board of Trade had to intervene to prevent a general railway strike by forcing the railway companies to accept boards of conciliation for the negotiation of wages. Then the boom faded and in 1908 and 1909 unemployment was back again to 7·7 per cent (see Appendix 5, p. 441). After 1910, however, there ensued a more longlived boom which brought unemployment as low as 2·1 per cent in 1913 and the way was open for an angry confrontation which had been brewing for some years.

The trouble began in November 1910 when a miners' strike over pay at Tonypandy in South Wales was soon joined by the pits of the Cambrian combine. This did not end until August 1911 by which time the country was seething with industrial disruption in the fierce heat of the summer of that year. In June 1911 seamen and firemen struck at Southampton and within a week the fever had spread to Cardiff, London and the northern ports; in August a railway dispute at Liverpool was followed within a few days by a national stoppage. All this was accompanied by looting, rioting and savage fighting to prevent the employment of blackleg labour. In the main the government tried desperately to maintain control with the use of the police, despite the urgent appeals of local authorities for the dispatch of troops. At Tonypandy one miner was killed, for which Labour ever afterwards blamed Winston Churchill, then Home Secretary—an unfair charge, since he had held back on bringing in the Army. In some areas, however, troops did have to be called in; on 15 August at Liverpool they opened fire on rioters, killing two, and four days later at Llanelli two more were killed. Llanelli was a particularly ugly episode involving five nights of violence during which there were more deaths when a van of gunpowder exploded.

Gradually Lloyd George, aided by G. R. Askwith, an official of the Board of Trade, managed to quell the disorders by processes of conciliation that usually entailed wage increases. Then in October 1911 the Miners' Federation put up a demand for a district minimum wage and in February 1912 this led to a general coal strike for a national minimum. The miners, however, were to be defeated by their own apparent power; the effect of their strike was so disastrous for workers in other branches of industry that they gave up their claim and returned to the pits in April. In May there was further trouble in the Port of London when lightermen, dockers and carters struck over the question of working with non-union labour. By August this, too, had collapsed, but in 1913 a further outbreak of strikes among a variety of factories in the Midlands did bring about increases in pay.

There were many consequences of this frantic period of unrest. The government had been drawn in increasingly to act as arbitrator between management and workers. A whole pattern of boards of conciliation was emerging in which wage levels were no longer to depend simply on the free play of the market. The violence of the times had necessitated this degree of intervention, but it was clearly difficult for the government in its role as the guardian of law and order to preserve an image of absolute impartiality. They did, however, do their best to preserve good relations with Labour. The payment of MPs had undone some of the harm done by the Osborne judgment, but there were many other forms of expenditure that faced the LRC, and in 1913 a Trade Union Act went some way towards meeting this difficulty by permitting unions to establish a political fund on the understanding that any member had the right to contract out of payment to this, if he wished.

The impact of the strikes on the trade unions was still greater. The figures for membership increased remarkably in these years—from two and a half million in 1909 to more than four million in 1913 (see Appendix 6, p. 442). The success of the earlier strikes was an obvious incentive to enrol. The provisions of the National Insurance Act may also have helped; most workers had now to register with an approved society, and by 1914 some 10 per cent of the 13 million employees registered under the scheme had done so through their unions. Probably a greater attraction was an awareness of the strength that came from size in numbers. In 1913, although the locomotive drivers' and firemen's union, ASLEF, and the Railway Clerks' Association remained outside, the three other main railway unions combined to form the National Union of Railwaymen (NUR), and it was significant that their total membership of 180,000 in 1912 had risen to 257,000 by the end of 1913.

The greatest lesson of all for the trade unions had been that the independent action of one union alone was not enough. The haphazard timing of strikes in different industries had proved harmful in that it might throw out of work thousands of other workers who were not then engaged in any dispute. The idea of working-class solidarity in industrial action had dawned and in October 1913 the miners at their annual conference formulated the scheme which was to be known as 'the triple alliance'. In future, miners, railwaymen and transport workers were to coordinate their efforts in a way that would have the maximum effect on industry. The scheme has sometimes been regarded as the first instance of syndicalism in Great Britain—a continental doctrine that aimed to make the representatives of the working class the true source of governmental power. In fact, like most of their countrymen, the trade unionists involved did not work on the basis of a formal philosophy. They were concerned to find an *ad hoc* solution to a problem of which they had suddenly become aware. There was certainly no great evidence of missionary zeal in the caution with which the relevant unions avoided any positive obligation to strike together; the 'triple alliance' was no more than an agreement to adopt a policy of mutual consultation before any of them decided to take individual action, and true working-class solidarity was to remain a dream for many years to come.

Nevertheless, the plan encouraged the railwaymen to return to the attack. In 1914 their assistant secretary, J. H. Thomas, gave notice of an impending demand for a forty-eight-hour week and a 5 shilling (25p) rise, with the threat that if this was not forthcoming, a general railway stoppage would begin on 1 November. Thus it is possible that Asquith's government was now on the verge of a new round of industrial battles in which the power of the 'triple alliance' would have been put to the test for the first time. As it was, the outbreak of war in August 1914 brought about an indefinite postponement and this new phase of working-class aspirations was not to develop until 1919, when the Liberal administration had vanished from the scene.

At the same time the government was being harassed by an outburst of violence from an entirely different section of society. In 1897 the National Union of Women's Suffrage Societies under Mrs Fawcett had been formed to promote the demand for the enfranchisement of women. This was an entirely respectable organization determined to pursue its aim through a legitimate policy of propaganda. In 1903, however, Mrs Pankhurst and her daughters Christabel and Sylvia broke away from this to form the Women's Social and Political Union which in 1905 developed a gradually mounting campaign of general obstruction. Their suffragettes shouted down political speeches at public meetings with cries of 'Votes for women'; they smashed windows in Downing Street and Whitehall; they made speeches after chaining themselves to park railings. Asquith and Churchill were both attacked with dog-whips and on one occasion a crowd of women stormed on to a golf course and attempted to undress the Prime Minister—an unusual political approach. Many, when arrested, went on hunger strike in prison and suffered the gruesome treatment of forcible feeding.

Their cause did have some sympathizers in the House of Commons and in 1907 and 1908 two private members' Bills attempted to establish feminine suffrage, but failed to survive. Strictly this was not a party issue, but there was one aspect that could not escape the notice of the Liberals. Enfranchisement for women on the same basis as the existing system of male suffrage would almost certainly favour the Conservatives, since women who were householders in their own right were mainly to be found among the richer classes. It was this consideration that caused Lloyd George and Churchill in 1910 to bring about the defeat of a third Bill drawn up this time by an all-party committee. In 1912 the government launched a new measure which would have increased the male electorate from 7·5 to 10 million and since this wider franchise might create a more equitable situation for all parties, it was suggested that an amendment should be added, granting women the vote on the same basis. The Speaker, however, ruled that this was contrary to correct procedure, and on this Asquith was happy to let the matter drop.

This final disappointment caused Mrs Fawcett to turn to Labour as the only firm supporter of feminine suffrage. Mrs Pankhurst's response was more dramatic. The suffragettes now embarked on a course of criminal violence. Churches and railway stations were set on fire; pictures in art galleries were slashed; a house that was being built for Lloyd George was blown up, and in 1913 a suffragette was killed when she threw herself under the King's horse at the Derby. There were many arrests, but the forcible feeding of those who went on hunger strike had by now aroused shocked comment and on one occasion in the Commons, George Lansbury, a Labour MP, had shaken his fist in Asquith's face and declared that he would go down in history as the man who tortured innocent women. Accordingly, in 1913, a new Act was passed, whereby prisoners who went on hunger strike would be released, only to be rearrested after they had recovered.

Few sections of society had fought for the right to vote with such selfless dedication, and later, when women had been enfranchised, the suffragettes could argue that their fanaticism had brought the question inescapably to the fore. Even so, the actions of the Pankhurst group probably reinforced the prejudices of a male society. It may have been as well for their cause that the outbreak of war in 1914 brought their campaign to a patriotic standstill and in the end it was the recognition of their contribution to the war effort that gave women the vote.

2. Ulster and the third Home Rule Bill

All this tempestuous violence from workers and women was soon to be eclipsed by one other scene of tribulation not unfamiliar to the Liberals. Asquith had now to pay the price of Irish support in the House of Commons. The third Home Rule Bill, introduced in April 1912, was not greatly different in its general form from its predecessor of 1893. An Irish legislature consisting of a nominated Senate of forty and an elective assembly of 164 was to be established at Dublin to concern itself purely with the internal affairs of Ireland. Ultimate sovereignty, including direct control over external relations and matters affecting the whole of the United Kingdom, still lay with Parliament at Westminster, where the Irish were to have a reduced representation of forty-two seats. The Bill thus gave a reasonable degree of autonomy and was regarded by many as a pilot scheme for arrangements that might later be made for Scotland and Wales.

The crux of the problem was the attitude of the Protestant population who predominated in parts of Ulster. To them Home Rule meant subordination to a Roman Catholic government at Dublin. Home Rule, it was declared, was Rome Rule, and now that the House of Lords could no longer be an effective ally the Conservative Opposition in England took up this genuine sense of anxiety as the sole remaining means of preserving the Union—a policy that was to bring them dangerously close to encouraging open rebellion.

By this time the Conservatives had a new leader. The loss of three successive general elections had weakened Balfour's position within his own party. He had not participated in the scene in the House of Commons in July 1911, when the Prime Minister had been shouted down for half an hour, and he had no sympathy with this new face of political life. Consequently, when by the autumn of that year he knew that intrigue was at work to remove him from the leadership, he was content on 8 November to announce his resignation. The choice of his successor lay between two rivals—Austen Chamberlain and Walter Long—but when this produced deadlock, the only solution was a third candidate, Bonar Law, whom both would support.

This decision marked a radical departure for a party which had for so long been the preserve of the Salisbury family. Bonar Law was a Canadian Scot who had returned to Glasgow to become a wealthy ironmaster. He had only been an MP since 1900, but had held office for three years as Parliamentary Secretary to the Board of Trade during Balfour's administration. He was a dour melancholy figure and he only accepted the leadership of the party at the persuasion of his friend Max Aitken, later Lord Beaverbrook, another Canadian of Scottish extraction, who after becoming a millionaire by the age of thirty had gained a seat in the Commons in the election of December 1910. Before the meeting at the Carlton Club, Aitken attempted to groom Bonar Law for his new role. 'You must talk like a great man, behave like a great man.' 'If I am a great man,' commented Bonar Law gloomily, 'then a good many great men must have been frauds.'[1] Still, he knew what was expected of him. 'I am afraid I shall have to show myself very vicious, Mr Asquith, this session,' he remarked to the Prime Minister on their way to the House of Lords to hear the King's speech in February 1912. 'I hope you will understand.'[2]

Meanwhile, the Ulstermen had already acquired a leader of their own. In February they chose Sir Edward Carson, a lawyer from Dublin, who had been Solicitor-General during the last five years of the Conservative administration. Characteristically, Carson took the bull by the horns. In September 1911, as soon as the passing of the Parliament Act had brought the likelihood of Home Rule appreciably closer, he announced to the Ulster Unionists: 'We must be prepared . . . the morning Home Rule is passed, ourselves to become responsible for the government of the Protestant Province of Ulster.'[3]

In parliamentary terms the course of the Home Rule Bill was easily predictable. It was bound to pass the House of Commons, equally bound to be rejected by the Lords. By the middle of 1914 after being passed three times in the Commons, it must inevitably become law and thus for two years, while the politicians engaged in futile exchanges, the Bill lay on the agenda of the House like a time-bomb ticking away the days before an explosion into civil war.

In Ireland both sides built up their forces. In January 1912 Carson had established a citizens' army of Ulster Volunteers, which by March 1914 numbered 84,000, and in September 1912 he collected almost half a million signatures for a 'Solemn Covenant' which utterly denied the authority of any future Dublin parliament. The Irish nationalists did not respond immediately to this, content to rely upon the passing of the Bill, but at the end of 1913 more radical elements began to raise a force of Irish Nationalist Volunteers, which by the middle of 1914 was said to number 100,000, many of them resident in Ulster.

In view of this rising tension it is natural to ask why no scheme for partition was put forward as a possible solution. In fact, a Liberal amendment had been suggested in June 1912, proposing that the four indubitably Protestant counties in Ulster, Antrim, Armagh, Derry and Down, should be excluded from the arrangements for Home Rule, but this had been accepted by neither party. There were several reasons for this. First, partition would necessitate the definition of a boundary and the Ulster Protestants would not accept the loss of the counties of Tyrone and Fermanagh, whose populations were mixed, and throughout most stages of the struggle would have insisted on all nine counties of Ulster including Cavan, Monaghan and Donegal, which were purely Catholic. Second, the Ulstermen and the Conservative party were not really interested in partition at all. The question of Ulster was really being raised as a means of blocking the introduction of Home Rule and it was important that there should be no solution to it. Third, John Redmond, the leader of the Irish nationalists in the Commons, knew that he dared not settle for anything less than Home Rule for the whole of Ireland, since his hold on his party was already weakening, and movements such as Arthur Griffith's Sinn Fein, and Patric Pearse's Irish Republican Brotherhood were threatening to take matters out of his hands with a demand for outright independence.

It was understandable that the Conservative party should be so determined to maintain the *status quo* in Ireland; this had always been their policy. And in the context of Irish history and of the emotions aroused by the religious issue it was even understandable that Protestant Ulstermen should think in terms of physical resistance to the establishment of Catholic rule. What was startling was the extent to which the Conservative leadership was prepared to give active encouragement to the possibility of such resistance. On Easter Tuesday 1912 Bonar Law was present with seventy MPs at a great march past in Belfast, and on 29 July at a Conservative gathering at Blenheim Palace he declared: 'I can imagine no length of resistance to which Ulster can go in which I should not be prepared to support them and in which, in my view, they would not be supported by the overwhelming majority of the British people.'[4] It seemed that His Majesty's leader of the Opposition was advocating an open defiance of the authority of Parliament.

A more legitimate aspect of the Conservative resistance was their demand that Home Rule should not be passed without a general election. They argued, somewhat dubiously, that this had not been an issue at the time of the election of December 1910. It was with this in mind that Bonar Law turned to King George. In May 1912 he suggested that the royal veto, unused for two hundred years, might be unearthed as a means of stopping the Home Rule Bill; and a few months later he wrote a memorandum proposing that in the present disturbing circumstances the King would be acting within his rights if he dismissed the Prime Minister. Either eventuality would ensure the general election to which the Conservatives pinned their hopes, and in August 1913 George V who was deeply troubled by the situation, did take up these points with Asquith. Not surprisingly the Prime Minister replied emphatically that the constitution did not permit the King to act in these ways.

By the beginning of 1914, when all negotiation had failed and it seemed that nothing could stop the Home Rule Bill from becoming law, the Conservatives saw a further chance of forcing an election. If Protestant Ulster resisted by setting up Carson's provisional government, the Army would have to be called in to carry out an occupation. All military discipline, however, depended on the annual passing of the Army Act, and early in 1914 the Lords were seriously considering amending this in such a way that it would not be possible to use troops in Ireland.

There was another issue raised by the likelihood of military coercion. Among the army units in Ireland many of the officers were Protestant Irish whose homes were in Ulster, and the prospect of their having to go into action against their own people might well prove intolerable. As early as September 1913 King George had put an anguished question to Asquith: 'Will it be wise, will it be fair to the Sovereign as head of the Army, to subject the discipline, and indeed the loyalty of his troops, to such a strain?'[5] Bonar Law seized on the same point with reckless relish and in a speech at Dublin on 28 November 1913 made a telling reference to James II. 'In order to carry out his despotic intention the King had the largest army which had ever been seen in England. What happened? There was no civil war. Why? Because his own army refused to fight for him.'[6] This was rash. He could be said merely to be warning the government of a practical difficulty, but it was also easy to read into his words an incitement to mutiny.

Indeed, there took place in March 1914 an episode that suggested that this was no idle hypothesis. By now the government and the Ulstermen each suspected the other of contemplating a coup, even before the Home Rule Bill had become law. Orders had been issued from London affecting the disposition of troops in Ulster and the protection of military stores, and on 19 March Carson in the House of Commons challenged the government to use its forces in Ulster. He then left the House dramatically, with his followers, and it was imagined (incorrectly) that he intended to set up the projected provisional government in Ulster forthwith. That same evening Churchill at the Admiralty dispatched the 3rd Battle Fleet to the isle of Arran only sixty miles away from Belfast.

These latest developments convinced General Sir Arthur Paget, the Commander-in-Chief in Ireland, that the government was contemplating immediate hostilities and he now took the first step in the incident known as the 'mutiny at the Curragh'. Having gained what he thought was an authorization from the War Office, he summoned his senior officers to the Curragh barracks in Dublin and informed them that all officers whose homes were in Ulster would be allowed to disappear for a short time and that all others who were not prepared to participate in any military operation in Ulster would have the option of dismissal from the service. On this fifty-seven out of seventy officers in the 3rd Cavalry Brigade under General Gough chose to be dismissed and the War Office was informed of their decision.

Obviously no government could tolerate such a bargain with its armed forces. Court martial was the natural consequence for any officer who refused to obey orders, but the situation was so tense that Asquith felt bound to handle the crisis as quietly as possible. At first he hoped to damp the whole episode down, maintaining that it had arisen from an honest misunderstanding, but these tactics were wrecked when Gough and Sir Henry Wilson, an Ulsterman, who was Director of Military Operation at the War Office, insisted on a statement in writing from Colonel John Seely, the Secretary of State for War, that officers would not be required to take action to impose the policy of the Home Rule Bill. Asquith was now left with no choice. He publicly repudiated Seely's statement, and the resignation of Seely, Sir Spencer Ewart, the Adjutant-General, and Sir John French, the Chief of Staff, duly followed. Asquith took over the War Office himself. 'The Army will hear nothing of politics from me,' he said, 'and in return I expect to hear nothing of politics from the Army.'[7]

It remained to be seen whether this bargain would hold. Already in March the cabinet had suggested a scheme whereby the counties of Ulster might vote themselves temporarily out of Home Rule, but this was not acceptable to Ulster, nor to the Irish nationalist party. Then on 24 April 1914 the Ulster Volunteers defied a recent embargo on the importing of arms into Ireland with a gun-running operation at Larne, which enabled them to acquire 35,000 rifles and 3 million rounds of ammunition. Thus, when on 26 May the Home Rule Bill had the third reading of its third passage through the House of Commons, Ulster seemed poised on the brink of civil war.

Asquith would go no further than his proposals in March, but in the hope of finding some escape at the last minute King George pressed for a conference of leading members of all parties at Buckingham Palace. The conference opened on 21 July, and since the situation was now so desperate, there was at last some serious consideration given to the possibility of partition. The old problem of the boundary, however, remained insuperable and the conference eventually broke up on 24 July, defeated by what Winston Churchill called 'the muddy by-ways of Fermanagh and Tyrone'. Two days later the realities that lay behind the deadlock were re-emphasized when an Irish Nationalist gun-running operation at Howth on Dublin Bay brought about a clash with British troops, in which three civilians were killed and thirty-eight wounded.

Release was to come from an entirely different quarter. On 24 July the cabinet, wearily turning over further solutions to the Irish riddle, was informed by Sir Edward Grey of Austria's ultimatum to Serbia (see

p. 92). Within a few days the quarrelling factions of Ireland were to be dwarfed by a stupendous cataclysm involving the whole of Europe. Before this a sense of proportion at last asserted itself. All parties agreed to suspend their conflict, and the question of Home Rule was set aside for the duration of the war; at the same time the suffragettes transferred their energies to support of the war effort, and the projected strike of the railwaymen was cancelled. It seemed that the mounting difficulties of the Liberal government had been temporarily resolved by the greatest tragedy of all.

9

Sir Edward Grey and the Approach of War 1906–1914

The advent of the Liberal government had made little difference to the new direction of British foreign policy. In a speech in the City of London during the last months of the Conservative administration Sir Edward Grey had already announced his full support of the Anglo-Japanese treaty and of the Anglo-French *entente*, and in January 1906, almost immediately after taking office as Foreign Secretary, he had repeated to the German ambassador his predecessor Lord Lansdowne's warning that Great Britain would stand beside France in the Moroccan crisis (see p. 50). Continuity had thus been preserved, but in subsequent years Grey's interpretation of the *entente* remained cautious and limited, reflecting the highly delicate balance that he was attempting to maintain for Great Britain in her relations with the Great Powers.

There were at this time in British government circles two schools of thought on the situation in Europe. The first was based on a deep mistrust of Germany. As early as 1902 Lord Selborne had commented in a memorandum: 'We cannot safely ignore the malignant hatred of the German people or the manifest design of the German navy.'[1] And in January 1907 a member of the Foreign Office, Eyre Crowe, produced a carefully argued warning of the danger from Germany. To this faction the obvious conclusion was the need to push ahead with naval expansion and to reach a positive military alliance with France. In contrast to this, the other school of thought disliked the Anglo-French entente and hoped for some firm understanding with Germany which would include a relaxation of the naval race.

Grey himself did not wholly accept either of these views—hence the complexity of his foreign policy. He was naturally determined to prevent a German predominance over the entire Continent, but he was loathe to take Great Britain positively into the Franco-Russian camp, since a hardening of the two blocs of Great Powers could only add to the political tension. Furthermore, the Liberal government, traditionally

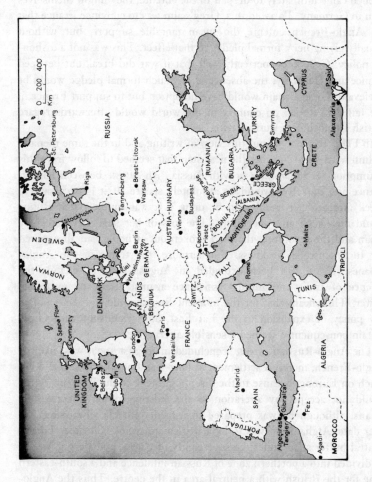

I EUROPE IN 1914

keen to reduce the amount of money spent on the services, still hoped to avert an Anglo-German naval race. For this it was essential that the door to negotiation with Germany should be kept open, and an unqualified promise of support to the French would finally place any naval agreement with Germany out of reach. On the other hand, if the French came ultimately to despair of the entente, they might themselves turn to Germany. To avoid this, Grey's aim was to convince France that the Anglo-French entente did mean tangible support, but without actually giving her a formal pledge to that effect. This was not a dishonest policy; Grey knew perfectly well that if war did break out between France and Germany, the absence of any such formal pledge would be irrelevant. Great Britain would have no option but to support France; if she failed to do so, no country in the world would afterwards regard British friendship as worth having.

In February 1906 he put this view in writing and in the same memorandum went on to consider the next step that seemed to follow from this assumption—a *rapprochement* with Russia. 'An *entente* between Russia, France and ourselves would be absolutely secure. If it is necessary to check Germany, it could then be done.'[2] It was unlikely that Russia would miss such an opportunity. The loss of her fleet, her defeat by Japan and the revolution that had broken out at home had all exposed her to a sense of weakness. Furthermore, the terms of the Anglo-Japanese treaty had been extended in August 1905 to include the defence of India and mutual assistance against attack by even one Power. This meant that for the moment Russia could not contemplate any policy of expansion in the Far East, and friendship with Great Britain consequently seemed a sensible alternative.

The Anglo-Russian *entente*, concluded in August 1907, was, like the Anglo-French, merely a settlement of long-standing disputes. It did not touch on Europe, because to the disappointment of the Russians, Grey would not accept any alteration to the existing ruling affecting the Straits, although he was prepared to consider further discussion at a later date. Afghanistan was to be a British sphere of influence, Tibet a neutral buffer state under the sovereignty of China, and Persia* was to be divided into a northern zone of Russian influence and a south-eastern zone for the British with a neutral area in the centre. Thus the Anglo-Russian *entente* considerably eased any threat to the Indian frontier and for the moment, at least, frustrated any German hopes of drawing Russia on to the side of the Central Powers.

In later years the Germans always maintained that the creation of the

---

* The name was changed to Iran in 1935.

triple *entente* meant that Germany was now encircled by a ring of hostile Powers. Even if this had been so, it could be argued that such a situation had only been brought about in response to earlier German policy, but in any case the triple *entente* was far from possessing that solidarity which Grey had hoped might effectively restrain further moves by the Central Powers.

In particular, neither Great Britain nor France was immediately prepared to underwrite Russian interests in the Balkans. There the competition between Austria and Russia had been renewed after the end of the Russo-Japanese war. A projected Austrian railway scheme had aroused Russian fears that Constantinople and the Straits might come under a control hostile to her interests. Russia had, too, a new foothold to protect; in 1903 a palace revolution in Belgrade had brought to the throne of Serbia Peter Karageorgević whose government promptly abandoned the earlier pro-Austrian policy and turned instead to Russia, drawing on French support for money and munitions.

At first, Aehrenthal and Izvolski, the Austrian and Russian foreign ministers, attempted to act in cooperation. Aehrenthal wanted formally to annex Bosnia and Herzegovina, already under Austrian occupation since 1878, as a show of strength against Serbia; Izvolski was prepared to accept this if he could gain a European agreement on the opening of the Straits to Russian warships. The two came to an understanding over these respective aims in September 1908, but when a few weeks later Aehrenthal announced the annexation of Bosnia and Herzegovina long before Izvolski had been able to negotiate any revision of the Straits settlement with Great Britain and France, the Russians knew that they had been tricked. Serbia, their *protégé*, protested strongly at the annexation of a region that contained many Serbs and looked to Russia for support, but it was the Central Powers who stood firm. The French were more interested in reaching a further agreement with Germany over Morocco; the British would not go beyond a moral condemnation, and the Russians could not face the only alternative, an international conference, since this would reveal to the Serbs that they had been prepared to condone the annexation under certain conditions.

Although the Bosnian crisis did not lead to war, its consequences were nevertheless considerable. It convinced the Russians that if they were to retain Serbia as a client state, they dared not let her down again. It encouraged the Serbs to think in terms of acting more on their own initiative in their struggle with Austria, and in 1909 a secret organization known as the Black Hand was formed for the purpose of fostering anti-

Austrian propaganda and sabotage in Bosnia. Technically, the Black Hand had no official status, but since one of its leaders, Colonel Dimitriević, was chief of the Intelligence Department, a dangerous situation was created whereby the Serbian government could not control its activities, yet was sufficiently closely involved to be implicated in them. Lastly, the trial of strength had produced a correspondence between Moltke and Conrad von Hötzendorff, the German and Austrian Chiefs of the General Staff, in which Moltke had promised full German support if Austria should find herself at war with Serbia supported by Russia—a gloss on the Dual Alliance of 1879 which Bismarck had always been careful to avoid.

So far as Russia was concerned, the outcome of the Bosnian crisis suggested that the triple *entente* had only limited advantages. Almost at the same time, however, the development of the Anglo-German naval race made it clear to the British that the entente Powers dared not allow them to appear too limited. In 1906 a gesture by the Liberal government, reducing the plans for the building of new dreadnoughts to only two in the naval estimates for 1907–08, had met with no response in Berlin. On the contrary, in February 1908, the German Reichstag passed a new naval law envisaging the annual construction of four capital ships for the next four years, and by the end of that year it was the British Admiralty's belief that the productive power of Krupp's was such that Germany might even be building in excess of those figures.

The subsequent naval scare in Great Britain had many repercussions. As has been seen (p. 65), the need to increase the number of dreadnoughts under construction had a marked effect upon Lloyd George's budget of 1909, which led ultimately to the attack on the power of the House of Lords. The official attitude towards Germany hardened and in 1908 a subcommittee of the Committee of Imperial Defence declared: 'The possibility of a surprise attack being made upon this country during normal diplomatic relations is not sufficiently remote to be ignored.' Still more striking was the public response to the growing threat from Germany. 'Never since I have been in office,' commented Sir Edward Grey, 'has opinion here been so thoroughly wide awake with regard to Germany and on its guard as it is now.'

In April 1909 Germany did offer to reduce her naval armament on terms. The price was to be an Anglo-German agreement, whereby neither of them would join a coalition hostile to the other and each would observe benevolent neutrality in the event of either being involved in war. It was a revival of the propositions of 1901, but this time with a note of menace; the German navy had become a weapon to blackmail Great Britain into abandoning her existing ententes. 'It is in fact an invitation to help Germany to make a European combination,' commented Grey, 'which could be directed against us when it suited her so to use it.'[3] The British Foreign Office was convinced that its object was to create a breathing space for Germany until her navy had reached its full strength, and their suspicions can be seen to be justified when at a conference at Berlin in June 1909 the German Chancellor Bülow stated that 'an understanding is advisable in order to get over the danger zone between the present time and the time when our fleet is built'.[4]

A rather useless negotiation did, however, continue for a while, until in 1911 the German government embarked upon another attempt to shatter the Anglo-French *entente*. The scene once again was Morocco. Here the French were by now almost ready for the *coup de grâce*, and in May 1911, after domestic disturbances in which the Sultan was driven out of his capital Fez, they made use of the traditional excuse of restoring order to occupy the city. The German government, who reckoned that the French had not honoured earlier agreements about German economic interests in Morocco, protested and on 1 July sent a gunboat to Agadir as a symbol of their determination to receive compensation, which, they declared later, was to be most of the French Congo.

The second Moroccan crisis emphasized the full delicacy of the Anglo-French *entente*, already suggested in the first crisis in 1905. As before, the issue for the British was not simply a question of facing up to German truculence; it involved the much more sinister possibility that France might not be prepared to rely upon her vague friendship with Great Britain and would come to terms privately with Germany. There were renewed fears that the Germans might gain an Atlantic naval base at Agadir, and when conversations had been proceeding for some time between France and Germany without any reference to Great Britain, the cabinet in London authorized Grey to warn the German ambassador that the British would not recognize any new arrangement until there had been consultation with them. This view was strongly underlined by Lloyd George on 21 July, when he made a great speech at the Mansion House announcing that Great Britain refused to be treated 'as if she were of no account in the Cabinet of nations'—a warning as much to the French as to the Germans. At the time the speech added greatly to the sense of crisis, but in the outcome it enabled the French to reduce the demands of the Germans, who eventually expressed themselves satisfied with two much smaller strips of Congolese territory as compensation for France's position in Morocco.

The Anglo-French *entente* had survived the Agadir crisis, but Grey was still no nearer to finding a way of reconciling it with a private agreement with Germany over the naval competition, and in the autumn of 1911 German plans for a supplementary naval law giving the German Navy a ratio of 2:3 in capital ships with the British Navy brought the issue to a head again. It was clear that there would have to be a renewal of negotiations—not a prospect that Grey viewed with any relish. 'Their way of beginning a conversation', he had written to the American president Theodore Roosevelt after Agadir, 'is to stamp upon your foot to attract your attention when you aren't looking, and then they are surprised and very annoyed when the conversation doesn't go smoothly afterwards.'[5]

Nevertheless, early in 1912 Lord Haldane, who had gained his peerage in the previous year, went to Germany where it was hoped he might reach agreement with the more conciliatory faction in Berlin. The exchanges, however, broke down once more over the German desire for a promise of benevolent neutrality and in March 1912 Winston Churchill, who had become First Lord of the Admiralty in the previous year, introduced naval estimates that allowed for maintaining a 60 per cent superiority in dreadnoughts as long as Germany abided by her present navy law, and for building two ships for every German one that went beyond that limit.

Thus the British could not escape from the naval race and the only immediate effect of the Haldane mission had been to increase the mistrust in the minds of the French. Still lacking a firm promise of British support in the event of war with Germany, this was perhaps not unnatural. Now, however, the failure of the latest Anglo-German negotiations did have the effect of drawing the British and the French into closer partnership. In July 1912 French generals in conversation with Sir Henry Wilson, Director of Military Operations until 1914, gained an agreement that if the two countries found themselves at war, all available British forces would be dispatched to a concentration area in France whose precise location was to be the subject of future discussion—a momentous decision that eventually led to Great Britain's immense involvement on the western front throughout the First World War. At the same time Anglo-French naval conversations of 1911–12 resulted in the French concentrating the bulk of their forces in the Mediterranean, while the British moved back to their home waters with the development of new bases at Scapa Flow and Cromarty. The implication of this was that France's Atlantic and Channel coasts would depend for their defence on the British Navy, while in the Mediterranean the British would rely on the French; thus, whatever the

political hesitations implicit in the *entente*, Anglo-French naval dispositions were now coming close to a combined operation.

For the anti-German faction in London these developments did not
go far enough. 'Were it possible to conclude a naval arrangement both
with Russia and France,' wrote Sir Arthur Nicolson, Permanent Under-
Secretary at the Foreign Office, 'I am sure that our position would be
more secure—and it is probable that Germany, in view of such a strong
naval combination, would be disposed to slacken her rate of construction.'[6] For many in the cabinet, however, it seemed that the new arrangements went a good deal too far, possibly restricting the government's
freedom of political manoeuvre, and Winston Churchill, considering the
distribution of French naval forces, commented anxiously on 'the moral
claims which France could make upon Great Britain if attacked by
Germany'. It was largely in response to this that in November 1912
Grey stressed in writing to Paul Cambon, the French ambassador in
London, that in an emergency their two governments would merely
consult each other and were in no way committed 'to action in a contin-
gency that has not arisen and may never arise'.[7] The situation was thus
highly anomalous—indicative of the divided nature of British foreign
policy—with the generals and admirals acting as if there existed between the two countries an alliance which the British government was at
pains to deny.

While Great Britain's agreements with France were merely growing
confused, her relations with Russia were positively deteriorating. Since
1909 Russia's confidence had been restored with an expansion of her
armed forces and by now she reckoned that the British were so in need
of her friendship that she could safely ignore the 1907 agreement over
Persia. There Russian agents were moving into the central neutral
zone and it seemed that Russia was on the verge of taking over a large
part of the country. For the anti-German school of thought this
simply represented an unfortunate price which Great Britain must
accept—a view strongly voiced by Nicolson at the Foreign Office,
principally because he regarded the possible enmity of Russia as an
even greater danger than that of Germany. 'We should put up with
perhaps occasional annoyances in Persia,' he wrote to the British ambassador at St Petersburg in April 1913, 'in order to remain on the best
footing with Russia.'[8] To Grey and Asquith, however, these Russian
designs were something more than an occasional annoyance, and although
a meeting between Grey and Sazonov, the Russian foreign minister, at
Balmoral in September 1912 did help to mend relations, the issue of
Persia continued to be a source of friction until 1914.

Naturally, mounting Anglo–Russian tension strengthened the arguments of the other school of thought who wished to go over to a wholehearted reconciliation with Germany, and from 1912 there was a marked improvement in Anglo–German relations. The naval question was no longer so disruptive, since the British, having at last regretfully accepted the challenge, recognized that they could outbuild Germany. At the same time the Colonial Secretary Lewis Harcourt, a strong advocate of friendship with Germany, was able to undertake a series of conversations which by 1914 had led to a proposal for the partitioning of the Portuguese colonies, although the objections of Portugal made it unlikely that this would come to anything. More productive were negotiations over the projected Berlin–Baghdad railway, which culminated in a convention signed in May 1914, allowing Germany control of the line as far as Basra in return for British control of shipping in the Persian Gulf.

None of these oscillations were in themselves likely to lead to war. The real danger lay in the mounting armaments and the general sense of chauvinism on the Continent. In March 1913 a German Army Bill aimed at a military expansion that might outdo the Russians; the French, conscious of their smaller population, could only retaliate by extending their length of compulsory military service to three years. In the shipyards of Great Britain and Germany the naval race went on. 'The situation is extraordinary,' wrote Colonel House, the personal agent of the American president on a mission in Europe. 'It is militarism run stark mad. Unless someone acting for you can bring about a different understanding, there is some day to be an awful cataclysm. There is too much hatred, too many jealousies.'

Of these hatreds and jealousies, there were two of long standing that were to lead to the final explosion: Austria's fear that her own position was threatened by the development of Serbia as the champion of the Slav world; and Russia's fear that Austrian schemes for economic expansion through the Balkans and the growth of German influence at Constantinople would eventually place the control of the Straits in hostile hands. The events that led to the fatal heightening of their fears began with a new assault upon the territories of Turkey. The Austrian annexation of Bosnia and the French acquisition of Morocco encouraged the Italian government to seize Tripoli in September 1911; in March 1912 Serbia and Bulgaria made an alliance preparatory to a partition of the remaining Turkish lands in the Balkans, the nucleus of a Balkan league which Greece and Montenegro were later to join. And in April 1912 the closing of the Straits by Turkey in the course of her war with

Italy had such an impact on Russian commerce that the Russian government realized they must work in close harmony with the Balkan league which might soon become the new guardians of the Straits.

The French were naturally nervous over the extent to which their Russian ally had committed herself to a Balkan adventure. At a time, however, when the confused state of the Anglo-French entente left them still uncertain of British support, they dared not weaken the Franco-Russian alliance, and it was unlikely that they would be able to persuade Russia to modify her policy. Indeed, in August 1912 the French premier, Poincaré, on a visit to St Petersburg went so far as to extend France's undertakings to Russia. The original agreement of the 1894 alliance, which had been purely defensive, had stipulated French assistance in the event of Russia being attacked by Germany or by Austria supported by Germany. It was clear by now, however, that the most likely course of events was that a German attack on Russia would only come after Russia had gone to the aid of a Balkan state invaded by Austria. Would the Franco-Russian treaty be operative in these circumstances? Poincaré assured the Russians that it would, and in so doing he established a link which, if taken in conjunction with the Moltke-Conrad correspondence in 1909 (see p. 86), completed the two dangerous chains of commitment in the rival systems of alliance.

There followed two Balkan wars. In the first, from October until December 1912, the states of the Balkan league were completely successful in driving out the Turks from most of their European territories; in the second, from June until August 1913, Bulgaria, suspicious of her allies, attacked Serbia and Greece to no avail and at the end was deprived of most of the ground that she had recently gained. In all this the Balkan states had acted largely on their own initiative—a new factor in the politics of the Eastern Question. Austria feared that Serbia might gain an Adriatic coastline, Russia that Bulgaria might actually occupy Constantinople. As a consequence, at the end of the first of these wars the Great Powers, conferring in London, were able to agree on imposing a mediation in May 1913, whereby the creation of a new state of Albania deprived Serbia of the Adriatic coast. The defeat of Bulgaria in the second war added considerably to Serbia's territory, but for the moment at least the Powers seemed prepared to accept this.

Less than a year after the end of the second Balkan war the Archduke Francis Ferdinand, heir to the Habsburg throne, was assassinated by a Bosnian Serb at Sarajevo in June 1914. Since this event was to lead to the final outbreak of European hostilities, it is reasonable to ask why diplomacy was unable to handle this crisis, when in the previous year the Powers had been able to face up to the dangers created by two Balkan wars in a spirit of rational cooperation. The answer is that in 1913 the Powers had genuinely wished to settle the implications of a situation that was initially of the Balkan states' own making, whereas the crisis of 1914 tempted Austria into a policy which precluded any peaceful solution. Basically the story is a very simple one. The assassination, the work of the Serbian Black Hand, occurred on 28 June; the Austrian government presented an overwhelming and humiliating ultimatum to Serbia on 23 July; the Serbs, advised by Russia to give way, accepted the ultimatum in almost every particular; the Austrians declared themselves unsatisfied and declared war on 28 July.

Two factors explain the pattern of these events. First, the Austrian government had finally decided that they could no longer live with their neighbour, Serbia. Conrad von Hötzendorff, the Austrian chief of staff, had long advocated a war to destroy her; Berchtold, the Austrian premier, had by now come round to his way of thinking and the assassination at Sarajevo seemed to provide the perfect excuse. Second, this new policy of a local war with Serbia could never have been envisaged, had it not been for the wholehearted support that the idea received from Berlin. On 8 July the German Emperor, William II, promised that 'he would stand loyally on the side of Austria-Hungary'. Of all his diplomatic interventions in the course of that unfortunate reign this was the most crass and the most deadly.

The kindest explanation of William's action is that it was based on a gigantic miscalculation: the belief that an Austrian attack on Serbia could remain a purely local war. This could only assume that Russia would remain inactive. Yet in the previous year Bethmann Hollweg, the German Chancellor, had already pointed out to Berchtold that 'it will be nearly impossible for Russia passively to watch military action by Austria against Serbia without a tremendous loss of face', and since then Russian alarm at the appointment of a German general to command the Constantinople army corps at the end of 1913 had emphasized the continuing sensitiveness of Russian reactions. It seems impossible to escape the conclusion that the German government must have known that there was a serious risk of general war, however much they may have been thinking in terms of a purely local one.

Indeed, among the German military there were many who believed that a major clash between the German and the Slav worlds was inevitable; Moltke had said as much to Conrad in February 1913, and in that case the growing military power of Russia suggested that it would be best for Germany 'to wage a preventive war in order to beat the enemy while we still have some chance of winning', as Moltke remarked in the early summer of 1914. Others had also foreseen this dangerous possibility. 'Can Germany afford to wait till Russia becomes the dominant factor in Europe', wondered Sir George Buchanan, the British ambassador at St Petersburg in March 1914, 'or will she strike, while victory is still within her grasp?'

Towards the end of July, when Russia, apparently preparing to stand by Serbia, embarked on partial mobilization, the German government began to speak in terms of mediation. By now, however, the race over mobilization had become a factor in itself. Moltke, anxious lest the Russians would get too far ahead, pressed for German mobilization on 29 July, but Bethmann Hollweg was determined to hold back until Russia had first committed herself to a general mobilization. Similar pressure from the Russian military staff on Tsar Nicholas brought this about on 30 July. On the next day Germany also mobilized, and on 1 August declared war on Russia.

It is hard to know whether the existence of the Franco-Russian alliance and the *ententes* would at this point have brought in Great Britain and France on the side of Russia. The French had hung back, only ordering a partial mobilization on 30 July and withdrawing their troops some six miles from their common frontier with Germany. In England, on the night of 29 July, the British fleet, on orders from Winston Churchill, had moved secretly through the Channel and then northward to its war station at Scapa Flow, but this concentration was only a precautionary measure against the long-dreaded sudden torpedo attack which might deprive Great Britain of her principal means of defence. The cabinet saw little prospect of public opinion accepting a war in defence of Serbia and, despite French pressure, it was not until 2 August that a naval guarantee of the northern coasts of France was given. In Berlin William still had hopes of neutrality in the west, but the issue was finally settled by the German generals. Moltke insisted that it would be technically impossible to dismantle the Schlieffen plan (see p. 47); war with Russia must mean the unleasing of the great attack on France through Belgium. Accordingly, France must be provoked into declaring war, but when she would go no further than refusing to promise neutrality, Germany declared war on her on 3 August and followed this up with an ultimatum to Belgium demanding that German forces should be allowed through on their way to attack France. With the violation of Belgian neutrality on 4 August, the British declaration of war followed on the same day.

This was a desperately bitter moment for Sir Edward Grey. 'The lamps are going out all over Europe,' he remarked to a friend that night in his room at the Foreign Office; no man could have hoped more earnestly to keep them lit. It was said afterwards that he might have pressed more forcefully for mediation, yet it is clear that until the last minute the Central Powers had no interest in mediation. It was said, too, that if he had openly joined the French earlier, the German government might have thought twice. The problem here for Grey was that he was a member of the government of a constitutional democracy, and the cabinet, Parliament and the country would have been hopelessly divided over such a policy. In any case, the German government knew that Great Britain could not watch the defeat of France nor the violation of Belgian neutrality, both of which were implicit in the Schlieffen plan; the truth was that, given the size of the British Army, the German military were not greatly concerned about the possible intervention of Great Britain.

The only remaining question is whether Great Britain need have entered the war at all, since there was no guarantee to the French to this effect. From the moment that he had taken office, however, Grey had been convinced that a German hegemony on the Continent must at all costs be avoided, and it had been this assumption that had caused him to cling to the Anglo-French *entente*, determined to prevent France succumbing to German pressure. The declaration of war on the side of France was only the ultimate implementation of that policy and the German invasion of Belgium had at last given him the moral justification that would make such a step acceptable to British public opinion.

II

The First World War
1914–1918

Asquith's War Administration:
August 1914–May 1915

At eleven o'clock on the night of Tuesday, 4 August, the British ultimatum to Germany expired and as Big Ben struck the hour, the crowds in Downing Street and Parliament Square burst into singing 'God save the King'. It is strange now to recall the joyful excitement with which the outbreak of war was welcomed in London, as it was in Paris and Berlin. 'Now, God be thanked Who has matched us with His hour', wrote Rupert Brooke.[1] War seemed a romantic adventure to those who had never experienced it, and in any case it would all be over by Christmas. They could not know that four weary Christmases were to pass, as the civilization of nineteenth-century Europe was torn apart amid a nightmarish slaughter of millions of men, and that many of those who celebrated that day in an orgy of patriotic fervour were to die in the mud of the western front.

For the British the plunge into a major European war was so novel that it demanded almost too much of the imagination of the men at the centre of events, and in the hasty preparations of the first few months many of the assumptions of peacetime still tended to predominate. First, the declaration of war was seen as a decision taken by the Liberal government, and although the Commons had given their full agreement, there was as yet no question of forming a coalition. John Redmond had pledged the support of the Irish Nationalists, but the struggle over Ulster (see p. 80) had been too recent and too bitter for Conservatives immediately to work in harmony with Liberal ministers. The most that Bonar Law could offer was a party truce in which the Opposition would forgo most of its normal functions.

This was a somewhat half-hearted arrangement for mobilizing a united war effort, leaving the Conservatives in the position of silent spectators. 'We are expected to give a mute and almost unquestioning support to everything done by the government,' complained Lord Curzon in January 1915; '. . . the government are to have all the advantages, while we have all the drawbacks of a coalition.'[2] And even this degree of cooperation seemed uncertain when, in September 1914, Asquith decided to shelve the Irish Home Rule Bill by placing it on the statute book with the proviso that it would be inoperative until after the war. In the circumstances it was probably the most sensible thing to do, but to the Conservatives Asquith's action appeared to be one further step towards putting Ulster under the rule of Dublin, and after hearing Bonar Law accuse the Prime Minister of bad faith, they walked out of the House.

The Conservatives, at least, believed firmly in the war. Labour with its element of pacifists and international Socialists was less single-minded. Although strongly critical of the diplomacy that had led up to the outbreak, the majority of the parliamentary Labour party were prepared to give their support, but their leader Ramsay MacDonald would not, and on his resignation Arthur Henderson was elected to take his place. The parliamentary committee of the TUC also supported the war, but the Labour party executive seemed likely to be influenced by the ILP, who on 13 August had issued a manifesto extending sympathy and greeting to German Socialists. 'They are no enemies of ours, but faithful friends.' In the event, a majority of the executive agreed to back the recruiting campaign, but the prospect of the working classes in arms against each other was genuinely a terrible one for many; it virtually killed Keir Hardie, who died in 1915, and the potential crisis of conscience in their ranks was bound to make Labour's support of the government somewhat equivocal.

Meanwhile, the Liberal government had a free hand, but was not too sure what to do with it. This was the second legacy of the days of peace. Essentially the conduct of a war of this magnitude required a flexible structure of supreme command, within which the Prime Minister, the cabinet, the political and service heads and the commander-in-chief in the field would all have clearly defined roles. At present such a structure simply did not exist, and although in fairness to Asquith it must be said that a satisfactory solution was never found at any stage of the war, it would be hard to imagine anything less workable than the makeshift arrangement which the Liberal government contrived in 1914.

At first the Committee of Imperial Defence acted as a war council; then, in November 1914, a special cabinet committee was formed for this purpose, consisting of the Prime Minister, the Foreign Secretary, the Secretaries of State for War and India, the First Lord of the Admiralty, the Chancellor of the Exchequer and Arthur Balfour. Neither of these bodies had any precise relationship with the rest of the cabinet and it was hardly surprising that intrigue should flourish amid a scene of interdepartmental confusion.

At a personal level the situation was complicated by the presence of Lord Kitchener whom Asquith at once made Secretary of State for War—a non-party appointment which would please the Conservatives as well as the nation, for whom his name was something of a legend. Whatever his later failings, Kitchener began his task with considerable energy and farsightedness. To the astonishment of the cabinet he at once predicted that the war would last three years, gained their assent to the raising of an army of at least a million men and embarked on a campaign for recruiting volunteers which by the end of September had provided 750,000 men.

It was difficult, however, to fit Kitchener into any scheme of constitutional control. 'Your Country Needs You' his posters announced beneath his piercing eye and pointing finger, but Kitchener himself did not appear to feel any need for his civilian colleagues. He clearly had little use for the cabinet and refused to divulge secret information at their meetings mainly on grounds of security. 'If they will only all divorce their wives,' he commented later, 'I will tell them everything,' but even this condition would hardly have been adequate in view of Winston Churchill's dinner-table chatter with Violet Asquith or Asquith's daily letters to Miss Venetia Stanley. Nor was Kitchener's relationship with his military colleagues much better. He was far from seeing himself as a mere political minister of the crown; rather as some sort of supreme commander-in-chief as befitted a senior field-marshal— a view hardly acceptable to the Chief of the Imperial General Staff or to Sir John French, the designate commander of the British Expeditionary Force (BEF).

Some of these difficulties might have been overcome, if Asquith had been able to supply another requirement of a wartime government— strong personal leadership. Here again the more leisurely attitudes of nineteenth-century government prevailed, with Asquith acting as the chairman of a group of departmental ministers. He 'dealt with questions not as they arose', complained Lloyd George, 'but as they were presented to him—always, essentially the judge'. The services must look after the war, for which the Commons had voted them a credit of £100 million. There must, of course, be certain other forms of state intervention (see p. 134): insurance of shipping, the issue of £1 and 10 shilling (50p) notes, government control of railways, shipping and transport; but although the Defence of the Realm Act (DORA) gave potentially wider powers than these, there was little conception of mobilizing the whole of British industry in a coordinated war effort; supply was largely by private contract and the cry was 'business as usual'. 'Mr Asquith, do you take an interest in the war?' asked Lady Tree; and Asquith, imbued with what his son called 'an excessive belief in the power of the unspoken word',[3] may well have had only himself to blame for the implied criticism.

There was a further legacy from the prewar years: the ultimate destination of the British Army. As has been seen (p. 54), there had been considerable debate and exploration of the types of strategy open to the British in the event of war, but there had been no combined planning at a general staff level between the Army and the Navy, and by the time the War Council met on 5 August at No. 10 Downing Street, the Belgians were already fighting desperately against the German on-slaught. At this moment of crisis the discussion could only take one direction. The possibility of an independent landing at Antwerp was ruled out by the Admiralty who would not guarantee the protection of the longer sea route, and it was decided that all six regular infantry divisions as well as the cavalry—the entire British Army—should be dispatched to France, where they would concentrate at Maubeuge, de-spite the misgivings of Kitchener who had correctly guessed the line of the German thrust and would have preferred Amiens. Thus, in this *ad hoc* manner the British took the first step towards their territorial com-mitment to northern France, which was eventually to draw nearly five and a half million of their men into the western front.

Embarkation followed at once; the Channel crossings were success-fully carried out and by 20 August four divisions of the expeditionary force had already assembled near Maubeuge under Sir John French, who now found his troops caught up in the great tide of the German advance. It was only during these first weeks that the fighting in France bore any resemblance to the war of movement to which the general staffs of Europe had hitherto devoted all their thought. The Schlieffen plan (see p. 47), aimed at the speedy defeat of France, was at last about to unfold. The opening of the campaign had of necessity been slow, since it involved the German capture of Liège, whose forts commanded the gap between the Dutch frontier and the Ardennes, but once these had fallen, the moment was ripe on 18 August for the line of four German armies pivoting on Luxemburg to begin their great sweep through the southern half of Belgium into the plains of north-eastern France (map, p. 103). The Belgian army after frantic resistance fell back northwards on Antwerp. The French in the meantime had gone ahead with their own plan of attack into Lorraine on 14 August, but after a week had been seriously repulsed. Thus for the first few days of their advance von Kluck's 1st Army on the extreme right of the German wheeling movement through France did not have to contend with any resistance, only endless marching.

This was not to last. By now Joffre, the French Commander-in-Chief, had realized the need to redeploy and General Lanrezac was asked to move his 5th Army northwards to link up with the British at Maubeuge. Despite local difficulties—neither commander spoke the other's language and Lanrezac had an ill-concealed contempt for British military prowess—the two armies advanced side by side. On 22 August von Kluck, learning to his surprise that the British were in the field somewhere in front of him, planned to outflank them, but von Bülow, commanding the 2nd German Army on his left, forbade him to extend the line any further west. A frontal attack was the only alternative and on 23 August, among the coalfields outside Mons, British forces had their first encounter with the German Army. The outcome was a tribute to their peacetime training. The expeditionary force, a tiny fragment in this tense battle of giants, fought off the onslaught with superb fire control and marksmanship, until 'with bloody losses', said the official German history afterwards, 'the attack gradually came to an end'.

What pleased Sir John French less was to discover that night that Lanrezac had already given orders for withdrawal. This had largely been dictated by the fact that the French 4th Army on his right was also pulling back, and it meant that the British, too, must now retreat to avoid encirclement; on 26 August the 2nd Corps, its men too exhausted to march any more, stood momentarily to repulse von Kluck at Le Cateau and then continued to fall back.

As the German advance continued, however, a gap was beginning to appear between the armies of von Kluck and von Bülow, and Joffre now saw his chance to throw the Germans off balance. On 29 August Lanrezac, with Joffre breathing down his neck at headquarters, halted to renew the attack against von Bülow at Guise. This was to be a crucial engagement; von Bülow at once appealed to von Kluck, who accordingly turned towards the south-east to close the gap between them. The great German wheeling movement was now swinging down to the east of Paris, and with this departure from the Schlieffen plan the German right flank was exposed to the blow which Joffre could deliver from the region of Paris with the recently formed French 6th Army.

Sir John French, meanwhile, was in the depths of despair. Mistrustful of his ally, conscious of his heavy casualties and the exhaustion of the survivors, and feeling himself being pushed ever southwards away from his Channel bases, he dispatched a message to London that he must withdraw from the line in order to refit. Reactions were immediate;

Lord Kitchener donned his field-marshal's uniform, was rushed across the Channel in a destroyer and in a furious interview at the embassy in Paris ordered French to keep his troops in the line.

This was as well, for the campaign had reached its turning-point. The issue now rested on the nerve of two men. At Luxemburg Moltke, the German Commander-in-Chief, only in fitful communication with his forces and harassed by the thought that the French Army was still intact, sensed the danger of the situation. At Bar-sur-Aube, Joffre, sitting under an apple tree in a school playground, pondered on whether the Germans, who were now across the Marne, had gone far enough to be caught in the trap. By 4 September it seemed that the moment had come and on the next day the French, striking on the German western flank with their 6th Army and from the south with their 5th, opened an offensive designed to encircle von Kluck.

As the battle of the Marne raged, the gap between von Kluck and von Bülow grew wider and into this gap marched the British Army, cautiously exploring the ground and puzzled to find no enemy at all. It is hard to say whether a more energetic exploiting of this penetration of the German line would have made much difference to the eventual outcome. As it was, Joffre failed to destroy his opponent, but he gained a strategic victory, when by 8 September Moltke's nerve had broken and the Germans began a general retreat. The two exhausted groups of armies moved painfully northwards, and then after Erich von Falkenhayn had replaced Moltke, a series of outflanking movements by the German right wing, countered in turn by the Allies, led the opposing forces swiftly back towards the Channel coast.

The fate of the ports now hung in the balance. This question was to be settled principally by the first battle of Ypres, but it was also vitally affected by a separate episode which took place behind the main line of the fighting. The Belgian army, which had fallen back on Antwerp, was relying on the forts that ringed the main citadel, but by 27 September the Germans, determined to capture Antwerp, had brought up giant howitzers which proceeded to knock out these forts one by one. So serious was the damage that on the night of 2 October the Belgian government decided that they must evacuate Antwerp immediately, while a line of retreat westwards to Ostend was still open to them.

The receipt of this news caused consternation in London, where it was considered vital that Antwerp should hold out until it was relieved by the Allied forces in France. Accordingly, it was agreed that Winston Churchill, who already had some marines in the vicinity, should go at once to Antwerp, where by the afternoon of 3 October he had persuaded

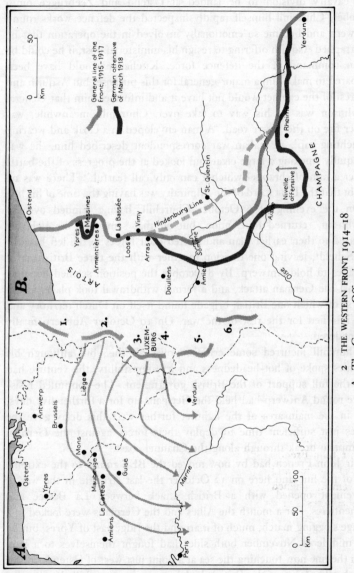

2 THE WESTERN FRONT 1914–18
A. The German Offensive in 1914
B. The deadlock and the final offensives

the Belgians to stand firm, promising a reinforcement of three naval brigades. At the same time Kitchener was able to offer one infantry and one cavalry division to be landed at Ostend and Zeebrugge on 6 October. Churchill himself rapidly inspected the defence works round Antwerp and became so emotionally involved in the operation that he telegraphed Asquith offering to resign his ministerial post, if he could be given command of the defence force. Kitchener would have been prepared to make him a major-general for this purpose, but Asquith and the rest of the cabinet would not have it and informed him that General Rawlinson was on his way to take over. Churchill, meanwhile, was under fire on the Lierre road. 'A man enveloped in a cloak and wearing a yachting cap', an Italian war correspondent described him, 'he was tranquilly smoking a large cigar and looked at the progress of the battle under a rain of shrapnel which I can only call fearful.'[4] There was no doubt that the First Lord of the Admiralty was having the time of his life.

On the evening of 6 October Churchill, having handed over to Rawlinson, returned to London, but on that same day the Belgians reverted to their earlier plan and shifted their forces to the left bank of the Scheldt, leaving one division together with the three British naval brigades to hold Antwerp. By 8 October the position seemed hopeless against the German attack, and a formal withdrawal took place, in the course of which one British brigade found itself on Dutch territory and was interned for the rest of the war. On 10 October Antwerp finally surrendered.

Churchill incurred some criticism over all this, but although his enemies spoke of hot-headedness and irresponsibility, the venture had had the full support of the British government. The continued resistance round Antwerp had held the Germans up for a further five days, and in the main area of the fighting further west this delay gave the Allies just sufficient time to deploy their forces against the German attempt to break through along the Channel coast.

Sir John French had by now moved the BEF round to the extreme left of the line and here on 12 October the last struggle in the war of movement opened with a British attack between La Bassée and Armentières. For a month the Allies and the Germans were locked in a savage slogging match, much of it around the ridge east of Ypres, but by the middle of November both sides had fought themselves to a halt, with the line now touching the sea at a point just west of Ostend. In this first battle of Ypres the British had lost 50,000 men, killed, wounded and missing; the old professional army of peacetime was no more, and the need to reinforce from the troops of Kitchener's New Army was to swallow up more and more of British manpower in an effort to retain the Ypres salient which had been saved at so great a cost.

In the west, the last vestiges of the Schlieffen plan had been shot to pieces on the Marne. Even in the east its implementation had not saved the Germans from the task of having to fight simultaneously on two fronts, contrary to what its author had intended. In August the Russians had advanced into East Prussia and so alarmed Moltke that on 25 August two corps were switched from the western offensive to the eastern front, where at the end of the month the Russian attack was smashed at the battle of Tannenberg. Meanwhile, further south the Austrians had also been engaged in heavy fighting with the Russians and by the beginning of October had been flung back in Galicia, the line only becoming stabilized when the Germans came to the rescue of their ally with a counter-offensive.

Overseas events went almost entirely in favour of the British. To the surprise of the Germans the Empire stood firm. The Dominions all declared war on their own initiative and dispatched forces to the aid of the mother country, Canadian units arriving in England, Australians and New Zealanders (the Anzacs) in Egypt. The South African prime minister, Louis Botha, whose previous military experience had been gained against the British in the Boer War, organized an expedition for the conquest of German South-West Africa, while to the north Togoland was occupied fairly quickly. The other German colonies in Africa lasted rather longer; the capture of the Cameroons took some eighteen months, while in German East Africa Lieutenant Colonel von Lettow-Vorbeck conducted a remarkable campaign throughout the whole of the war. In the Pacific there was little hope for the German islands. The Australians took New Guinea and the Bismarck archipelago, the New Zealanders occupied Samoa, and Japan, who declared war on 23 August, helped herself to the Marshall, Caroline and Mariana archipelagoes (map, p. 379), at the same time taking by assault the German-held area of Kiao-Chow on the mainland of China.

In the early months at sea there were one or two small actions, in which the Germans enjoyed a momentary success. Their battle-cruiser, the *Goeben* and the cruiser, *Breslau*, in the Mediterranean gained refuge in Turkish territorial waters. In the Pacific the *Emden*, a light cruiser, bombarded Madras and Penang before being sunk by the Australians. At the end of October the British battleship *Audacious* was sunk by a mine off the Irish coast, a loss which the Admiralty tried to keep secret until after the war. Then, at the beginning of November, a German squadron under Admiral Graf von Spee sank a weaker British force off

Coronel on the coast of Chile; this was a serious blow and Vice-Admiral Sturdee was sent at once with two battle-cruisers to the Falkland Islands, where they were coaling when von Spee arrived with the intention of destroying the naval base there. This time it was the British who had the superior guns and only one ship of the German squadron managed to escape. Even this better news was overclouded, however, when German battle-cruisers slipped into the North Sea to shell Scarborough and Hartlepool in December.

To the British public, hungry for the Nelson touch, there was something unsatisfactory about it all. They wanted Britannia to rule the waves and did not notice that she did. The continuous transporting of troops across the Channel, the more hazardous operations around Antwerp and the safe passage of Canadian forces across the Atlantic, all put that beyond doubt. By the end of the year German freight had been banished from the seas; the fate of the German colonies was sealed by the fact that no reinforcements could be sent to them, and throughout the war the Navy kept the British Isles safe and fed and her armies overseas supplied.

The principal role of the Navy, however, was as unobtrusive as it was momentous. The greatest threat was the presence of the German High Seas Fleet at Wilhelmshaven and in the face of that the British Grand Fleet, under the command of Admiral Jellicoe, was tied to the east coast of Great Britain with its main base at Scapa Flow and lighter forces at Harwich, in the Thames estuary and along the Channel. A false move here could have meant the loss of British security in a single afternoon, as Winston Churchill said of the later battle of Jutland; equally it could mean the end of the German fleet. Thus the paradox of Anglo-German naval competition in the prewar years was that the fleets had grown too big to risk an encounter; the stakes were too high and for four years the North Sea became a no-man's-land, while the two navies watched each other in a constant war of nerves.

The escape of the *Goeben* and the *Breslau* in the Mediterranean was to have one profoundly significant consequence. It helped to bring Turkey into the war on the side of the Central Powers. A treaty to this effect had been signed on 2 August, but the uncertainty of the fighting on the eastern and western fronts had caused Turkey to hold back. It was only a takeover by the pro-German party under the Turkish war minister, Enver Pasha, that gained the two German ships permission to enter the nominally neutral waters of the Dardanelles, and then at the end of October Turkey took the final step with a naval excursion into the Black Sea, in which Russian ports were bombarded.

The entry of Turkey into the war was highly relevant to a debate over future strategy which had developed in London between the so-called easterners and westerners. The issue had arisen initially over the new circumstances that prevailed on the western front. Here, as the two sides battered themselves to a standstill, it had quickly become apparent that the trench gave the best protection from shellfire for the infantry, and from the Channel coast to the Swiss frontier the armies had dug themselves in, creating a continuous line of opposing earthworks. Thus for an attacker flanking movements were ruled out and any frontal advance would have to be made through barbed wire entanglements under heavy machine-gun fire. The only solution the military could devise was a vast preliminary bombardment which was supposed to destroy the enemy wire and machine-gun posts, but as the war progressed this method was found to be ineffective and appallingly costly in lives. Kitchener was never at ease with this new style of trench warfare, and in January 1915 he wrote to Sir John French despairing of the likelihood of any break-through: 'The German lines in France may be looked on as a fortress that cannot be carried by assault and also that cannot be completely invested, with the result that the lines may be held by an investing force while operations proceed elsewhere.'[5]

This deadlock on the western front was the basis of the case put forward by the easterners who believed that it was essential to open up a new theatre of operations. They argued that by becoming an adjunct to the French, the British Army had lost that independence of action which naval power could give. 'Are there not other alternatives,' asked Winston Churchill, 'than sending our armies to chew barbed wire in Flanders?' Churchill himself had dallied with the idea of landing a strong force on the German North Sea coast to capture the Kiel canal and to inveigle Denmark into joining the Allies. Sir John Fisher, whom Churchill had recalled at the age of seventy-three to the post of First Sea Lord, nursed a pet scheme for a landing on the Baltic coast. Now the Turkish declaration of war added a new dimension to the dreams of the easterners: an assault on Constantinople, which would knock Turkey out, open up a new supply route to Russia and hold back Bulgaria from joining the Central Powers.

To the 'westerners' these arguments all ignored the fact that the war could not be won until the German Army had been defeated and that the place for this lay in the west. Even if an expedition in the east were at first successful, this could only mean that the Allies would eventually be confronted by a major part of the German Army on a Balkan front, where the ground would be favourable for defence and the problems of supply for the Allies infinitely greater. There was hard, though unpalatable, sense in the westerners' case, but when one considers the eventual slaughter in the west it is understandable how attractive some alternative might seem. Certainly the government was torn in doubt over this controversy, although most of the military were westerners in sympathy. Asquith, as usual, could see both points of view, and perhaps as a consequence the early months of 1915 saw an attempt to satisfy both groups simultaneously—a disastrous policy that led directly to the fall of the Liberal government.

In France Joffre was determined on a two-pronged attack on the sides of the great bulge of the front line (map, p. 103). The first part of this—a thrust northwards in Champagne—was broken off in March 1915 after the loss of some 80,000 men. The second—eastwards in Artois—was to have the help of Sir John French, who accordingly launched an independent attack on Neuve Chapelle on 10 March. During the first three hours the British advanced a thousand yards on a front of 4,000 yards, but the exploitation of this initial success failed to materialize and at the end of three days' fighting, during which they lost nearly 13,000 men, they had got no further and the battle was broken off. On 22 April the Germans launched their own assault against the British, and using poison gas for the first time, pushed them back some three miles in the second battle of Ypres, a murderous struggle which cost both sides together a total of more than 100,000 men. On 9 May the French attempted a new advance on Vimy Ridge. On the same day Sir Douglas Haig, commanding the 1st Army, made an assault on Aubers Ridge which came to nothing and on 11 May followed this up with a second further south at Festubert, which produced a gain of three-quarters of a mile after a fortnight's fighting.

The principal effect of these engagements was to bring to a head a great controversy over shell production, since the policy of heavy bombardment was demanding more shells than were being produced. For months Lloyd George struggled with Kitchener on this score, but it was not until April 1915 that he became chairman of a new cabinet committee on munitions, from which Kitchener was carefully excluded. In the meanwhile the shortage did give the generals a weapon for their own defence, and as he watched the beginning of the Festubert battle from a church tower, Sir John French resolved on a highly irregular move. He drew up a case against the government for failing to maintain the necessary supply, and handed it to Colonel Repington, the military correspondent of *The Times*. The information was in the press on Friday 14 May—a single salvo which was largely instrumental in bringing down the Liberal administration, aided by another shock that the government sustained at the same moment.

While Sir John French's forces had been locked in these ineffective assaults, the plans of the easterners had also come to unhappy fruition. At the beginning of 1915 Churchill's enthusiasm for a naval attack on the Dardanelles was strengthened by an appeal from the Russian Tsar for some kind of demonstration by the Allies which might make Turkey relax her pressure in the Caucasus. Kitchener, too, gave some support to such a scheme, although he did not see how he could provide any troops for it for some months. Churchill, however, was content to envisage a Dardanelles campaign as a purely naval venture. He had been deeply impressed by the destruction which the German howitzers had wrought on the Antwerp forts, and he reckoned that a force of old battleships could silence the Turkish gun emplacements on the shores of the Straits and open a way into the sea of Marmara and thence to Constantinople. The scheme was gallant, romantic and immensely hazardous; it assumed that a naval expedition, lacking any military support, could bring about the surrender of Constantinople and perhaps the whole of Turkey. It was hardly surprising that Sir John Fisher blew hot and cold; he loved the thought of action, yet he feared any reduction in the forces of the Grand Fleet which might have to meet the German High Seas Fleet in the North Sea, and he was certain that it was wrong for the Navy to move through the Dardanelles without the support of the Army.

On 28 January 1915 Asquith took the decision. The Navy was to commence its forcing of the Straits on 19 February. Thus there was still no question of a combined operation; this only developed as an after-thought, when in the middle of February Kitchener agreed to release the 29th Division for this purpose. As if this was not late enough, he then changed his mind and only finally acquiesced on 10 March. It was not until the third week of March that these forces were embarked, preceded by their commander, General Sir Ian Hamilton, who set off for the Aegean furnished with only the vaguest instructions to act in conjunction with the Navy if he was needed.

In the meantime, Admiral Cardan had begun the independent naval operation on 19 February as ordered, and throughout the next four weeks his forces edged their way up the Dardanelles (see map, p. 203). The shore batteries were engaged; then trawlers acting as mine-sweepers would clear the waters they had covered, and the ships would move forward to bombard the next forts. By 5 March Cardan had penetrated some eleven miles to the point where the Straits narrowed to a breadth of three-quarters of a mile and the minefields were at their thickest. The prospect was not good. Bombardment at long range from the sea had not silenced the shore batteries; the Turks had in addition a number of mobile howitzers and attempts by the trawlers to sweep the Narrows on three separate nights were frustrated by heavy fire under searchlights which the ships were unable to knock out. On 18 March Admiral de Robeck, who had now replaced Cardan, launched an assault in daylight. Again the guns were bombarded, this time from closer range, but the minesweepers could still not get through and after one battleship had blown up, two had been sunk by mines and three others seriously damaged, de Robeck decided to disengage.

As it turned out, this was to be the end of the independent naval action. In London the War Council were all in favour of pressing on, if de Robeck agreed, but at a conference with Hamilton off the island of Lemnos on 22 March, the admiral declared that he must have military support. This was bound to entail a fatal delay. The hasty dispatch of Hamilton's troops had meant that their stores were utterly unready for an immediate landing and Hamilton knew that he must first move his force to Alexandria for a reorganization. Thus the invasion of the Gallipoli peninsula could not begin before a further month had elapsed —ample time for Liman von Sanders, the head of the German military mission, to make his dispositions.

Hamilton's plan was for the 29th Division to land at five separate points at Cape Helles, while the two divisions of the Anzac Corps, already in Egypt, should land further north at Gaba Tepe, later known as Anzac Cove. There were to be two feints—a French division taking Kum Kale on the south side of the entrance to the Dardanelles and the Royal Naval Division making a demonstration much further north at Bulair.

The invasion was launched on 25 April. At Cape Helles a Turkish division was dug in and played havoc with two of the landing forces as they set foot on the beaches. At Gaba Tepe the Anzacs were confronted first by high cliffs, then by the Turkish reserve division which its commander, Mustapha Kemal, flung in on his own initiative. For weeks savage fighting ensued, but for the invaders it was all in vain; as the Turks strengthened their forces, the British and Anzac armies were held in their cramped beachheads in one more deadlock of trench warfare, which by 9 May had cost them 20,000 casualties.

In London Churchill was still undaunted, but by now the apparent failures on the western front and in Gallipoli were about to converge upon the government. On 14 May *The Times* published Sir John French's complaint about the shortage of shells; on 15 May Sir John Fisher, stung by

Churchill's determination to draw more ships away from home waters for the Gallipoli expedition, sent in his resignation. It was his ninth, but this time he meant it. On this Bonar Law reckoned that he could no longer hold back his Conservative Opposition, already chafing at the silence imposed upon them, and on 17 May he paid a short visit to No. 10 Downing Street to demand the establishment of a coalition government.

His price was to be the removal of Churchill and Lord Haldane. The Conservatives could now use the fiasco of the Dardanelles to give vent to their resentment at Churchill's leaving them for the Liberals in 1904. Haldane's crime was that he had been educated partly in Germany which he had once declared to be his spiritual home. This was not as dastardly as his enemies made out. The atmosphere of Queen Victoria's court had naturally been German, and among the upper middle class who had grown up before the *entente cordiale* there were many ties with Germany. German spas had been popular holiday resorts and at the turn of the century it had been in Germany rather than in his own country that Edward Elgar's music had first been recognized. In the new mood of wartime, however, when even royalty had felt compelled to change the family name to Windsor, and when all German works of music had ceased to be played, Haldane could expect little mercy.

Churchill always maintained afterwards that Asquith could have countered Bonar Law by allowing open debate in a secret session of the House of Commons, when the news from Italy, now on the verge of joining the Allies, would have greatly strengthened his hand. Asquith, however, gave way. Churchill, protesting vigorously, was transferred to the Chancellorship of the Duchy of Lancaster and for many years was to be hounded with the cry of 'Gallipoli'. Haldane went without protest and without any word of consolation from Asquith.

The Liberal government resigned and a coalition was formed, although still under the leadership of Asquith. Of the Liberals Sir Edward Grey remained at the Foreign Office and Lloyd George, supported by the press campaign over the shell shortage, headed a new Ministry of Munitions. Of the Conservatives Bonar Law became Colonial Secretary, Lord Curzon Lord Privy Seal and Austen Chamberlain Secretary of State for India, while Balfour succeeded Churchill at the Admiralty. Labour, too, was given representation with Arthur Henderson as President of the Board of Education with a seat in the cabinet. In this way the last Liberal government, which had swept into power with the great electoral triumph of 1906, came to an end; the stresses of war had proved too much for it and before long these were to be a factor in the eclipse of the Liberal party itself.

11

Coalition Under Asquith:
May 1915–December 1916

T he forming of the Coalition government was to give Asquith a
further eighteen months as Prime Minister. During that time,
however, the most dynamic contribution to the war effort came
from Lloyd George at the Ministry of Munitions. The new department
grew quickly to a staff of 25,000 civil servants and by the end of the war
numbered 65,000 with more than three million workers under its control. This was a task ideally suited to Lloyd George's restless energy. He
was determined to produce armaments far in excess of what even the
service departments were demanding, and when a cabinet committee
was set up to check this, it got no further than one meeting. 'I suppose,
sir,' said his secretary, 'that means the end of your programme.' 'No,'
replied Lloyd George, 'it means the end of the committee.'[1] He
recruited businessmen into the department and cut ruthlessly across
existing arrangements at the War Office and the Admiralty; he toured
the factories appealing directly to the workers to surrender some of the
safeguards which their unions had won for them, and seeking to convince them that they too were part of the front line. 'Plant the flag on
your work-shops. Every lathe you have, recruit it. Convert your machinery into battalions.'[2] He showed a fine ungentlemanly grasp of the
requirements of total war, a sense of personal leadership, of extrovert
commitment, and it is easy to understand how he could eventually oust
Asquith from the premiership. 'In war,' Bonar Law had warned
Asquith, 'it is necessary not only to be active, but to seem active', and
by December 1916 Lloyd George had made it clear that he was the man
to take the country to victory.

In the diplomatic sphere the Coalition government began its career
by reaping the benefits of a long and difficult negotiation which brought
Italy on to the side of the Allies. Her price, written into the secret treaty
of London in April 1915, was to be the Tyrol, Istria and northern
Dalmatia, and in 1917, when the Allied statesmen had got to work on
the Asiatic territories of Turkey, a section of Asia Minor was added to

this (see p. 162). Indeed, the Turkish empire was becoming a useful bargaining counter in the diplomacy of war. Russia had already been promised Constantinople and the Straits—a revolutionary change in British foreign policy, prompted by the need to encourage Russia to withstand the pressures to which she was exposed, even though such a concession at once put any positive agreement with Greece out of reach.

Beyond this the rest of the year 1915 was disappointing for the Allies. The Italians duly embarked on a campaign against the Austrians, but despite four major assaults along the river Isonzo were unable to make any headway. In Gallipoli things went from bad to worse: in August a new landing at Suvla Bay (map, p. 203) seemed to offer every chance of success, but the attack moved with appalling slowness; the troops became pinned down in yet another beachhead, and an attempt to break out from Anzac cove came to nothing.

Meanwhile, on the eastern front a major Austro-German offensive had been launched in May and had swept through Russian Poland; on 5 August Warsaw fell and by October the Central Powers were established on a line from Riga to the Carpathians. These advances finally persuaded Bulgaria to enter the war against the Allies, and as a consequence Serbia's eastern frontier was now open to attack. In October a combined invasion from the north and the east drove the Serb army into retreat and although Greece agreed to allow an Anglo-French force to land at Salonika, this did little to help the Serbs who eventually had to find their way to the Albanian coast where they were evacuated by Allied ships.

Thus in the east the Central Powers had made great gains and there was to be no compensating success for the Allies on the western front. In July, despite a decision to the contrary at an Allied conference at Calais, Kitchener agreed in private conversation with Joffre to join him in an autumn offensive. This, as before, was to consist of a double thrust through Champagne and Artois, and when it was launched on 25 September, the usual pattern prevailed. Heavy artillery bombardment was inadequate to smash the barbed wire and machine-guns of a German defence in depth. Haig's 1st Army did make some penetration on the first day of the battle of Loos, but the untried New Army divisions had been held too far back in reserve and when they did eventually follow up, the Germans had recovered and were ready for them. The battle dragged on throughout October and then petered out, the British having made some small advance at a cost of 60,000 men.

This failure at Loos finally brought the question of the high command to a head. Haig had earlier been asked by Kitchener to correspond with him, unknown to Sir John French—an extraordinary procedure to which King George had objected strongly. Haig now had a legitimate grievance, since French had refused to allow him to have command of the reserve divisions, and he was convinced that the initial attack at Loos had created a shortlived gap in the German line which, if it had been exploited immediately, would have led to a major victory. 'I do not think that after Loos D. H. and French can work satisfactorily together,' wrote Haig's Chief of Staff. 'One or other will have to go elsewhere.'³ Haig certainly unburdened himself in letters to Kitchener and in conversation with Lord Haldane and King George, when they visited his headquarters. All this was later depicted as intrigue by an officer against his own Commander-in-Chief, but at least Haigh could argue that he had been asked to express his view and in a war in which thousands of men were dying in useless charges across no-man's-land this was no time for etiquette.

By the end of the year the decision had been taken and Sir John French was replaced by Sir Douglas Haig as Commander-in-Chief. At the same time Asquith was very conscious of the need to find a new CIGS who would be strong enough to stand up to Kitchener and had decided on General Sir William Robertson, at present Chief of Staff to the BEF. Robertson at once showed his mettle by demanding that he alone should be responsible to the War Council for all matters of military strategy and that the Secretary of State for War should confine himself to matters of administration and recruiting. This was exactly what Asquith wanted and Kitchener, after a struggle, agreed to conform.

Haig was to hold his appointment until the end of the war, Robertson until February 1918. They were men of very different background—Haig, the son of an old Border family, Clifton, Oxford, Sandhurst and a commission in the Hussars; Robertson, the son of a village postman, rising from the ranks of the Army, the first ever to reach the position of general and later field-marshal—yet in personality they were rather similar: dour, hard-working, unflinching. Both could present a case clearly and precisely on paper; neither of them could express himself effectively in conversation. 'I've 'eard different,' was Robertson's brusque retort to any view with which he disagreed, and politicians endeavouring to plumb the military mind were confronted in these two men with a model of tight-lipped non-communication.

The crisis over the military command in the west had coincided with a fierce debate in the cabinet about Gallipoli. Bonar Law, Lloyd George, Carson and Austen Chamberlain, supported by many of the military, were in favour of evacuation; Asquith, Balfour, Curzon and Churchill urged reinforcement and a renewal of the attack. The dispute did at least provide an excuse for sending out Kitchener, whose presence in London was becoming increasingly irksome, to view the scene at first hand, and it was during his absence in November 1915 that Asquith, temporarily taking over the War Office, had made his dispositions for the appointments of Haig and Robertson. On his return Kitchener advocated evacuation and at the end of the year the troops in the three beachheads were successfully withdrawn, despite the blood-curdling picture of the massacre that such an operation would entail, conjured up by Churchill and Curzon.

The closing of the Gallipoli front ended the one serious strategic effort of the 'easterners'. This did not mean, however, an end to the dispatch of many troops to theatres of operation outside France. A large inactive army was being built up at Salonika. Another army in Egypt protected the Suez Canal and eventually marched eastwards across Sinai to carry the war against the Turks into Palestine. In Mesopotamia another force under General Townshend advanced towards Baghdad from Basra and then fell back on Kut (see map p. 203) where it was besieged and finally surrendered in April 1916. Politically these ventures were to be of some significance after the war; at the time they did little to hasten the defeat of Germany and drained off more than a million troops whom Robertson, an uncompromising 'westerner', would have dearly liked to have in France.

The difficulties for the government at home were not limited to the question of Gallipoli and the reorganization of the military command. Lloyd George at the Ministry of Munitions was overcoming the shortage of shells, but there remained the more sinister requirement of men. At first the recruiting of volunteers had given the Army as many as could be trained, but by now the supply was slowing down and Robertson calculated that to maintain the seventy British divisions he would need an intake of 130,000 a month. The issue of conscription was inescapable. In fact, the House of Commons and the country were prepared to accept this, but Asquith misjudged the feeling, influenced by the objections of several members of the cabinet who, even at this stage of the war, saw conscription as an unwarrantable form of state intervention. As a consequence he felt his way towards it with a series of compromise measures which only culminated in a Military Service Act as late as May 1916, applying to all men between eighteen and forty-one. Had conscription come earlier, it might have saved the best of those young volunteers whose lives were thrown away on the western front in the first half of the war; as it was, it did create some order and control in the organizing of the armies and ensured that workers in essential occupations were unable to join up. In this way the nation moved a step further towards total war, as one more principle of nineteenth-century liberalism was abandoned.

Wisely, conscription was not extended to Ireland,* where it was important not to disturb the uneasy truce. The placing of the Home Rule Act on the statute book, albeit in suspended operation, had already awoken anxiety in Ulster; and the appearance of Conservatives in the Coalition government had created corresponding misgivings in the south that the Act might remain permanently a dead letter. In the main, however, the bulk of the Irish were prepared to accept the policies of Carson and John Redmond for a united effort to win the war and some 135,000 Irish volunteered to serve with the British forces.

The leaders of Sinn Fein thought differently. They looked to Germany. Here Sir Roger Casement, formerly an official in the British consular service, had been trying to raise a force of Irish volunteers from the prison-of-war camps and in 1916 plans were laid for a revolt in Dublin, aided by a German shipment of arms. In the event the German ship was intercepted and Sir Roger Casement was arrested shortly after he had landed on the Irish coast from a U-boat. On this some of the leaders attempted to call off the rising, but others were determined to press on, even though they knew that it could only be a hopeless gesture. On Easter Monday 1916 they captured several key points in Dublin and proclaimed an independent Irish republic, but after four days of fighting British troops forced them to surrender.

Thus far the Easter rising with its open allegiance to Germany had gained little sympathy among the Irish. It was the British authorities who gave Sinn Fein the psychological victory they sought. Casement was brought to England, tried on a charge of treason and hanged. More significant, fifteen of the leaders of the rebellion were tried by court-martial and shot. Asquith hastened to Dublin too late to stop the executions, agreed to allow Lloyd George to try to undo the damage by offering immediate Home Rule for all of Ireland except for six counties of Ulster, and then, despite the support of Bonar Law, Balfour and Carson, backed away in the face of diehard Conservative opposition. Thus Ireland continued to be ruled from Westminster and the dead of the Easter rising came to be seen by many of the Irish as men who had shown the way after all; Sinn Fein began to increase their numbers and the position of John Redmond with his insistence on parliamentary

* It was eventually applied in Ireland in April 1918.

procedures was seriously discredited (see p. 182).

There was one other incidental consequence of the Irish negotiation. It saved the life of Lloyd George who, before this, had been intending to accompany Kitchener on a visit to Russia. Kitchener sailed without him and on 5 June was drowned, when his cruiser sank in rough seas after striking a mine. The country was shattered by this news; the cabinet had rather more mixed feelings, although they would not have spoken as explicitly as Lord Northcliffe who declared: 'Providence is on the side of the British Empire after all.'

The summer of 1916 hardly seemed the occasion for such optimism. Since the end of February the Germans in the west had been engaged in a fearsome offensive against the fortress of Verdun, gradually extending the attack throughout the surrounding district; for months an appalling slaughter continued, as the French under General Pétain fought a fanatical resistance. The 'hell of Verdun' is by now a cliché, but a justifiable one, swallowing up, as it did, 315,000 French and 281,000 Germans; and soon the British, too, were to have their own traumatic experience in the battle of the Somme.

Since the beginning of 1916 it had been agreed by Joffre and Haig that there should be a combined offensive and although Haig would have preferred Flanders, the eventual battleground lay further south in the region of the river Somme. This seems to have had no tactical purpose, merely the convenience of being the junction point of the British and French armies, although as the grim struggle around Verdun continued it was soon apparent that the British would have to carry much of the burden. Haig's plan was that after a prolonged bombardment eleven divisions would attack on a front of some eighteen miles. With this weight of assault he hoped to maintain sufficient impetus to break right through the German line, and then to exploit this success with five cavalry divisions which he had waiting in reserve.

The bombardment which began on 24 June lasted an entire week and then on 1 July at 7.30 on a beautiful summer morning the eleven divisions of Kitchener's New Army, with five French divisions on their right, went over the top. Before they were half-way across no-man's-land, the awful realization had dawned. The German dug-outs had been sunk too deep into the chalk for the shelling to touch them; the German troops sheltering in them might be dazed or concussed, but as the bombardment lifted, they could still run with their machine-guns up the steps to the emplacements above and the whole area of the British advance became a vast killing ground. In places the German trenches were reached, but in the course of this single day the British lost 57,000 men, of whom 19,000 were killed.

Haig at first had no idea how badly things had gone and in any case was determined to persevere. So the Somme campaign wore on, battle after battle, some a little more successful, gaining a few hundred yards, all appallingly costly in human life. Haig would not relent. In September he determined to use the first tanks with which he had been supplied; they were a great success, but the assault only gained a mile and a half and victory still eluded him. The weather had now broken and the land over which the troops fought had become a quagmire; yet the fighting went on until November, when a blizzard finally brought it to an end.

The battle of the Somme cost the British 418,000 men in casualties. It had destroyed the largest army of volunteers ever raised and it left a memory that haunted the survivors for the rest of their lives. In later years Haig and his staff incurred immense criticism for this carnage. Some of it, perhaps, is unfair; the troops were inexperienced, and better tactics could have reduced casualties, as the French showed. Haig simply had to fight with what he had got. Yet when that is said, there does seem to have been an appalling unawareness at headquarters of the conditions under which the troops were fighting, an ignorance that heavy bombardment did not destroy barbed wire or deep dug-outs, and an obstinacy in persisting when all surprise had been lost and the methods in use proved ineffective.

It could be argued that, given the conditions of the western front, little variation on the themes of bombardment and frontal assault was possible. The truth was that the pre-1914 military mind was desperately inelastic and slow in devising or even accepting new methods to cope with the novel circumstances of trench warfare. It was not, for example, until August 1915 that the War Office was prepared to sponsor the manufacture of trench mortars, not until the autumn of 1915 that the first steel helmets were issued. If men had to advance against machine-guns, it might be sensible to design bullet-proof vehicles whose caterpillar tracks could take them over mud and enemy trenches. H. G. Wells had already suggested this in a short story as early as 1900. Yet even when the western front had taken shape, the military remained intensely suspicious about the idea of tanks. It was Winston Churchill, always eager for a new approach, who actually put up Admiralty funds to finance their trial development. Lloyd George was delighted with them at a secret demonstration in February 1916, but Kitchener still seemed **unc**onvinced and Robertson had grave doubts. It must be added that

Haig was enthusiastic at once, asked for as many as possible, and the day after their first use in action in September 1916 requested the supply of a thousand. Even so, his employment of them was criticized as a premature and ineffective divulging of the secret to the enemy. In fact, this alarm was unnecessary, since the German general staff were as shortsighted as their British counterparts and during the war, at least, never grasped the significance of the tank.

On the sea that summer there was not disaster, only disappointment. Admiral Jellicoe had been more cautious than Haig; battleships were less expendable than men and the security of Great Britain more immediately dependent on them. The initiative that led to the only major naval engagement in the war, the battle of Jutland, came from the German Admiral Scheer. Hoping to entice some of the British ships into the North Sea, he had challenged them with a couple of sorties in March and April, and then at the end of May sent Admiral Hipper's battle-cruisers towards the Norwegian coast to act as bait to draw the attacking British ships on to the German High Seas Fleet lying in wait off Denmark. The British, who were in possession of the German code, picked up the signals and Jellicoe resolved to give the appearance of falling into Scheer's trap as a means of drawing the German fleet in turn on to the British Grand Fleet, which accordingly put to sea on the night of 30 May.

The plan worked. Admiral Beatty's battle-cruisers engaged Hipper's force on the afternoon of 31 May and allowed themselves to become involved with Scheer's High Seas Fleet as Jellicoe's fleet was approaching from the north-west. There was, however, to be no new Trafalgar. 'Chatfield, there seems to be something wrong with our bloody ships today,' Beatty remarked to his flag captain, observing two of his battle-cruisers knocked out and his own on fire. Jellicoe knew what was wrong. The German gunnery was highly accurate and the armour protection of the British ships inadequate, and the further dangers of mine, torpedo and U-boat convinced him that he dared not risk an all-out action. Scheer, too, was worried that he might be cut off from return to the German coast. Thus both admirals were content to fight a couple of tentative actions, after which the German High Seas Fleet was able to make good its escape homewards. The British had suffered heavy losses, but their fleet still stood guard over the North Sea and although the Germans claimed a famous victory, they certainly did not act on that assumption and after Jutland turned instead to a greater concentration on the U-boat campaign.

Jutland and the Somme had proved indecisive and the murderous deadlock had by now encouraged talk of a negotiated peace in some quarters. At the end of the year approaches were made to both sides by President Wilson, who had been re-elected in November 1916 on a promise to keep the United States neutral—a policy he knew would be impossible, if the war continued much longer. In England a left-wing organization, the Union of Democratic Control, which included Ramsay MacDonald and E. D. Morel, favoured negotiation and had support from the ILP. Even in the cabinet Lord Lansdowne circulated a paper advocating peace on the basis of a general return to the situation before the war. These efforts, however, were isolated and ineffectual. They never influenced the policy of the Allied governments, and they were certainly unacceptable to the Germans who, by December 1916, had just overrun the most part of Romania three months after the Allies' promise of Transylvania had tempted her to make an ill-advised entry into the war.

The British as a whole were determined to fight on to final victory. The only doubt centred on Asquith's continued leadership, and although he had never countenanced negotiation, the rumours about peace talks weakened his position still further. By the autumn there was growing support for Lloyd George, now Secretary of State for War, whom Carson and, later, Bonar Law encouraged by Sir Max Aitken, were prepared to back.. The final crisis came on 1 December when Lloyd George proposed to Asquith that the supreme direction of the war should be placed in the hands of a War Council of three, of which he, Lloyd George, would be chairman. Asquith, well aware that this would leave him Prime Minister only in name, hastily sounded the opinion of Conservative and Liberal ministers and eventually rejected the proposal. On this Lloyd George resigned. Asquith retaliated by also resigning, but he had over-estimated the strength of his position. King George consulted Bonar Law and on his advice sent for Lloyd George who at the age of fifty-three became Prime Minister on 7 December 1916 at the darkest hour of the war.[4]

12

Coalition Under Lloyd George: December 1916–November 1918

On the military front the war administration of Lloyd George is a long story of disaster only turning at the end to rapid and decisive victory. 1917 was to be an appalling year for the Allies: two bloody and ineffective offensives on the western front, a mutiny in the French army, headlong retreat on the Italian front and the collapse of Russia into revolution and eventual peace with Germany. This was to be followed in March 1918 by a German offensive in the west which by the summer had come within an ace of success. Then suddenly at the beginning of August the German force was spent. The Allies, taking advantage of the new mobility on the western front, counterattacked and were able to maintain their advance, until by November 1918 the German government had been compelled to accept an armistice.

It might be thought that the heroic endurance and terrible bloodshed exacted from the soldiers would have been matched at home with a loyal unity of effort behind the inspiring war leadership of the new Prime Minister. In fact, Lloyd George was involved throughout almost the whole period in a fierce struggle of wills. He was at odds with Haig and Robertson, whose stolid monosyllabic utterances created a temperamental impasse for the agile mind of the Prime Minister. 'Haig', he wrote afterwards, 'was devoid of the gift of intelligible and coherent expression.' He mistrusted their ability, refusing to 'bow the knee to this military Moloch'. He hated the western front, epitomized for him by the ghastly losses in the battle of the Somme. He strove constantly to find the means of holding Haig in check, schemed for some unified system of command to which the British Commander-in-Chief would be subordinated, and by the beginning of 1918 was even thought to be keeping troops back in England for fear that Haig would otherwise throw them away in one more useless offensive. Thus Haig, imperturbable and dedicated, wrestled with his own problems, knowing all the time that the Prime Minister longed to be rid of him and was restrained only by the fact that there was no one suitable to replace him.

The bitterness of the struggle was heightened by the Prime Minister's own sense of insecurity. Intrigue had brought him to power; it might also remove him. The Liberals had split, roughly half the party following Asquith into Opposition, and Lloyd George had now to rely entirely on his old enemies, the Conservatives, in the Coalition. It was perhaps natural that he should constantly be sensing a possible conspiracy against him in the circles of what in later years came to be called 'the establishment'. The erstwhile radical Chancellor of the Exchequer felt himself under attack from the lobbying of Conservative clubland and the enmity of the military hierarchy, strongly supported by the Northcliffe press; he trusted no one and as a consequence was hardly trusted by anyone himself.

His first act was to revise the structure of the central direction of the war. There was to be no more doubt over the relationship of the cabinet and the successive types of War Council that Asquith had used. Lloyd George resolved this problem immediately by getting rid of the cabinet itself in its peacetime form. In future there was to be a small war cabinet of five: himself, Curzon as Lord President of the Council, Bonar Law as Chancellor of the Exchequer and Arthur Henderson and Lord Milner each without any specific office. Other ministers might sometimes be summoned to give their advice, but in the main their task was to get on with running their departments, while the war cabinet as the supreme national executive got on with running the war.

He established a cabinet secretariat under Sir Maurice Hankey, so that minutes should now be taken at cabinet meetings—a remarkable innovation in British constitutional practice. He also built up his own private staff, who worked in huts at the back of No. 10 Downing Street, known as the 'garden suburb' and strongly suspected of being the Prime Minister's means of short-circuiting routine departmental channels. He cut through the inhibitions over state interference and set up six new ministries: shipping, labour, food, national service, food production and information. He even hoped to achieve a greater concentration of effort by creating an imperial war cabinet including the prime ministers of the Dominions, and although this did not come to much, he was able to persuade Jan Christian Smuts, the South African Minister of Defence, to accept a seat in the British war cabinet.

His relations with the services were tempestuous from the start. The first major issue was occasioned by the menace of the German U-boats. As early as the beginning of 1915 the Germans had opened an intensive submarine campaign, sinking merchant ships on sight, as Fisher had predicted before the war. In May 1915 many American passengers lost their lives when the British liner *Lusitania* was sunk, and in August the subsequent fear of American reactions had caused the Germans to modify their policy of sinking without warning. After the battle of Jutland, however, it was clear that their main hope at sea lay in submarine warfare and the figures for Allied losses rose from 109,000 tons in June 1916 to 368,000 tons at the beginning of 1917. This success encouraged the German admirals to reiterate their appeals for a return to unrestricted submarine activity, and in January 1917 William II and the German chancellor, Bethmann Hollweg, gloomily aware that this would probably bring the United States into the war against them, gave their assent. Both sides in this controversy at Berlin were proved right. Total losses of Allied and neutral shipping rose immediately to 540,000 tons in February alone, followed by 593,000 tons in March; and in April 1917 the United States finally declared war on Germany.

This sharp increase in sinkings provoked a similar encounter between admirals and politicians in London, but here it was not the Prime Minister who surrendered. Carson, First Lord of the Admiralty, accepted the view of Jellicoe, now First Sea Lord, and of other senior admirals that the only hope lay in intensifying the naval attack on the U-boats. Lloyd George, impatient for some more positive solution, pressed for the institution of a system whereby all merchant ships would sail in convoy, protected by a naval escort armed with anti-submarine devices. The admirals resisted. They wildly overestimated the number of ships that would be involved, mistrusted the seamanship of captains in the merchant navy and objected that convoys would be too slow and would present an easy target. Lloyd George was not to be stopped. Characteristically he went behind the admirals to sound opinion among more junior officers, found them favourably disposed and on 30 April, after gaining the backing of the war cabinet, went in person to the Admiralty to push through the adoption of the convoy system. By September it was in full operation and showed its worth at once with a marked drop in the loss of merchant shipping and an increase in the number of submarines sunk.

The episode had convinced Lloyd George that all was not well at the Admiralty and he was now determined to get rid of both Carson and Jellicoe. The difficulty was that the removal of Carson, a leading Conservative, might be politically disruptive, and the manoeuvring by which the changes were eventually brought about is supremely illustrative of the caution with which Lloyd George had to proceed. He used all his guile. The war cabinet were persuaded and Haig, who was home on leave and had a poor opinion of Jellicoe, proved an unusual ally whose influence with the King was invaluable. In July Carson was cajoled into exchanging the Admiralty for a seat in the war cabinet and in December Sir Eric Geddes, who had replaced him, finally dismissed Jellicoe, on which Carson resigned from the government, ostensibly over the Irish question.

In this instance Haig's support had been won by his genuine doubts about the measures for dealing with U-boats. It did not point to any better relations with the Prime Minister, with whom he and Robertson had had a furious encounter earlier in the year. This had occurred when Lloyd George's objections to a new offensive on the western front were overcome by General Nivelle, who had now taken over from Joffre as the French Commander-in-Chief. Nivelle was an eloquent speaker, could converse in English and believed that he had the answer for 1917—an attack on the Aisne front in which a heavy artillery bombardment would be followed by a deep creeping barrage. Lloyd George's heart was warmed by the fluency and charm of Nivelle; the particular attraction, however, was that this offensive, which would be predominantly French, might provide an opportunity for establishing a unified command which would keep Haig in check by placing him under the orders of the French Commander-in-Chief.

Accordingly, on his own initiative Lloyd George suggested this arrangement to the French. He did give a vague intimation of such a development at a meeting of the war cabinet, but Robertson had been told that he need not attend and the first that the British military knew of it was at an Allied conference at Calais, where the French, prompted by Lloyd George, put forward the new proposal. Haig and Robertson were aghast and protested so furiously that Haig was eventually allowed a compromise whereby the French should only enjoy a general power of direction for the coming campaign, from which Haig could release himself if he felt that the safety of his army was threatened. The whole episode represented Lloyd George at his most devious. He seemed to be in conspiracy with the French against his own Commander-in-Chief, who returned the compliment by making full use of his line of communication with King George.

Against this background of mistrust and intrigue among the leaders the troops were once more launched into battle. The plan was for the British on the left of the French to distract the Germans with a preliminary attack. By the middle of April they had succeeded in capturing Vimy Ridge, but the main Nivelle offensive, beginning on 16 April, was thrown off balance by the Germans' voluntary withdrawal to the newly constructed Hindenburg line. After a fortnight of heavy casualties, when no breakthrough had been achieved, it was brought to an end, and Nivelle, a victim of his own confident promises, was replaced by General Pétain.

For the time being there were to be no further French offensives. The Nivelle venture proved to be the last straw for the French Army, which had suffered appalling losses in the past three years. In May there began a sporadic mutiny affecting units in some fifty-four divisions and throughout the summer Pétain laboured to restore discipline, a task which he accomplished with a mixture of firmness and concession. The need to prevent the Germans from taking advantage of the French disarray, however, gave Haig a strong argument in favour of mounting an offensive of his own—a long-cherished scheme for a breakthrough in Flanders. In London he had the support of the Admiralty, worried about the U-boat bases at Zeebrugge and Ostend, and although Lloyd George's temporary acceptance of 'westernism' had been rudely shocked by the failure of Nivelle, the war cabinet eventually agreed somewhat reluctantly to let Haig go ahead.

The outcome was the third battle of Ypres. It began encouragingly with the capture of the Messines Ridge in June. Then the main attack in July repeated the pattern of so many earlier engagements; the bombardment failed to destroy the German positions; the defence was in too great a depth, and when the weather broke in August and the shellfire wrecked the drainage system of this low-lying land, the soldiers found themselves fighting in a sea of liquid mud. By the beginning of October even the generals were advocating breaking off the attack, but Haig would not give up. It was claimed in his defence long afterwards that the plight of the French Army forced him to go on; in fact, the mutiny by now had been quelled and the real reason for continuing was tactical, the need to establish a final line on the Passchendaele ridge rather than on the exposed slope in front of it. Thus the struggle in the mud and rain went on for another month, until the Canadians took the unrecognizable ruins of Passchendaele on 6 November. Four months of fighting; an advance of four miles; 240,000 casualties—the worst fears of Lloyd George seemed to have been confirmed.

At least on the western front the British had gone forward and the French had re-established their armies sufficiently to hold the line. In Italy, however, there was disaster when at the end of October the Germans broke through at Caporetto and the Italians were driven back in rout some seventy miles as far as the river Piave, where they were reinforced by British and French divisions.

Only in the east could the British find any consolation. Throughout 1917 a new expeditionary force in Mesopotamia had advanced up the

Tigris and by November had reached a point a hundred miles to the north of Baghdad. At the same time an Arab revolt against the Turks, fostered and coordinated by a young peacetime archaeologist, T. E. Lawrence (see p. 162), had gathered momentum and in July the port of Akaba (map, p. 203) was captured by the tribesmen. The principal army in this area, under the command of General Allenby, advanced into Palestine, defeated a combined German and Turkish force at Beersheba and early in December 1917 occupied Jerusalem. Here at least was success, but it was a long way from the crucial scene of operations and was in some ways a liability in that it created a mistrust among the French, who not unnaturally suspected that the British had designs on the Middle East.

There was by now a new factor with which the governments had to cope: a war-weariness bred of the inescapable sense of deadlock in which the whole of Europe was bleeding to death. It had played havoc with the French Army in the summer. It had given some impetus to the first stage of the Russian revolution that ended the Tsarist monarchy in March, and after the new Russian government had attempted one more ill-fated offensive in the summer of 1917, it gave growing strength to the appeal of the Bolsheviks who seized power in November with the intention of taking Russia out of the war.

Although British opinion still stood comparatively firm, the Bolshevik claim that all the belligerents were engaged in a war of annexation and imperialism did strengthen the criticism already expressed by left-wing groups such as the ILP and the UDC (see p. 120). An unofficial gathering at Leeds in June 1917 demanded peace negotiations as well as the establishing of workers' and soldiers' councils. The Labour party would not accept the idea of government by Soviets, but they were attracted by the idea of an international Socialist conference which was to meet at Stockholm to discuss appropriate peace terms. Arthur Henderson strongly supported this, to the annoyance of his cabinet colleagues, and when on 10 August the Labour party conference, swayed by his fervent advocacy, voted in favour of sending delegates, his position in the government became so difficult that he resigned from the war cabinet, though remaining leader of the parliamentary Labour party.

This sense of uncertainty about the purpose of the war came mainly from the left, but there was too a voice from the right when Lord Lansdowne revived the proposals for a negotiated peace which he had put forward twelve months before. This time he made them public; in November 1917 he published in the *Daily Telegraph* a letter suggesting that Germany might keep her eastern gains, if she would renounce those in the west as well as her navy and her colonies. Almost immediately afterwards all these doubts on the right and the left were suddenly strengthened, when the Bolsheviks published the secret treaties of the Allies, and the charge that the war was being fought for annexations seemed no longer to be an empty one.

It was clear to the government, faced with this crisis of conscience, that there was a need for a statement of war aims of unimpeachable highmindedness. President Wilson had already broached the subject in his message to Congress at the beginning of December, and at the end of the month a Labour conference produced a statement demanding an end to secret diplomacy and stressing the need for eventual reconciliation with Germany. Lloyd George was not to be outdone. On 5 January 1918 at a conference of trade-union leaders he renounced all schemes of annexation and put forward the main lines of a future settlement: the return of Alsace and Lorraine to France, the independence of Belgium, the creation of a Polish state and autonomy for the nationalities of the Habsburg empire. Three days later President Wilson announced his Fourteen Points, a fuller development of similar themes, which were to be the basis of any negotiation with Germany.

All these statements did something to set minds at rest at home; they did not bring the end of the war any nearer, since the German and Austrian governments considered that their military position was too strong to warrant their taking them very seriously. And in March 1918 the vast territorial losses imposed on Russia by the Germans with the treaty of Brest-Litovsk convinced the west that the defeat of Germany remained the only feasible goal.

In the course of all this Lloyd George had returned to his scheme for a unified command. In November 1917 he had managed to establish a supreme war council at Versailles composed of military representatives from Great Britain, France, Italy and the United States. The general conception was sound enough, but Haig and Robertson guessed rightly that the plan was simply a means of setting up a rival authority to their own, and their hostility, supported by that aura of influence in high places with which the military invested themselves, led to this new council having no more than advisory powers.

The final clash came in February 1918, when Lloyd George returned to the attack by taking up a proposal for the creation of a general Allied reserve under the control of an executive committee headed by the French general, Foch, at Versailles. This was a direct challenge to Haig and Robertson, since such a reserve would give the Versailles council a hold over all strategy on the western front. Robertson was adamant, but this time Lloyd George called the military bluff. He threatened resignation himself and it was Robertson who had to go, being replaced as CIGS by the voluble and politically minded Sir Henry Wilson, a man much more to Lloyd George's liking. Haig was prepared to submit, but the victory was largely theoretical, since neither he nor Pétain was prepared to contribute any troops for the creation of the new reserve, and at Versailles Foch remained a general without an army.

Behind all this manoeuvring two thoughts predominated in Lloyd George's mind: how to hold Haig back from any further costly offensives; and at the same time how to bring the deadlock in France to an end. Within a few weeks the Germans had supplied the answer to both these questions. For them this was the last moment for a decisive blow against the Allies in the west, before the build-up of American forces in Europe and the growing effects of the blockade put victory out of reach; on 21 March 1918 Ludendorff launched his great offensive.

The first attack fell on Gough's 5th Army near St Quentin. The British line was more lightly held here and the Germans were aided by fog. The principal factor, however, was their own tactics, refusing to be held up by British strongpoints, but moving round them and thus never losing the momentum of their advance. Within a few days Gough's shattered army had been pushed back miles towards Amiens. A fatal gap had been created between his forces and the French on his right and on 24 March Haig learnt to his horror that Pétain, always a pessimist, was already considering falling back on Paris and assumed that the British would be making for the Channel ports.

This was to be Haig's most impressive moment of decision. There was only one answer to Pétain's defeatism. They must both place themselves under a supreme Allied commander who would be prepared to fight. He telegraphed London and on 26 March, at a conference at Doullens attended by representatives of the British and French governments, Haig made his offer. 'If General Foch will consent to give me his advice, I will gladly follow it.' Thus ironically the subordination of the British Commander-in-Chief to a French Supreme Commander, for which Lloyd George had struggled so long, came about at the request of that Commander-in-Chief himself. Lloyd George had wanted it for fear of Haig's desire to attack; and now Haig invited it for fear of Pétain's desire to retreat.

The next four months were to see desperate conflict as Ludendorff lunged out in one direction after another. On 28 March a new German attack to the north of the original penetration was checked and a little later this first offensive was closed down, since the German troops had advanced too far ahead of their artillery and transport. In April a new storm burst upon the British forces on the Flanders front, Operation Georgette, which thrust towards Hazebrouch to the south-west of Ypres and wrung from Haig his famous order of the day: 'With our backs to the wall and believing in the justice of our cause each one must fight on to the end.' Foch shifted his reserves north and by the end of the month the possible breakthrough to the Channel ports had been checked.

Ludendorff still regarded Flanders as the battleground where the final success must come, but with the growing concentration of Allied reserves in that area it was vital to stage a diversionary offensive which would draw them back again to the south. Accordingly at the end of May a new attack thrust down towards the Aisne and was so successful that by 3 June the Germans were on the Marne. Such an advance was too tempting. Torn between the needs of his future offensive in Flanders and the desire to exploit this recent victory which had brought the Germans once again close to Paris, Ludendorff hung on too long in this sector and on 15 July launched a further attack aimed at encircling Rheims.

As it turned out, this was to be the last spurt of the German advance. The attack was held and three days later a French counter-offensive broke through the long dangerously exposed side of the German salient. The news reached Ludendorff just as he was making his preparations for the conclusive thrust in Flanders, which as a consequence had to be postponed. In fact, it was never to take place. On 8 August Haig, who had been preparing for his own attack from the region of Amiens since May, struck first and with his advance of four miles with tanks and infantry the retreat of the German Army had begun.

These months of tension, as the Germans had seemed about to smash their way through to victory, were also a time of severe political danger for Lloyd George. As soon as Ludendorff's offensives had been launched, he had immediately rushed all available forces across the Channel, but the justifiable suspicion that before this he had been withholding troops from Haig now laid the Prime Minister open to attack. As the Allied soldiers fought on with their backs to the wall, Lloyd George's foes began to mass; the military fumed at the recent removal of Robertson; in the House of Commons the Asquith Liberals awaited their chance and at the beginning of May it seemed that it had come.

A month before, in reply to the charges that he had denuded Haig of necessary troops, Lloyd George had stated in the Commons that 'the army in France was considerably stronger on 1 January 1918 than on 1

January 1917'. There was consequently a sensation when on 7 May General Sir Frederick Maurice, until recently Director of Military Operations at the War Office, wrote a letter to *The Times* positively accusing the Prime Minister of lying. Bonar Law proposed a judicial enquiry, but Asquith demanded a Select Committee of the House of Commons. It was a rash step, for in the subsequent debate in the House Lloyd George was able to play his trump card. The figures on which he had based his statement had come from Maurice's own department at the War Office. In fact, those original figures had been erroneous and a corrected version had later been sent to the Prime Minister, but whether he had ever seen this has remained a matter of some doubt. At the time Lloyd George certainly made no mention of it. His answer to the House seemed incontrovertible and not surprisingly the Opposition lost the motion by 293 votes to 106.

With Haig's successful counterattack the growling of the critics died away. Ludendorff himself had no doubts that after 8 August a German victory was impossible. His main hope now was to stave off military defeat, but Haig, who at last could do justice to his ability as a general, was determined to avoid a new deadlock. He and Foch scented victory for that autumn, unlike the government in London, who did not believe that it could come before 1919 and still cautioned Haig not to embark on any too costly offensive. A succession of blows from the British, French and American armies hammered on the salients created by the original German advance; Ludendorff fell back on the old Hindenburg line, but by the end of September the Allied armies had broken through. At the same time there came the news that the Bulgarians, defeated by the Salonika force, were suing for terms, and on 29 September Ludendorff declared at a council of war at Spa that Germany must ask for an armistice.

Throughout October desperate political manoeuvring ensued. The Germans seized on the Fourteen Points and communicated direct with President Wilson—an approach much mistrusted by Lloyd George and Clemenceau, French premièr since the previous November. These two conferring in Paris knew that the German Army was still intact, and were determined that the conditions of the armistice should ensure that Germany would not be capable of any further military resistance, whatever the final terms of the peace might be. In conjunction with Foch it was agreed that France, Belgium, Alsace, Lorraine and Luxemburg must be evacuated immediately, that the Allies should occupy the Rhineland as well as bridgeheads on the east bank of the Rhine and that the German Navy should be interned. 'It is unconditional surrender,' commented the German war minister, but the generals could offer no alternative. At five o'clock in the morning on 11 November in a railway carriage at Rethondes in the forest of Compiègne the German delegation signed the armistice and at eleven o'clock that morning the sound of gunfire on the western front finally died away.

13

The Impact of War

1. The psychological shock

The impact of the Great War cannot be measured simply in terms of casualty lists or statistics of destruction. The young men who in the first romantic flush of excitement had flocked to the recruiting offices had been possessed with an impatience to get to the front before the war was over. They had their wish, and in the long years of trench warfare they were to endure a nightmare that was beyond the conception of those who had grown up in the peace of the nineteenth century.

The scene where all these illusions died was that comparatively narrow strip of territory running from the Channel to the Swiss frontier along which the armies of the Allies and Germany faced each other across a hundred yards of no-man's-land. The front line trench, protected by a barbed-wire entanglement some twenty yards out, was dug in a zigzag of bays and traverses to a depth of about six feet with a fire step for sentries. This was connected by communication trenches with the support line some 200 yards back, where troops off duty could rest in dug-outs which were like caves burrowed out of the earth of the trench walls; and beyond this, further communication trenches led back out of sight of the enemy.

When the line was quiet the infantry lived amid the cramped and filthy confines of the narrow trenches under periodic bombardment of shells and mortars, the occasional sweeping fire of a machine-gun or the single aimed shot of a sniper. When the communication trenches were too shallow, smashed or waterlogged, movement was only possible at night; it was then that rations and supplies were brought up by troops temporarily in reserve and the wounded could be sent back on the perilous pain-racked journey to the field dressing station; small wiring parties would go out to repair or strengthen their own barbed-wire entanglement; others would creep out close to the enemy line in search of information; or sometimes, after a hole in the enemy wire had been made by artillery fire, a fighting patrol would launch a small attack on a part of the line opposite, flinging hand grenades down into enemy trenches or dug-outs in the murderous confusion of the darkness.

These were merely the routine circumstances, the times which the official communiqués described as 'all quiet on the western front'. The major offensives usually began at dawn—a movement of thousands of men across no-man's-land in the face of the machine-guns that the preceding artillery bombardment never seemed to have silenced. Throughout this hell men struggled only to contain their fear and fatigue. For a shilling (5p) a day they soldiered on amid the rats and lice and the shattered corpses of their friends, knowing that desertion could only mean the firing squad.

The extraordinary thing is that the morale of the British Army never broke, that even after the Somme, Passchendaele and the German offensive of March 1918 they could go forward again to win the remarkable series of victories in the last months of the war. It is less surprising that many should wish to express their bitterness at being engulfed in a demonic world known only to them. For Wilfred Owen, who served for nearly two years in the trenches before being killed a week before the armistice, it was the pity of war that overwhelmed him. 'Hideous landscapes, vile noises, foul language ... everything unnatural, broken, blasted; the distortion of the dead, whose unburiable bodies sit outside the dug-outs all day, all night, the most execrable sights on earth. In poetry we call them the most glorious.'[1] For Siegfried Sassoon, who served with great gallantry on the western front before returning home to denounce the wickedness of war, there was a sharper sense of anger at the incompetence of staff officers who lived remote from the men whom they condemned to suicidal attacks:

> *If I were fierce and bald and short of breath*
> *I'd live with scarlet majors at the Base*
> *And speed glum heroes up the line to death.*[2]

Owen, too, could turn to anger at the thought of the civilians at home waiting for victory:

> *You shall not hear their mirth:*
> *You shall not come to think them well content*
> *By any jest of mine. These men are worth*
> *Your tears. You are not worth their merriment.*[3]

This last was not entirely fair. The patriotic belligerence of those at home was not likely to be damped by a censored press that gave little impression of life in the trenches. In any case, as the months wore on, the glory of war died in the hearts of many civilians, chastened by the arrival of the hospital trains and the endless casualty lists, and the new mood was captured in a novel by H. G. Wells, *Mr Britling Sees It Through*, published in 1916. This was essentially a record of civilian experience, but those who worked in the hospitals saw something of the true price of war, as Enid Bagnold described in her *Diary Without Dates* in 1918.

The personal accounts of the survivors of the western front could not come until the years after the war, but then they came in full flood. Most of the writers had served as officers and for them, at least, there had been some relief from the harshness of military discipline when out of the line, but the fundamental experience of war had been the same for all ranks. Sad, bitter or simply reminiscent, they were the work of men haunted by the fear that they had known and the carnage that they had seen. Some chose a fictional form such as A. P. Herbert's *The Secret Battle* (1919), Frederic Manning's *Her Privates We* (1930), or R. C. Sherriff's play *Journey's End* (1929). Others turned to autobiography, for example Robert Graves's *Goodbye to All That* (1929) and Edmund Blunden's *Undertones of War* (1929).

These are some of the better-known writers, but there were many others, all perhaps searching for some therapy through literary expression for the trauma that they had suffered. As one of them wrote, they were 'united by a secret bond and separated by a mental barrier from their fellows who were too old or too young to fight in the Great War'. They could never forget. They sought to dispel an illusion and they did not write in vain. The memory of the western front was to create a great divide in time for the British and was eventually to play its own part in shaping the policies of the 1930s.

2. The machinery of war

The civilian population only slowly became aware of the real nature of the western front. Equally, it was a little time before the full extent of the requirements of modern war was grasped. At first the government hoped to use its powers merely to steer the existing institutions of free enterprise in the direction of a concerted effort. About 20 per cent of civilian shipping was requisitioned and railways came at once under state control, although their management remained unchanged. A special commission took charge of the supply of sugar, but apart from this and the direct purchase of meat from abroad by the War Office, the supply and price of food was left largely to the free play of the market, and as late as October 1916 Walter Runciman announced in the House of Commons: 'We want to avoid any rationing of our people in food.' Even over the vital question of munitions the government was loath to interfere, until the shell scandal in the early months of 1915 left them no option.

The Ministry of Munitions, set up under Lloyd George in May 1915, gave the country its first glimpse of the comprehensive planning that twentieth-century warfare demanded, and from December 1916, when he assumed the premiership, the process was constantly to accelerate. A new ministry took charge of all shipping. Lord Devonport was appointed food controller, later to be succeeded by Lord Rhondda, and the county agricultural committees, established at the beginning of the war, were stimulated into bringing a further three million acres under the plough by 1918, with the aid of the Women's Land Army. By February 1917 government control had already been established over all coal-mines, and a year later an Act of Parliament deducted 80 per cent of the excess profits of the mining companies in tax. By November 1917 the price of all principal foodstuffs had been fixed; in the spring of 1918 a general food rationing system was extended throughout the whole country, and the government was by now responsible for the purchase of 90 per cent of imports and the marketing of 80 per cent of food consumed at home. Thus, however slow the start may have been, the last years of the war were to witness a revolutionary extension of state management in the control of productive capacity, the purchase of raw materials and the restriction of capital expenditure.

The greatest testimony to this new era of collective organization and mass production was that, despite the absence of nearly six million men mobilized in the armed forces, British industry maintained its peacetime level of output and in certain spheres greatly increased it. The country's steel-making capacity rose by a half, the numbers employed in the iron and steel industry by a third; and the need to import foreign ore was greatly reduced by the widespread development of open-hearth furnaces which made it possible to use the ore of the east Midlands. After the first year of the war government control over enlistment reduced the serious drainage of the skilled work force in the mines and the engineering trades; coal production, which had at first dropped sharply, was to some extent restored, reaching 228 million tons by 1918, although this figure was still 60 million below that for 1913; and in engineering there was marked expansion, particularly in the machine-tool industry.

Under government sponsorship there came, too, a somewhat belated recognition of the significance of scientific research for British industry.

The needs of war naturally stimulated rapid developments in aviation and wireless, but serious deficiencies in many other types of technological products led to the establishment of a committee of the Privy Council 'for the promotion of scientific and industrial research', and by 1917 this had grown into a fully fledged department with its own minister and a budget of a million pounds. This, together with the work of the medical research committee, might at least suggest a change of method; how far it reflected a change of heart at the military level was a matter of doubt in the mind of H. G. Wells, as he suggested in his *Experiment in Autobiography*:

> We and our like with our bits of stick and iron pipe and wire, our test tubes and our tanks and our incalculable possibilities, came to these fine but entirely inconclusive warriors humbly demanding permission to give them victory—but victory at the price of all that they were used to, of all they held dear. It must have been obvious to them, for instance, that we hated saluting; we were the sort that might talk shop in the mess; we had no essential rigidities, no style; our loyalties were incomprehensible; our effect on 'the men', if men had to be instructed, might be deplorable.[4]

The most startling aspect of the war effort was its cost. In the financial year 1913–14 government expenditure had amounted to £197·5 million; by 1918–19 this had risen to about £2,500 million—more than twelve times as much. To help meet this, income tax rose in the course of the war from 1 shilling and 2 pence (6p) in the pound to 6 shillings (30p) and with eventual increases in wages and the lowering of the exemption limit more than three times as many incomes had become liable to the tax by 1919. Supertax was also increased and an excess profits duty levied on firms, so that, in all, the £94 million yield from direct taxes in 1913–14 had grown to £508 million in 1917–18. Indirect taxes rose less, but in 1915 Reginald McKenna, the Chancellor of the Exchequer, introduced import duties on motor-cars, cycles, watches and clocks. The exigencies of wartime had thus created the first breach in the nineteenth-century doctrine of free trade, although the immediate motive was to cut down unnecessary imports rather than to establish a system of protection. None of this, however, was adequate to meet the full expenditure and the government fell back on loans through war bonds and other issues at an average rate of interest of 4·6 per cent. By 1919 the national debt had risen from £650 million to £7,500 million, mostly the total deficit on the war budgets.

These financial arrangements, which would have struck an Edwardian as utterly appalling, were largely internal. Abroad, Great Britain's international position did not appear to have changed significantly for the worse. The value of her exports dropped only slightly and although that of her imports was doubled during the war, this was largely offset by a sharp rise in her earnings from shipping and insurance services; the balance of payments remained favourable. The financing of the war did, however, involve the sale of about £300 million of her foreign assets. To meet the rest of the cost she borrowed £1,365 million, principally from the USA and Canada, but her own loans to her European allies and to the Empire exceeded this by some £350 million—a reasonably comfortable situation, although war debts were eventually to prove a somewhat unreliable investment (see p. 210).

The more immediate concern of the government was to ensure that the detailed consequences of these changes should not have a damaging effect on labour relations which had been so disturbed before the outbreak of war. There were two questions that needed careful attention: the effect of inflation on wages, and the inroads that government control might make on the position of the trade unions.

Inflation may have been slightly encouraged by the government's issue of £1 and 10 shilling (50p) notes in place of sovereigns and half sovereigns at the beginning of the war, but the real cause was the scarcity of civilian goods, which in the absence of any serious price control before 1917 opened the door to profiteering. By that time the cost of living had almost doubled and wage levels had lagged significantly behind, since the trade-union leaders did not wish to put pressure on the government with strike action, and the scarcity of labour, which might otherwise have put wages up, was largely overcome by an influx of women to the factories, where they were paid at a much lower rate.

The other problem was the question of 'dilution'. It has already been seen (p. 36) that in the years before the war employers in many industries had hoped to increase output at lower cost by a rationalization of the production lines and the introduction of new machines which could be tended by semi-skilled or unskilled labour. The skilled workers had naturally regarded this as a serious threat to their own position, but the needs of war now made such a development inevitable. The supply of skilled labour simply was not adequate to cope with the enormous expansion of certain industries and the government, previously an arbitrator in the peacetime disputes over this issue, now became the principal organizer of 'dilution'.

Considering the potential explosiveness of these questions, the war years were remarkably free of industrial unrest. In February 1915 an engineering strike on Clydeside and, later that summer, a strike in the South Wales mines were both resolved by agreements over pay; in May 1917 the fear of 'dilution' led to the biggest engineering strike of the war, involving over 100,000 workers in the North and the Midlands. All these stoppages were mainly due to the efforts of the shop stewards who were now acquiring a new power of local leadership, since it appeared to many of their followers that the central organizations of the trade unions had been taken into wartime partnership with the government.

In the main, however, this partnership triumphed. Negotiations at a national level persuaded most of the unions to acquiesce over many innovations in the interest of promoting the war effort, on the understanding that these concessions were purely temporary and that the government would do its best to meet outstanding grievances. Thus the Treasury agreement of March 1915 was succeeded that summer by the Munitions of War Act which prohibited strikes and lock-outs in the relevant industries, enforced compulsory arbitration in all disputes and made provision for 'dilution' with the admission of unskilled men and women into the work shops. Subsequent Acts extended these terms to more and more branches of industry and with the introduction of conscription the government assumed a comprehensive control over the entire manpower of the country, including the revision of wage scales on a uniform national basis.

By and large, the promise that these were all emergency wartime measures was kept. Indeed, the postwar government was as anxious to denationalize the industries and services that it controlled as the trade unions were to regain their old powers of independent negotiation. Some changes, however, were lasting. Wages for unskilled labour were to remain much closer to those of the skilled worker. The employment of women in industrial, commercial and clerical occupations was to continue, although their work was usually of lower status and with lower pay. The Summer Time Act, whereby the British put their clocks forward one hour to gain an extra hour of daylight in the summer evenings, became a permanent institution, and even the public houses, whose opening times had been strictly curtailed to avoid distraction from war work, did not revert to their earlier freedom. But these few relics of the experience of wartime were small compared with the impact of the precedent that it had established, and the thought of what could be achieved by a degree of state control inconceivable before 1914 was to linger on, preserving a memory as telling as the horror of the western front.

III

The Immediate Problems of Peace 1918–1922

14

Party Prospects and the General Election of 1918

At eleven o'clock on the morning of 11 November 1918 in the streets and squares of London, excited crowds gave vent to a frenzy of exultation. 'There prevailed everywhere', wrote an eye witness, 'an irresistible impulse to let business go hang, to get into the streets and yell and sing and dance and weep—above all, to make oneself supremely ridiculous.'[1] Along the line of the western front the emotion was too overwhelming for rejoicing, only a numbed incredulous relief; but although the expression of it varied, the same unbalancing thought gripped soldier and civilian alike. The most terrible of wars had at last come to an end.

That night Winston Churchill, already a connoisseur of the historic moment, dined with Lloyd George at No. 10 Downing Street 'in the large room from whose walls the portraits of Pitt and Fox, of Nelson and Wellington and—perhaps somewhat incongruously—of Washington then looked down'.[2] It was a time for many new decisions. For Lloyd George the coming of peace clearly emphasized the isolation of his position, created by his seizure of power in the middle of the war. He was a man without a party. His main hope, therefore, was to continue at the head of the Coalition government after an immediate general election while public confidence in his leadership was at its height. There was certainly a good case for the dissolution of Parliament. The state of emergency had meant that the existing House of Commons had remained unchanged for eight years. Earlier in 1918 the Representation of the People Act (see p. 145) had greatly extended the franchise and ought to take effect as soon as possible; most compelling of all, it could be argued that government spokesmen at any peace negotiations must be invested with the authority of a recent electoral decision.

Lloyd George's first obstacle was the opposition of George V, who considered it unwise to hold an election at a time of social and economic dislocation. The King argued, too, that many servicemen would be deprived of a chance to vote in an election held so early, owing to faults in the preparation of the new registers. Lloyd George had already dismissed Hayes Fisher, the minister responsible (later to be consoled with a peerage and a directorship in the Suez Canal company), but he had no intention of being deflected by this difficulty and the monarch's constitutional advice had to give way to the will of his Prime Minister.

It was hardly possible to adopt the same attitude towards Bonar Law. It could well be that the Conservatives would reject the idea of campaigning as a Coalition government under the continued leadership of Lloyd George. Indeed, many of them saw this as the moment to break free. The Liberals were in poor shape; Labour was still at an early stage of development, and a general election must surely bring a great Conservative victory. To Bonar Law's mind, however, the overriding consideration was Lloyd George's popularity throughout the country. 'Remember this,' he told a meeting of Conservative MPs on 12 November, 'that at this moment Mr Lloyd George commands an amount of influence in every constituency as great as has ever been exercised by any Prime Minister in our political history.'[3] This view may perhaps illustrate a tendency in the Conservative party to overestimate the electoral appeal of a great war leader immediately after the end of hostilities; in 1945 they suffered defeat when relying excessively on the magic of Winston Churchill's name, and in 1918 it is possible that they missed an opportunity through a similar assumption that Lloyd George would carry all before him.

Nevertheless, there were more subtle aspects of the question than that. With the resumption of normal political life new social forces, accelerated by the war, would be seeking expression, and while the full implications of this were still emerging, all parties were in a state of some uncertainty. It was hard to tell how they would eventually regroup themselves. In October Bonar Law had written to Balfour: 'our party on the old lines will never have any future in this country', and it might be safer to keep Lloyd George with them, while the party leaders tried to discover what the new lines were to be. Furthermore, the postwar years would probably be difficult and the label of a Coalition might be an effective shield against any opprobrium which would otherwise fall on a Conservative government.

This might be sound strategy, but it did not resolve the problem of tactics. A peacetime Coalition would have to cope with party conflicts that had been shelved during the war, and three issues in particular seemed sure to divide Liberals and Conservatives: tariffs, Ireland and the Welsh Church, which had been disestablished at the same time as the passing of the third Irish Home Rule Bill.* Here Lloyd George

* Also like the Irish Bill it was to be inoperative until after the war.

appeared at his most equivocal. He accepted the possibility of a policy of imperial preference, although he would not agree to a tax on food; over Ireland he promised that he would never employ force to coerce Ulster into accepting rule from Dublin, which could only mean that he did not envisage the implementing of the Home Rule Act (see p. 75) as it stood; and although he would compromise rather less over the Welsh Church, he was prepared to reconsider some of the financial clauses of the Act.

Once these arrangements had been made, Bonar Law announced to Conservative MPs on 12 November that the party would fight the forthcoming election in support of the Coalition alongside the Lloyd George Liberals, and on the dissolution of Parliament it was agreed that the official Coalition candidates should be identified by a joint letter from Bonar Law and Lloyd George. This was no more than a means of giving guidance to the electors who might otherwise clash at a constituency level, but it was hotly abused by Asquith who referred to the letter as 'the coupon', a reference to wartime rationing. It was also maintained that Bonar Law struck a hard bargain in putting up 364 Coalition Conservative candidates in comparison with Lloyd George's 159 Liberals, but Lloyd George actually had great difficulty in finding many more on whom he could rely; in any case there were also concessions on the Conservative side, since several prospective Conservative candidates had to withdraw to make way for a Coalition Liberal.

The decision to continue the Coalition after the war was to have momentous consequences. It meant that the breach in the Liberal party was to remain unclosed. Asquith's Liberals were to fight the election of 1918 in opposition to Lloyd George's government and this hardening of the divide was an essential element in the rise of Labour, when the Liberals were unable to provide a viable alternative to Conservative rule. Asquith and Lloyd George have each been blamed for the failure to reunite their party. At the time of the armistice Liberals, uneasily aware of the Prime Minister's negotiations with Bonar Law, sent two delegations to Lloyd George petitioning him to reach agreement with Asquith, and after consultation with Bonar Law Lloyd George responded by offering Asquith the position of Lord Chancellor and a place for some of his colleagues in the administration. Asquith refused, and his critics maintained that out of pique he had thrown away a chance of eventually reconciling the two wings of the party. In answer to this, Asquith's supporters claimed that Lloyd George's distribution of 'the coupon' had been based on the voting of Liberals in the Maurice debate (see p. 130) in May 1918 and had thus sacrificed any possible restoration of party unity for the sake of building up his own personal following.

The Liberal split, however, was not merely the result of individual rivalry. Those who had gone into Opposition in December 1916 had remained genuinely at variance with the Coalition government over a number of domestic issues: the McKenna duties, the extension of conscription to Ireland in April 1918, and some of the clauses in the Representation of the People Act. Asquith himself had not led the way in this; indeed, the Maurice debate was the only one in which he had given his official support, but the attitude of the rank and file among his section of the Liberals made it clear that the gulf was real, and these political considerations ruled out any attempt on his part to bring them back into the Coalition by accepting office. Equally, Lloyd George's distribution of 'the coupon' is not of prime importance; an examination of the figures has revealed that these do not tally precisely with the voting in the Maurice debate, but it would be surprising if that debate had not indicated the rough alignment of opinion among the Liberals. They had fallen back into that state of disunity to which they had been prone before 1906, and the distribution of 'the coupon' had done no more than reflect this.

Meanwhile, as the Liberals remained divided and the Conservatives clung to Lloyd George, the Labour party announced its intention of leaving the Coalition immediately. This was the outcome of a vote at a party conference in London on 14 November. The Labour MPs—the Parliamentary Labour Party—had actually been in favour of remaining with the government; they saw little prospect of success in campaigning against a Bonar Law–Lloyd George combination, and they believed that there should be some Labour representation at the peace conference. J. R. Clynes, who held office as food controller, fought hard to resist the motion, but the majority of the delegates had little faith in Lloyd George, and Bernard Shaw voiced this mistrust in the most significant political speech of his life: 'Mr Clynes has come from Mr Lloyd George and done the best he can. I ask you to send Mr Clynes back to him with the message: "nothing doing!" '⁴ Clynes himself was obedient to the will of the conference and resigned from the government. Four other wartime Labour ministers, including G. N. Barnes, who later attended the Paris peace negotiations, refused; they formed the leadership of a very small Coalition Labour group in the subsequent election, but eventually faded from sight—politicians who had backed the wrong horse.

This decision by the Labour party to resume independence followed on a series of developments over the previous eight years that had greatly heightened its potential. The Parliament Act of 1911 had already concentrated all legislative power on the House of Commons; the payment of MPs in the same year had removed a great financial obstacle to the growth of a large Labour representation there, and now in the last year of the war there had come two further measures which completed the transformation of the political arena.

The most obvious feature of the Representation of the People Act of 1918 was that it brought about a great increase in the size of the electorate from seven million to more than twenty million. This was largely the result of enfranchising women over the age of thirty, but it was also assisted by the establishment of a simple six months residential qualification for all males who had reached the age of twenty-one, in place of the more complicated stipulations of rate-paying and lodger tenancies. Men who had served in the war could vote at nineteen, although conscientious objectors, by a spiteful and undemocratic clause, were disenfranchised for five years. This extension of the franchise was not likely to shift the balance in the agricultural areas and richer urban districts held by the Conservatives, but it could well mean an opportunity for Labour in the larger industrial regions.

Most of the other rearrangements also tended to favour Labour. The Act sharply curtailed the extent of plural voting (see p. 12)—a blow for the more affluent. Henceforth, only the university seats and the occupation of business premises would allow the elector an extra vote, and all polling was to take place throughout the country on the same day. The amount of financial expenditure permitted for each electoral candidate by the Corrupt Practices Act of 1883 was reduced by more than half, and the administrative costs of the returning officer were to be paid out of the public funds. A redistribution of seats ended the old distinction between county and borough and divided the entire country into single-member constituencies of roughly similar population, thereby increasing the representation of industrial cities. Finally, to discourage the growth of small freak parties whose presence in the Commons would have an unstabilizing effect, all candidates for election were required to pay £150 deposit, which would be forfeited if the candidate failed to gain one-eighth of the votes cast in that constituency. This last ruling naturally operated in favour of the parties already in existence, which might otherwise have seen some of their strength drawn off into splinter movements at a time of political uncertainty. It might militate slightly against a party like Labour which still had its way to make, but far more against a party which became divided, and between 1918 and 1959 794

Liberal candidates forfeited their deposits in comparison with 151 Labour.

The other measure of marked significance for the future was the devising of the Labour party constitution which received official approval in January 1918. Until then the party had simply been a federation acting through a variety of affiliated societies, largely trade unions, together with others coordinated by the ILP and the Fabian Society. The purpose of the new constitution was to transform Labour into a political party on a national basis with local branches in every constituency. An overwhelming argument in favour of this step, as Arthur Henderson pointed out at the annual conference, was the prospect of an immensely increased electorate containing many sympathizers who, if they did not belong to a trade union or some Socialist society, would be unable in the existing situation to participate in the shaping of the postwar Labour movement.

This aim was set out in the second clause of the new constitution which stated that 'the Labour Party shall consist of all its affiliated organizations together with those men and women who are individual members of a local Labour party and who subscribe to the constitution and programme of the party'.[5] The annual party conference would thus include delegates elected by the trade unions, Socialist societies and local Labour parties, but of these every trade-union delegate would enjoy the advantage of having one vote for every thousand members of his union—the system of the card vote already introduced in the TUC in 1895 (see p. 36).

The function of the conference would be to debate matters of general policy and, more particularly, to elect the twenty-three members of the national executive, the central decision-making body of the party. The crux here was the distribution of places reserved on the executive for the various organizations that made up the Labour party. There were to be thirteen representatives of the affiliated organizations, but since none of these places were specifically earmarked for the Socialist societies or trades councils, it was possible for the card vote of the trade unions to exclude them entirely from the list of nominations. Indeed, the trade unions could with the unanimous vote of their thirteen representatives control the national executive, a price which Henderson had to pay in order to gain the inclusion of five representatives of the new local Labour parties who were to be nominated by their own organizations. The remaining five places were reserved for four women and the treasurer, all of whom could be nominated by any affiliated organization.

In some sections of the party the terms of this constitution had aroused misgivings which ultimately proved to be justified. The trades councils soon dwindled into political insignificance. The ILP, whose central body had clearly seen that the new constituency Labour parties 'will come into competition with the branches of the Independent Labour Party', did eventually lose its role as the chief propaganda and organizational agency at the local level. The trade unions, too, might find their position overshadowed by a massive national structure, although they would still be called upon to finance the bulk of the increased costs.

Most significant of all, the Parliamentary Labour Party (PLP) might find their independence of manoeuvre in the House of Commons hampered by the demands of a more broadly based executive. In the same way as the Conservative and Liberal parties had had to wrestle with their national associations in the 1880s (see p. 29), they fought hard to preserve their freedom of action and an amendment eventually established that at the time before an election the principal issues should be defined *jointly* by the PLP and the national executive. This, however, did not lay down any further procedure in the event of disagreement. Many assumed that a special meeting of the annual conference would be the final arbiter, as happened in November 1918, when Labour MPs were taken out of the Coalition against their wishes. On the other hand, there was one clause in the constitution that left the PLP a loophole by defining their function 'to give effect *as far as may be practicable* to the principles from time to time approved by the party conference'. With this delicate imprecision the tension between the parliamentary party and their extra-parliamentary organization was to remain a recurring and fascinating feature of Labour history in the twentieth century.

The constitution of 1918 was not only concerned with the creation of a political party on a national basis; it also included a specific statement of Socialist doctrine. Before this, it had been one of the remarkable aspects of the Labour movement that none of its official pronouncements had ever dared to do so for fear of frightening off the larger non-Socialist trade unions. It is the measure of the general tendency towards an acceptance of such ideas that the new constitution declared that the Labour party proposed 'to secure for the producers by hand and by brain the full fruits of their industry and the most equitable distribution thereof that may be possible upon the basis of the common ownership of the means of production and the best obtainable system of popular administration and control of each industry and service'.[6]

The full implications of this clause were to be debated at the first meeting of the annual conference under the new constitution in June 1918. Sidney Webb had already circulated copies of his *Labour and the New Social Order*, which set out a series of objectives for later Labour governments. He demanded the universal enforcement of a national minimum standard of living for all citizens, making the government responsible for a general wage level and for providing full employment, if necessary by organizing programmes of public works. He wanted a democratic control of industry by public ownership under the supervision of Parliament, thereby ruling out the notions of workers' control which were being advocated in various forms of Guild Socialism and Syndicalism. He envisaged a revolution in national finance which through heavier taxation of higher incomes would facilitate the creation of a system of social services and finance fuller provision for education and scientific research. It was the doctrine of the welfare state, implying social change consistent with the evolutionary outlook of the Fabian Society, but avoiding the remorseless philosophy of the class struggle which formed the basis of Marxism. At the conference the national executive put forward for discussion twenty-six policy resolutions closely based on Webb's statement, and all twenty-six were carried virtually without amendment—an extremely significant occasion, made more memorable by the appearance of Kerensky, the Russian ex-premier, who delivered a speech in Russian and implanted a formal kiss on the cheek of an embarrassed Arthur Henderson.

As it turned out, the election campaign of 1918 was a very undistinguished affair. All parties began by talking in terms of homes fit for heroes; all came to be drawn into promises of harsh treatment for Germany under pressure from the newspapers and public opinion. In the Coalition manifesto Lloyd George had carefully avoided any mention of reparations, but the whole country seethed with an unforgiving anger and no politician dared ignore the danger of being labelled pro-German. Within a week Lloyd George had been led on to state at Newcastle that 'Germany must pay the costs of the war up to the limit of her capacity to do so'. Some of his colleagues were more blatant. 'I am for hanging the Kaiser,' announced G. N. Barnes, the Labour Coalitionist, and on 9 December Sir Eric Geddes coined a famous phrase, when he declared at Cambridge that Germany should be squeezed 'until you can hear the pips squeak'. 'Mean brutal talk degrading to the electorate,' commented Beatrice Webb,[7] but it was what the electorate wanted, and the final Coalition election manifesto differed greatly from the first, demanding the trial of the Kaiser, the punishment of those responsible for atrocities and the imposition of reparations on the Central European Powers. The workings of democracy at the end of a bitter war were not a pretty sight.

The election was held on 14 December and resulted in an immense victory for the Coalition. They won 478 seats, composed of 335 Conservatives, 133 Lloyd George Liberals and ten Coalition Labour. The Asquith Liberals were utterly shattered, winning only twenty-eight seats, and Asquith himself was not returned. Labour improved their position with sixty-three seats, although there were many defeats for the leaders of the party who had been associated with the pacifist wing— Ramsay MacDonald, Philip Snowden and George Lansbury. The vast majority of Labour MPs in the new House were trade-union candidates, twenty-five of them from the Miners' Federation; and in the absence of Henderson, who had also lost his seat and did not get back to the Commons until August 1919 on a by-election, William Adamson, a Scottish miner, took over the leadership of the Parliamentary Labour Party. The Irish vote was almost entirely captured by Sinn Fein (see p. 182); they won seventy-three seats in Ireland, but since in accordance with their national aims they refused to attend at Westminster, their absence had the effect of increasing the relative strength of the Coalition.

Not too much could be deduced from the voting at this moment. The poll had been low—slightly more than 50 per cent of the electorate— and the emotional issues in the campaign irrelevant to the normal struggle of party politics. One earlier emotional issue, however, seems to have made remarkably little impact. Women were now entitled to stand for Parliament, but although sixteen did so, only one was successful. This was Countess Markiewicz (Constance Gore-Booth), a Sinn Feiner, who consequently did not take her seat; it was only later in 1919 that Lady Astor became the first woman to sit in the House of Commons.

Labour had done well, capturing one-fifth of the poll, however disdainfully Beatrice Webb might speak of their representation in the new Parliament, and they could probably have done still better, if more of the serving soldiers had been able to vote. This was to be an important element in the Labour victory of 1945 (see p. 384). The principal fact demonstrated by the election, however, was that the Coalition majority was a thinly disguised victory for the Conservatives. From now on Lloyd George was dependent on them; he could not even threaten a reunion with the remnant of the Asquith Liberals, even supposing that a reconciliation with Asquith had been possible, since on the present balance of seats in the Commons this would have gained him nothing. For the moment it seemed that the Conservatives had taken their Prime Minister prisoner; the question now was whether during the next four years the feverish activity of Lloyd George might not yet reverse that situation.

15
Peace-making and Its Implications

'Walking through the beautiful forests of Versailles,' said Lloyd George in a speech at the Guildhall on the eve of the armistice, 'the leaves were falling, but not these alone. Empires and kingdoms, kings and crowns were falling like withered leaves.' The dominions of Turkey and Austria were in varying states of dissolution; Russia had already lost most of her western territories by the Treaty of Brest-Litovsk in March 1918, and now Germany awaited in her turn the terms which the Allies would impose on her. For the rulers the end had already come. The entire imperial family of Russia had been shot by the Bolsheviks in the summer of 1918; the last Habsburg emperor Karl and the German Kaiser William II had both abdicated and gone into exile; only the Turkish sultan was to linger on for a further four years of ineffective rule.

In January 1919 the leaders of the victors were slowly assembling for the peace conference in Paris. By the following July many of them had departed after the signing of the Treaty of Versailles with Germany, but the work of the conference continued until January 1920 as peace was concluded with the other enemy states, the whole becoming known as the Versailles settlement.

Comparisons with the congress of Vienna of 1814 were inevitably frequent and often odious. Few treaties have incurred the degree of criticism that was later heaped on Versailles, but in fairness to the men of 1919 it is worth remembering that they were grappling with problems of a unique complexity that virtually defied a satisfactory solution. In the first place, they had to contend with forces of nationalism and public opinion which the congress of Vienna had largely been able to ignore. Eastern Europe at this moment was alive with all those nationalities that had grown increasingly vociferous throughout the nineteenth century. In the latter stages of the war the Allies had made use of these seeds of disruption against their enemies, and they had now to reap a harvest of excited and mutually antagonistic national movements, each of which believed that its hour of destiny had come.

The politicians of the west were themselves answerable to their own domestic organizations, and the power of the press in continuing to work up a patriotic hatred of the enemy was enormous. Indeed, Lord Northcliffe had had hopes of exercising even greater influence. 'What do you think that fellow Northcliffe has just had the impudence to demand?' remarked Lloyd George to Carson. 'He told me I must make him a member of the peace delegation. I told him to go to hell.' Even if he was not to be in the delegation, Northcliffe could not be discounted. 'The Junkers will cheat you yet', announced the *Daily Mail* every day at the head of its leading article and the problems of statesmanship were greatly increased by the need to show the public that the Junkers had not succeeded in doing so.

A second factor was the presence of the United States at the conference in the person of President Wilson himself. Author of the Fourteen Points, determined to establish a League of Nations within the framework of the settlement, and convinced that he could curb the cynicism of European diplomacy with the doctrine of national self-determination, President Wilson suffered harsh treatment for his efforts during these months in Paris. He was lampooned by the French press, and lampooned more lastingly by J. M. Keynes, the British economist who was the representative of the Treasury at the negotiations. 'He had no plan, no scheme, no constructive ideas whatever for clothing with the flesh of life the commandments which he had thundered from the White House. He could have preached a sermon on any of them or have addressed a stately prayer to the Almighty for their fulfilment, but he could not frame their concrete application to the actual state of Europe.'[1] Thus, although the President had announced on his arrival: 'this is a peace conference in which arrangements cannot be made in the old style', the more earthy aspirations of Clemenceau and Lloyd George made the old style ultimately inescapable.

A third issue which had no counterpart in 1814 was the existence of a Communist government in Russia, offering the example of an alternative form of society which might spread westwards, as it did momentarily in Bavaria and Hungary, if a swift and effective settlement of Europe were not achieved.

Finally, there was the anomalous state of the negotiations with Germany. The Germans had made their initial approach to the United States on 4 October 1918, accepting the Fourteen Points as a basis for a political settlement. Great Britain and France at first played no part in the exchange of notes between President Wilson and the German government and it was only on 23 October that they were informed of the situation. Lloyd George and Clemenceau did not by any means agree with the whole of the Fourteen Points, but after a long argument with Colonel House, Wilson's representative in Paris, they were only able to gain a Memorandum of Reservation affecting the freedom of the seas and stipulating compensation by Germany for all damage suffered by civilians, and this was duly communicated to the Germans by Wilson on 5 November. A further confusion arose over the fact that the Fourteen Points were mainly in the form of general principles. A more precise definition involving several important modifications was devised at Paris and approved by the President on 30 October, but was never sent to Germany, who had not asked for any clarification. And on 11 November, after the Germans had received an invitation to apply for armistice terms, the military agreement for the cease-fire which they signed with British and French representatives made no mention of the nature of the political settlement. Thus even before the war was over, the position was sufficiently ambiguous for the moral validity of the eventual settlement to be called into question and for the Germans later to be able to raise the cry of deception.

When all these problems have been allowed, however, there was certainly much that was unsatisfactory about the management of the negotiations in Paris. To some of those who were present it seemed that the conference that was to set the affairs of the world in order was having some considerable difficulty with its own. A number of factors had delayed its opening until two months after the armistice—the President's need to address Congress on 2 December before his departure for Europe, the British general election and the uncertainty of the domestic scene in Germany—but although this should have provided an excellent opportunity to make the preliminary arrangements, the conference eventually opened on 18 January 1919 with little idea of the procedure to be adopted, no programme of matters to be discussed and, indeed, no clear conception of the nature of its task.

The French had originally envisaged two stages: peace with the enemy states followed by a general congress to deal with the whole international scene. This had been the pattern of events in 1814, but nothing so logical materialized in 1919. Discussion drifted on in an atmosphere of industrious informality at the Quai d'Orsay and in the hotels of the ministers and their staffs, and eventually by the end of March it was clear that the findings of the fifty-eight subcommittees on all aspects of European problems were so interwoven with the terms to be presented to the defeated countries that the two stages could not be disentangled; consequently, at no time did neutral or enemy states take part in the negotiations.

The central decision-making body was a council of ten—the American President and his Secretary of State Robert Lansing, the prime ministers and foreign ministers of Great Britain, France and Italy and two delegates from Japan. This proved unwieldy and there eventually emerged a council of four consisting of the four heads of government, excluding the Japanese, with a council of five for the foreign ministers. This still left the problem of language. French had normally been used in diplomatic circles, except when Disraeli had addressed the congress of Berlin in 1878 in English, but the British and the Americans now claimed that the number of English-speaking delegates made it appropriate for English to be recognized as a second official language at the conference. Thereupon, considerations of prestige as well as convenience caused the Italian premier Orlando to insist upon Italian as well. As it turned out, this concession did little good; Lloyd George and President Wilson spoke only English, and since Orlando's only other language was French, he was incapable of conversing with them except through an interpreter. As a result he was haunted by the fear that Italian interests were being ignored, and when in April the other three met separately to discuss the Adriatic, he announced his immediate return to Rome. For the moment the council of four had become a council of three.

These complications over procedure, however, were only minor compared with the actual problem of devising peace terms with Germany. The difficulty here lay in the fundamental divergence of views between Great Britain and France. For the British the situation at the end of the war had already answered most of their immediate requirements. The German colonies had been taken in the course of the fighting and the terms of the armistice had ensured the evacuation of Belgium and the internment of the German fleet at Scapa Flow. Thus fears for their own security were quietened; indeed, the immediate circumstances which had led to the Anglo-French *entente* in 1904 now no longer existed for the British. They were naturally conscious of the possibility of a revival of German power, but they hoped that this might be made less likely through the redevising of the map of eastern Europe, as Balfour had suggested in October 1916, 'diminishing the area from which the Central Powers can draw the men and the money required for a policy of aggression'. Otherwise, their concern was to avoid any wide commitment on the Continent which might hinder a speedy disarmament and a restoration of peaceful relations.

For the 40 million inhabitants of France the terms of the armistice had done little to create any permanent security against the 58 million of Germany.* Furthermore, the end of the First World War was to give Germany a relatively greater preponderance on the Continent, since two former Powers could no longer play a part on the European scene; Austria had disintegrated and the re-emergence of Poland meant that Russia had no common frontier with Germany across which she could act as an effective ally for the French, as she had in 1914. This last factor, consequent on the creation of a Polish state, had already been anticipated by Balfour in a speech to the Imperial War Cabinet in March 1917. 'If Germany has designs in the future upon France or the west, I think she will be protected by this new state from any action on the part of Russia and I am not at all sure that that is to the interests of western civilization.' But after the Bolshevik revolution in November 1917 the west had strong reasons for wanting Poland to shut Russia off and the weakening of the French position was unavoidable. Since any renewal of the Franco-Russian alliance of 1894 would serve little purpose, the only alternative for France now was to make an ally of the new Poland; yet Polish military power was hardly an adequate substitute and in any case it was unlikely that France would be able to pour into Poland the 16 billion francs of investment that she had lavished on Russia between 1887 and 1917.

It was therefore understandable that Clemenceau should be obsessed with the security of France for the future. 'He had one illusion— France,' wrote J. M. Keynes, 'and one disillusion—mankind, including Frenchmen and his colleagues not least.'[2] The image of 'the Tiger', the old man with his parchment face, heavy white walrus moustache and deep fierce eyes, has come to symbolize the determination of France that Germany should never again be able to ravage French soil, a determination that the British in their later disgust at the treaty and irritation with the French were inclined to see as a simple desire for revenge.

Given the new situation in the east, French security on her own borders could only be achieved in one of two ways. The first was rapprochement, as happened after the Second World War, but although this was strongly advocated by the British and the Americans, it was unacceptable to Clemenceau. The second was the creation of a situation on the western border of Germany whereby she could always be held

* This was the figure of Germany's population after the settlement.

in check and it was in pursuit of this that Marshal Foch, early in 1919, proposed that the German frontier should be pushed back to the line of the Rhine. This would mean that, in addition to the restoration of Alsace and Lorraine to France, the German Rhineland territories lying to the west of the Rhine should become a separate state, not annexed to France, but under an Allied military occupation of indefinite duration. President Wilson and Lloyd George both strongly opposed this, believing that it could only create lasting German resentment, and instead they eventually persuaded Clemenceau to accept a temporary Allied occupation of the Rhineland, which was to remain a part of Germany, although permanently demilitarized, in return for an Anglo-American guarantee for France against any future German aggression.

In fact, French misgivings on this score turned out to be justified. In March 1920 the American Senate rejected the Treaty of Versailles and with this lapsing of the joint guarantee the British withdrew theirs as well; a later British offer in 1921 did little to meet French requirements, not even envisaging general staff conversations between the two countries. In the prewar experience of the British combined military arrangements could become as binding as any formal treaty, and thus the French were left to maintain a lone watch over Germany, uneasily aware that she might eventually become too powerful for them.

The problem of reparations revealed another division between Great Britain and France. It was certainly normal practice for a defeated country to pay an indemnity to the victor, who hoped in this way to recover the cost of the war effort. In 1919 the French and the Belgians could argue that their lands had suffered enormous material damage in the course of four years' fighting, whereas there had been virtually none on German soil; hence their primary interest was a payment by Germany in gold and raw materials. The British delegation, however, knowing that their country was dependent on a flourishing world trade, regarded German economic recovery as an essential part of a general European revival and were fearful lest the saddling of Germany with a vast debt might hinder that process.

This was the view of the experts, but British politicians, conscious of the press and the promises made in the recent general election that Germany would pay, could not stand in the way of the French demands. Instead, they joined in the hue and cry. Lloyd George's first suggestion was that national claims on the sum to be raised from Germany should be settled according to the financial amount that each of them had contributed to the war. This was not likely to be successful, so he moved on to demand compensation for the cost of pensions to the disabled and war widows, and Smuts was eventually able to persuade President Wilson to accept this. And so the sum with which Germany was to be charged continued to increase, until it was apparent that no final figure could be established before the peace treaty was signed; nor was there any agreement on the amount that Germany would actually be capable of paying.

One aspect of the economic problem, however, did demand an immediate solution: the supply of food to Germany. The terms of the armistice had stipulated a continuation of the blockade and in later years critics accused the Allies of cruelly prolonging the period of near starvation in Germany. This was not the aim of the Allies at all. Their purpose had been simply to ensure that the German government did not make use of the armistice to replenish their stocks of war material for a subsequent renewal of hostilities; it did not preclude any controlled scheme for allowing food to be brought into the country. Nevertheless, there was a delay of some four and a half months after the armistice before food trains could enter Germany.

The reasons for this lay in the international wrangle over the way in which the supply was to be arranged, rather than in any conscious malice. By the end of the war the Americans had produced a surplus of foodstuffs which they were keen to export, but they insisted that Germany should pay cash for them. The British, too, believed that the Germans should be fed, but demanded that Germany should surrender her mercantile marine for the delivery of supplies and a clause to this effect was inserted in the renewal of the armistice in January 1919. The Germans, however, were as determined to cling to their shipping as they were to their remaining gold reserve of £120 million; equally, the French, who wanted the German gold reserve for reparation payments, had no wish to see part of it pass into the pockets of American farmers and in the supplementary armistice of December 1918 had prohibited Germany from disposing abroad of any of her financial assets.

In the consequent deadlock that continued throughout the early months of 1919 the Americans and the British were adamant over payment in gold and the use of German shipping, and had thus to deal with French and German objections. By now the shortage of food in Germany was desperate and the climax came at a meeting of the Supreme Economic Council on 8 March, when Lloyd George made an impassioned intervention. 'The creeping lethargy of the proceedings was thrown off,' wrote Keynes, 'as he launched his words with rage',[3] insisting that French resistance to the release of German gold must be dropped so that the supply of food might begin. Clemenceau surrendered and so, too, did the head of the German delegation at Brussels, when he gave his assent to the use of the merchant fleet. Thus at last food began to enter Germany some three months before the signing of the Treaty of Versailles, at the expense of German gold and more bruised feelings between the British and the French.

Anglo-French differences were not the only complications during these months in Paris. Italy was eager to gain her reward for entering the war on the side of the Allies. Originally this was to consist of the Tyrol, Istria and a part of the Dalmatian coast, as well as an area in the southern half of Asia Minor (map, p. 203), which had been given more precise definition in 1917 and included Smyrna. All this would have represented a spectacular advance in that policy of Mediterranean expansion on which Italy had embarked in 1911 (see p. 90), but throughout the conference Orlando was convinced that the promises would not be fulfilled. These fears were by no means unfounded. Trieste and the Tyrol were to come to Italy, but the doctrine of national self-determination put Istria and Dalmatia beyond her reach; and Lloyd George had other plans in mind for Asia Minor (see p. 162). The eventual withdrawal of Orlando from the conference symbolized a lasting sense of discontent over the peace settlement which was to have a significant effect upon Italy's political alignments in later years. Well might Ludendorff comment at the time: 'Versailles had shown that there is no unity among the Allies. In ten years Germany will have risen again and providing she keeps the Allied camp split and wins over one or two nations to her side, she can win back all she has lost.'

Nevertheless, the outlook for Germany at this moment was bleak. Slowly through all the discord the terms of the treaty were taking shape. The territory that she was to lose consisted of Alsace and Lorraine, which were returned to France, a small border area of Eupen and Malmedy given to Belgium, northern Schleswig to Denmark, Memel to Lithuania, and the provinces of West Prussia and Posen to create an outlet to the sea for Poland (map, p. 159). Not one of her colonies was to be restored. The British Dominions had been allowed their own representation at the conference and South Africa intended to hold German South-West Africa, as did Australia the German half of New Guinea. Great Britain kept German East Africa; Japan received the German islands in the Pacific north of the equator and took over the former German sphere of influence in Shantung on the mainland of China. At home Germany was to have virtually no navy and no air force at all, and her army was to be restricted to 100,000 men recruited on a voluntary basis. As had been agreed, the Rhineland remained perman-

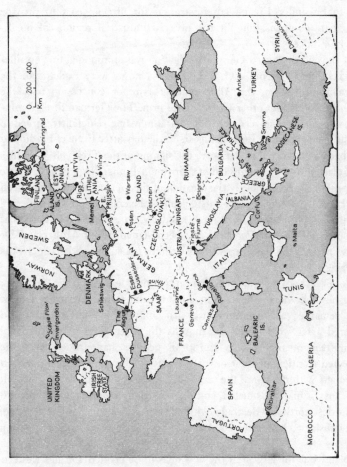

3   EUROPE AFTER THE PEACE OF VERSAILLES

ently demilitarized, including the east bank of the Rhine to a depth of 50 kilometres, and the Allies were to station an occupation force there for the next fifteen years. To justify the charging of reparations a clause was included in the treaty by which Germany accepted responsibility for causing the war; the final figure had to await the findings of the Reparations Commission, but in addition to this, the area of the Saar was to be under French administration for fifteen years to provide immediate compensation for the ravaged industrial regions of north-eastern France.

At the end of April a German delegation was summoned to Versailles to receive these terms. For several weeks notes were exchanged, the Germans protesting, the Allies making a minor concession over the eastern frontier, but otherwise standing firm. The German foreign minister resigned; the government fell, but a new one reluctantly agreed to accept. And so, on 28 June, five years to the day after Francis Ferdinand had been assassinated in Sarajevo, the signing of the Treaty of Versailles took place in the crowded Hall of Mirrors in Louis XIV's palace, where forty-eight years previously the creation of the German empire had been proclaimed. 'Suddenly from outside comes the crash of guns thundering a salute,' wrote Harold Nicolson in his diary. 'It announces to Paris that the second Treaty of Versailles has been signed by Dr Müller and Dr Bell. Through the few open windows comes the sound of distant crowds cheering hoarsely.'[4]

Not everybody felt like cheering on that day, least of all the Germans. Still, however harsh they might consider the terms, Germany had at least remained a European power. In contrast, her ally Austria had suffered a far worse fate. For months the delegations of the national committees of the eastern European peoples had argued over the projected frontiers of their new states and at the end the incorporation of Galicia within Poland, the creation of Czechoslovakia, the acquisition of Transylvania by Romania, and the inclusion of Bosnia, Dalmatia and territories north of Belgrade within Serbia to form a new kingdom of Yugoslavia, had reduced Austria and Hungary to two tiny rump states.

Poland was the largest of the new ones to be created. On her western frontier the Treaty of Versailles had established her corridor to the sea with Germany's cession of West Prussia and Posen, although this was not as extensive as she would have wished. A plebiscite ensured that Germany would retain upper Silesia, and the port of Danzig with its almost entirely German population was not given to Poland, but became a Free City under a League of Nations commissioner. Lloyd George was responsible for both these modifications, since he was a little suspicious of a possible Franco-Polish hegemony in Europe and it consequently became part of his policy to prevent the creation of too powerful a Polish state. There were also economic grounds for having Danzig as a Baltic port available for British commerce, and Germany's retention of upper Silesia would aid an economic recovery which Great Britain regarded as important in her own interest.

The eastern frontier of Poland was harder to establish. The Poles claimed the frontier of 1772 (before the first partition) arguing that they would stand guard for Europe against Russian Bolshevism. The western Powers decided that the disputed city of Vilna should go provisionally to Lithuania, but the rest of Poland's eastern frontier was ultimately to be settled by a Russo-Polish war (see p. 175). In the course of this the Council of Ambassadors in Paris suggested on 8 December 1919 a line running very roughly along the old eastern frontier of Poland when she had been under Russian rule; and when in July 1920 Lloyd George made a similar proposal, sometimes known as the Curzon line, the Poles, hard-pressed by the Russians, accepted this. The Russians, however, refused a truce on this basis, but were then thrown back and in 1921 the Treaty of Riga established a frontier some 200 miles to the east of these earlier proposals.

One further empire had still to be dismantled. Turkey, the sick man of Europe, whose decease had been regarded as imminent throughout the nineteenth century, was at last about to succumb, and the international rivalries which had previously helped to keep her in existence now combined to tear her apart. The British naturally reckoned to consolidate their line of communication to India; the French were suspicious of British plans to undermine their influence in the Middle East; Italy and Greece were competing over territorial designs on the eastern Mediterranean. Ironically the one absentee was Russia, still too involved in her own domestic turmoil to be able to force her way into the schemes for the final partition of her old enemy.

The Treaty of Sèvres was eventually signed with Turkey in August 1920. Inevitably this included a new agreement over the Straits whose control had been a key question in the past. Throughout the nineteenth century Great Britain had always resisted any Russian move in this direction, but the new alignment after the Anglo-Russian *entente* of 1907 and the need to keep Russia in the war had led her to offer the Straits to the Tsar in 1915 (see p. 113). The Bolsheviks, once in power, had renounced this agreement, along with all others, as symbols of an imperialist past, and the Treaty of Sèvres now declared that the Straits were to be demilitarized and placed under an international commission; this implied complete freedom of navigation for all types of vessel in peace or war, a risk which the British had never wished to accept in the past and only acceptable now in view of the weakened condition of Russia.

In territory all that was left to Turkey by the treaty was the northern half of Asia Minor. The southern half had originally been earmarked for Italy, but over this Lloyd George was able to accomplish a remarkable alteration. He had become enamoured of the idea of a close working relationship with Greece, where the pro-German King Constantine had been replaced by his young son Alexander, whose prime minister Venizelos was strongly pro-British. Accordingly Lloyd George insisted that the Greek government was to have the right to administer the Smyrna* region in southern Asia Minor for the next five years. Since this contained a considerable Greek population, the argument of self-determination was on his side and the Italians suffered one more disillusionment. Greece was also to acquire Gallipoli, the Aegean isles and eastern Thrace to within twelve miles of Constantinople. France and Italy were too much in need of British support over their respective aims in the Rhineland and the Adriatic to be able to resist this development, and the challenge to Lloyd George's Greek policy was eventually to come from Turkey herself, when a military revolution brought an end to the rule of the Sultan and ultimately led to a radical revision of this section of the Treaty of Sèvres.†

In Asia the division of Turkish territories was complicated by the hopes for independence among the Arabs who, in June 1916, had risen in revolt against their Turkish overlords (see p. 126). This Arab rising had been preceded by a long correspondence between the British High Commissioner in Egypt and Sherif Hussein of Mecca, in which it had been agreed that after the war there should be independence for all the Arab regions, a promise complicated by confusing qualifications over ill-defined areas in Syria, Palestine and lower and upper Mesopotamia. The Arab revolt duly broke out and soon developed into a major insurrection under the guidance of a small group of British officers commanded by Colonel T. E. Lawrence. Indeed, the next two years were to create a unique aspect of the First World War, more akin to the partisan movements in the second; the decisive battle, which brought about the defeat of the main Turkish forces at Megiddo in September 1918, was fought by General Allenby, but at the same time the Arabs under Lawrence had swept up as far north as Damascus, a success which

* Now known as Izmir.
† The full consequences of the settlement with Turkey are dealt with in Chapter 18.

naturally convinced them that they had won their independence them-selves.

Lawrence was almost the only wartime commander to emerge with an aura of romantic heroism. His adventures in the desert captured the public imagination in Great Britain, intrigued by the slight boyish figure of the scholar-soldier who had lived as an Arab among the Bedouin. Paris, however, was less romantic, as Lawrence found when he arrived at the conference, hoping to see his *protégé* Feisal, a younger son of Hussein, made king of an independent Arabia. 'He would glide along the corridors of the Majestic Hotel,' wrote Harold Nicolson, 'the lines of resentment hardening around his boyish lips, an undergraduate with a chin.'

The problem facing Lawrence was that a good many other promises had been made during the war as well as to Sherif Hussein. The Sykes–Picot agreement of May 1916 had divided the northern Arab areas into Allied zones of administration and influence—Mesopotamia for Great Britain, Syria for France; and in November 1917 the Balfour declaration had announced that the British government viewed 'with favour the establishment in Palestine of a National Home for the Jewish people and will use their best endeavours to facilitate the achievement of this object'. The Sykes–Picot agreement and the Balfour declaration were not entirely compatible, and both were likely to clash with the hopes for unity and independence which Sherif Hussein had nursed, although the British claimed that they had expressed reservations over the affected areas in the arrangements which they had made with him at the beginning of 1916.

In the event, the French and the Arabs gained rather less than what they had expected. By the Treaty of Sèvres the main part of the Arabian peninsula was granted independence under Sherif Hussein ruling at Mecca; in the northern area the French were given a mandate over the Lebanon and Syria, where Feisal became King (see p. 191), and a British mandate was to extend over Palestine and Mesopotamia* (map, p. 203). Egypt was not included in this partition, since it was assumed to be under British control. Clearly in this side of the Versailles settlement the British had made immense economic and strategic gains. The oil-fields of Mesopotamia represented the richest section of the Turkish empire and the great strengthening of the land route to India marked a successful outcome to the long intermittent struggle which had been one feature of British relations with France and Russia throughout the nine-teenth century and which the *ententes* of 1904 and 1907 had been designed to settle.

* Now known as Iraq.

The Versailles settlement was at least a relatively swift attempt to cope with the problems of a whole world in a violent state of transition. It could hardly hope to find a satisfactory solution to them all; in the end it did not prevent a second great war with Germany and thus in practical terms it may be considered a failure.

In certain respects, however, the peace-makers, harassed by every kind of distraction, did arrive at imaginative and sensible conclusions. It was fashionable to complain later that the diplomats had balkanized Europe, but the truth was that the peoples of eastern Europe were determined to be balkanized, and although the Allies had been reluctant to give official recognition to the nationalist movements before 1918, the circumstances at the end of the war had left them little option. Assuming that any federal solution was out of the question and that the new states had to be created, the frontiers which were established for them took most factors into account, so far as this was possible. In the middle of the Second World War an American historian wrote: 'Hard as it is to visualize in 1941, it would not be surprising if the negotiators of the new Versailles were to recreate Poland and Czechoslovakia with something like the original boundaries.'[5] Indeed, except for the shift westwards in the position of Poland, the map of eastern Europe after 1945 (p. 397) was not so remote from that created in Paris in 1919.

What the peace-makers could not avoid was the existence of mixed populations that were bound to hamper the evolution of the new small states, and their attitudes were not yet sufficiently inhumane to countenance a policy of wholesale evictions with which the problem of minorities was handled in 1945. Nor could they escape the fact that the new states could only hope for true independence so long as Russia and Germany remained weak; once each of these had recovered, the countries that lay in between were bound to fall under the aegis of one or other of them, as the old rivalry reasserted itself. The men of 1919 could devise frontiers, but they could not destroy the harsh forces of eastern European political life.

The main hope for the future was centred on President Wilson's scheme for a League of Nations. The aim of this assembly of delegates from the nations of the world, with its headquarters at Geneva, was to create a forum in which all international disputes might be resolved peaceably. Idealist in conception, this proved impotent in practice and doomed to failure. The American Senate rejected the President's proposal; Germany and Russia were excluded, and with Great Britain and France as the two most powerful members it was natural that the League should seem in the eyes of the defeated merely an instrument of the victors—'a League not to end sovereignties but preserve them', as H. G. Wells wrote several years later.[6]

Indeed, it was soon clear that the peace settlement had not reduced the intensity of international animosities; if anything, it had added to them. Poland was eventually to seize Vilna from Lithuania and resented Czechoslovakia's possession of Teschen. Czechoslovakia, Romania and Yugoslavia were antagonistic towards Hungary, from whom each of them had extracted territory. Of the older Powers France suspected Great Britain of having deserted her in Europe and cheated her in the Middle East, while Italy saw herself betrayed by the Allies, robbed of that part of the Adriatic coast which had gone to Yugoslavia and of the promised territory in Asia Minor.

Yet all this was as nothing compared with the anger felt by Germany over the terms of the Treaty of Versailles—'this instrument of boundless extortion and abject humiliation', as Adolf Hitler called it in *Mein Kampf*. Germans protested that the peace was a *Diktat*, that the Fourteen Points, on which they had based their original negotiations with the United States, had not been respected and that the doctrine of national self-determination had sometimes been invoked, sometimes infringed, simply to deprive them of territory. Memel and Danzig were both German cities, and although the 6·5 million German-speaking Austrians and the 3 million Germans of the Sudetenland on the western border of Czechoslovakia had all formerly been under Habsburg rule, the Allies' proclaimed principle suggested that they should now be included within Germany, if that was their wish.

It was true that there had been some departure from the Fourteen Points; open covenants had not been openly arrived at; tariff barriers remained and were to increase, and 'the free open-minded and absolutely impartial adjustment of colonial claims' had turned into the confiscation of all German colonies, together with a partition of Turkish possessions among the Powers. Against this it could be said that Great Britain and France had never accepted the Fourteen Points in their entirety and had never concluded any agreement with Germany on that basis. Indeed, the German government had largely been responsible for this confusion by opening its initial negotiations purely with the United States. In any case, the principal German territorial losses—the return of Alsace and Lorraine to France and the creation of a Polish corridor— had both been stipulated in Wilson's proposals.

Over the more detailed settlement of frontiers in eastern Europe the Allies had had to consider a good many factors as well as national self-determination in order to make each new state a viable political and economic entity. Memel had been needed as a port for Lithuania, and the mountainous regions of the Sudetenland were to provide Czechoslovakia with a militarily defensible western frontier. Danzig, at least, had been established as a Free City, although on practical grounds it could have been given to Poland who had no other port on the coast of the Polish corridor and had consequently to build one of her own. There was, however, one blatant example of a denial of national self-determination to be seen in Austria, now shorn of her non-German Habsburg territories. Here, early in 1919, the Austrian government, supported by a strong majority, requested incorporation in Germany, but the proposal was rejected outright by the Allies. This might seem less justifiable, but it was not likely that the Allies would allow a substantial extension of the frontiers of Germany which would then have enclosed half of Czechoslovakia, and in view of the harshness of the terms which the Germans had recently imposed on Russia with the Treaty of Brest-Litovsk, they hardly had a right to expect it.

A more questionable aspect of the settlement was to be found in the economic clauses, mainly because the eventual size of the reparations demanded was absurdly heavy. It was over this that the first serious criticism of Versailles was heard outside Germany, when in 1919 J. M. Keynes published a denunciation in his book *The Economic Consequences of the Peace*. Although generally uneasy about the morality of the settlement, the principal stimulus of his attack came from the outraged feelings of a professional economist that the Allies should insist on payment that Germany could not possibly make, and that in demanding it they might disrupt the chances of a rapid economic recovery throughout Europe. 'This treaty,' he wrote in a separate article, 'ignores the economic solidarity of Europe and by aiming at the destruction of the economic life of Germany it threatens the health and prosperity of the Allies themselves.'[7] In addition, there was no way of forcing Germany to pay, short of total military occupation. The controversy continued long after it had ceased to be a significant question and even during the Second World War a young Frenchman, while temporarily in the United States, produced a reply entitled *The Economic Consequences of Mr Keynes*.

In Great Britain it was the political consequences of Mr Keynes that were more immediately relevant. As wartime hatred died away, his book helped to sow a seed of doubt in the minds of the British about the fairness of the whole settlement. Idealists and pacifists naturally regarded the treaty as unjust; the Labour party had condemned the terms in May 1919, declaring that the Germans would become 'a people

of serfs working for their conquerors in arms'—an inaccurate predic-
tion, as it turned out. Some of the right wing also had their objections,
wishing to enlist Germany against Russia; thus in March 1920 Winston
Churchill wrote in a memorandum to Lloyd George: 'since the armistice
my policy would have been, "peace with the German people, war on the
Bolshevik tyranny" ', suggesting that any treaty with France should be
dependent on the French modifying their treatment of Germany. Genuine horror at the thought of any further war, a growing sense that
Germany had legitimate grievances, a wish to use Germany as a bulwark
against Bolshevism—these were the attitudes that governed later British
reactions to the Treaty of Versailles, and they were to lie at the root of
the policy of appeasement in the 1930s (see p. 297).

At the time, however, Lloyd George had little difficulty in getting the
treaty ratified by the House of Commons. Indeed, the British might well
feel satisfied with the immediate situation. All they wanted now was to
return to a prewar state of prosperity. Yet in the long term it is clear
that this could never be. The war had brought to a head many of the
factors that had been quietly undermining British predominance before
1914. The precarious state of the European economy and the strengthened position of new competitors, the United States and Japan, were
both to contribute to a relative weakening of Great Britain's situation.
She had made colonial gains, but the spread of local nationalism in Asia
and, later, in Africa was to add enormously to her political burden and
to make the growth of empire a doubtful asset; her Dominions, too, now
spoke with an increasing independence and initiative. Even the security
of her own shores was not absolutely certain; the German Navy, which
had once seemed to represent the greatest threat of invasion, was now no
more, but the war had created a new danger, the rise of air power, and
command of the sea was no longer the only safeguard against attack.
The British victory had temporarily ended a threatening German
hegemony on the Continent; it could not restore a position which had
already been under attack before the war began.

16

Industrial Unrest and the Dream of Working-class Solidarity

'In the autumn of 1919, in which I write, we are at the dead season of our fortunes,' wrote J. M. Keynes in his *Economic Consequences of the Peace*. 'The reaction from the exertions, the fears, and the sufferings of the past five years is at its height. Our power of feeling or caring beyond the immediate questions of our own material well being is temporarily eclipsed.'[1] It was as if the entire nation were in a prolonged state of shock; the years of casualty lists, totalling 750,000 dead and 1,700,000 wounded, created a feeling of having lived through some nightmare unthinkable to men and women who had grown up in the peace of Victorian and Edwardian England. The lightheaded vindictiveness that came with victory was to fade fairly quickly; the sense of horror and loss did not. One in every eleven men between twenty and forty-five was dead, including many of promise and ability, and the poignant thought of all that waste haunted the survivors, as they lived on in the subsequent decades. 'I am beginning to rub my eyes at the prospect of peace,' wrote Cynthia Asquith in October 1918. 'I think it will require more courage than anything that has gone before. It isn't until one leaves off spinning round that one realizes how giddy one is. One will have to look at long vistas again, instead of short ones, and one will at last recognize that the dead are not only dead for the duration of the war.'[2]

The nation had suffered more than shock and loss; it was exhausted and undernourished. Small wonder that the epidemic of Spanish flu, which raged from the last months of the war until the early part of 1919, should claim the lives of 150,000 people in England and Wales. It was in this dead season of their fortunes that British society and government had to cope with all the strain and frustration of a readjustment to peacetime conditions and it is hardly surprising that bitterness and unrest should be a predominant feature of these immediate postwar years.

Industrial unrest was not merely the consequence of the war; the fierce outburst of violence in 1911–13 and the forming of the 'triple alliance' of miners, railwaymen and transport workers in 1913 (see p. 73), all pointed to an independent antecedent. What the war had done was to establish a background in which brute force was accepted as the sole arbiter. In Russia civil war raged; in Hungary a Soviet government was established under Bela Kun, until ejected by Romania; in Italy the poet D'Annunzio had occupied Fiume with a private army in defiance of the Versailles settlement, and Mussolini was founding his Fascist party. Along the south coast of the Baltic German Freikorps and local national and Communist groups fought their vicious battles; in Berlin the German Communists (Spartakists) were massacred by government forces and in Bavaria another shortlived Soviet government succumbed to the right-wing groups. 'This is the end and the beginning of an age,' wrote H. G. Wells in *Mr Britling Sees It Through* in 1916. He had said it with hope, but 'the war to end war' was a misnomer from the day the armistice was signed, and it was hard now to recapture that sense of moral crusade so pronounced in the early years of hostilities.

The government which Lloyd George formed in 1919 took into account the rapid disappearance of many of the wartime ministries, but did not include many new faces. Bonar Law, Lord Privy Seal, was also leader of the House of Commons, Lord Curzon Lord President, Austen Chamberlain Chancellor of the Exchequer, Balfour Foreign Secretary, Winston Churchill Secretary for War and H. A. L. Fisher President of the Board of Education. The most striking appointment was that of F. E. Smith as Lord Chancellor at the age of forty-seven. The flamboyance of a brilliant personality had often aroused a sense of antagonism in established circles, and King George had expressed some doubt when his name was submitted. Unabashed, F. E. Smith was duly sworn in as Lord Chancellor and assumed the title of Birkenhead—not of the Atlantic, as had been suggested in the legal profession.

As it turned out, the major personal complications arose over the Foreign Office. Balfour was attending the peace conference and Lord Curzon had to stand in for him in London, not an easy situation for a man of Curzon's commanding temperament; and it was no better when he succeeded Balfour in October 1919. Lloyd George clearly intended to be his own Foreign Secretary and before long he was at odds with Curzon over his Greek policy (see p. 162). 'He wants his Foreign Secretary to be a valet, almost a drudge,' Curzon complained in a letter to his wife in 1921, but he was too prone to an air of contemptuous superiority to gain much sympathy from his colleagues, although his exasperation was certainly understandable. Later British Prime Ministers in the century—Neville Chamberlain, Churchill and Eden— have also been accused of excessive interference with the work of their Foreign Secretaries; Stanley Baldwin was thought not to have interfered enough. Probably a correctly balanced relationship is difficult to achieve and there seemed little prospect of it with Lloyd George, who had not the temperament for an Asquithian detachment and in any case needed a personal success for the sake of his own political future.

The first troubles for the government arose over demobilization. Under Milner, Churchill's predecessor at the War Office, a scheme had been devised whereby men with key jobs in industry should be the first to be released. This was a rational attempt to prepare the way for absorbing the eventual onrush of ex-servicemen into employment, but it overlooked the fact that these key jobs had already kept many of their holders out of the Army for much of the war. The government seemed to be operating on the principle of 'last in, first out', and there were angry scenes of near-mutiny. Thousands of troops at Folkestone and Dover refused to re-embark for France; mass demonstrations were held in London; at Luton the town hall was set on fire and at Calais rioting soldiers seemed barely under military control.

At this point Lloyd George in the course of appointing his new government gave the War Office to Churchill, shifting Milner to the Colonial Office. On 29 January 1919 a new order of demobilization was published, based on age and length of service. From then on demob- ilization proceeded at the rate of 10,000 men a day, until by the end of the year 4 million had been released, most of them being reabsorbed into industry without any need for the free insurance against unemploy- ment with which they had been provided.

Civilian problems were less easy to resolve. The immediate economic background to postwar unrest was a shortlived boom; the shipping lanes were now open, most countries throughout the world needed to replen- ish their stocks and for the moment purchasing power was available. This sudden revival of trade naturally helped to provide employment for the ex-servicemen, but it also gave a sharp acceleration to the process of inflation that had been developing throughout the war. By December 1918 the cost of living had risen by 125 per cent of what it had been in July 1914; by March 1920 this figure had reached 176 per cent and although wages also rose, they did not succeed in keeping pace in many trades.

Thus the primary concern of the trade unions in the first two years after the war was over wage increases and the length of the working day, and they were by now in a far stronger position from which to make their claims felt. Total membership had risen from 4 million in 1913 to nearly 8 million in 1919 (see Appendix 6, p. 442); larger amalgamations were soon to emerge—the Transport and General Workers' Union in 1921 under Ernest Bevin, the General and Municipal Workers' Union in 1924—and the growth of the shop stewards' power during the war (see p. 138) had strengthened the radical tendencies in the whole movement. The Labour party was naturally sympathetic, but they would have preferred to concentrate on the question of nationalization, as this was already partly embodied in existing wartime controls and their principal aim was to resist the government's plans to hand the mines and the railways back to private ownership.

Both these issues, pay and nationalization, were to feature predominantly in a series of industrial troubles to which government reactions varied greatly. At the end of January 1919 the Clydeside shop stewards, failing to gain a forty-hour week, called a strike which spread throughout the surrounding area. Glasgow became a scene of revolt amid demonstrations and the hoisting of the red flag, and the government moved in tanks and troops, although the actual clashes were with the police. The strike, condemned at union headquarters, was over by 11 February and three of the local leaders, William Gallacher, Emmanuel Shinwell and David Kirkwood, received short prison sentences for 'inciting to riot'.*

This was strong action, but soon a more extensive conflict seemed to be impending. In January the Miners' Federation demanded a 30 per cent increase in wages, a six-hour working day and nationalization under a mining council, half of whose members would represent the miners. The rejection of these demands was followed by a strike, and the announcement of the recreating of the 'triple alliance' with the railwaymen and the transport workers suggested that there might be nationwide implications.

With other pay claims pressing Lloyd George stalled. To reach a general agreement on conditions of labour he set up a national industrial conference of employers and trade unionists. The unions of the 'triple alliance' refused to attend, but months of debate did eventually produce proposals for a forty-eight-hour week and a minimum-wage commission, although further negotiation had collapsed by the middle of 1921 before any legislation had been passed.

To ward off the more immediate threat from the Miners' Federation, Lloyd George offered them a royal commission on the mines under Mr Justice Sankey, a High Court judge. It was obviously important that the

* All three later became MPs; Shinwell and Kirkwood both eventually moved to the House of Lords. This prospect was not open to Gallacher who represented the British Communist party.

composition of the commission should be acceptable to the trade unions, and Lloyd George, back briefly from the peace conference at Paris, spent an evening dining with the Webbs at Lord Haldane's to discuss the matter. Eventually it was settled that the commission would consist of representatives of the owners and of the miners, as well as Sir Leo Chiozza Money, R. H. Tawney, the economic historian, and Sidney Webb himself.

On 20 March 1919 the interim report of the Sankey Commission recommended a pay increase of two shillings (10p) a day, a seven-hour working day and some form of national purchase or joint control of the mines. This had the desired effect of getting the strike notices withdrawn, but the final outcome was less satisfactory. A commission including so many divergent interests might well have failed to produce any report at all. In fact, it produced four. Sankey wanted state ownership of the mines; the miners wanted workers' control; the private owners wanted private ownership and one industrialist, Sir Arthur Duckham, wanted amalgamations of privately owned collieries. Confronted with such a wealth of conflicting advice, Lloyd George was well placed to declare that the government was unable to act. In August he officially renounced any plan for nationalizing the mines and after the rejection of the Duckham plan by the Miners' Federation the last traces of the Sankey commission simply faded away.

The unrest continued. In June 1919 the cotton operatives went on strike, in August the police in London and Liverpool, and in September the ironfounders. In September, too, there began a renewed dispute with the railwaymen, when Sir Auckland Geddes, President of the Board of Trade, carefully retaining the recently improved rates of pay for engine-drivers, proceeded to lay down reduced rates for almost all other grades of railway worker. J. H. Thomas, MP for Derby and parliamentary general secretary of the NUR, leaped to the attack, and on 26 September a rail strike began. The government appealed for volunteers. Two demobilized majors drove the first strike-breaking train from London to Manchester and everywhere railway enthusiasts rushed to seize a heavensent opportunity. Once again Lloyd George stalled and the strike ended with an agreement that there should be no change in wage rates for a year and that they would only be reduced after that, if the cost of living dropped below 110 per cent of the prewar level, which seemed unlikely in this period of boom.

Thus far, the abandoning of nationalization and the government's search for temporary solutions amid a series of skirmishes naturally tended to alienate large sections of the working class, confirming the

mistrust that Bernard Shaw had expressed at the Labour party conference in November 1918. To many it seemed that the radical Chancellor
of the Exchequer of the prewar period had succumbed to the attitudes
of a House of Commons which, as a friend remarked to Keynes after the
general election, appeared to consist of 'a lot of hard-faced men who
look as if they had done very well out of the war'. Lloyd George,
however, was determined to handle the situation with restraint, and
while the strikes remained sporadic, he did his best to try to play the
situation down. 'Throughout the discussion,' wrote Tom Jones* of a
cabinet meeting in February 1920, 'the Prime Minister did a lot of
unsuspected leg-pulling, as he does not believe in the imminence of
revolution and more than suspects the War Office of trying to increase
the army along these lines.'[3]

There was nevertheless the danger of a more ambitious form of industrial
action. The idea of the 'triple alliance' conjured up for some trade unionists
a dream of working-class solidarity which might impose its will by the
threat of a total stoppage of work throughout the country. Against this
doctrine of the general strike the government, for all its delaying tactics and
occasional retreats, was prepared to fight. 'We shall beat them—we control
the food,' Lloyd George had said to the Webbs. A committee of the cabinet
had been formed at the beginning of 1919 at the time of the Glasgow riots,
and in September 1919 a scheme was devised whereby the country was
divided into twelve regions, each with a special commissioner through
whom essential services could be kept running during an emergency.

The resources of the government were not the sole obstacle to the
implementing of a general strike. Working-class solidarity itself was to
remain for the most part only a dream. Wage claims in one trade might
attract sympathy in other trades, but did not inspire a united strike
action throughout the country. Demands for nationalization were
weakened by the debate over workers' control or state control, and the
fragmented nature of British trade unionism hampered the creation of a
central organization that was vital, if solidarity was to be effective. Even
if it could be achieved, a natural conservatism made many trade-union
leaders uneasy over the implications of such a step. To use the kind of
pressure they were contemplating would be an attempt by a sectional
interest to dictate to a government answerable to a duly elected House of
Commons, and they were by no means sure of claiming a right to
challenge the sovereignty of Parliament. 'The unfortunate tendency
today is to assume that we can hold the state up to ransom at any time,'
J. H. Thomas told a meeting of railway strikers in February 1919. 'We

* Assistant Secretary to the cabinet.

may succeed and achieve our object, but if we did it at the expense of the state, then as citizens we would have destroyed all our claim to citizenship.' 'He is a good and loyal man,' commented George V in his diary;[4] extreme Socialists naturally thought somewhat differently.

Despite these misgivings there was one concerted effort to coerce the government by this means as early as 1920—an incident all the more significant in that it affected foreign policy. The issue arose out of the continuing war between Russia and Poland. After the Bolshevik revolution the Allies had established a combined force in the extreme north of Russia based on Archangel and Murmansk. The motive behind this had been primarily military, owing to the Bolshevik determination to make peace with Germany, but it also sprang from political dislike of the new regime and it had been hoped later that these troops would be able to link up with other anti-Bolshevik forces operating in the south and east of Russia. Winston Churchill had been particularly vehement over the need to intervene on this front. 'His ducal blood,' wrote Lloyd George, 'revolted against the wholesale elimination of Grand Dukes in Russia.'

In 1919, however, even Churchill had conceded that 'the invasion and occupation of Russia at the present time is not considered to be a practical proposition'[5] and after General Ironside had made one last unsuccessful effort to threaten St Petersburg, the Allied forces were withdrawn. In the same year the Poles under Pilsudski took the opportunity to push eastwards and looked eagerly for support from Great Britain and France, but Lloyd George and Clemenceau had by now agreed that they would not become involved in sending further aid to anti-Bolshevik elements, 'whether in the form of troops, war material or financial aid'.[6] In January 1920 the cabinet endorsed this decision.

So too did Labour, but their reactions to the situation in eastern Europe were rather more complex. The revolution of 1917 establishing the dictatorship of the Bolshevik party in Russia had finally divided the entire Social Democrat movement throughout Europe, and the anti-Bolshevik attitude of many of the left was firmly stated in a resolution passed by a large majority at an International Labour Conference held at Berne in January 1919: 'A reorganized society more and more permeated with Socialism cannot be realized, much less permanently established unless it rests upon triumphs of democracy and is rooted in the principles of liberty.'[7] The Labour party was entirely in accord with that view and was constantly to reject applications for affiliation made by the British Communist party, founded in 1920.

Nevertheless, for people of left-wing inclinations the recent events in Russia appeared to represent the beginnings of an attempt to create a

Socialist society, and although they might not wish to follow exactly the same course, they were bound to watch its development with a benign interest, knowing that its very existence was anathema to their own opponents. Consequently Labour's desire that there should be no intervention against Russia was based on emotional as well as practical grounds, and they were not absolutely convinced that the government was sincere in its declaration that there would be none.

Thus, when a new Polish offensive was launched at the end of April 1920 leading to the capture of Kiev, there were deep suspicions among most Labour MPs that the Poles had had some assistance from Great Britain. These were by no means allayed, when on 6 May Bonar Law assured the Commons that no moral or material support was being given; and they were very largely confirmed a fortnight later, when Ernest Bevin's London dockers refused to load munitions bound for Poland on a ship appropriately named the SS *Jolly George*.

Almost immediately afterwards the crisis came to a head with a new development in the course of the war. In June the Russians opened an offensive of their own, which the Poles were unable to check. Despite diplomatic pressure that Russia should rest content with the Curzon line (see p. 161), the Red Army pushed on far west of this and was soon threatening Warsaw. This reappearance of the Eastern Question under a Bolshevik guise at once altered the attitude of the Coalition government. The British and the French hastily conferred at Hythe and agreed to send supplies to the Poles, and on 5 August Lloyd George warned the Commons that military action might be necessary to preserve the independence of Poland.

At this point the Labour party and the TUC made their stand. On the same day as the Prime Minister's statement they announced the setting up of a Council of Action to use 'the whole industrial power of the organized workers' to prevent any military action by the government, and 350 local councils were established to implement the 'hands off Russia' movement. The unanimous belief among the members of the Council was that Poland had brought her troubles on herself and that Russia did not intend to destroy Polish independence. If the cabinet continued with its warlike attitude, then it must be incapacitated by a general strike, which, in the view of the *Daily Herald*, the Labour newspaper, would shatter the government in forty-eight hours.

In the event the matter was never put to the test. The Poles, who had now received support from the French, mounted a counterattack on 16 August, won the battle of the Vistula and pushed the Russians back far east of the Curzon line to a point where the frontier was eventually established after an armistice signed at Riga in October 1920. Thus the question was settled before the British had embarked on any intervention.

It is clear that the change in the military situation rather than threats of an industrial stoppage had been the decisive factor in the ending of the crisis. In any case, it does not seem that the great support for the Council of Action represented a purely working-class solidarity. A secret Intelligence report at the time stated: 'on every hand ex-servicemen are saying that they will never take part in any war again',[8] and this prevailing emotion spread far beyond the bounds of any sectional interest or any particular political allegiance. Labour persisted, however, in the claim that they had demonstrated their collective power to hold the government in check and this new confidence was to play its part in the events of 1921.

In the autumn of 1920 the conflict shifted back to more familiar territory. A new pay claim by the miners gained only hesitant support from the other two groups of the triple alliance, but the government authorized a temporary increase, at the same time taking advantage of the situation to strengthen their hand for the future with the passing of the Emergency Powers Act.

It seemed likely that they would soon have need of it. Already in December 1919 the financial authorities, alarmed at the rapidly growing inflation, had restricted note issue and in the following April raised the Bank rate to 7 per cent. Unfortunately the effect of these measures coincided with the collapse of the short postwar boom. The recovery of shipping and peacetime trade had ended the scarcity of foodstuffs and raw materials, and the index number of prices, which had stood at 265 in April 1920, fell to 155 in 1921 and to 131 in 1922. This new recession was naturally accompanied by a sharp rise in unemployment; the 619,000 of December 1920 had increased to two million by June 1921 and did not drop to 1·5 million until a year later.

At this point, on 15 February 1921, the government announced the restoration of the control of the mines to the owners. This was part of their policy of dismantling of wartime apparatus and would also relieve them of an unprofitable commitment. The owners, aware of dwindling markets (see p. 213) and uncompetitive prices, at once declared substantial reductions in wages. The Miners' Federation, now faced with a double challenge over pay and nationalization, insisted on a national pool of wages which might protect the living standards of the miners. The owners rejected this and imposed a lock-out on 1 April, whereupon the Miners' Federation called a strike and appealed to the railwaymen and transport workers of the 'triple alliance'. The Council of Action in the previous year had suggested to enthusiasts that working-class solidarity was strong enough to challenge the government's foreign policy; now surely it could deal effectively with the mine-owners. The government's response to this at the end of March was to proclaim a state of emergency.

The executives of the other unions of the 'triple alliance' were sympathetic, but nervous. They feared the full implications of a national struggle; they were doubtful over the outcome of negotiations, when they were not in a position to control the miners' demands, and there was even a lack of unanimity within the Federation—Herbert Smith, the president, uncompromising; Frank Hodges, the secretary, seeking a more flexible approach. On 8 April 1921, however, the leaders of the alliance did agree to a strike in cooperation with the miners, which was to begin on 12 April. It was a reluctant decision, and when negotiations were reopened, they postponed the date until Friday 15 April. Then on 14 April there seemed a further chance of escape, when Frank Hodges suggested at a meeting of MPs that the miners would probably accept a temporary settlement, while the question of a national pool was under discussion, and Lloyd George at once gave strong support to the proposal. When the miners' executive rejected this by one vote, the other unions were quick to seize on the excuse that this decision was unreasonable, and on 15 April they finally called off the strike with which they had promised to support the miners.

Black Friday might well seem the death knell of the hopes for a united working-class movement crushing the resistance of the employers. 'A wasteful futility', Beatrice Webb called it in her diary. 'The trade union officials are not "fit to govern"; they are not even equal to their own extremely limited business of collective bargaining with the strike or the sanction.'[9] The momentary unanimity over the Polish war had been misleading, for it had drawn support from a nationwide warweariness. Now the purely industrial contest over miners' pay revealed all the uncertainties of establishing a firm front with other large unions. It revealed, too, the almost total lack of practical preparation for combined action. There was no central organizing or negotiating body which could speak with authority or fight a general campaign, and when the crucial moment arrived, the 'triple alliance' was shown to be no more than a friendly arrangement based largely on wishful thinking.

For the miners the strike went on until June 1921 when they were forced to surrender to the employers' terms, although later government intervention in the form of subsidies and agreements over wages and profits did something to make the situation more tolerable. Among the workers the abandoning of the miners caused considerable recrimination and J. H. Thomas, whose natural flamboyance had brought him to the fore, was assailed as a Judas, although he had been by no means alone in his doubts; Ernest Bevin had been equally opposed to taking action. The whole affair had illustrated the two attitudes contained in the world of trade unionism: the one which saw the work as an unrelenting struggle between employer and employee, the other which regarded their organizations as national structures whose power must be matched with restraint and responsibility, aiming essentially at partnership rather than conflict.

This defeat for the working-class movement, coupled with the growth of unemployment, made short work of the subsequent intermittent strikes over falling wages. There were demonstrations by the unemployed in many northern towns, and in November 1922 the first hunger march on London. All was in vain and there seemed no way of shaking the Coalition government from pursuing a predominantly Conservative policy. All thought of shifting the system of wartime controls on to a permanent basis of nationalization was abandoned. After the mines the railways were handed back to private ownership in August 1921, although the many private companies were to be amalgamated into four great systems—the Great Western, the Southern, the London, Midland and Scottish, and the London and North-Eastern—a parallel to the unsuccessful Duckham proposal for the mines. The agricultural wages board, the trade boards of 1909 to investigate sweated labour, and the Civil Service arbitration board all disappeared in a holocaust of wage-fixing apparatus.

At the same time a cry was raised by the Conservatives that the economic depression necessitated cuts in governmental expenditure. In February 1922 a committee under Sir Eric Geddes proposed a series of ruthless economies, and government departments, whose size represented for some a form of Socialist bureaucracy, fell away before the Geddes 'axe'. Only a few features of the developing machinery of state were spared in this onslaught. Five new ministries survived—Air, Pensions, Health, Labour and the Forestry Commission as well as the Medical Research Council and the Electricity Commission. The Rent Acts of 1915 and 1920, protecting tenants from eviction or unreasonable increases in rent, held firm until their repeal by the Conservatives in 1957.

The Education Act of 1918, devised by H. A. L. Fisher, was less fortunate. Fisher had established a general school-leaving age of fourteen, allowing local authorities the option of raising it to fifteen. There were also to be part-time 'continuation' schools beyond the age of fourteen, nursery schools and an additional two hundred state scholarships to send poorer boys to the universities. The Geddes axe played havoc with much of this, cutting back school building, wiping out the 'continuation' schools and the new state scholarships, and depriving local authorities of their option over the school-leaving age. At the end all that remained of the Fisher Act was free universal education up to the age of fourteen.

Lloyd George could, however, claim credit for at least two measures which pointed in the other direction. He had been determined that the promise of 'homes fit for heroes' should be honoured, and in 1919 Dr Addison, the Minister of Health, drew up the Bill that was to put this into effect. In form the Housing and Town Planning Act was an echo of much nineteenth-century social legislation in that its working was initially based on the local authorities, who were to carry out surveys of their housing needs and then to proceed with an appropriate building programme. The general scope of the plan, however, was far beyond the means of any local authority and the bulk of the cost was to be borne by the Exchequer, apart from what could be raised by an extra penny ($\frac{1}{2}$p) on local rates. This financial involvement enabled the minister to demand that council houses should be equipped with baths, despite remarks that the poor would only keep the coal in them, and rents were fixed with an eye to the tenant's ability to pay, ranging from 5 shillings (25p) a week in rural areas to 12 shillings (60p) a week in parts of London. An additional subsidy was made available for private enterprise builders who were prepared to undertake similar construction.

The theoretical implications of the Act were startling. The provision of adequate housing as a governmental responsibility seemed a total departure from the Victorian ethic of self-help. In all, Addison was able to build 213,000 houses, a considerable achievement but inadequate to meet a demand that was constantly increasing, since young men were no longer held back from early matrimony by life in the trenches. Unfortunately Addison was not allowed to complete his task. Rightly in a hurry to build, he had been doing so at the time of the boom, when prices were high, and as the cry of government extravagance was raised, Lloyd George disowned his colleague; Addison was forced from office and the subsidies duly ended, ironically at a moment when the ensuing slump would have reduced the cost of building by more than half.

The second assumption of governmental responsibility lay in the field of unemployment insurance. The Act of 1911 had restricted the scheme to the building, engineering and shipbuilding trades, although during the war it had been extended to all who were working in trades relevant to the war effort. Now in 1920 a new Act covered all wage-earners except non-manual workers earning more than £250 a year, civil servants, soldiers, school-teachers, farm labourers and domestic servants. The employer, the employee and the state contributed between them a sum of 10 pence (4p) a week and this entitled the worker to an unemployment benefit of 15 shillings (75p) a week for a maximum of fifteen weeks in any single year, provided that he had genuinely tried to find work and that at least twelve contributions had been paid.

As in 1911, this was an excellent solution to the problem of casual unemployment; it was no answer to a long-drawn-out depression with unemployed numbering two million by June 1921. Once the fifteen weeks had expired, a man could only resort to Poor Law relief, which was financed by a local rate. In the poorer areas, where unemployment was heaviest, boroughs were simply incapable of coping with this burden, and in London the borough of Poplar, whose council was controlled by Labour, challenged the government by paying 33 shillings (£1.65p) for a man and his wife and financed this by refusing to pay the contribution that they owed to the London County Council—an act of defiance which led to the mayor, George Lansbury, and the thirty councillors being sent to prison for a month.

The government might not wish to tolerate the independent action of the Poplar councillors. They were, nevertheless, soon to be driven to instituting something very similar on a national scale. With more than a million people dependent on outdoor relief from the Poor Law it was decided in 1921 that the Exchequer should finance 'unconvenanted benefit' for two periods of sixteen weeks each. Dependants' allowances were also introduced; these were so small—a weekly sum of 5 shillings (25p) for a wife and 1 shilling (5p) for every child—that Labour MPs walked out of the House in protest, when it was proposed. Nevertheless, although the 'unconvenanted benefits' were in theory supposed to be an advance to be covered by future contributions, the plain fact was that the government had departed radically from the basis of the earlier schemes. 'Unconvenanted benefit' was a form of national dole responding to human need rather than the mathematical calculations of an insurance policy operating on an actuarial basis, and, as with the Housing Act, the cost of this was to be shouldered by the whole country rather than by the local area of residence.*

The implications of these measures may have seemed revolutionary; in their immediate consequences, however, their effect was mainly con-

* There were a number of technical alterations in the operating of the scheme in subsequent years, including the name of the benefit which later became 'extended', and then 'transitional'.

servative. They made unemployment just bearable; malnutrition and
enforced idleness were less likely to lead to open revolution than the
prospect of outright starvation might have done. Society as a whole,
reckoning complacently that the workless had only themselves to blame
and that they had been dealt with generously, could now accept the
existence of a mass of unemployed as a fact of life. Declining industries,
sure of a pool of cheap labour, could linger on, and the trade unions,
who by the end of 1921 had already spent £7 million in unemployment
relief and whose membership by 1925 had dropped to 5·5 million, had
now to walk warily, conscious of the precariousness of all employment.
It was indeed a new age, but one remote from the hopes that had
sustained men in the trenches of the western front.

17

The Irish Question

'The mode and thought of men, the whole outlook on affairs, the grouping of parties, all have encountered violent and tremendous changes in the deluge of the world,' said Winston Churchill in 1922, 'but as the deluge subsides and the waters fall, we see the dreary steeples of Fermanagh and Tyrone emerging once again.'[1] As John Bright had said of Russia in another context, Ireland was always there. And now to the complications of international settlement and industrial unrest that beset the Coalition government there was to be added the bitterness of an Irish war of independence.

John Redmond, the leader of the Irish nationalist party in the House of Commons until his death in 1918, had once warned that 'if the constitutional movement in Ireland disappears, the Prime Minister will find himself face to face with the revolutionary movement and he will have to govern Ireland by the naked sword'. This is precisely what happened. A convention summoned by Lloyd George in 1917 had produced no concrete results, the Home Rule Act remained inoperative and in the general election of 1918 the Irish Nationalist party, lacking anything to show by way of recent achievement, was almost entirely eclipsed. Immediate outright independence was the promise of Sinn Fein, and they won seventy-three seats, including ten in Ulster, whereas John Dillon, Redmond's successor, gained only seven and failed to be returned himself. If national self-determination rested on a majority vote, the Irish had established an overwhelming case for independence.

This was the last constitutional move made by Sinn Fein. In their election programme they had stated that they would immediately secede from Westminster, and although forty of the elected candidates were still under preventive arrest after the extension of conscription to Ireland in 1918, a rump of twenty-seven Sinn Feiners met in January 1919 in the Mansion House in Dublin. Here they established themselves as the parliament of Ireland—the Dail Eireann—under the presidency of Charles Burgess, who amid the surge of national fervour had translated his name into the Irish form of Cathal Brugha. They issued a unilateral declaration of independence, ratified the proclamation of Saorstat Eireann—the Irish republic of the Easter Rising (see p. 116)—and promptly sent delegates to Paris as representatives of a separate sovereign state, although Lloyd George was able to persuade President Wilson to withhold recognition on the grounds that this was a manifestation of a purely domestic upheaval.

By the spring of 1918 the Dail numbered fifty-two after the release of the Irish from prison and the new government had acquired an armed force through the transforming of the Irish Nationalist Volunteers (see p. 77) into the Irish Republican Army (IRA) with Michael Collins as its director of organization. Collins, who later distinguished himself as a magnetic and capable leader of the resistance movement, carried out his first coup in engineering the escape of Eamon de Valera from Lincoln jail. De Valera had been a leader in the Easter Rising of 1916, but had been saved from execution by his American citizenship, and now on his return to Ireland became president of the Dail in place of Cathal Brugha.

At a governmental level Sinn Fein continued to emphasize the independence of Ireland. No report was sent to the English local government board, new Irish courts of law were set up and de Valera departed on a propaganda tour of the United States. This last naturally won immense support from the Irish-American section of the population but it proved a disappointment to extreme anti-British sentiment, since de Valera was cautious over the extent to which Ireland would break off international relations with Great Britain, once her independence had been recognized, and he talked of the possibility of an Anglo-Irish treaty along the lines of the existing treaty between the USA and Cuba.

At the same time Collins had raised funds for the purchase of arms and there now began a long period of sporadic attacks on the Royal Irish Constabulary and the British Army in Ireland. Neither of these bodies could cope with a guerrilla war in which their assailants, not wearing uniform, concentrated on ambushes and isolated killings, melting away afterwards amid a local population that was almost entirely sympathetic. It was a pattern of warfare which the Boers had developed after their formal resistance had been broken, one with which the world was to become increasingly familiar in the twentieth century. The Royal Irish Constabulary, stationed in small units scattered over the whole country, were particularly vulnerable and by the spring of 1920 they had been forced very largely to evacuate the south and west of Ireland.

At first the British government had been too preoccupied to take much notice, but as Sinn Fein seemed to be settling down to a *fait accompli*, demand for an active suppression of the movement began to make itself heard from the Conservatives in the cabinet, as well as from Sir Edward Carson and Sir Henry Wilson, Chief of the Imperial General Staff. In August 1919 Sinn Fein and the Dail were declared illegal; Sir Hamar Greenwood, who was appointed Irish Secretary in April 1920, proceeded to create an auxiliary division consisting of ex-officers and to reinforce the Royal Irish Constabulary by recruiting ex-servicemen, who with their khaki uniforms and black belts became known as the Black and Tans.

For some twelve months the IRA and the Black and Tans fought a merciless war, as martial law was declared in one county after another. Much of the literature inspired by this unhappy period came from the Irish side. The poems of Yeats, the plays of Sean O'Casey and the stories of O'Flaherty later captured the pathos as well as the brutality of war; at the time, the accounts of Erskine Childers, the author of *The Riddle of the Sands* (see p. 51), an Englishman who had thrown in his lot with the Irish, depicted more immediately the savagery of the Black and Tans. The British had the advantage of numbers—40,000 in 1920 against 15,000 IRA, of whom only a third could be active at one time; the Irish had the advantage of local support and information about British moves through leakages at almost every level. It was a war of espionage and betrayal, a war whose horror lacked the anonymity of the western front and became a personal vendetta of revenge among the combatants, in which civilians often suffered and few prisoners were taken. In all, 230 British were killed and three times that number of Irish.

Lloyd George was still confident that he could win. 'We have murder by the throat,' he said in November 1920, but apart from military suppression, the precise nature of a solution to the Irish question remained as obscure as ever. In the course of the year the government did at least make another attempt to devise one: the Government of Ireland Act, which was finally passed in December 1920. This measure took the step of decreeing partition: two parliaments with powers of separate government for northern and southern Ireland, centred respectively on Belfast and Dublin. Northern Ireland was to consist of the six Ulster counties, Armagh, Antrim, Down, Derry, Fermanagh and Tyrone, thus excluding the other three Donegal, Monaghan and Cavan with their strong Roman Catholic majorities. The two Irelands were still to be within the United Kingdom with a reduced representation at

Westminster; they were separate, yet there was to be a Council of Ireland to deal jointly with matters such as railways, fisheries and contagious diseases, and the hope was expressed that most of these measures would be temporary, a preliminary to the establishment of a united government for the whole country.

The ingenuity of the Act only succeeded in disappointing both Ulster and the South. Neither side cared for partition. Ulster wanted a continuation of the nineteenth-century system; Sinn Fein would only hear of total independence for all Ireland. The practical reactions, however, were different. Sinn Fein ignored the Act. Ulster reluctantly accepted it, since it did at least free them from the threat of rule from Dublin. 'We, therefore, have made up our minds,' wrote Carson to Birkenhead in November 1920, 'that in the interests of Ireland, Great Britain and the empire the best and only solution of the question is to accept the present Bill and to endeavour to work it loyally.'[2]

Thus, out of this stage of the imbroglio there did emerge the system whereby Northern Ireland was to be governed for the next fifty years. The north accordingly went ahead with elections in May 1921; forty Unionists were returned and Sir James Craig became prime minister. Twelve Sinn Feiners were also elected. These included such figures as de Valera, Collins and Arthur Griffith—largely a gesture of defiance, but still significant, since it pointed to the presence of the Roman Catholic population included within the six counties of Northern Ireland. In the South Sinn Fein mocked the whole thing by holding their own elections for a new Dail, in which they gained 124 out of the 128 seats.

Meanwhile, the war dragged on and as the stories of atrocities and counter atrocities spread and the activities of the Black and Tans became increasingly discredited, British public opinion, already sickened by the long years of the western front, began to demand a political settlement. Liberal newspapers were understandably opposed to the war and in February 1921 Asquith demanded a truce, as the Labour party had already done in the previous month. More striking, Conservative opinion was beginning to move in the same direction. The Northcliffe press took up the cry, Wickham Steed, the editor of *The Times*, being particularly concerned that Anglo-American relations might suffer; similarly, Lord Beaverbrook,* the apostle of the British Empire, was anxious over offending Irish elements in Canada and Australia.

King George V himself had watched the events in Ireland with growing distress. 'It seems to his Majesty', wrote Lord Stamfordham, 'that in punishing the guilty we are inflicting punishment no less severe upon

* Sir Max Aitken's title since December 1916.

the innocent.'³ As a constitutional sovereign he was of course largely powerless, but after a conversation with General Smuts, it did seem that there was one contribution that he could make and on 22 June 1921, when he opened the first Belfast parliament elected under the Government of Ireland Act, he uttered a deeply felt appeal for peace and reason.

These pressures on the government at home were matched by anxieties felt by the leaders of Sinn Fein. By now they were uneasily aware of a movement towards agrarian Socialism that was growing among their rank and file. More particularly, they knew that they could not keep up an effective fight much longer; the IRA had virtually exhausted their ammunition and Collins admitted afterwards that they could not have lasted another three weeks. Thus by July 1921 both sides were ready to talk and after insisting that this must be preceded by a truce, de Valera himself came to London under a safe conduct.

The peculiar problem for Lloyd George was that a settlement with the Sinn Fein might so shock Conservative sentiment that it would wreck the Coalition on which his political position depended. Despite the swing in public opinion there were many Conservative supporters of Ulster who resented the very idea of negotiation and could not accept the thought that a Prime Minister, who the previous November had claimed to have murder by the throat, should now apparently be prepared to take it by the hand.

Lloyd George's hopes for finding a way out of this quandary were based on an offer of Dominion status for Ireland, on condition that the six counties of Ulster were excluded and remained part of the United Kingdom. This might come sufficiently close to the Government of Ireland Act to avoid a split in the cabinet and he worked hard to bring Birkenhead and Churchill round to his way of thinking. In one respect he was fortunate in that Bonar Law, whose views on Ireland had not changed since his active and somewhat questionable support of Ulster in 1912, had retired for reasons of health in March 1921 and had been replaced as leader of the Conservative party by Austen Chamberlain, who would certainly do his utmost to preserve the Coalition.

Sinn Fein did not prove so amenable, and in their conversations Lloyd George's position was weakened by the truce which de Valera had shrewdly demanded, as once this had been announced it was unlikely that British opinion as a whole would accept a return to a policy of force. Thus the negotiations were like a game of poker, each playing for high stakes from a poor hand. Both threatened a renewal of hostilities if the talks broke down, and each knew that in his own case he would hardly be able to carry out the threat.

The initial exchanges made little headway. De Valera was unimpressed by the idea of Dominion status, preferring simply 'external association', and in any case was determined to be on his guard against the wily charm of the Prime Minister. 'Negotiating with De Valera,' complained Lloyd George, 'is like trying to pick up mercury with a fork.' De Valera suggested that he should use a spoon, but by the end of this first round nothing had been agreed and de Valera returned to Ireland.

In October, after an effort to reopen the discussions, a new Irish delegation of five, including Griffith and Collins, came to London. This time de Valera stayed in Ireland, probably because he wished to be in a position to keep a check from Dublin on any eventual proposals. The team which Lloyd George selected to confront them included Austen Chamberlain, Sir Hamar Greenwood, Birkenhead and Winston Churchill. The presence of Greenwood, who was naturally hated by the Irish, was likely to be an embarrassment, but in fact relations remained cordial and it was not long before Birkenhead and Churchill had conceived a most remarkable friendship and respect for Collins and Griffith.

Personal relationships, however, did not make the struggle any easier. Lloyd George clung fervently to the idea of Dominion status, which he regarded as vital for the military and naval defence of Great Britain, and to gain this he was prepared at one moment even to consider a trial period during which Ulster would be under the rule of Dublin. In Belfast Sir James Craig, to whom the suggestion was communicated on 10 November, naturally found it totally unacceptable, as did Bonar Law, who had now returned from abroad. Conservatives generally reacted with vociferous alarm and the life of the Coalition seemed to hang in the balance. In the House of Commons Lloyd George had to fight off attacks on the government, and in the middle of November it took all the efforts of Austen Chamberlain and Birkenhead to hold down a revolt at the Conservative party conference at Liverpool.

The Conservatives could not be ignored and Lloyd George now swung back to coercing the Irish into acceptance of the exclusion of Ulster. He used bluff—the threat of war; he used deceptive hints—a suggestion through Tom Jones to Collins that a revision of the boundaries would leave Ulster so small that she would be unable to remain outside southern Ireland. Finally, at 7.30 in the evening of 5 December he presented his ultimatum with characteristic panache. 'I have to communicate with Sir James Craig tonight: here are the alternative letters I have prepared—one enclosing the articles of agreement reached by His Majesty's Government and yourselves, the other saying that the Sinn Fein representatives refuse the oath of allegiance and refuse to come within the Empire. If I send this letter, it is war, and war in three days. Which letter am I to send?'⁴ Some five hours later after anguished debate the Irish delegates came back to Downing Street to give their consent and in the early hours of the morning the agreement was signed.

The terms of the settlement were very simple and not unreasonable, indicative of the way in which the route to the commonsense solution in politics is usually by a winding stair. In return for the recognition of the Irish Free State the Irish accepted Dominion status and the swearing of an oath of allegiance to the Crown. They were to be liable to a share of the public debt of the United Kingdom. Coastal defence was to be in British hands for the next five years, after which the Navy was to have the use of the harbour of Berehaven, Queenstown, Lough Swilly and Belfast Lough. Ulster was allowed one month during which she could contract out of the Irish Free State and in that event the boundary commission, to which Lloyd George had referred, would define the frontier of Northern Ireland.

At Westminster the settlement caused no difficulties. Bonar Law had not seriously intended to destroy the Coalition, only to use the threat as a means of saving Ulster from southern Irish rule. The Irish treaty satisfied him on that score at least and the House of Commons ratified the agreement by 401 votes to 58. In the Lords there were angry exchanges between Carson and Birkenhead, but here too the government gained a large majority. Thus, at the end of the most brutal period of Anglo-Irish relations the knot seemed at last to have been unravelled and Lloyd George had avoided the disaster which had overcome so many British governments attempting to handle the Irish problem in the past.

In Northern Ireland the Belfast government exercised its right to opt out of the Irish Free State the day after the treaty was signed and continued to work under the arrangements of the Government of Ireland Act. In the Irish Free State the troubles were not yet over. De Valera would not accept partition and when in January 1922 the Dail ratified the treaty by a narrow margin, he resigned and was succeeded by Arthur Griffith as President.

For the next year southern Ireland was torn by a civil war between the Treatyites, as they were called, and the IRA. Once again it was a war of ambushes, conspiracy and betrayal, and in the course of it many of the leading figures succumbed. Griffith died of heart failure; Cathal Brugha was killed; so, too, was Michael Collins, as he himself had predicted. 'I may have signed my actual death warrant,' he had said to Birkenhead on that memorable night in Downing Street, when agreement had been reached. For once the British were not involved, although there was an echo of the Irish question, when Sir Henry Wilson, now no longer CIGS, was shot down in a London street by IRA gunmen. Throughout the upheavals, however, the Dail continued to work out its new constitution, which was approved by the British parliament in December 1922, and a few months later, in May 1923, de Valera decided to accept the situation and issued a proclamation of truce.

There was still to come one last twist in the story which might well seem to vindicate his mistrust of the settlement. In 1925, when Lloyd George was no longer in power and a Conservative government ruled in Great Britain, the boundary commission on which Collins had pinned his faith proved a disappointment for the Irish Free State. It made little change to the frontier of Northern Ireland and the six counties remained largely intact. For years to come this was to be a source of grievance among southern Irish nationalists, who in any case resented the whole idea of partition. And in Ulster the presence of a Roman Catholic minority was watched carefully by the Belfast government, relying on the arrangement of electoral constituencies and a franchise dependent on a property qualification to reduce the efficacy of the Catholic vote. Lloyd George might reckon that he had solved the Irish question; Protestant and Catholic Irishmen appeared unlikely to see it in quite the same light.

18

The Aftermath of Peace-making

1. The Middle East and India

In the summer of 1918 the Senate of the United States refused to ratify the Treaty of Versailles. This withdrawal from the affairs of Europe, as well as from President Wilson's own scheme for a League of Nations, marked the opening of a new period of American isolationism. The British sometimes deplored this abandoning of world responsibilities; yet in effect it came close to their own attitude. Throughout most of the nineteenth century Great Britain had been wary of any political commitment on the Continent and it was only the challenge of German power before the war that had drawn her reluctantly into Europe. She had had nothing to gain there and now that the German threat appeared to be extinguished, British governments would have liked nothing better than to have returned to a nineteenth-century policy of detachment. For the general public the loss of three-quarters of a million dead meant simply that involvement did not pay. In government circles there was a different motive. Victory in Europe should now free Great Britain to concentrate on her true centre of interest—the defence of India and the control of the oilfields in the Middle East.

The end of the war had brought Great Britain to a more powerful position in southern Asia than ever before, since the partition of the Turkish empire had given her the opportunity to establish a direct control over Iraq (the new name for Mesopotamia) and Palestine. This preponderance was to be hampered by two factors. The first was of long standing. Throughout the nineteenth century the security of India and, much later, the development of oil had meant an inevitable mistrust of intrigue by the Russians along their southern frontiers in Asia. Anxiety over Persia, Afghanistan and Tibet had been allayed by the Anglo-Russian entente of 1907, but this had only come about at a time when the attitude of the Central European Powers had suggested a greater danger. Once that danger had gone, the earlier concern over Russia was bound to revive, and, the collapse of Turkey had made it imperative for Great Britain to establish herself in Arab territory before others anticipated her there. Fear plays as great a part as greed in the acquisition of empire, and apprehension over the consequences of a power vacuum loomed large in British calculations; it helped to draw her into the Middle East, and when after the Second World War she no longer had the strength to remain, it left her worried and unsure, inspiring one last unhappy effort to return with the ill-fated Suez expedition of 1956 (see p. 427).

The second more recent complication was the spread of the doctrine of national self-determination. If there was still to be empire, it must be empire in a new guise, unrepressive, conciliatory, and masking itself behind phrases such as 'a mandate from the League of Nations'. Any failure in this direction could only mean that the new governments of the Middle East would eventually turn to Russia. The history of the Balkans before the war had shown too well how small countries could depend for survival on playing off one great Power against another, and the balkanization of the Middle East was not likely to prove any exception.

In the territories which Great Britain and France had gained from the Turkish empire (map, p. 203) there was trouble almost at once. In Syria and the Lebanon the French were particularly nervous over the cry of Arab nationalism, which might find some response in their North African possessions, and after falling out with King Feisal, they finally evicted him from Damascus in 1920 and set up instead a highly paternalist system of rule over the whole area. In Iraq the British were faced with a similar outburst of unrest, when the Iraqui suspected that they had merely exchanged one imperial master for another. There was, too, the further difficulty which the Balfour declaration had created for the British by establishing the Jewish National Home in Palestine. For the Arabs, many of whom still lived there, this was not merely an intrusion; the growing volume of Jewish immigration made it also a threat, and from now on the Holy Land was likely to be a scene of unholy turmoil, always bedevilling Anglo-Arab relations.

Military power enabled the British to suppress the outbreak in Iraq, but could not in itself supply a satisfactory political solution. This was to be the task of Winston Churchill, who was moved from the War Office to the Colonial Office in February 1921 with responsibility for Middle Eastern affairs. Churchill went to Cairo and among others took with him T. E. Lawrence, who had previously retired in high dudgeon to a fellowship at All Souls'. They succeeded in negotiating a settlement so adroit that British interests on this part of the Middle East were to remain reasonably secure for the next twenty-five years. Feisal, who had acquired the image of a martyr to western imperialism, was made King of Iraq, despite the anger of the French, and another of Lawrence's wartime companions, Nuri-el-Said Pasha, was to act as his chief adviser, all on the understanding that there would be a swift advance to absolute independence. British troops were mostly withdrawn, while a more unobtrusive hold was to be maintained through a few scattered Air Force bases. In this way the government attempted to work in harmony with Arab nationalism, which they hoped might acquire a pro-British flavour at Baghdad, where the King and the richer middle class would realize the value of continuing to work in conjunction with Great Britain.

Peace in these regions was still endangered by the constant raiding across the indeterminate area of the inland frontier of the Jewish National Home in Palestine. The immediate need seemed to be definition and control, and in 1922 the British carved out of the eastern region of Palestine a new Arab kingdom, the Trans-Jordan, under Abdullah, Feisal's elder brother. This was to act both as a buffer between Iraq and Palestine and as a means of containing the expanding area of Jewish settlement; and for the time being it completed the organization of the recent British gains from the Turkish empire.

Technically Egypt had also been a part of that empire and the British position there had always been somewhat anomalous. The idea that they were holding it as a mandate from the Turkish Sultan had long ceased to be even a fiction, but they had continued to govern, while denying that they were in formal occupation at all. During the war Egypt had been declared a protectorate, but it was unlikely that this would go unchallenged; like the Irish, the Egyptian nationalists reckoned that national self-determination began at home, and in March 1919, after the British had refused to accept a separate Egyptian delegation at the Paris peace conference, a revolt broke out which could only be suppressed by a proclamation of martial law.

Ideally the British wanted a solution on the pattern they eventually achieved in Iraq. In August 1920 Lord Milner suggested a scheme to Zaghlul Pasha, the nationalist leader, whereby Great Britain would recognize the independence of Egypt, if she were allowed 'such rights as are necessary to safeguard her special interests'. This, of course, referred to the Suez Canal and would entail the stationing of British troops in specified localities in Egypt. This proved unacceptable to the Egyptians. In July 1921 conversations were resumed between Lord Curzon and Adly Pasha, the Egyptian prime minister, and it is possible that Curzon would have reached agreement but for the resistance of his colleagues.

'The cabinet are all much stiffer than I am in the matter,' he wrote to his wife, 'and I am sure that we shall have an absolute rupture with another Ireland in Egypt.'[1]

Ultimately negotiations broke down and Adly Pasha resigned. A new Egyptian ministry was formed on the understanding that the protectorate had been abolished, but in March 1922 Curzon published a manifesto stating that, until a treaty had been signed to this effect, matters concerning the defence of Egypt and the administration of the Sudan were 'absolutely reserved to the discretion of His Majesty's Government'. This was followed by a Note to foreign Powers warning them off any interference. Thus Egypt gained a limited independence, but was unable to rid herself of the presence of the British Army which remained to ensure that Curzon's Note was not merely an empty diplomatic gesture.

Untidy though the situation in Egypt might be, the Coalition government had on the whole been successful in blunting the edge of the various forms of Arab nationalism in the former territories of the Turkish empire; they could reckon that by a combination of tact and firmness they had devised an economical and effective system for safeguarding British interests in the Suez Canal and the oil wells of Iraq. In the territories that lay between Iraq and India their hopes of creating a corresponding sphere of influence were to be disappointed.

The Anglo-Russian convention of 1907 (see p. 84) had already recognized Afghanistan as a British sphere of influence and during the war the Amir, Habibullah, had remained sympathetic to the Allied cause. In February 1919, however, he was murdered and his son, Amanullah, reckoning that there was little now to be feared from Russia, embarked on an attack on India. This was totally routed by British forces, but the government in India was at this time so disturbed by domestic unrest that they sought an easy way out and formally abandoned all claim to control Afghan policy. Thus, in an astonishing way Amanullah gained political victory out of military defeat and at once used his new freedom to sign a treaty of friendship with Russia in February 1921.

Similarly, Persia was to escape from British control. The Persian government had every reason to regard the European Powers with suspicion. The Anglo-Russian convention had smacked of partition; in 1911 an agreement between Russia and Germany for linking the Baghdad railway with a future Persian railway had emphasized Russian control over the northern zone and the publication of tsarist secret treaties by the Bolsheviks in 1917 had revealed that the Anglo-Russian

Treaty of 1915 (see p. 113), promising Constantinople and the Straits for Russia, had also stipulated the inclusion of the neutral central zone of Persia within the British sphere of influence. Furthermore, although not a combatant during the war, Persia had become a battleground for Russian, British and German and Turkish forces and after her territory had been ravaged by all sides, found at the end that the British were virtually in occupation.

It was against this unfavourable background that Lord Curzon hoped to persuade the Persians to accept an arrangement which would establish yet another type of protectorate. In the cabinet the only voice of opposition was that of Edwin Montagu, the Secretary of State for India, who maintained that such a scheme would be an affront to Muslim feelings. Curzon, who regarded himself as an expert on Persia, felt that Montagu's objection was also an affront to himself. At the time Montagu gave way and in August 1919 the treaty was duly signed. Persia was recognized as an independent sovereign state, while Great Britain would supply her with officers to reorganize the Persian army, financial advisers, a loan of £2 million and assistance over the construction of railways. There were also promises that the Persian frontier would be revised and compensation paid for damage suffered during the war.

The Persian government had accepted all this on the assumption that Great Britain was the predominant power. It soon became apparent, however, from serious unrest in Ireland, Turkey, Egypt, Iraq and India, that this predominance was not entirely unquestioned, and before long Persia was made aware that Great Britain's old rival in this area was not to be discounted. In May 1920 the Russians moved across the Caspian to the southern shore and established a local government on Persian soil, which the British forces were not strong enough to dislodge. There was a natural conclusion to draw from this, and the Persian prime minister declared that the treaty of 1919 was 'in suspense'. Lord Curzon was very hurt, but there was little that he could do. The Russians followed up their move with the offer of extremely attractive terms, and in February 1921 Reza Khan, who had once served in the Cossack Brigade, carried out a coup in Teheran, setting himself up at the head of a new government. He wasted no time. The Anglo-Persian Treaty was finally denounced and a new treaty signed with Russia; and four years later, after driving out the reigning sovereign, Reza Khan established himself as the Shah of Persia.

Thus far, the Coalition government had been coping with the complications of a changed situation. In India very little had changed. The

Congress party and the British Raj had continued to gyrate in a reasonably friendly manner around the questions of developing greater autonomy and in August 1917 the British government had publicly committed itself to 'the progressive realization of responsible government in India as an integral part of the British Empire'. This was certainly the sincere hope of Edwin Montagu during his five years as Secretary of State for India, but as always the moderate view was harassed by the extremes on either side. The resident British in India with strong support in the Conservative party believed firmly in keeping the natives in their place; the Indian nationalists, growing increasingly powerful in the Congress party, thought only in terms of outright independence from foreign rule.

By this time the Congress party was coming increasingly under the leadership of Mahatma Gandhi, a wizened emaciated Indian lawyer, who with his toothless grin and simple dress combined the aura of an eastern holy man with the ambitions of a political agitator. His principal weapon for achieving independence was a policy of civil disobedience, which he insisted must always remain non-violent, and the British authorities now found themselves confronted with the irritation of a saintly obstructiveness. Gandhi's doctrine was a strange mixture of conservatism and radicalism; conservative, in that he thought that the future of India lay in small village communities which must be encouraged to develop their own rural industries, such as the spinning of cotton cloth; radical, in that he recognized that independence would hardly be feasible, unless there could be a reconciliation with the Muslims, and, among the Hindus, some modification of the caste system.

It was inevitable in the highly charged atmosphere of the postwar period that there should be trouble. In February 1919 Gandhi persuaded the Congress party to launch a programme of passive resistance. In the Punjab this became a good deal more than passive, with mob riots and attacks on buildings and British personnel. In April 1919, at Amritsar, General Dyer determined to restore order by opening fire on the crowd: 379 Indians were killed and over 1,000 wounded. Dyer maintained that he was not merely concerned to check the riot, but to set such an example as to end the outbreaks in other regions as well.

In fact, the episode merely hardened the hearts of many Indians against their imperialist rulers and proved a great support for the Congress party. The repercussions, however, went far beyond that. General Dyer was removed from his command by the commander-in-chief in India and placed on the retired list, but when Edwin Montagu confirmed this decision, the more imperialist section of the

Conservatives in the House of Commons rushed to Dyer's defence. They disliked Montagu anyway, because of his Jewish origin, and they mistrusted his attitude towards the future of India. In July 1920 there ensued a bitter debate in the House. Montagu was adamant. 'Are you going to keep your hold upon India by terrorism, racial humiliation and frightfulness,' he asked, 'or are you going to rest it upon the good will and the growing good will of the people of your Indian empire?' The cabinet supported him, and Bonar Law was able to calm the Conservatives sufficiently to get the House to agree to Dyer's retirement by 230 votes to 129—in contrast to the House of Lords, who backed Dyer with a majority of 43, declaring that his treatment was 'dangerous to the preservation of order in the face of rebellion'. The fierceness of the controversy only serves to illustrate the difficulties that confronted any politician attempting to handle the problem of India; the hopes for a liberal compromise seemed constantly to be at the mercy of the forces represented by Gandhi and Dyer.

For the moment, however, Montagu was able to press on with his plans. In 1918 a report which he had produced with Lord Chelmsford, the Viceroy, had outlined a new scheme of government and although this was later rejected by the Congress party, it formed the basis of the Government of India Act, which was passed in 1919. This was an attempt to establish the roots of parliamentary processes in Indian society, but it did leave a great deal of power still in the hands of the British. The central advisory council (see p. 58) was transformed into a two-chamber elective assembly representative of the Indian population, but its powers were extremely limited, as in matters of justice, police, finance and defence the executive remained responsible only to the Secretary of State for India. Some control over education and public works was, however, entrusted to the Indian ministers, who were to be responsible to eight provincial legislatures. It was a fairly cautious step forward along the road to self government—too cautious a step and too long a road in the view of the Congress party, who undid some of its full effect by boycotting the provincial elections, which thus failed to gather in the full potential of Indian political life.

'Would the peoples of India be happier if you ran the country?' the Prince of Wales, later George V, had asked when on a State visit to India in 1905. 'No, Sir, I do not say they would be happier,' replied the president of the Congress party at that time, 'but they would have more self-respect.'[2] This was the crux. British rule was not harsh, but it meant the presence of an upper class of British soldiers and civilians who kept themselves aloof with a galling sense of social superiority. The

memsahib and the club lay at the heart of British India; governmental
legislation might be framed in terms of gradual integration and, indeed,
in the administration got some way towards this; yet everyday life was
based on a nameless sense of *apartheid*. It was this feeling that E. M.
Forster captured in his novel *A Passage to India*. It was reflected, too, in
a comment by Edwin Montagu after a visit to India. 'Again I say that
the social question, the fact that civil servants are willing to work with
Indians, but not to play with them, the fact that Boxwallah will have
nothing to do with them has really brought the present political situation upon us.' These were the imponderables against which enlightened
politicians had to work; on the one side, the excitements of mob
violence; on the other, what an English novelist described as the tone of
a woman's voice which has destroyed empires.

2. Naval power and the Far East

On 21 June 1919, one week before the signing of the Treaty of
Versailles, the German High Seas Fleet, interned at Scapa Flow, sank
to the bottom, scuttled on the orders of its commander, Admiral von
Reuter. Thus dramatically a major factor in the worsening of Anglo-
German relations before the war had literally disappeared from sight.
For the British Admiralty, however, the fundamental problem of maintaining naval predominance in the world was still acute. Japan, another
island empire, had acquired the Marshall, Caroline and Mariana
archipelagoes previously held by Germany, and the planning of a large
postwar shipbuilding programme seemed likely to make her the principal naval power in the central and western Pacific. By the end of the
war the United States, too, had established a naval strength that she did
not intend to relinquish, and in December 1920 the British Admiralty,
who since the turn of the century had serious doubts over their ability to
maintain the 'two power' principle (see p. 48), was now forced to con-
fess that 'the utmost we can hope for in the near future is to possess a fleet
as large as that of any other single Power'. It remained to be seen whether
financial stringency would allow even this 'one power' standard.

One solution, already proposed in June 1918 at an Imperial War
Conference, had been the pooling of the Dominions' navies under an
imperial naval authority, but this was rejected by the Dominions' prime
ministers, who felt that it would infringe their own independence. They
did, however, agree on the need for cooperation and in 1919 Lord
Jellicoe embarked on a long tour of investigation to India, South Africa,
Australia, New Zealand and Canada, ending with a short visit to

Washington. Much of Jellicoe's reports assumed the possibility of eventual war with Japan, and although the Admiralty did not act immediately on many of his suggestions, the construction of a naval base at Singapore was considered with an eye to the defence of the whole of the Far East and, in particular, of Hong Kong.

Most of these issues formed the agenda of another Imperial Conference which was opened in London in June 1921, but no agreement was reached on any of them. In discussion over the question of the Anglo-Japanese alliance, which was due shortly to expire, Australia and New Zealand favoured its renewal, while Canada insisted that it should end. Similarly, although the principle of cooperation was reiterated, little was settled over the distribution of the expense of a combined naval policy. Thus, when in July President Harding of the United States issued an invitation to the major naval Powers for a conference at Washington on the limitation of armament, this seemed to provide a happy excuse for deferring any statement of conclusions.

The main motive behind the American proposal was not merely the fear of Japanese power in the Pacific, but also the need to prevent a renewal of the Anglo-Japanese alliance which would otherwise force the United States to outbuild the combined fleets of Great Britain and Japan. The Washington conference, which Balfour attended as the British delegate, was consequently concerned with replacing this alliance with a four-power treaty between the United States, Great Britain, Japan and France, laying down an agreed ratio for the size of their respective navies. The ratio of tonnage for capital ships was eventually settled at: USA 5, Great Britain 5 and Japan 3, with France and Italy at 1·75 each—a limitation which the French only accepted after some dispute. In effect, by 1925 after the Powers had slimmed down their fleets in accordance with the treaty, the British had a total tonnage in capital ships of 580,450, the Americans 525,800 and the Japanese 301,320.

The conference established a similar ratio for aircraft-carriers, although slightly higher for France and Italy, and an upper limit of 10,000 tons per ship for battle-cruisers, but could arrive at no similar arrangements over submarines, largely because of the obduracy of the French. In the Pacific the Japanese island possessions of Formosa, the Pescadores and southern Sakhalin, as well as the recently acquired German islands, were to remain unfortified, on the understanding that the United States would not fortify the Philippines and Guam, nor the British Hong Kong, although there was to be a special exemption for Singapore (map, p. 379).

The Washington conference may thus be regarded as a landmark in the history of twentieth-century Britain. First, she had now officially admitted the end of that period of naval predominance which she had been able to assume throughout the nineteenth century, although the agreement merely recorded a fact which the new circumstances in the world made inescapable. Second, she had abandoned the Anglo-Japanese alliance, which in 1902 had been the first step out of her previous isolation. She had now to depend instead upon a rather vague partnership with the United States, and there were some who looked back wistfully to the old Anglo-Japanese alliance as a more effective mainstay of British interests in the Far East.

In its detailed provisions, the Washington conference accomplished rather less than was imagined. Its principal achievement, assuming that one could rely on the good faith of the Powers, had been to limit the construction of vast battleships, but these were already becoming outdated by the development of the submarine and aircraft in naval warfare. There was no restriction on the number of battle-cruisers and the competitive instinct made it probable that the Powers would build up to the 10,000 ton limit. Lastly, the geographical distances from their respective bases meant that the lack of fortified islands in the Pacific was bound to give Japan the advantage over the other Powers. The Washington conference had at least temporarily ensured British naval parity with the United States, and it had done something to avoid an armaments race in the Pacific, but it was perhaps a little optimistic of Balfour to see its work as an 'absolute unmixed benefit to mankind which carried no seeds of future misfortune'.[3]

3. Genoa and Chanak

Meanwhile, peace-making in Europe was not yet complete. The Russian–Polish war had continued until 1920 (see p. 175); the official relationship between Russia and the other Powers of Europe had still to be established; the wrangling over German reparations was no nearer to solution, and in Turkey new developments suggested that the Treaty of Sèvres would not be of long duration.

It had been Lloyd George's hope at Paris that by delaying the final assessment of the figure due from Germany in reparations the passage of time would allow more moderate counsels to prevail; and the various amounts suggested by the west did drop from £24 thousand million in 1918 to a definite sum of £6,600 million put forward by the reparations committee in April 1921. The intervening months had brought many angry scenes at a succession of conferences when the British had tried to persuade the French to reduce their demands, while German stone-walling had only strengthened French determination to hold on. In March 1921, when the Germans had defaulted on an interim payment, Duisburg, Ruhrort and Düsseldorf on the east bank of the Rhine were occupied and customs duties levied by the occupying forces on imports and exports. Eventually, under threat of an occupation of the whole of the Ruhr, a new German government resumed payment, but this back-ground of economic upheaval had an ominous effect on the value of the German mark, which in the course of 1921 fell from 224 to 1,020 to the pound.

At the end of 1921 Lloyd George attempted a new approach which might create a broader context for the whole question. Since a basic factor in France's intransigence was her sense of insecurity, he returned to the possibility of some kind of Anglo-French military pact. At Cannes in conversation with the French premier, Briand, he also suggested the summoning of a world reconstruction conference at Genoa, where among other things Russia's position might be regularized. As usual, he was optimistic and his relations with Briand proved good enough even to survive an absurd game of golf, which revealed that the French premier had never in his life played before.

Almost immediately afterwards, however, Briand, whom French political circles regarded as a captive of Lloyd George's wiles, fell from power and was succeeded by Poincaré. 'While Clemenceau was a tiger, he had charm and understanding,' wrote Lord Beaverbrook many years later. 'He was a good tiger. Poincaré was also a tiger, but he had no charm, no warmth and a rigidity of outlook that was quite inflexible.'⁴ Preliminary negotiations over an Anglo-French security pact were hopeless from the start. Poincaré demanded a general guarantee of all French interests in the peace settlement, including the right for France to 'forestall the danger of indirect German aggression'; at the Foreign Office Lord Curzon made it clear that Great Britain would not go beyond the maintenance of France's eastern border, reckoning that any wider guarantees would only result in extending French predominance throughout Europe.

Over Russia Poincaré was equally adamant, insisting that her govern-ment must honour tsarist debts and accept international supervision of the protection of the property of foreign residents. The Russian issue was also delicate ground in Great Britain. Winston Churchill threatened to resign if any agreement was reached with the Bolsheviks, and the Northcliffe Press became extremely hostile. 'I suppose you will be meeting Lenin and Trotsky there,' said George V dubiously to Lloyd George, before he set off for Genoa. 'Your Majesty,' replied Lloyd George, 'I have to meet all kinds of people in your Majesty's service.'[5]

Altogether, the prospects were fairly poor for the conference when it opened on 10 April 1922, attended by the representatives of thirty-four nations. Poincaré himself did not come, but he had stipulated to the French delegate that there was to be no discussion of matters relating to the peace treaties or disarmament. Against this inauspicious background Lloyd George used all his charm and dexterity to gain the admission of Germany and Russia to the committees of the conference. 'Is Germany a nation of 63 million people, and Russia with 120 million people to be left standing on the doorstep until we call them in?'[6] It was all in vain. Within a week the alternative development he had feared had taken place. The Russian and German delegates, Chicherin and Rathenau, withdrew to Rapallo to sign a German–Soviet treaty, in which the two countries mutually recognized their regimes and gave up all financial claims against each other. This Rapallo treaty was followed a little later by a secret military agreement enabling Germany to prepare a larger armed force than that allowed by the Treaty of Versailles. To the other countries the fears over Germany and Russia voiced by Poincaré seemed fatally confirmed. The Genoa conference continued for a further six weeks, but there was little more that Lloyd George could do, and the great world meeting which he had hoped might heal the wounds of war fell away into an inconclusive silence.

The disappointment at Genoa did not in itself bring about the downfall of Lloyd George. This was to come later in 1922 after a new crisis over the Turkish situation. It has already been seen (see p. 162) how at the end of the war, after the young King Alexander of Greece and his prime minister Venizelos had been established at Athens, Lloyd George had conceived the idea of fostering Greek power in the eastern Mediterranean. To do this he had shattered Italy's hopes of gaining the southern section of Asia Minor, offering it instead to Greece, and in May 1919 the Greek government with the active encouragement of the British Prime Minister sent a military force to occupy the city of Smyrna (now Izmir; map, p. 203).

The problem created by this policy was that while the Turks might accept the loss of their Arab possessions, a partition of the Turkish mainland of Asia Minor would almost certainly stimulate a nationalist movement challenging the decrepit rule of the Sultan and confronting the Allies with a more active resistance. Such an outcome seemed all too likely, when shortly after the Greek occupation of Smyrna a Turkish army officer, Mustapha Kemal, forced the election of a grand national assembly, in which his party was strongly represented, and from his base in Ankara organized attacks on French and Italian troops in the interior of Asia Minor.

Lloyd George received plenty of warning of this danger. Admiral de Robeck, the high commissioner at Constantinople, advised mild terms for the Sultan, and in London Lord Curzon, even before he became Foreign Secretary, had been circulating memoranda advocating that the whole of Asia Minor should remain Turkish, while Constantinople and the Straits should be internationalized under a commission of the League of Nations. In April 1919 he had said: 'When it is realized that the fugitives are to be kicked from pillar to post and that there is to be practically no Turkish empire and probably no Caliphate at all, I believe that we shall be giving a most dangerous and most unnecessary stimulus to Muslim passions throughout the eastern world and that sullen resentment may easily burst into savage frenzy.'[7]

Lloyd George, however, persisted, and in response to Kemal's attacks the British occupied Constantinople in March 1920 and ejected his supporters from the national assembly. On this a remnant of them established their own assembly at Ankara and elected Kemal their president, who was now declared a rebel by the Sultan. In June Kemal advanced on the Bosphorus, but was driven back under a naval bombardment from British warships and at the same time Greek troops began to press eastwards from Smyrna. This Allied alignment with the Greeks was finally consolidated in August 1920 by the Treaty of Sèvres (see p. 161), which in its partitioning of the Turkish empire gave to Greece eastern Thrace, Gallipoli, the Aegean islands and the right to administer the Smyrna region for the next five years—a direct challenge to the Kemalists who were now determined to expel the Greeks from Smyrna and eastern Thrace.

The hardening of Turkish national feeling largely confirmed Curzon's original opinion and in the autumn of 1920 Lloyd George suffered a new diplomatic setback through a rather odd circumstance. In October the young Greek king Alexander died as a result of a bite from his pet monkey. In the subsequent elections, which centred on the question of succession, Venizelos fell from power and the pro-German Constantine, Alexander's father, was restored to the throne. The return of Constantine was bound to affect Greece's popularity in the west, and although Lloyd George continued to support her in his schemes, British public opinion was becoming doubtful and the French government began positively to turn towards the Turks.

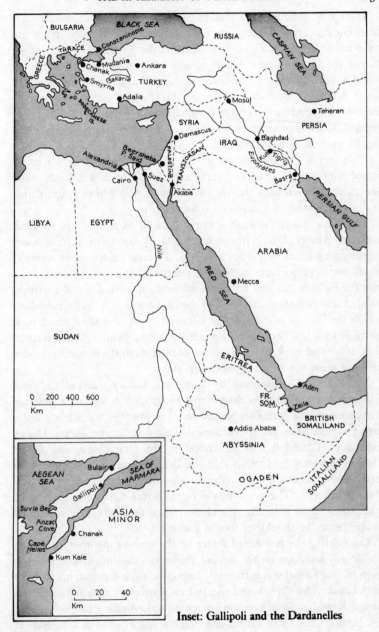

Inset: Gallipoli and the Dardanelles

4   THE PARTITION OF THE TURKISH EMPIRE

These new attitudes were soon to be strengthened by further military developments. In February 1921 a conference in London failed to resolve Greek and Turkish differences over the Treaty of Sèvres and in March the Greeks began a new offensive aimed at Ankara. After an initial advance, however, they were defeated on 7 August by Kemal's forces defending the Sakaria river and this Turkish victory encouraged the French to make a secret treaty with Kemal in October, giving up the parts of Asia Minor and northern Syria which they occupied and offering to provide him with military supplies. The Greeks still held a sizeable area of the Smyrna region, but in the summer of 1922 Kemal, armed with French guns and aeroplanes, could open a full campaign against them, eventually driving them out of Asia Minor entirely and occupying the city of Smyrna on 9 September.

The ruin of Lloyd George's schemes for a Greek empire now entailed a greater danger. Greek troops evacuated by sea from Smyrna were hastily reorganized in Thrace and Kemal's army, inspired by victory, thrust north, preparatory to crossing the Straits and driving the Greeks into the Balkans. All that lay between them and their foe was a narrow band of territory along each side of the Bosphorus and the Dardanelles, which the Treaty of Sèvres had declared to be a neutral zone, now guarded by a few British and French battalions. Would Kemal respect this? It seemed unlikely, as his forces drew close to the boundary by the crossing point at Chanak (now Canakkale).

Lloyd George, supported by Churchill, Balfour, Birkenhead and Austen Chamberlain, was determined to stand firm against a possible Turkish incursion into Europe, and on 11 September Kemal received a direct warning from the Allied commissioners in Constantinople. On 15 September Churchill sent an appeal to the Dominions, and Lloyd George suggested to Curzon that the Balkan countries, too, might be persuaded to resist a Turkish advance across the Straits and into eastern Thrace beyond. 'The press might howl,' wrote Churchill afterwards, 'the Allies might bolt. We intended to force the Turk to a negotiated peace, before he should set foot in Europe.'[8]

Considering the few Allied forces on the spot—supported, it is true, by British warships on the sea of Marmara—this might seem a rash gesture, but Kemal was sufficiently impressed to desist from his advance on Chanak. The French and the Italians, however, already inclined to favour Kemal, ordered their own forces to retire to the European side of the Straits. Once again British and French policies seemed hopelessly at variance, but Curzon rushed to Paris and after tense exchanges with Poincaré managed through Italian mediation to reach agreement that the British and French military commanders should open negotiations with Kemal at Mudania. At this point, when a peaceful solution seemed possible after all, a revolution in Greece drove King Constantine again into exile. Kemal, reckoning that this would create a revival of pro-Greek feeling in the west, resolved to lose no time and advanced once more on Chanak. Here his army confronted the small British detachments which were the only military force that stood between him and the European mainland.

Lloyd George was determined that matters should not be left in doubt, and on 29 September the cabinet issued an ultimatum threatening war if there was no immediate Turkish withdrawal. Lord Curzon was strongly opposed to this, considering it unnecessarily hazardous. Indeed, had it been delivered, Great Britain might well have become involved in a purposeless war which the Russians could possibly turn to their advantage by offering assistance to Turkey. Fortunately at Constantinople General Sir Charles Harington and the British High Commissioner, now Sir Horace Rumbold, shared Curzon's views, and with courageous decision failed to deliver the ultimatum. Talks with the Kemalists continued. Despite persuasion from the French, Harington refused to withdraw from the neutral zone and eventually on 11 October the Turks agreed to an armistice on the understanding that eastern Thrace would be occupied by Allied forces before being handed back to Turkey.

The final arrangements with Turkey, involving a revision of the Treaty of Sèvres, were to be completed at Lausanne in the following year (see p. 224). For Turkey this was the beginning of a new era, symbolized by the departure of the last of the sultans in a British battleship bound for Malta in November 1922. For the Coalition government in Great Britain, too, the episode had its implications. The heroic aspects of the stand at Chanak made little appeal to a British public, sickened by further rumours of war. 'We cannot alone act as the policeman of the world,' wrote Bonar Law in a highly significant letter to *The Times* on 6 October. 'The financial and social condition of this country makes that impossible.'[9] The flourish with which Lloyd George had carried out this latest adventure in foreign policy proved to be the last straw for those Conservatives who found the Coalition irksome, and his moment of triumph turned almost at once to personal defeat. By the time the Sultan set sail for Malta, Lloyd George had already gone from No. 10 Downing Street. Neither of them was ever to rule again.

IV

The Pursuit of Recovery
1922–1929

19

The Postwar Economy

Throughout the 1920s the British dreamed of recovery, but year after year the fulfilment of that dream continued to elude them. The struggle to export was greater than ever before and the problem of the workless appeared to be insoluble. It is true that there was a very gradual revival from the depression on which the country had entered in the summer of 1920; yet a hard core of well over a million unemployed persisted throughout the decade. In many people's eyes it was all a sad departure from the years before 1914, which they now saw as a golden age of prosperity and security, and they imagined that in some obscure way the war was responsible for this economic dislocation.

In fact, the postwar situation merely emphasized the dangers to which the economy of Great Britain had been exposed before 1914 (see p. 21), and conditions in the 1920s were largely due to that legacy and to the government's attempts to cope with it. The official attitude to the problem rested on a belief in the free working of the economy, whereby the laws of supply and demand provided a natural self-regulating mechanism. There had in the past been periodic occurrences of unemployment, but these were thought to be incidental to the operating of the trade cycle. According to this theory, prosperity would lead to a boom until some form of overproduction would eventually bring about a fall in sales in certain areas of the market. This would be met by reducing wages and laying off men at work, and the resultant drop in purchasing power would soon make itself felt over the market as a whole; the snowball of depression would continue to run downhill with growing unemployment, falling prices and a lack of incentive to invest. Eventually, however, businessmen judged that the low point of the slump had been reached and that costs had dropped far enough for it to be worth reinvesting. Then, with the consequent increase in employment and returning optimism the market would begin to expand again; prices would rise and the economic process move gradually to its next period of boom. Economists differed over the precise factors that were decisive in the collapse of a boom or the emergence from a slump, but most were agreed that the pattern was an automatic one in which the extremes were temporary aberrations from a situation in which reasonably full employment could be expected.

Consequently, when depression came in 1920 it was thought by most men in government circles that it was only necessary to wait for the natural rhythm of the trade cycle to right the situation. In the meanwhile, it was vital to re-establish the main features of the prewar economy. State intervention in any programme of restructuring was out of the question and it has been seen how by 1921 much of the wartime governmental machinery had been dismantled and the various concerns handed back to private management. Equally there could be no abandonment of free trade. The notion of protection was incompatible with economic liberalism and in any case the general election of 1906 had shown that it could be politically dangerous.

Otherwise, the immediate concern was over solvency. In the nineteenth century a nation's finances had been seen in the same light as those of a family: a belief in thrift, hard work and the need to live within one's income. This philosophy of a nation of shopkeepers had been expressed in personal terms by Charles Dickens's Mr Micawber: 'Annual income: twenty pounds. Annual expenditure: nineteen nineteen six. Result: happiness. Annual income: twenty pounds. Annual expenditure: twenty pounds nought and six. Result: misery.' The country that showed a loss at the end of the year was living above its income and this was felt to be morally as well as economically abhorrent. Hence the budget was not to be regarded as an instrument for the manipulation of the economy. It was merely the account sheet of the government for the coming year, and it must balance. Thus in the 1920s, since falling personal incomes were producing less revenue from income tax, government expenditure must also be reduced and as a consequence most of the budgets of these years were deflationary.

Similarly in her trade throughout the world Great Britain must retain a favourable balance of payments. The annual average surplus of about £200 million which she had enjoyed before 1914 was now somewhat reduced. Theoretically her total overseas investments had increased during the war, since her lending to her European allies and to the Empire had considerably outweighed her borrowing from the USA and Canada (see p. 137). Unfortunately much of this lending turned out to be a bad debt, because in the postwar situation many European countries were unable to make repayment. They depended on German reparations to finance this and, as Keynes had predicted, these were not always forthcoming. In addition, the Bolshevik government had no intention of honouring the £568 million which the British had lent to tsarist Russia. As a consequence, Great Britain found herself paying out more in settlement to her creditors than she was receiving from her own debtors, at a time when she had already sold £300 million of her long-term foreign assets to meet the expenses of the war.

The bulk of these assets, however, remained, and the interest payments, as well as the return from services such as shipping and insurance, did enable her comfortably to bridge the gap between imports and exports. Indeed her imports, primarily of food, increased sharply in the 1920s; but this made relatively little impact owing to the continuing decline in food prices throughout the world at this time. For nearly every year between 1923 and 1930 Great Britain showed a surplus on her balance of payments, and although this was only half of what it had been before 1914, an annual average of some £90 million could still be invested overseas.

Thus, by their own lights, the governments of those years were doing what was required of them. The budgets were balanced; the pound was being safeguarded by a deflationary policy which would avoid the disaster of wild inflation that brought ruin to many in Germany in 1923; a careful eye was being kept on the balance of payments. Yet if the general position of the country appeared satisfactory, this was in odd contrast to the plight of the unemployed. The imbalance was all the more marked in that unemployment was not evenly spread over the entire country, but concentrated in regions such as South Wales, the north-east of England and parts of Lancashire, where old-established industries had provided the principal means of livelihood for whole areas. The fundamental assumptions of financial policy meant, however, that governments, faced with this, could only advocate a policy of retrenchment and economy, a temporary acceptance of unemployment and of the need for lower wages and profits in an effort to remain competitive in the overseas markets. Imbued with the Micawber philosophy, they waited patiently for the trade cycle to turn up.

It now seems clear that they were likely to wait in vain. If there is to be full employment, the general consumer demand has to be great enough to absorb the whole of the productive capacity of the working population. This demand does not merely imply a desire for the goods and services offered; for it to be effective, the consumer must also possess a purchasing power sufficient to pay for them, and the extent to which this effective demand falls short of absorbing the total productive capacity will be reflected in the number of unemployed. The difficulty for Great Britain was that by the 1920s both the size of the working population and its potential productivity had grown, and if she was to have full employment, there had to be a correspondingly increased demand for her goods at home and abroad. Instead, the postwar economy of Great Britain pointed to a decline rather than a rise in demand, since at home the reduction of government expenditure brought about a fall in domestic purchasing power, and abroad her nineteenth-century export market was under serious pressure. In these circumstances a body of unemployed could easily become a permanent feature of society.

The first of these factors, the drop in government expenditure at home from about £2,500 million in 1918–19 to £1,000 million in 1920–21, was only to be expected with the end of the war. Had it been accompanied by a fall in direct taxation, the shrinking of sales to the government might have been balanced by an increase of consumption by the private citizen with more money in his pocket. The government, however, was determined to pay off the vast debts that it had incurred during the war, and to meet this, income tax, which by 1918 had risen to 6 shillings (30p) (see p. 136), remained at 5 shillings (25p) as late as 1922 and only came down to 4 shillings (20p) in 1925. Thus the private citizen did not have the money with which he could make his demand effective. Of course, the repayment of debt within the country should have put more money in circulation, but whereas the level of taxation needed to make this repayment prevented any rise in consumption power throughout the entire country, the richer section of the population now being repaid was more interested in investing its capital abroad.

The second factor reached back to the years before the war. It had long been evident that Great Britain was no longer the workshop of the world, but by now Germany, Japan and the United States were not her only rivals. Other countries, protecting their new industries behind tariffs, were able to undercut British exporters and to enter the general competition to export outside their own frontiers. Such economic development implied a wide range of more sophisticated technological demands and this could have offered opportunities for a country with a well-established industry. It meant, also, that the British would have to move away from their old spheres of production, in which too many countries were becoming self-sufficient, and concentrate instead on new forms of manufacture. Clearly this would not be easy. Types of factory could not be changed at the stroke of a pen and the labour force was not sufficiently mobile to move to a different part of the country which such a restructuring would entail. It was a long time before this readjustment came about and during the postwar period British businessmen, looking for increased demand, continued to seek it in their earlier fields of economic power, where they were now least likely to find it.

The bulk of the unemployed came consequently from the older export industries. The coalminers were particularly vulnerable, since with the development of new forms of power—electricity and oil—the world consumption of coal, which had been growing by 4 per cent per annum until 1914, only increased by 0·3 per cent after the war. The mineowners were confronted with a competition from Poland and Germany at a time when their former Russian market was closed to them and when their pits were becoming less economic to work (see p. 71). In 1913 a labour force of a million miners had raised 290 million tons of coal, of which 97 million tons had been exported. By 1924 that labour force had acquired an additional 200,000 men; yet in the last years of the 1920s only an annual average of 150 million tons was raised, of which 50 million tons was exported. It was small wonder that the coalminers, who before the war had been among the most highly paid of the working class, should in the interwar years be near the bottom of the wage scale and the most prone to prolonged unemployment.

The peculiar feature of coal was its partial obsolescence. Other older industries were not obsolete, but were confronted with an international competition that deprived them of their nineteenth-century supremacy. In 1914 the annual steel output of India, China, Japan and Australia had amounted to 360,000 tons; by 1922 it had reached 858,000. Similarly, British shipbuilding, after the initial postwar boom, saw its tonnage under construction drop by December 1922 to one-third of the figure for April 1921, partly because Swedish and Dutch yards were found to be more efficient and the Japanese very much cheaper.

The figures for textiles reveal the same pattern, as former markets succumbed to domestic producers. Between 1913 and 1922 the number of cotton power-looms in India and Japan grew from 120,000 to 200,000, and foreign markets began to be invaded by China, Brazil, Japan, Italy and India. The export of British piece goods fell from 6,5000 million square yards in 1912 to 2,000 million square yards in 1937, and this was reflected in a corresponding decline in the numbers employed in textiles, which between these years fell from 621,000 to 288,000.

The problem of exports was largely one for the industrialists to resolve, but in 1925 the government added to their difficulties by the decision to return to the gold standard. This had been in operation throughout the nineteenth century and had meant that any pound note could be freely exchanged for gold at the Bank of England. The necessary concomitant had been a fixed rate of exchange with the currency of any other country also on the gold standard, and in 1913 the pound sterling had stood at approximately 4·86 American dollars. In 1919 it seemed that the fixed rate of exchange might hamper immediate postwar recovery and the government had temporarily suspended the gold standard with the result that the value of the pound fell some way below its former level in terms of dollars. This, in effect, was a devaluation of the pound, and thus the price of British exports, when measured in some foreign currencies, became cheaper and hence more attractive to prospective purchasers abroad.

There was, however, among many economists and men of the City a great nostalgia for a return to the gold standard. It was regarded as an essential feature of a stable economy, and when the Suspending Act of 1919 expired in 1925, it was decided that the nation's finances must once more be based on gold. Several other countries did the same, but were careful to fix their rate against the dollar at a lower level than before the war. In Great Britain most financial advisers, including the Governor of the Bank of England, Montagu Norman, were adamant that to return to the gold standard at a lower rate would ruin confidence in the City of London in its lucrative position as the world's financial centre, since foreign investors in sterling would suffer a reduction in the worth of their holdings when measured in dollars. Consequently in 1925 the country returned to the gold standard at the prewar exchange rate between the pound and the dollar. This victory of the financiers could only be at the expense of the industrialists. The selling price of British exports went up accordingly and the only hope of competing lay in reducing production costs, which must mean cuts in wages.

The re-establishment of the gold standard was the supreme symbol of the dream that recovery meant a return to the ideals of the nineteenth century, an attitude fundamentally submissive to the trend of the world economy. But among younger politicians and economists there was a general body of ideas challenging this submissiveness which left more than a million of the nation's labour force unemployed. Impatient of the past, they conceived a new adventurous form of state intervention, whereby the economy could be expanded by schemes for internal development based on credit or some kind of financial manipulation. If, for example, the government could prime the pump through the financing of public works, such as road building, then the new purchasing power among the men thus given employment would create a greater domestic market which in turn would draw many more back into employment. In other words, the snowball of depression, which kept men out of work, could be checked and be made to roll in the opposite direction through governmental initiative, and the temporary deficit in the budget that this might entail would be outweighed by the long-term advantages of expansion.

In 1925 Oswald Mosley (see p. 269), in collaboration with John Strachey and Allen Young of the ILP, produced a statement *Revolution by Reason* which envisaged a national plan for the stimulation of industrial production, including the bulk purchase of raw materials by the government and the nationalization of banks, through whom credit could be expanded. Another publication, *The Living Wage*, produced by the ILP, proposed to increase domestic purchasing power with family allowances and minimum wage rates, all to be financed by printing more money. In 1927 the Liberal committee, greatly aided by J. M. Keynes, was working on a book, *Britain's Industrial Future*, which suggested establishing some general agency of cooperation between private enterprise and the state. At the same time there was among the Conservatives a group of younger MPs—Robert Boothby, Harold Macmillan, Oliver Stanley—who pressed for greater state interference in the economy. Naturally the details varied, and it was not until 1936 that J. M. Keynes published his *General Theory of Employment, Interest and Money*, which was to provide the theoretical justification for a new governmental financial policy, but the general aspirations of the mixed economy, which was to predominate in the 1950s and 1960s, had already been voiced.

It is clear that the debate did not run on party lines. Rather it reflected a gulf between the older and the younger men. And for the time being it was the older men who held the reins of power. In April 1929 Winston Churchill summed up the Treasury view: 'Whatever might be the political or social advantages, very little additional employment and no permanent additional employment can, in fact, and as a general rule, be created by state borrowing and state expenditure.' Thus there was to be no risky financial experimenting in the 1920s, only the hope that the cloud of unemployment would somehow disperse. It would not; even a world boom towards the end of the decade barely affected Great Britain, since the demands which it stimulated were different to those which her outmoded export industry could supply, and the subsequent world slump after the Wall Street crash in New York in 1929 was to show that depression had not yet done its worst.

20

The Parties in Flux 1922–1924

1. The fall of Lloyd George: October 1922

In the autumn of 1922 the Coalition, on which the political life of Lloyd George depended, was brought to an end by a revolt of Conservative MPs. It had in many ways been a remarkable premiership; few prime ministers have had to cope with a task of such magnitude as had confronted him during the first four years of peace, and the manner in which he had turned from organizing the war effort to dealing with the appalling complexities of the aftermath is a testimony to his energy and resilience.

Nevertheless, these were unhappy times. The difficulties were such that the solutions were bound to be untidy and incomplete, and the individualist spirit in which Lloyd George had conceived them was a constant gamble against mishap. At home the slump had brought higher unemployment. In Europe relations with France appeared in tatters, and the fiasco of the Genoa conference had merely served to throw Germany and Russia together. In Ireland the civil war between the IRA and the Treatyites revived the doubts that had beset the Conservative party in 1921; further afield, British influence in Persia and Afghanistan seemed eclipsed and the Washington treaties were regarded by many as an open admission of the decline of British naval power. Finally, over Chanak the Prime Minister had seemed ready to plunge the country into a war for which there was little public support.

There were also personal aspects of Lloyd George's government that aroused criticism. It was considered to be too clever, not entirely trustworthy, even by some of his colleagues. 'Sucking his pencil at cabinet meetings,' wrote Leo Amery in his memoirs, 'Stanley Baldwin [President of the Board of Trade since 1921] felt ill at ease with the combination of intellectual brilliance with the cynical lack of political or moral principle which he sensed in Lloyd George and the dominating group among his colleagues.'[1] The more staid thought that they could detect an odour of corruption amid the workings of the Coalition government—particularly over patronage. The sale of honours and peerages was, of course, an accepted method of swelling party funds, but Lloyd George may have been a little over-enthusiastic in virtually operating a tariff—£12,000 for a knighthood, £50,000 and more for a peerage—and in 1922 there was a debate in both Houses of Parliament, when the choice of some of the recipients was reckoned to be particularly dubious. In fact, as a partner in the Coalition the Conservative party received its financial share in these transactions, although even some of this seems to have been diverted into the Lloyd George fund which inevitably struck a more personal note—'to promote any political purpose approved by the Right Honourable David Lloyd George'.

The fall of the Coalition government was not simply due to a desire to jettison Lloyd George. It was motivated by a change of view within the Conservative party over their political strategy for the future. In 1918 it had seemed dangerous to dispense with the Coalition; by 1922 it was becoming apparent to many Conservatives that it would be equally dangerous to continue with it. This was indeed an important moment of decision for all parties, and any miscalculation could prove disastrous. The whole spectrum of electoral appeal had broadened enormously with the establishment of universal suffrage and the growth of the Labour party, and the popular vote was now ranged along a line of political sentiment in which shades of opinion moved by indefinable degrees from dark blue to bright red.

The urgent task for each party was to come to grips with these new imponderables and to capture the broadest possible spread of opinion that would remain politically viable. How far could Labour with its new constitution extend to the centre of the line without losing the support of the extreme left? Could a recreated Liberal party capture the centre together with the more moderate wings of left and right? Or could the Conservatives forestall the Liberals in this without the loss of their own right wing? This was more than a scramble for votes. If the British system continued to function on the basis of two major parties, as seemed probable, one of the three was destined to split and to cease to be a political power. The issue was not merely electoral victory, but survival.

The most significant feature of these new ideas was that they threatened to divide the Conservative party. The desire for change came from the rank and file, whereas the Conservative leaders, Austen Chamberlain, Birkenhead and Balfour all wished to continue with the Coalition as the most promising course for the future. 'My object', wrote Chamberlain to Lloyd George in January 1922, 'has been to lead the Unionist [Conservative] Party to accept merger in a new party under the lead of the present Prime Minister and including the bulk of the old Unionists and old Liberals, so as to secure the widest and closest possible union of all men and women of constitutional and progressive views.' In other words, he hoped to capture a broad bracket of support for a party in the centre.

To his critics this policy, which Chamberlain continued to advocate throughout the year, seemed to embrace the very danger that they wished to avoid. The Conservative party would divide. Those who were prepared to follow Chamberlain into the new group would almost certainly find that their original identity as Conservatives was soon lost under the leadership of Lloyd George. Those who remained outside would be the extreme right, probably destined for years in the wilderness. Nor did it seem to the critics that Chamberlain's scheme would preclude the possibility of an advantage for Labour. 'Having a party composed of everyone who was not Labour, with Labour as the only alternative,' said Bonar Law, 'will inevitably have the effect of making a Labour government some day.'[2]

For months signs of revolt continued to grow. Lord Salisbury had stated as early as June 1921 in a letter to the press: 'The fact is, the Coalition government no longer possesses the full confidence of the Unionist [Conservative] Party.'[3] By the summer of 1922 Conservative junior ministers were seriously questioning the wisdom of continuing the Coalition and were reprimanded in a tactless and arrogant manner by Birkenhead. 'We dispersed,' wrote Leo Amery, 'most of the juniors spluttering with indignation.'[4] And a similar restlessness among a group of back-benchers under Sir Samuel Hoare added a third element to the number of dissidents.

It was a cabinet decision that brought the issue to a head. The annual conference of the Conservative party, due to meet on 15 November 1922, seemed likely to vote in favour of ending the Coalition, and to forestall this the Conservative leaders agreed in October that there should be an immediate general election, in which their party would campaign in a continuing coalition with Lloyd George. Initially this decision was taken without any consultation with their own organization, but angry protests from Sir George Younger, the party chairman, eventually pushed Austen Chamberlain into agreeing that he would accept a vote on the question at a meeting of Conservative MPs to be held at the Carlton Club. This, he reckoned, might offer a fair chance of success, since the principal members of the cabinet were still on his side. So far the only resignation had been Stanley Baldwin's from the Board of Trade, and the Conservative dissidents might lack sufficient strength in personalities to create an alternative government.

His hopes were upset by a succession of events during the next few days. On 14 October Lloyd George had made a speech at Manchester denouncing Turkey and France, and Lord Curzon, regarding this as totally destructive of his foreign policy, sent in his resignation. The Conservative anti-coalitionists now had a potential Foreign Secretary. Then on 19 October news of a by-election result at Newport deprived the coalitionists of one of their strongest arguments. An anti-coalitionist Conservative won the seat against Liberal and Labour opponents—an indication that the Conservatives campaigning on their own could win a general election. The final blow was the decision of Bonar Law, strongly urged by Lord Beaverbrook and Wickham Steed, the editor of *The Times*, to return to active political life and to attend the Carlton Club meeting to speak against the Coalition.

All this only hardened the determination of the Conservative cabinet ministers to preserve the Coalition. 'This thing is wrong,' cried Balfour. 'Is the lead of Law and Curzon to count as everything and the advice of the rest of us as nothing? This is a revolt and it should be crushed.' It proved impossible to crush. At the meeting at the Carlton Club, on Thursday 19 October, Chamberlain and Balfour did their best to sway the 275 Conservative MPs who were present, but it was clear from the start that the general feeling was against them and after two striking speeches from Bonar Law and Stanley Baldwin the motion to end the Coalition was carried by 185 votes to 88. 'We are beaten, we must resign,'[5] declared Chamberlain, after he had rushed back with the news to Lloyd George, who had been awaiting the outcome at No. 10 Downing Street, and that same afternoon the Prime Minister submitted the resignation of his government to King George, recommending him to summon Bonar Law.

The decision of the Carlton Club meeting has sometimes been depicted as the work of a reactionary clique within the Conservative party. In fact, it was the result of an open debate among MPs, which revealed that the cabinet ministers who supported the Coalition had lost touch with the shift of opinion within their own party. In this sense it was a highly democratic occasion in which the leadership had been shown to be ultimately dependent upon the general body of the parliamentary party. It only remained now to see whether the decision had been the right one for the Conservatives, and as all sides made hurried preparations for a general election in November, the pattern of party politics for the future still lay in the lap of the gods.

2. Bonar Law's administration: October 1922–May 1923

The gaining of the premiership, for most men the supreme goal in political life, did little to relieve Bonar Law of his air of dour melancholy; if anything, it grew deeper. 'You want me to look cheerful?'[6] he said to the photographers who swarmed to his house on the announcement of the news. It was almost asking too much. He was weary, in poor health, and the loss of his two sons in the war had snapped some vital string of further ambition. He had been an adroit politician, a skilful committee-man, but even at the height of his power, never a colourful character; he had few interests in life outside chess, at which he was an expert player; he read only detective stories. And now at the end of his life he embarked with gloomy reluctance on the premiership, held it until May 1923, when his doctor diagnosed cancer of the throat, and died a few months after his resignation. 'It is fitting,' said Asquith after his funeral at Westminster Abbey, 'that we should have buried the unknown prime minister by the side of the unknown soldier.'[7] Indeed, Bonar Law is probably the least famous of all British prime ministers; yet by a chance of history this unassuming man in the last months of his life stood at the centre of events that were to settle the political pattern of the next two decades.

His first problem was how to form a government at all. The full extent of any significant division in the Conservative party created by the Carlton Club decision would only be revealed in the general election. The effect on the leadership was already apparent. Only three members of the previous cabinet—including Curzon and Baldwin— agreed to serve under Bonar Law, and the absence of unrepentant Coalitionists, such as Chamberlain, Balfour and Birkenhead, was hardly a healthy situation—one which Bonar Law was determined should only be temporary. 'Do you think that I or Curzon imagine we can rule the country with the sort of people that will be left to make up a cabinet after the break tomorrow?' he had said on the day before the Carlton Club meeting. 'I must have Austen and F. E. [Birkenhead] back at the first possible opportunity.'[8]

In the meantime he did his best, producing a rather heavily aristocratic cabinet: one duke, two marquises, one of them Curzon, who became Foreign Secretary again, one earl and three viscounts. Stanley Baldwin suggested that Reginald McKenna should become Chancellor of the Exchequer, but on his refusal Baldwin himself accepted the post. Leo Amery became First Lord of the Admiralty, and outside the cabinet

Sir Samuel Hoare was made Air Minister and Neville Chamberlain Postmaster-General. 'The second eleven', they were called by Winston Churchill—an understandably jaundiced view, since he was just recovering from an operation, to find that 'I had lost not only my appendix, but my office as Secretary of State for the Dominions and Colonies'.[9]

The next question was whether the second eleven could win the general election. Bonar Law himself, while never doubting the rightness of his decision to end the Coalition, was all too aware that the situation was precarious. The displaced Conservative ministers would give him no support; Asquith's Liberals, although still unable to end the quarrel with Lloyd George, were clearly determined to seize the opportunity to re-establish their party and entered 325 candidates; Labour looked forward to gaining the electoral fruits of their new constitution. It was characteristic of the Prime Minister that he should counter all these vigorous excitements with the simple promise of 'tranquillity', putting aside the question of protection, to the disappointment of Lord Beaverbrook, and declaring in his Conservative manifesto that the nation's first need was 'to get on with its own work with the minimum of interference at home and of disturbance abroad'. The contrast to Lloyd George could hardly have been made more explicit. 'We are asked to choose,' said Asquith's daughter Violet, 'between one man suffering from sleeping sickness and another from St Vitus' dance.'[10]

In the event, sleeping sickness had the more profound appeal. At the election on 15 November Bonar Law's Conservatives gained a remarkable victory, winning 345 seats which gave them an outright majority in the House of Commons—rather larger than their popular vote would seem to warrant, owing to the complications of a many-cornered fight. The Asquith Liberals won only sixty-two seats, and the Lloyd George Liberals and Coalitionists fifty-four. In contrast to this, Labour came back with 142 seats; Ramsay MacDonald, Philip Snowden and George Lansbury all made their return to the House, and among those who had entered it for the first time were Clement Attlee, A. V. Alexander, Arthur Greenwood, Emmanuel Shinwell and Sidney Webb.

The most significant aspect of the 1922 election was that it supplied a complete vindication of the Carlton Club decision. The Conservative party had successfully challenged the personal ascendancy of Lloyd George and despite the opposition of some of its leading figures, had retained sufficient unity to emerge as the principal party to oppose the growing hopes of Labour. The gamble which Bonar Law had refused to take in 1918 had paid off; the polarization of Conservative and Labour, which was to become the fundamental assumption in British political life throughout subsequent decades, was now firmly established and the Liberals had failed to capture the strong central position from which they had hoped to keep the other two parties at bay.

The second striking feature was the growth of Labour itself. Their popular vote had risen from 2·3 million to 4·2 million, and although the winning of 142 seats, which nearly doubled their representation before the election, may have been partly assisted by the fact that Liberals and Conservatives had been divided among themselves, their achievement pointed none the less to the value of the broader base that the party constitution of 1918 had given them. It had had a further consequence. The more variegated nature of the Labour electorate was now reflected in the composition of the new Parliamentary Labour Party. After the 1918 election the sixty-three Labour MPs had included forty-eight trade unionists; now this proportion was radically changed, since the non-trade unionist element amounted to more than a third, representing either the ILP or their local Labour constituency organizations.

This change meant that Labour would no longer be a purely working-class party, although that did not necessarily suggest that its policies would become less extreme. On the contrary, the new middle-class supporter could be more doctrinaire and intellectually aggressive than the older type of trade unionist. The emergence, however, of a truly national representation in the House of Commons, coupled with its very size, lent new emphasis to that earlier dispute between the Parliamentary Labour Party and the national executive. At the party conference in 1920 Emmanuel Shinwell had declared that 'the parliamentary party was the property of the Labour movement'. Even then, this view had been hotly contested by J. R. Clynes, and it was unlikely after 1922 that the much larger number of Labour MPs, conscious of their strong and varied ties with their constituents, would be prepared to submit to dictation from an extra-parliamentary organization.

It was not only a new political pattern that was emerging in these months; both parties were on the verge of selecting new leaders, whose personalities were to add their own particular gloss to that pattern. For Labour this meant simply the election of a new leader of the parliamentary party by the Labour MPs. Arthur Henderson, the man whose work in hammering through the acceptance of the party constitution in 1918 was largely responsible for the enhanced position of Labour, had failed to be returned by his constituency and was thus not eligible. Neither Adamson nor Clynes was thought to have given a sufficiently powerful

lead during the postwar period, and it was Ramsay MacDonald, drawing on the support of the ILP, who was elected by a very narrow
majority.

Thus MacDonald, in all probability, would eventually be the first
Labour Prime Minister—an appropriate climax to all his past services to
the working-class movement. Since his appointment as secretary of the
Labour Representation Committee in 1900, he had nursed the party
through its early stages; he had already acted as leader of the
Parliamentary Party from 1911 to 1914, and his pacifism during the war,
which had cost him his seat in the 1918 election, was evidence of his
moral courage. Even Beatrice Webb, who could be caustic about Labour
leadership, gave him a qualified blessing in her diary.

Certainly he looked the part for a potential national leader. He was a
man of immensely commanding presence, tall, handsome, and with a
remarkable power of rhetoric. There was a visionary note in his public
speeches, a Celtic persuasiveness in their romantic idealism often lacking in the more prosaic utterances of his colleagues; and with this he
could always win a working-class audience. Equally, he could charm his
way through an international conference or a society drawing room, and
he adored both. In fact, it is doubtful whether high or low ever really
knew him, for his was an aloof complex personality, a little vain and
defensive, perhaps on account of his humble origins and illegitimate
birth. Three years after the death of his wife in 1911 he wrote: 'I have
no close friend in the world to share either the satisfaction of success
or the disturbance of defeat.' Although his appeal was mystically
revolutionary, the personal attitude of the man himself was always one
of strict constitutionalism. Under him it was certain that Labour policy
would be absolutely parliamentary; to critics in his own party it seemed
that it would not even be Socialist, and the Clydeside MPs soon had
reason to regret their support which had helped to bring him to the top.

The future leadership of the Conservative party was not to be settled
so easily. Since assuming office Bonar Law had acted with energy and
discretion. Although he retained the cabinet secretariat under Sir
Maurice Hankey, he dismantled much of the apparatus—the 'garden
suburb'—by means of which Lloyd George had been able to interfere in
the work of most departments of state; and the Irish Free State Bill,
which ratified the constitution of southern Ireland, was passed without
any reawakening of last-ditch opposition. He had made it clear, however,
that he would not be in office long and there could soon be no escape
from the problem of finding his successor.

The peculiar feature of the situation was that the leading

Conservatives, who would otherwise have been the most likely candidates, could not be considered for the moment, since they had clung to the Coalition. Thus, if Bonar Law retired before they returned to the party, the field for the choice of his successor would be absurdly narrow. Of those who were available the most distinguished was Lord Curzon. The only other possibility was Stanley Baldwin who, although he had entered the House of Commons in 1908, had been an obscure backbencher until 1917 and had only held cabinet office since 1921. Much might depend upon their achievements in their respective spheres during the subsequent months, and in the light of the eventual outcome it is ironical that Curzon was about to win his greatest diplomatic triumph, whereas Baldwin as Chancellor of the Exchequer was to be involved in an unhappy tangle with Bonar Law.

In November 1922 Curzon set off for Lausanne, where an international conference was assembling to make a final settlement with Turkey. He did not go with any great sense of confidence. The pro-Greek schemes of Lloyd George had already thrown France and Russia into alignment with Turkey and this could strengthen Turkish resistance to the British plan to hand over to Iraq the disputed border territory of Mosul (map, p. 203)—an issue in which prestige and oil-fields were both at stake.

In fact, Curzon's handling of the conference was to be a masterpiece of shrewd negotiation from a poor position. He first succeeded in drawing France and Italy over to his side and weakened Russo-Turkish relations by playing on the old question of the Straits. Then he set about demolishing Turkey's case for the possession of Mosul. It would constitute a strategic threat to Iraq; Turkey had not the slightest claim on ethnic grounds and he challenged her to put the whole matter up for arbitration by the League of Nations. In the end, although the Turks still had not surrendered when Curzon returned to London, the moral victory was clear. In the summer of 1923, after the conference had been resumed, the Treaty of Lausanne gave the Turks some concessions. Their possession of the Smyrna region in Asia Minor was recognized and they regained eastern Thrace, but the question of Mosul was to be referred to the League of Nations, who eventually granted the territory to Iraq.

Curzon's success was all the more striking in that he had been hampered by a sudden outburst of alarm in London that his efforts to gain Mosul for Iraq were becoming too aggressive. 'Mosul,' declared the *Daily Express*, 'is not worth the bones of one single British soldier.' To Bonar Law it was Chanak all over again—a far cry from his policy of tranquillity—and he wrote firmly to Curzon that there could be no question of going to war with Turkey.

'The feet of the prime minister were glacial,' commented Curzon bitterly, 'positively glacial',[11] but Bonar Law had good reason to avoid the risk of foreign adventures at this moment, since on another front Anglo-French relations had finally broken down. In 1922 Germany had again defaulted in her payment of reparations to France and Poincaré was determined that this time French troops should occupy the whole of the Ruhr in order to extract direct payment in kind (see p. 238). All British attempts to dissuade him came to nothing and on 11 January 1923 French troops crossed the Rhine to occupy Essen. Bonar Law flatly refused to participate and with this *rupture cordiale* the two nations had openly parted company.

Meanwhile, Stanley Baldwin had rather less to show than Lord Curzon. As Chancellor of the Exchequer he had been concerned almost at once with the problem of the American debt. As has been seen (p. 137), Great Britain had borrowed from the United States in the course of the war, but had lent a good deal more to her other Allies. In order to simplify the situation, Balfour, while temporarily in charge of the Foreign Office in August 1922, had proposed to the continental debtors that Great Britain would cancel all debts to her, except for the amount that she needed to meet her own debt to the United States. In December Bonar Law took this suggestion a step further, when he declared that that amount must be forthcoming before British payment to America could be made. 'I am sure there is no one in the world who will doubt that from the point of view of justice it cannot be right that we alone should make payment.'[12]

The American government, however, was demanding the funding of the British debt, regardless of other circumstances, and in January 1923 Stanley Baldwin, accompanied by Montagu Norman, Governor of the Bank of England, sailed to the United States to open the negotiations. The discussions centred around the rate of interest, originally fixed at $4\frac{1}{2}$ per cent. The Americans were prepared to lower this, but when they offered $3\frac{1}{2}$ per cent for a period of sixty-one years, the British cabinet still found this too high. Baldwin then asked for 3 per cent. The Americans agreed to this for an initial period of ten years, after which it would rise to $3\frac{1}{2}$ per cent, and Baldwin, considering that this was the best offer he could get, advised acceptance. Bonar Law, however, would not hear of it; he did not wish to go beyond $2\frac{1}{2}$ per cent and still maintained that in any case all arrangements should be dependent on reciprocal payment to Great Britain by her continental debtors. Baldwin was consequently instructed to say that he was not authorized to accept such an offer and he was to return to London for further consultation.

This direct division of opinion between the Prime Minister and his Chancellor of the Exchequer was hardly aided by a somewhat unfortunate press conference which Baldwin gave after his ship had docked at Southampton, when in an unguarded moment he stated that the offer ought to be accepted. There followed a few days later a long cabinet meeting at which Baldwin struggled to rally his colleagues against Bonar Law's view that if better terms were not forthcoming, the American debt should be repudiated. In the end the cabinet, informed of general support in the City, decided in favour of acceptance of the terms and Bonar Law knew that if he still held out for repudiation, he would have to resign. In his bitterness at this moment it must have been a tempting thought, but under persuasion from his colleagues he put it behind him. Parliament had yet to open; the question of his successor was still unsettled and it would be wrong to jeopardize the future of his party at a time when it was just emerging successfully from a period of serious crisis.

And so sadly he continued with his administration. If he could hold on long enough, there was a chance that the Coalitionist Conservatives would return to the fold, after which it would be possible for Austen Chamberlain to succeed him. Fate, however, was not to allow sufficient time for such a development. His health was deteriorating. The loss of his voice and excruciating pain in his face persuaded him at last to go on a Mediterranean cruise, but as his condition grew worse, this had to be cut short, and at Paris a medical examination revealed that he was suffering from an incurable cancer of the throat.

Thus the choice after all could only be between Curzon and Baldwin. Of the two, Curzon was much the more experienced and had just achieved the greatest success of his career. Against that, it was hardly appropriate to the democratic tendencies of the age for the Prime Minister to be a member of the House of Lords, an idea certainly not acceptable to Labour. More important, his haughty manner had made him many enemies; most of his cabinet would be antagonistic, and Bonar Law himself had recently been upset by a characteristically high-handed and arrogant correspondence with him.

Although the decision lay technically with King George, the advice of the retiring Prime Minister would normally have been conclusive. Bonar Law himself believed that it ought to be Baldwin, but expected that it would have to be Curzon and, unable to cope with the complexity of the situation in his distress, asked to be excused from being consulted. The

King did not wish to press a dying man and consequently, instead of advice, there was only speculation over what Bonar Law really wanted. There were many who claimed to know. A memorandum supporting Baldwin, drawn up by Lord Davidson, Parliamentary Private Secretary to the Prime Minister, was presented to the King by Colonel Waterhouse as representing Bonar Law's own views. Lord Salisbury was similarly convinced that Law wanted Curzon. Balfour, strongly opposed to Curzon, was content merely to express his own opinion, and rose from a sickbed in order to do so.

In the end George V, feeling his way through the conflicting evidence and relying ultimately on his own common sense, decided on 22 May to send for Baldwin. This was a staggering blow for Curzon, but he mastered his emotion. On the next day he wrote courteously to Baldwin agreeing to serve under him as Foreign Secretary and on 28 May it was he who made the formal proposal that Baldwin should be elected leader of the Conservative party.

Amid all the chances of political life few men have attained supreme power so unexpectedly and so fortuitously. Stanley Baldwin became Prime Minister for two reasons; first, because Austen Chamberlain was not available at the time when Bonar Law's health finally gave way; second, because the principal Conservatives could not stand the thought of serving under Curzon. Of course, some only saw Baldwin as a stop-gap. Probably few imagined that he would be at their head until his retirement in 1937. Yet once he was in power, Baldwin revealed two enormous sources of strength. He proved an extraordinarily skilful politician, knowing exactly how to divide his opponents. His inaction could be deadly—'the most formidable antagonist whom I ever encountered', commented Lloyd George. On the other hand, his public image was almost exactly the reverse of this. Increasingly people warmed to the sight of this stolid, portly, pipe-smoking imperturbable figure who seemed to carry with him an aura of old England. His speeches were laced with little bits of homespun philosophy and he was the first politician to master the art of the radio talk—intimate, cosy and reassuring. 'I am not a clever man,' he loved to say. 'I know nothing of political tactics.' Perhaps he even believed it himself; certainly his listeners welcomed the simple note of honesty and common sense, and in electoral appeal he soon showed that he could outdistance all his party rivals.

Thus the scene was set—Conservatives under Baldwin versus Labour under MacDonald; and the personalities of the two men, whom chance had thrown up as their leaders, were to have a marked impact on the nature of the conflict. Both were moderate men determined to keep the extremists of their respective parties under control; neither was a great man of action. Paradoxically each of them would have fitted comfortably into the centre party which the Carlton Club decision and the election of 1922 had ruled out. With their successive administrations during the interwar years it was unlikely that anything very startling was going to happen, hence the sense of drift at a time when the economic and political state of affairs seemed to demand firm acts of decision. Each ultimately paid a price for his mildness: Ramsay MacDonald denounced as a traitor to his party when he formed the National government in 1931, Baldwin blamed on a national scale after his retirement for not resisting the early demands of Hitler.

Yet, whatever their failings, they did between them make one great contribution to the country. At a time when fanaticism on the Continent was to lead to upheaval followed by authoritarian rule, they stood firm by the requirement of constitutional government and they did what they could to blunt the edge of class war that could so easily have predominated in the clash between their two parties. Of course, for those who believed in radical change or diehard conservatism this philosophy of the sedative was utterly frustrating, and to the unemployed the advantages of tranquillity must have seemed dubious. For the bulk of the population, however, a commuter existence in suburbia was preferable to revolution, and if the period of Baldwin and MacDonald appears low-powered and unenterprising, these two men, who had just emerged through the intrigues and vicissitudes of party politics, came close to reflecting the general will of the country.

3. Stanley Baldwin's first administration: May 1923–January 1924

The beginning of Stanley Baldwin's leadership of the Conservative party could hardly be called encouraging. In May 1923 he assumed office at the head of a government with a powerful majority in the House of Commons, which could have remained unchallenged until 1927. Yet before the year was out, he had chosen to fight a further general election on a highly controversial issue for which his party was quite unprepared, and suffered such a serious loss of seats in the Commons that in January 1924 he was forced to resign and make way for the first Labour administration. It was a defeat that naturally delighted his critics and could have brought his leadership of the party to a speedy close.

The reason Baldwin embarked upon this adventurous course was that he hoped to do something to reduce unemployment, which in October

1923 stood at more than 1,300,000. He suddenly became convinced that the only way to achieve this was through some form of protection, enlarging the home market for industry by imposing tariffs on imported articles of foreign manufacture. He may have been influenced by the Commonwealth premiers, who were actually in conference at this time and who constantly advocated imperial preference. Baldwin, however, did not contemplate placing taxes on imported foodstuffs, particularly meat and wheat, which such a scheme would demand. That really would mean political suicide. Indeed, import duties on manufactured goods would be risky enough; ever since their electoral defeat in 1906 the Conservatives had understandably fought shy of tariff reform (see p. 42) and except for a tax on one or two enumerated articles established during the war (see p. 136), Great Britain had remained a free trade country. It had been with this in mind that Bonar Law during the election of 1922 had promised not to introduce protection, a pledge that now made it necessary for Baldwin to refer to the electorate if he was to go ahead with his plan.

It is possible that his motives were more political than economic. Lloyd George was on his way back from a triumphant tour of North America and Baldwin suspected that he was preparing a campaign for imperial preference which might win over some of the Coalitionist Conservatives, before Baldwin could get them back into the party and thus close the wounds inflicted by the Carlton Club decision. 'The Goat . . . was on the water,' he said long afterwards, '. . . I had information that he was going protectionist and I had to get in quick.'[13]

The effect of this new demand for protection was immediate. The Liberals rallied in defence of free trade, as they had done in 1906, and Lloyd George and Asquith swung back momentarily into alliance. At least Austen Chamberlain and Birkenhead were now hardly likely to join a revived Liberal party and they did actually campaign on behalf of the government, while remaining outside it; yet if this was Baldwin's purpose, it had only been gained at the serious risk of reuniting the Liberals, thus threatening to squander the fruits of all Bonar Law's work.

Respect for Baldwin's political guile was such that other complex and highly implausible motives were also suggested after the event. Some Labour MPs so mistrusted him that they thought he was trying to give the Liberals a chance to re-establish themselves as a viable alternative to Labour, while others reckoned that he had purposely courted disaster, so that a brief Labour administration might discredit itself and thus facilitate a great Conservative resurgence.

Whether Baldwin deliberately courted disaster or not, he certainly achieved it. Austen Chamberlain reckoned that Baldwin had 'said enough to arouse all our opponents to their fullest activity. He has not yet said enough to give guidance to his friends and to rally their enthusiasm to his support'. The reunited Liberals were in full cry, drawing happily on Lloyd George's political fund. Labour set their face against protection, arguing that it would raise the cost of living, but were careful to stress their separateness from the Liberal party by concentrating on a capital levy, social welfare and, less insistently, the question of nationalization. In contrast to this, Conservative party workers had to struggle with the dismay of free trade Conservatives, who protested that they had been told nothing of their leader's sudden change of policy.

In the outcome the general election of December 1923 brought about a fall in Conservative seats to 258. Labour won 191, much of their gain being in the Great London area; the combined Liberals won 159, of whom the bulk were supporters of Asquith. This change was largely a parliamentary one, not reflecting any radical shift in the popular vote of 1922, but its consequences were nevertheless momentous, since it meant that no single party could now maintain a government without some working arrangement with one of the other two.

Everything rested with Asquith and he was deluged with appeals from the right to form an alliance with the Conservatives in order to keep Labour out. 'You would be amused if you saw the contents of my daily post-bag,' he wrote on 28 December; 'appeals, threats, prayers from all parts and from all sorts and conditions of men, women and lunatics, to step in and save the country from the horrors of Socialism and Confiscation.'[14] Asquith, however, was not prepared to step in. He had no intention of taking the Liberals into partnership with a Conservative government now pledged to protection; he saw little danger in the formation of a Labour government with a minority in the Commons, and in January 1924, when the new Parliament had assembled, Liberal support of a Labour vote of no confidence brought an immediate defeat for the government. Baldwin at once resigned and on 22 January Ramsay MacDonald became Prime Minister.

For Stanley Baldwin himself the outcome could have meant more than the loss of the premiership. When the results of the election were known, there had been a desperate plot by the right wing of the party to persuade Balfour to replace him as leader and to make a deal with the Liberals as a means of avoiding a Labour government. Balfour, however, found this unacceptable; if Baldwin was to be ousted, he would prefer to serve under Austen Chamberlain. 'But I hope,' he wrote to Birkenhead, 'his friends will hesitate before they attempt to change horses while crossing the particular stream which threatens to overwhelm us. I have very imperfect sources of information, but nothing has reached me which suggests that the party as a whole, however bitter its feelings may be about recent events, at the moment desire the change.' His judgment proved sound. At a meeting of the party in February 1924, after Baldwin had agreed to drop the question of protection until public opinion was more prepared for it, his position as leader was overwhelmingly reaffirmed.

Thus Baldwin escaped the worst consequences of his miscalculation. The same could not be said of Asquith, whose tactics had given Labour their first opportunity to rule. 'He has sung the swan song of the Liberal party,' declared Austen Chamberlain in the Commons. 'When next the country is called upon for a decision, if it wants a Socialist government, it will vote Socialist; if it does not want a Socialist government, it will vote for a Unionist [Conservative].' Certainly the Conservatives now saw themselves as the main alternative to a Labour government and this prospect caused them at last to close their ranks. Within a few months, through the mediation of Neville Chamberlain, the dissidents, Austen Chamberlain, Birkenhead and Balfour had all returned to the party, and the Conservatives could reckon that they had survived the risk implicit in the break with the Coalition and could now face Labour with a united front.

21

The Trials of Labour I
The First Labour Administration
January–October 1924

The prospect of a Labour government came as a cold shock to many of the upper class who were not inclined to distinguish between the varieties of left-wing opinion. It was less than six years since the murder of the Russian imperial family; the Labour constitution suggested to the more nervous that the country was about to succumb to a Bolshevik regime, and the *English Review* voiced a general alarm when it spoke of the new government as 'the party of revolution' intent upon 'destroying the very basis of civilized life'.

Fortunately those at the centre of the political scene viewed the situation with greater equanimity. King George, who should have had most reason to dislike them, accepted his new ministers in the same spirit of paternalism that had marked his attitude towards the Irish. 'They have different ideas to ours, as they are all Socialists,' he wrote to his mother in February 1924, 'but they ought to be given a chance and ought to be treated fairly.'[1] Among the Conservatives Neville Chamberlain drew a more sardonic conclusion, regarding a Labour government as 'too weak to do much harm, but not too weak to get discredited'.[2] The crux of the matter was that the new government could not survive without the Liberal vote in the Commons, and as Asquith said at the National Liberal Club in December 1923, 'if a Labour government is ever to be tried in this country, as it will be sooner or later, it could hardly be tried under safer conditions'.[3]

Indeed, it was evident to many members of the Labour party that the chance of holding office which the election result had thrust upon them had come prematurely. Some had consequently been in favour of refusal; others advocated forming a government merely to put forward a defiantly Socialist programme which would purposely invite immediate defeat. The little group of leaders, however, who met for dinner at the Webbs in December, had resolved to take up the challenge and to work in conjunction but not in coalition with the Liberals. MacDonald's aim in this was to give his party experience of office and to show the country that Labour was fit to govern—'a testing of men and measures,' as Beatrice Webb wrote in her diary, 'before they are actually called to exercise majority power'.[4] In many ways it was a far-sighted decision, but the danger of such a course was that it must mean the avoidance of the more controversial types of legislation which a true Labour policy should entail; thus in demonstrating to the country as a whole that they were fit to govern, they might cause the working class to wonder whether there was any point in their doing so.

Clearly the selection of the cabinet was not going to be easy. 'No party since the Whig–Liberal combines of the middle of the nineteenth century,' said Lord Birkenhead, 'have been so heterogeneous as the present Socialist–Labour bloc.' There would have to be representation of most shades of opinion, but in view of the policy that MacDonald envisaged the more moderate element must predominate. During the Christmas break, when it seemed that the summons might be imminent, MacDonald departed north to Lossiemouth where he set about the task in consultation with Lord Haldane, a recent recruit to Labour. Out of the battle with the personalities involved, Arthur Henderson, whom MacDonald had hoped to leave in charge of the party organization, eventually secured the Home Office; Philip Snowden became Chancellor of the Exchequer, Clynes Lord Privy Seal and Deputy Leader of the House, and Sidney Webb President of the Board of Trade. MacDonald himself assumed the position of Foreign Secretary in addition to the premiership. Of the cabinet's twenty members seven were trade unionists and eleven could claim a working-class origin. Superficially, at least, this was a revolutionary change, but John Wheatley at the Ministry of Health was the only radical among them, and George Lansbury, whose incautious references to Charles I had upset King George, was left out.

And so on 22 January 1924 the Labour ministers, equipped with court dress hired from Moss Bros, set off for Buckingham Palace to kiss hands and to prove that they were fit to govern. Afterwards Beatrice Webb recorded in her diary: 'Sidney was chuckling over a hitch in the solemn ceremony in which he had been right and Hankey wrong; they were all laughing over Wheatley—the revolutionary—going down on both knees and actually kissing the king's hand. . . . Altogether we were a jolly party—all laughing at the joke of Labour in office.'[5]

The relative orthodoxy of Ramsay MacDonald and his colleagues was particularly emphasized by the first Labour budget. It might have been expected that this would give some indication of a new approach and memories of Lloyd George's budget of 1909 suggested that it would involve greater government expenditure. Instead, Philip Snowden produced the pure milk of Gladstonian Liberalism. An existing surplus of £48 million was ploughed back into reducing the national debt. Direct and indirect taxes were actually reduced through savings made at the expense of the Admiralty estimates—five cruisers rather than eight and a close to the fortifying of Singapore. In the interests of free trade the wartime McKenna duties (see p. 136) were swept away with the result that the growing motor-car industry was deprived of its protection from foreign competition. The duties on tea, coffee, cocoa and sugar were also lowered—an outright repudiation of any scheme for imperial preference—and there were reductions in entertainment duty, telephone charges and the tax on motor vehicles. No mention was made of any plans for public works which might provide employment, although Snowden does seem to have been contemplating that possibility for his 1925 budget. Thus in essence Snowden's attitude was that of a benevolent but thrifty nineteenth-century businessman and it was not unnatural that Asquith should congratulate him wholeheartedly on his work.

A second feature of the Labour administration was their apparent helplessness in the face of the problem of unemployment—the so-called intractable million. For years they had maintained that this was the fundamental flaw in the system of unrestricted capitalism. The force behind this cry, however, had been largely emotional; the mere presence of a Labour government, it was believed, would bring the solution naturally in its wake. 'We are going to make the land blossom like a rose and contain houses and firesides where there shall be happiness and contentment and glorious aspirations,' Ramsay MacDonald had announced in November 1923. It did not take long for the truth to dawn. 'Until you have been in office,' he said in the House of Commons in May 1924, 'until you have seen those files warning cabinet ministers of the dangers of legislation, or that sort of thing, you have not had the experience of trying to carry out what seems to be a simple thing, but which becomes a complex, an exceedingly difficult and a laborious and almost heartbreaking thing, when you come to be a member of a cabinet in a responsible government.' The admission was honest, but desperately sad. The basic problem that confronted the Labour government was not their dependence on the Liberal vote, but the simple fact that they had no notion of a remedy for unemployment.

All that they could do was to resort to palliatives to show that they still had the interests of the poor at heart. Rates of unemployment benefit were raised from 15 to 18 shillings (90p) for men, from 12 to 15 shillings (75p) for women, and from 1 to 2 shillings (10p) a week for each child; and the intervals of time between periods of 'extended benefit' demanded by the legislation of 1921 (see p. 180) were abolished.

There were two fields, however, in which the government was able to come closer to the fundamental philosophy of the Labour party. In education the aim had been stated in R. H. Tawney's *Secondary Education For All* in 1923 'that all normal children, irrespective of the income, class or occupation of their parents, may be transferred at the age of eleven plus from the primary or preparatory school to one type or another of secondary school and remain in the latter till sixteen'.[6] The Fisher Education Act of 1918 (see p. 179) had gone some way in this direction, but it had allowed the raising of the school-leaving age beyond fourteen to rest with local authorities. In any case, the Geddes axe had deprived them of that option and had seriously affected the school building programme which the establishment of secondary education necessitated; in 1923, 72·5 per cent of the eleven to fourteen age group were still lingering on in the old elementary schools.

Now, as soon as he was in office, Charles Trevelyan at the Board of Education removed much of the effect of the Geddes economies; approval was given for forty new secondary schools; the proportion of free places at grant-aided secondary schools was increased; the additional state scholarships to the universities were restored and raised from 200 to 300, and the grant for adult education was tripled.

His most significant measure was the establishment of a committee under Sir Henry Hadow to explore methods for the eventual implementing of a much fuller Labour education policy. Its report, which did not appear until 1926, advocated a secondary stage of education for all from the age of eleven plus either at grammar schools or at secondary moderns with a less academic bias, the school-leaving age being universally raised to fifteen after a period of five years. Some developments did follow from these proposals, before they were brought to a halt for a time by the economic crisis of 1931; during the course of the 1920s the total number of secondary schools increased by 50 per cent and by 1930 43 per cent of the places in these were free. The process, however, was gradual and piecemeal, hampered by the complications of working through local authorities, and it was not until 1944 that the Education Act (see p. 361) of that year finally established the main lines of the Hadow report.

Housing was the other field in which the Labour government was to make a decisive contribution. It was already established that government sponsorship of the building of houses was no longer a specifically Socialist policy. The general principle had been made clear by Dr Addison (see p. 179) in the postwar Coalition government, although his particular scheme had been killed by rising costs after completing 213,000 houses. Party differences in future would lie simply in the way in which the legislation was framed, and two successive Housing Acts, one produced by Neville Chamberlain as Minister of Health under Bonar Law in 1923, the other by John Wheatley at the same post in the MacDonald government in 1924, are neatly illustrative of Conservative and Labour attitudes towards the problems of social reform.

Both were reasonably successful, Chamberlain's Act being ultimately responsible for the building of 436,000 homes by 1929, Wheatley's more than half a million by 1933. Both recognized the need for government financial aid—Chamberlain offering a subsidy of £6 a year for twenty years for every home constructed, Wheatley £9 a year for forty years. Both laid down precise specifications severely limiting the size to what were thought to be the requirements of the working class. Beyond that their methods diverged. First, the Chamberlain Act did not envisage any government interference in the supply of labour and materials; this was a matter for the free market and private enterprise. Wheatley, on the other hand, began with a study of the building industry, showing that the full demand for housing would require an expansion of the labour force, which would only be possible with a long-term scheme. His Act thus laid down a fifteen-year programme and was preceded by agreements with the unions for shortening the length of apprenticeship to four years and extending the maximum age for taking on apprentices.

Secondly, the Chamberlain Act fought shy of any control of the ultimate disposal of the houses. The subsidy was offered direct to any firm in the building industry, although local authorities could apply if they could make out a case; and the houses would mostly be for sale, a fact which put them beyond the reach of a large section of the working class. Wheatley in his Act accordingly stipulated that all his houses were to be rented; the subsidy would be paid to the local authority who would establish a rent based on that paid in 1914 for working-class homes in the same area, although where the construction costs were greater than anticipated they might raise this. As it turned out, rents came to about 15 shillings (75p) a week, rather higher than what Wheatley had hoped.

The differences in approach are clear. Even so, the form of the Wheatley Act was a good deal less radical than the character of its author might have suggested. It did bring the prospect of a house closer to a more impecunious section of the working class than had been affected by the Chamberlain Act, but there would still be many who would be unable to afford these rents. Equally, it left the slums untouched, although the general level of living standards was bound to rise as more homes were built. His scheme bore few features of the state direction of labour and capital normally associated with Socialism. Local authorities had freedom to negotiate independently with building firms; and since the system of subsidies was a gradual one, it assumed that these authorities would in the first instance have to borrow the necessary money through normal financial channels, in contrast to the original Labour proposal of low interest loans from the government. Wheatley's measure was an interesting example of the extraordinarily undoctrinaire mildness of the British Labour movement; it was also a farsighted anticipation of those forms of planning in which employers, unions and local authorities were to be coaxed into cooperation under a very loose government control—the pattern of later twentieth-century legislation adopted by Conservative and Labour alike.

Apart from these measures in education and housing the domestic record of the first Labour administration was understandably bleak. In economic terms the question of unemployment defeated them; in political terms they did not have the strength in the Commons to act decisively, a circumstance of the moment which would have restricted the programme of any political party.

There was in addition to this one other problem which was always to be peculiar to a Labour government and which no majority in the Commons was likely to solve. The Labour party had begun as a working-class movement financed largely by the trade unions. This might lead to a certain haggling over the precise relationship of the Parliamentary Labour Party and the national executive dominated by the unions, but as long as Labour remained in Opposition, that relationship was not likely to become too confused, since the parties confronting them in the Commons represented in the main the employer class. The situation became very different when Labour assumed the responsibility of running the entire country, while the trade unions continued to concentrate on their own sectional interest.

On the day of Baldwin's resignation a strike of locomotive engineers and firemen began, but was eventually ended by the intervention of the general council of the TUC. In February 110,000 of Bevin's dockers struck for an increase in pay and a decasualization of their labour; they gained their demands within three days, but not before Colonel Wedgwood, a Labour minister, had warned their union that troops would have to be used in order to maintain essential supplies. In March the London tramway workers, whose wages had previously been cut, went on strike for higher pay and when this spread to the London underground railway, MacDonald declared that he would invoke the Emergency Powers Act, which Labour had criticized so bitterly when it had been passed in 1920.

Here was the supreme irony of the government's position. Ministers of the Crown found themselves in open conflict with the unions on whom their party depended for money and votes. MacDonald's statement was condemned by a joint resolution of the general council of the TUC and the national executive of the Labour party, and the unions remained quite unrepentant over the embarrassment they were causing their political leaders. 'Governments may come and governments may go,' said Ernest Bevin in April 1924, 'but the workers' fight for betterment of conditions must go on all the time.'[7] The tramway dispute ended a little later with a compromise between the employers and the union, facilitated by the introduction of a London Transport Bill in the Commons, but the apparent gulf between the political and industrial wings of the movement was to be a continuing difficulty for future Labour governments.

During most of his administration Ramsay MacDonald was principally concerned with foreign affairs, striving to bring an end to the French occupation of the Ruhr (see p. 225), looking for ways to strengthen the authority of the League of Nations and hoping to create better relations with Soviet Russia. The situation in Germany was the most urgent since the French occupation had stimulated a policy of passive resistance by the German government throughout most of 1923; internally this resulted in an economic dislocation, coupled with the collapse of the German mark in a violent inflation, and on the international scene the consequent coldness of Anglo-French relations was unlikely to be reduced by exchanges between Poincaré and Lord Curzon. The position had eased a little, however, when in September 1923 a new German chancellor, Gustav Stresemann, finally abandoned passive resistance, and in October the French agreed to participate in a committee under the chairmanship of an American general, Charles G. Dawes, to reframe the conditions of reparations.

At this point, when Labour came to power, Ramsay MacDonald was resolved to foster a new sense of harmony in Great Britain's dealings with France. This was a problem of some delicacy, since Labour had always stigmatized French rapacity in the Treaty of Versailles and disliked the whole policy of reparations. Despite this, conversations began fairly encouragingly, and in May 1924 MacDonald was suddenly assisted by a great stroke of luck, when Poincaré lost the French election and was succeeded by the radical Socialist Edouard Herriot. This made it far more probable that the French government would accept the Dawes plan, and in July MacDonald presided over a conference in London, where agreement was reached on the details of revitalizing the German economy and devising a new scale of payments and guarantees for reparations; the first stages of the evacuation of the Ruhr by the French were to follow on this.

For more positive achievements MacDonald looked to Geneva. One scheme, the draft treaty of mutual assistance, had to be turned down by the government, since it proposed that victims of aggression should be aided by other Powers in the same continent and the existence of the Dominions would have created an immense and complicated liability for Great Britain. Lest this rejection should give a wrong impression, MacDonald emphasized his faith in the League of Nations by coming to Geneva in September, together with Herriot, to address the Assembly and an alternative scheme, known later as the Geneva Protocol, largely the work of Arthur Henderson and Lord Parmoor, was put forward, whereby all parties to an international dispute must submit to compulsory arbitration. The Dominions were still uneasy over such a commitment; the left wing of Labour deplored the prospect of the armed force that sactions might require, but before MacDonald had had to grasp the nettle of ratification, he was spared by the fall of his government.

The desire to restore diplomatic relations with Soviet Russia was rather more realistic, but was to prove politically disastrous. This was by no means the first attempt. Lloyd George had already tried to pave the way for a renewal of trade relations with an Anglo-Soviet agreement in 1921, and had hoped at the Genoa conference in 1922 to restore Russia's position on the European scene. There should, therefore, have been nothing particularly sinister about MacDonald turning to a similar policy, but his efforts naturally strengthened suspicions among many Conservatives who were always inclined to regard the Labour party as the lackey of the Communist classes.

Almost at once the Labour government gave full diplomatic recognition to the Russian government, but the negotiations over trade came eventually to a standstill. The Russians wanted a large loan from the British government; the British insisted on Russian payment of tsarist debts repudiated by the Bolsheviks. In August, however, left-wing back-benchers mediated to produce a compromise. In return for the provisional promise of a loan a trade treaty was concluded whereby British exports were to enjoy most-favoured-nation treatment in Russia. The Russians were then to proceed to a settlement of their debts, after which the British loan would be forthcoming. It did not seem an unpromising arrangement, but the prospect of a government loan to Bolshevik Russia, whose Third International was a constant source of propaganda and potential conspiracy against British institutions, was too much for the Conservative press, who rose furiously to the attack. So, too, did Lloyd George, taking a reluctant Asquith with him, and it seemed that the Liberal–Labour alliance was unlikely to survive the autumn.

In fact, the government fell in October as a result of a muddle over a triviality. In August J. R. Campbell, the acting editor of the Communist *Workers' Weekly*, published an article appealing to soldiers not to open fire on workers. This gratuitous exhortation does not appear to have been relevant to any episode at the time, but the Director of Public Prosecutions decided to charge him with incitement to mutiny. A little later Patrick Hastings, the Attorney-General, recognized that there was hardly a case which would satisfy a jury and after consultation with MacDonald, ordered the prosecution to be dropped. This was a gift for the Opposition at a time when excitement was still running high over the Russian loan. Political intervention, it was said, was subverting the course of justice in the interest of Communist sedition. In October the Conservatives in the Commons demanded a vote of censure. Asquith proposed, instead, an investigation by a select committee of inquiry, but MacDonald would not compromise on such an issue, even at the risk of jeopardizing his relations with the Liberals, and declared the matter to be a vote of confidence. Inevitably Asquith's amendment was carried by a large majority and on 8 October MacDonald, deciding to appeal to the country, announced the dissolution of Parliament.

The heated electoral campaign that ensued was largely centred on one question. The Conservatives could not make much of Labour's failure to deal with unemployment, since their own record in this field had not been particularly successful, and most other aspects of MacDonald's administration had been too neutral to allow a charge of rampant Socialism. That only left Labour's attitude towards Russia as suggested by the Anglo-Soviet treaties, and the main theme of the Conservative campaign was a warning that a vote for Labour was a vote 'for handing this country over to the Communists and to Moscow', as Lord Curzon put it. Labour attempted to counter this with long reasoned statements about the treaties, and the annual conference of the party, which took place shortly before polling day, was careful to reject a further application for affiliation by the British Communist party and to exclude individual Communists as Labour parliamentary candidates. All their efforts, however, to quieten the nervousness over this emotional issue were suddenly shattered by the publication of the Zinoviev letter.

This letter, of which a copy reached the Foreign Office on 10 October, purported to be a communication signed by Zinoviev, the president of the Third International in Moscow, to the British Communist party and in addition to the usual admonition to prepare for armed insurrection urged British Communists to support the ratification of the Anglo-Soviet treaties. Ramsay MacDonald in the middle of a nationwide electoral campaign did not receive it until the night of 15 October and then ruled that its authenticity must be established before it was published. At the same time he set in motion the preparation of a draft note of protest to be delivered to the Russian *chargé d'affaires* in London in the event of authenticity being established. On 24 October, however, five days before the election, Sir Eyre Crowe, the Permanent Under-Secretary of the Foreign Office, who was convinced that the letter was not a forgery, learnt that the *Daily Mail* also had a copy of it and intended to publish it on the next day. On this without any authorization from MacDonald he decided to act on his own initiative and to publish the letter officially, at the same time dispatching the note of protest to the Russian *chargé d'affaires*.

The effect naturally was to heighten enormously the Red scare. It did not matter to most of the readers of the press that the letter spoke scathingly of the Labour government. At best it seemed that MacDonald was the innocent dupe in a plot which linked the Anglo-Soviet treaties with the Communist conspiracy for world revolution, and MacDonald himself, exhausted by electioneering and bewildered by the Foreign Office's precipitate action, took three days to produce some kind of reply in a speech at Cardiff.

The Zinoviev letter left a long legacy of bitter recrimination. Labour always maintained that it was a forgery, the Conservatives that it was genuine. Labour muttered darkly of a plot by the Foreign Office to undermine the government; the Conservatives accused the Prime Minister of attempting to suppress a document which would be politically embarrassing. On the whole, it would seem that the letter was a forgery, the work of white Russian *émigrés* in Berlin hoping to ruin Russia's chances of a British loan, although it would not have been inconsistent or improbable for the Third International to have produced such a letter. Certainly the men who passed it to the *Daily Mail* believed that it was genuine. And Sir Eyre Crowe not merely believed it, but honestly thought that he must forestall the *Daily Mail* to avoid later accusations 'that information vitally concerning the security of the empire had been deliberately suppressed during the elections',[8] as he told MacDonald on the day of publication. Even so, the fact that he made no attempt to consult MacDonald before acting is curious. Did he mistrust the Prime Minister? Or did he merely think that he knew best?

As it turned out, the Zinoviev letter did not greatly affect the result of the general election held on 29 October. It is true that the Conservatives gained a great victory with 419 seats, increasing their popular vote by 2·5 million to approximately 8 million. On the other hand, although Labour seats fell from 191 to 151, their popular vote actually rose by more than a million. Thus the real casualty was the Liberal party who dropped from 159 seats to 40, their popular vote falling from 4·3 million to 2·9 million. The new factor in the campaign had been the actual existence of a Labour government and the electorate had been deciding whether that government should continue. This had not been the issue in the election of 1923, when the voter who rejected Baldwin's bid for protection had not reckoned that by so doing he was opening the way for a Labour administration. Thus Austen Chamberlain's comment on Asquith's decision to support Labour at the beginning of 1924 appeared to be vindicated, and MacDonald's acceptance of the chance had done more than show that Labour could govern. It had finally consolidated the new orientation of British political life that had been emerging since the fall of Lloyd George's Coalition government.

22

The Trials of Labour II
The General Strike of 1926

'I am under no temptation to believe that the victory was the result of leadership,' said Baldwin modestly at a Conservative celebration at the Albert Hall in December 1924. It was a sentiment with which many of his critics would have agreed; yet there was no denying that the party had emerged very successfully from the period of flux. A big majority was to give them an uninterrupted term of five years and the membership of a large cabinet pointed to the healing of past wounds. Austen Chamberlain went to the Foreign Office, Birkenhead became Secretary of State for India and, on Curzon's death in 1925, Balfour took over as Lord President of the Council.

It was not only the Coalitionist Conservatives whom Baldwin had won back to the party. The turn of events also brought Winston Churchill over to his side. The Liberals' support of Labour had been anathema to Churchill and he never campaigned again under that flag. He won his seat for Epping in the election of October 1924 as a self-styled 'constitutionalist', and with Baldwin's renunciation of protection his drift back to the Conservatives quickened. It was not until a year later that he finally rejoined the party which he had abandoned in 1904, but before that Baldwin had established him as Chancellor of the Exchequer. From this position he could keep a watchful eye on free trade, although Churchill himself was never entirely at home in the world of finance. 'If they were soldiers or generals, I would understand what they were talking about,' he commented on his Treasury advisers. 'As it is, they all talk Persian.'[1]

For Labour the result of the general election was not in itself disheartening. Nevertheless, the sense of anticlimax created by the somewhat unexciting record of their first government led to considerable criticism of MacDonald's leadership. More particularly, there was natural dismay at the prospect of a long Conservative reign and in the following months the working-class movement turned back to greater reliance on industrial action, which was to culminate in a second great disillusionment with the failure of the general strike in 1926.

The fundamental reason for worsening industrial relations was the generally weakened condition of the British export market. In the previous year the coalminers' conditions of work had actually improved, since the German policy of passive resistance to the French occupation of the Ruhr (see p. 238) had allowed a short boom in the export of British coal. Thus, in May 1924, under the aegis of the Labour government there had been established a seven-hour day and a more favourable pay agreement which amounted virtually to a national minimum wage. This new arrangement, however, was out of date almost before it began, when with the French evacuation of the Ruhr the German coal industry came back to life.

It was at this moment that the Conservative government decided to return to the gold standard. The Suspending Act of 1919, which had temporarily taken the country off it, was due to expire in 1925 and during these years the value of the pound against the dollar had fluctuated a good deal below the prewar rate of $4·86. As has been seen (p. 214), orthodox economic thinking, strongly represented at the Treasury, maintained that it was vital to return to the gold standard as quickly as possible, since by stabilizing the rate at the higher prewar level and anchoring it to gold, sterling would be strengthened as a currency. It was only J. M. Keynes who stressed other consequences of a revaluation of the pound. The inevitable rise in the price of British exports abroad would have to be countered by a lowering of the costs of production through a reduction in wages, and Keynes forecast immediate suffering for the workers in export industries—almost certainly the miners in the first instance.

The orthodox view prevailed. In April 1925, when introducing his first budget, Winston Churchill announced that the government would not renew the Suspending Act of 1919. This meant that Great Britain had returned to the gold standard at the old prewar rate and it was not long before Keynes's forebodings, published in a pamphlet entitled *The Economic Consequences of Mr Churchill*, were proved correct.

The revival of the German mines had already had a disastrous effect on British coal exports which in the twelve months since the 1924 agreement had fallen by one-third. Now, with the prospect of the return to the gold standard adding to the selling price of exports the mineowners declared that, in order to meet this, they must revert to lower wages and on 30 June 1925 they gave their month's notice of the termination of the 1924 agreement. This the miners were determined to resist, even if the continuation of higher pay should mean greater unemployment, and at a meeting at Kingsway Hall in London on 3 July A. J. Cook, the belligerent Communist secretary of the Miners' Federation, who had replaced Frank Hodges in 1924, announced that they would accept no mediation from any quarter until the owners' notices had been withdrawn.

It was soon clear that this was not going to be just one more coal dispute. It was to involve the whole of the trade union world. On 10 July the general council of the TUC agreed to support the Miners' Federation and on 25 July ordered an embargo on the movement of coal by the railway and general transport unions in the event of the owners' notices coming into operation at the end of the month. This solidarity was aided by a widespread fear that the return to the gold standard was a prelude to a general attack on wages, and these suspicions were strengthened when it was reported that Baldwin had said in discussion with the miners' leaders on 30 July: 'all the workers of this country have got to take reductions in wages to help put industry on its feet',[2] although this statement was later officially denied by the government.

The threat of a national stoppage had its effect. 'The majority of the cabinet', wrote Sir Maurice Hankey to King George, 'regard the present moment as badly chosen for the fight, though the conditions would be more favourable nine months hence.' The diehard minority reckoned that the government's administrative arrangements were adequate for an immediate confrontation, but Baldwin felt that the country was not yet politically prepared for the dislocation that a general strike would entail and on 31 July—Red Friday—he climbed down. The miners' notices were suspended, a subsidy eventually costing £23 million was offered to the industry until the end of April 1926 and a royal commission on the coal industry was set up.

The *Daily Herald* and the working-class movement might rejoice over the apparent reversal of the Black Friday episode of 1921, but Baldwin was merely returning to the tactics of Lloyd George. He was playing for time and the subsequent nine months allowed Sir John Anderson to refurbish earlier schemes for the organization of maintenance of supply, if a general strike should ensue (see p. 173).

Meanwhile, the royal commission set to work under Sir Herbert Samuel. Unlike the Sankey commission of 1919, they did reach a unanimous verdict. Coal royalties should be nationalized, but there was to be no public ownership of the mines; instead the owners were to be encouraged to re-equip, to modernize, to amalgamate some of the smaller pits and to provide better working conditions. For the moment, however, the commission could see no alternative to a reduction in wages, since they regarded the continuation of the government subsidy as economically unsound.

Their report, which was issued in March 1926, sold 100,000 copies—a best-seller, which neither the owners nor the miners would buy. The owners were determined not to bargain; the miners were determined not to accept any reduction. By the middle of April all negotiations had reached an obstinate deadlock, despite all Baldwin's efforts to bring the two sides closer together. On 30 April the government subsidy and the owner's notices expired and on 1 May a national coal strike and lock-out brought the entire industry to a halt.

Would the TUC now go the whole way and support the miners with a general strike? Certainly they had considerable sympathy with them, but the problem of achieving working-class solidarity remained as great as in 1921. There was doubt over whether the general council of the TUC, under the chairmanship of Arthur Pugh, could assume responsibility for the entire negotiation, including, perhaps, concessions over the miners' wages. There was, too, uneasiness over the burden that other sections of the working class would have to shoulder. Railway and transport workers, for instance, would have to bear the brunt of concerted action and in the previous February Ernest Bevin had already expressed his misgivings: 'I have vivid recollections of the 1921 movement and even last July I did not feel too happy about what the rest of the unions were expected to obtain for the miners.'[3]

Despite these doubts the TUC could hardly stand aside from an attempt to mediate. On 29 April eight hundred delegates from the executive committees of 141 trade unions meeting in London voted in favour of taking up the miners' case. On 1 May the miners' leaders agreed to entrust the dispute to the general council, provided that they were consulted on any suggested terms, and during the first two days of the coal strike the general council and the government became engaged in a frantic search for a settlement.

Early on Sunday 2 May it seemed that some acceptable formula based on the Samuel report might be found, but there were further delays, because the miners' executive was not immediately available for consultation. Suspicious of another Black Friday, they had left London. The cabinet, who had assembled at noon on that day, were kept waiting and now had time to learn that the TUC had already sent out telegrams in preparation for a general strike. Then dramatically, at midnight, they heard by telephone from the editor of the *Daily Mail* that the compositors had refused to set up the type for a leading article condemning a general strike, and Baldwin decided that this was an unconstitutional interference with the liberty of the press. On this he broke off all further negotiations. Much has been made of the fact that when two delegates of the general council returned to No. 10 Downing Street in the early hours of the morning to deliver a letter of protest, the Prime Minister had gone to bed and did not see them. Actually this made little difference. There would have been time for talks on the next day, but although the general council was prepared to repudiate the action of the *Daily Mail* printers, the cabinet was now convinced that there could be no negotiation while there was any threat of a national stoppage. Accordingly, at midnight on Monday 3 May the general strike began.

It would seem clear that Baldwin's action in breaking off negotiations was decisive. The general council was desperately reluctant to embark on the strike; they had negotiated hard as soon as the miners had empowered them to do so and they might well feel aggrieved at Baldwin's final message to them. There had not perhaps been much hope in the various formulae put forward, since these had all included the probability of a reduction in wages or an increase in hours, and it was hardly likely that the general council would get the miners to swallow this. On the night of 2 May, however, Bevin with characteristic directness had cut through all the verbiage and had successfully proposed an entirely new framework: a national mining board composed of owners, miners, government representatives and others, who would work out a scheme for the implementing of all the proposals of the Samuel commission. So far as wages were concerned, they should decide 'what adjustments shall be made, if any, by all parties necessary to cover the interim period, subject to the maintenance of a national minimum and the Seven Hours Act'.[4] On the morning of 3 May the miners' leaders accepted this, even though the expression '*a* national minimum' might mean something different to the minimum established in the 1924 settlement. This was a major breakthrough and might well have averted the general strike, but since the government had now refused to negotiate in the existing circumstances, the proposal could not be discussed.

Why did Baldwin take this step? Certainly he regarded the position of a government arguing under threat of a general strike as abhorrent to the principles of democracy; he felt genuinely that the nation was being held to ransom by an extra-parliamentary force. The instance of the *Daily Mail* printers was hardly well chosen, since they had acted purely on their own initiative and were not supported by their union. The incident, however, strengthened the impression, already created by the news of the TUC telegrams, that the workers were stealing a march in putting their operation into action. As with the general staffs in July 1914, the chances of conciliation were wrecked by the race over mobilization and it was hard now for Baldwin to resist the right wing of the cabinet—Winston Churchill, Neville Chamberlain, Leo Amery and Joynson Hicks—all of whom wanted a straight fight with the workers to show who was really master.

And so now they had it. The general strike, which lasted for nine days until 12 May, did not mean a total stoppage, since many branches of industry were told to remain at work. Those who were called out were employed in transport, the railways, the docks, power stations, iron, steel and printing—a million and a half men—and considering the fragmented structure of British trade unionism it proved a remarkable demonstration of working-class solidarity which took even the TUC by surprise. Passenger and freight services on the railways fell away almost to nothing and out of 4,400 London buses only forty were running by the third day of the strike. Much of this was due to the energy and power of improvisation displayed by Ernest Bevin on the strike organization committee. 'He was the only one of the trade union leaders,' commented the *Sunday Express* afterwards, 'whose reputation was enhanced by the general strike.'

On the government side there was a surge of 30,000 volunteers on the first day to help run the emergency services, and Oxford and Cambridge undergraduates had the time of their lives—an interesting contrast to the left-wing attitudes prevalent at the ancient universities in the 1930s. The government's plans stood the strain. Road transport was able to keep the country fed. Seaside towns were used as ports and in the London docks submarines helped to supply essential electric power. In the absence of the national press the government produced its own newspaper, *The British Gazette*, in the offices of the *Morning Post*, a task given to Winston Churchill in order to keep him away from more directly belligerent action. The strikers also had their own, the *British Worker*, while at the BBC John Reith (see p. 257) struggled to maintain an image of neutrality in his control of the principal means of communication with the nation.

Despite this wholehearted sense of involvement on each side the atmosphere during the general strike was in the main remarkably good-tempered. Baldwin tried hard to avoid provocation and had the support of King George, who on one occasion intervened to stop a measure which would have prevented the unions from drawing their strike pay from the banks. The weather was fine; cricket matches continued to be played and few accounts of the strike omit the football match at Plymouth between the strikers and the police, at which the wife of the chief constable kicked off. This does not alter the fact that the strike had revealed a social war not far below the surface; there were ugly clashes with the police in London, in the north and in Glasgow; over 3,000 prosecutions were issued for incitement to sedition and for violence, and although no one was killed during the strike, there is no knowing how long this relative mildness would have lasted.

The confrontation brought with it that simplification of issues that comes with the outbreak of hostilities. Whatever his hesitations beforehand, Baldwin now stood implacably by his basic contention. He would not negotiate while the general strike lasted. 'The laws are in your keeping,' he stated to the country on 6 May in *The British Gazette*. 'You have made Parliament your guardian. The General Strike is a challenge to Parliament and is the road to ruin.' And as the government's emergency measures proved equal to the test, he could reckon that time was on his side.

So it seemed also to the TUC. Their aim all along had been to impose the continuation of negotiations and now the strike, far from forcing the government towards this, appeared only to postpone a settlement indefinitely. Local union funds were being drained by strike pay and there had been an ominous statement by Sir John Simon in the House of Commons on 6 May that a general strike was illegal and hence not protected by the Trade Disputes Act of 1906 (see p. 59). The longer strikers remained unemployed, the greater the threat of real violence seemed to grow and the general council of the TUC was very soon looking for some excuse to call the strike off.

The return of Sir Herbert Samuel from Italy brought a ray of hope. His offer to mediate was rejected by the government, but J. H. Thomas was quick to open up unofficial negotiations with him. By 10 May the general council decided that the main lines of the Samuel report would form a satisfactory basis, provided that any reduction in wages was made conditional on implementation of the reorganization recommended for the mining industry. Herbert Smith, the miners' president, refused to accept this, but the general council was determined to delay no longer.

At midday on 12 May their negotiating committee came to No. 10 Downing Street to see Stanley Baldwin. Ernest Bevin described how they were met by Horace Wilson at the door of the cabinet room: 'Wilson then said: "Well, Mr Pugh and Mr Thomas, what do you want to see the Prime Minister for?" They replied, "We want to see him on the position." The reply to this was, "You know the Prime Minister will not see you before the strike is called off." I said at the back, "For Christ's sake, let's call it on again, if this is the position." Thomas then said, "We have come to call the strike off," and we then went in and sat down.'[5]

The interview that followed was short. Baldwin would consider no terms; there was no mention of the Samuel report and when Bevin broke in to request the withdrawal of the owners' notices, Baldwin refused to commit himself. Thus the TUC got themselves out of the general strike on the basis of proposals which neither the government nor the miners were prepared to accept. It was unconditional surrender under a very thin guise. Bevin, at least, had no illusions. 'Something has happened,' he said, 'and the best way to describe today, if we are not quick, is that we have committed suicide.'[6] The general strike had failed; its only effect had been to harden Conservative resistance and to transform the cabinet into what Ramsay MacDonald called 'a very efficient, very faithful and very loyal sub-committee of the mine-owners'.

The aftermath was bitter. Each union had to make its own arrangements for a return to work. There were no safeguards against victimization; some unions were forced to pay compensation to the employers for breach of contract and many local strikes continued throughout the summer. The miners themselves were determined to go on alone and the rest of the working class watched them with conscience-stricken exasperation. It was all useless. By November 1926 the miners were forced to surrender to lower wages and longer hours, the government having passed an Act suspending the seven-hour day for the next five years. The agreement of 1924 had gone; nothing was done to implement the Samuel recommendations and with coal output halved for 1926 the industry seemed to be in a more parlous state than ever before.

The trade union movement, too, had suffered an appalling psychological setback. Since the 1890s there had existed the dream of a general strike as the last resort of the working class. Some had feared that there would be insufficient solidarity to make it possible; others, particularly among the leaders, had had qualms about its constitutional propriety, but all had assumed that if it were accomplished, a general strike would be bound to bring a government to terms. Over the question of the supply of arms to Poland in 1920 (see p. 175) Labour had claimed that the threat alone had been effective, although the issue had really been settled by the Polish victory in the battle of the Vistula. In 1921 Black Friday had demonstrated the difficulty of establishing working-class solidarity, not its inefficacy, if it could be achieved. But in 1926 the test had come and the lesson of that year was that the much vaunted weapon of a general strike was a broken reed—an expensive lesson which had cost the unions £4 million of their funds.

In 1927 the Conservatives celebrated their victory with the passing of a Trade Disputes Act. This declared that in future sympathetic strikes or strikes designed to coerce the government would be illegal. They would not enjoy the immunity afforded by the Act of 1906 and a court injunction could prohibit the use of trade-union funds in support of them. Peaceful picketing was defined much more rigorously and civil servants were forbidden to join a union associated with the TUC or the Labour party. The Act also included a clause whereby trade unionists wishing to contribute to the political levy, which was the mainstay of the Labour party's finances, would have to contract *in*, whereas until now by the Act of 1913 (see p. 73) payment could be assumed unless a trade unionist positively contracted *out*. This was purely a political move, since it was hoped that sheer inertia would reduce the amount paid in this way. It had already been proposed in 1925, when Baldwin had rejected it as a provocative measure, and its inclusion in the Act of 1927 is indicative of the way in which recent events had pushed him further to the right.

The Act certainly had a marked effect. Trade unions, fearful of heavy fines and damages in the courts, became extremely cautious, and men at the head of the movement such as Walter Citrine, J. H. Thomas and Ernest Bevin aimed now at a policy of compromise and reasonable cooperation. In the subsequent years strikes were far less frequent and the slight economic revival before the slump at the end of the decade made wage reductions unnecessary. With the continuing decline in world food prices the cost of living was still falling, so that the wage-earner, provided that he could avoid becoming one of the million unemployed, was relatively better off than he had been for a long time.

The political consequences were less clearcut. The change from contracting out to contracting in, coupled with the loss of the Civil Service unions, brought about a considerable drop in financial support for the Labour party whose numbers fell sharply. On the other hand, the openly partisan nature of the Act caused great resentment and stimulated the party organization to compensate for this loss by increasing their individual membership in the constituencies. Thus the Conservatives may have significantly aided the shift of the Labour party on to a national basis. This had been the purpose of the constitution adopted in 1918 and it forms an odd epilogue to the general strike, an unexpected bonus after the trials of Labour on the political and industrial fronts.

23

Recovery in Sight?

1. The hopes of the Locarno period

It had never been expected that the League of Nations could play much part in the settlement of immediate postwar problems, but by 1924 many of its ardent supporters believed that this panacea for all the world's ills should now come into its own. Superficially, at least, the last years of the decade did see the emergence of a new harmony and spirit of optimism in European affairs, but it is significant, in view of the later failure of the League, that this easing of international tension largely followed on the normal workings of diplomacy rather than from any great contribution from the new organization at Geneva.

Throughout its history the League was always to amount to a good deal less than the sum of its parts. Even its most pacifist advocates had recognized that if its decisions were to carry any weight, it must have some coercive power and the Covenant of the League had accordingly prescribed the collective pressure of economic and military sanctions against any country stigmatized as an aggressor by the Council. This statement of general principle, however, merely glossed over the practical difficulties involved in its application. In the first place, it was obvious that while Germany, Russia and the United States remained outside the League, no economic blockade could possibly be effective. 'Had we ever been able to foresee that America would not join,' wrote Sir Maurice Hankey to Lord Robert Cecil in 1924, 'I do not believe the Covenant could have included any sanctions or commitments.' It was also extremely doubtful how far member states would respond to an appeal from the League for military action, since the sheer extent of such an obligation might involve a country in hostilities in a part of the world where it had no vital interest at stake. The burden, too, was hardly likely to be equally shared, since Great Britain as the greatest naval power within the League would probably find herself charged with the task of policing the world, and Bonar Law's letter to *The Times* in 1922 had already voiced an understandable British reaction to that prospect—a view all the more strongly held by the various Dominions of the Empire. It had been these considerations that had caused the Labour government of 1924 to reject the draft treaty of mutual assistance (see p. 239), and although MacDonald and Henderson committed themselves to the Geneva Protocol as an acceptable alternative, this was bound to involve similar objections and in March 1925 it, too, was rejected by Austen Chamberlain, the Foreign Secretary in the new Conservative government.

The fundamental weakness of the League was that none of its members would seriously contemplate a surrender of national sovereignty and without that the only hope of success rested on good will and a calm international scene. This might be adequate to settle a dispute between Sweden and Finland over the Åland isles; it could not prevent Mussolini, the new Fascist leader of Italy, from bombarding and occupying Corfu in 1923 as a means of finding his own solution to a quarrel with Greece; nor could it have any effect on the fear and hostility that Germany aroused in France, who preferred to rely on a network of treaties with Belgium, Poland and Czechoslovakia.

Thus, old-fashioned diplomacy remained the principal instrument in foreign affairs. In the middle of the decade this did produce two relatively successful settlements: the implementing of the Dawes plan (see p. 238) in October 1924, and the Locarno agreements of 1925. The immediate consequences of the Dawes plan were certainly beneficial. It put the payment of reparations on a workable basis and the re-establishment of the Reichsmark created a new confidence in the German economy. The consequent influx of investment from the United States helped to produce a rapid expansion of German industry, and although this return of prosperity was dangerously dependent on short-term loans which might be called in at any moment, the mood at the time became markedly more cheerful, exhibiting a belief that the worst aspects of the aftermath of war were now past.

These hopes seemed to be confirmed by the settlement of the Locarno pact in the autumn of 1925. Proposals and counter-proposals over a guarantee of existing frontiers had multiplied during the previous years. In March 1925 Austen Chamberlain in his speech rejecting the Geneva Protocol suggested that as an alternative it might be possible to make 'special arrangements in order to meet special needs', and Stresemann, the German foreign minister, was quick to take this up. There were still many difficulties. France would have preferred a straightforward treaty of military alliance with Great Britain, which would underwrite her other treaties in eastern Europe; she was, too, still embroiled with Germany, refusing to evacuate Cologne after she had learnt of Germany's evasion of disarmament. Stresemann himself had to be careful not to antagonize Russia through any exclusive alignment with the west. In the end, however, a formula was discovered. The western frontiers of Germany, as well as the permanent demilitarization of the Rhineland, were collectively guaranteed by Great Britain, France, Belgium, Germany and Italy, while in the east Germany concluded arbitration treaties with Poland and Czechoslovakia.

For many, particularly in Great Britain, the signing of the Locarno agreements marked the opening of a new era of reconciliation and recovery. Immediately afterwards a preparatory commission for a world disarmament conference was set up. In 1926 Germany was elected to a permanent place on the League Council, although there was still an echo of the earlier resentments which Lloyd George had encountered at Genoa in the objections of Spain, Poland and Brazil, only silenced by the creation of three semi-permanent seats for them. And in January 1927 a further gesture of good faith was made towards Germany with the ending of the Allied Control Commission, despite its constant reports that the German government was continuing to evade the provisions for her disarmament stipulated in the Treaty of Versailles.

Certain features of the Locarno treaties should have held this wishful thinking in check. The confirmation of the existing frontiers could imply that the peace settlement which had established them was inadequate in itself. There followed no military staff talks to give practical effect to the guarantee, since these were virtually precluded by the collective nature of the agreement. In fact, the terms of Locarno had had to be carefully written around antagonisms and ambitions that could not be resolved. They did little to relieve the French of their sense of insecurity, and the separate arrangements over Poland and Czechoslovakia made it clear that the British had no intention of entering into any binding agreement east of the Rhine. Even the guarantee in the west was so vague as to be worthless, as Hitler was to demonstrate, when he reoccupied the Rhineland in 1936 (see p. 306).

The same concern with national self-interest played havoc with the preparatory commission for the disarmament conference. The United States, Great Britain and France argued endlessly over methods of assessing the size of armed forces, each demanding the one which would favour her own form of military organization. France insisted on some system of supervision, unacceptable to Italy and the United States, and in the summer of 1927 the British and the American naval chiefs fell out over a proposed cruiser strength which was inadequate for British needs. When the world disarmament conference (see p. 295) finally met in February 1932, the preparatory commission had been able to prepare nothing beyond rival sets of facts and figures.

However, although no universal formula was ever enunciated, Great Britain certainly did disarm during these years. The motive was economic and the justification was a decision taken by the cabinet in August 1919 that 'the British Empire will not be engaged in any great war during the next ten years'. This ten-year rule, which was not rescinded until 1933, was to be the basis of a dramatic reduction of all her armed forces. As early as 1919 Winston Churchill as Secretary of State for War and Air brought the RAF down to eighteen squadrons abroad and four at home, and during his time as Chancellor of the Exchequer from 1924 to 1929 he was engaged in long struggles with the Admiralty, whose annual estimates were eventually cut back to about £60 million.

Public opinion was on his side. The hatred of war and the rosy hopes of the Locarno period made the thought of all armaments abhorrent. The British preferred to put their faith in the Briand–Kellogg pact, a remarkable document signed initially by fifteen Powers in August 1928 and eventually by a total of sixty-five, all formally renouncing war as an instrument of national policy—a perfect symbol of the heady atmosphere of optimism that predominated at this time.

It would be wrong to mock the statesmanlike efforts of the triumvirate of foreign ministers, Chamberlain, Briand and Stresemann, in these years. They had done better than the League of Nations in moving towards an atmosphere of international cooperation. Austen Chamberlain was no longer in office when the Young plan, named after its American sponsor, proposed a reduction of German reparations, which was endorsed at The Hague in August 1929, but this, together with the Allied evacuation of the Rhineland five years ahead of schedule, was entirely in the spirit of his work; the French decision to bolster up their security by embarking on the construction of the Maginot line along their side of the Franco–German border may add a slightly sour note to this development, but it does at least serve to illustrate the deep feelings of mistrust with which he had had to contend.

2. The jazz age

It is as difficult to give a precise title to the 1920s as it is to define a Victorian or an Edwardian. 'The jazz age' was a phrase coined by Scott Fitzgerald and was inspired by the American scene; others have suggested 'the age of illusion' or 'the locust years' for the interwar period of British history, but on the whole the wail of the saxophone symbolizes quite satisfactorily the sense of a new era.

With all their virtues and faults the Victorians had sometimes been resented in the years before the war, but they had never been laughed at until Lytton Strachey published his *Eminent Victorians* in 1918. Among the younger people of the upper section of society the mood was brittle and cynical, a reaction against the war in which they had not served, and their antics formed the basis of the early novels of Aldous Huxley and Evelyn Waugh. As usual, the sense of difference was demonstrated most immediately in dress. For men the top hat and tail-coat faded into the lounge suit. Women's hair styles became short and boyish and their dresses tubular. Unlike their mothers, they ceased to have bosoms; instead, they had legs, as skirts rose giddily above the knee.

In fact, the break with the past was less emphatic than these superficial symptoms might suggest. It came more slowly and was in the main a continuation of processes at work before 1914. The population of the United Kingdom which, excluding the Irish Free State, had reached 44 million by 1921, was still growing, but, as before, this was principally due to the decline in the death rate. The birth rate was dropping much more sharply and the average number of children in a family had fallen from five to two. There was also a marked shift in the distribution of this population towards the south and into the towns. Landowners sold off unprofitable parts of their estates; farmers struggled with the world-wide fall in the prices of foodstuffs, and the number of agricultural workers dwindled. In contrast, salaried white-collar workers in industry and public administration almost doubled; these were mostly town-dwellers and as high-rise buildings were not yet the fashion, the dormitory suburbs spread outwards over the countryside and commuter services followed them. Between 1920 and 1929 the number of municipal buses had multiplied eight times and by 1930 there were over two million cars on the roads.

On the whole, the rich were a little less rich and employed slightly fewer domestic servants; the poverty of the poor was not quite so grinding, and in material terms the classes that lay in between had come a little closer to each other. Apart from this, however, much of Edwardian England lingered on. Despite the housing schemes of these years some 8 per cent of the population of England and Wales lived more than two to a room and in the cities this percentage was considerably higher. The slums vacated by those who gained council houses were soon occupied by others less fortunate. The bulk of children left school at fourteen and only about 7 per cent reached a secondary school. Universities catered for 30,000 students in England, 2,750 in Wales and 10,000 in Scotland, but of these Oxford and Cambridge still drew their undergraduates largely from the public schools. These figures differed very little from those before the war.

Probably the most striking aspect of the new urban culture was the growth of the cinema. This was the heyday of the silent film, immensely formative of fashion and common to all classes, but by the end of the decade the 'talkies' had arrived from America and before long only Charlie Chaplin remained silent. The cinema virtually killed the old-style music hall and little local theatres hurriedly turned over to showing films, just as the ornate picture palaces of the 1930s were to suffer from the onslaught of television after the Second World War.

Unlike the cinema, the advent of wireless in the home was a purely postwar phenomenon. In 1926 a private broadcasting company, established four years before under its general manager, John Reith, was transformed by royal charter into the British Broadcasting Corporation. Throughout the interwar years Reith, a Calvinist Scot, governed the entertainment of the nation in a spirit of highminded propriety. Radio announcers read the news in evening dress, church bells filled the intervals between programmes, and light variety shows, dance bands and plays of a middle-class background provided an innocuous fare. The BBC assisted in the growing standardization of spoken English, and although little opportunity was offered to contemporary composers, the established works of music reached a wider audience than ever before. Reith was certainly a great educational force in his time, but it was not education for the inquiring mind and all forms of religious and political controversy were barred.

In the field of literature D. H. Lawrence, James Joyce and Virginia Woolf were publishing their major works. Lawrence and Joyce both had some of their books banned on grounds of obscenity—hardly a necessary precaution, because very few people read them. The general public preferred the novels of Hugh Walpole or the crime fiction of Edgar Wallace, Agatha Christie and Sapper, and lending libraries, already well established before the war, continued to boom. The popular press was becoming increasingly national, competing for circulations that ran into millions. Most newspapers were of a conservative bias, but a left-wing publication, the *Daily Herald*, founded in 1912, was placed under the joint ownership of the Labour party and the TUC in 1922, although this did not enable it to escape constant financial difficulties.

Despite unemployment and industrial unrest Great Britain in the 1920s was a country of reasonable stability and contentment. There was less drunkenness and less church-going. Suburbia was the predominant feature of this society of commuters, cultivating their gardens and allotments and attending the local tennis or golf club. Many were conscious of having lived through hard times, but by now there seemed grounds for a quiet optimism. The war was a receding memory and it was comforting to think that there could never be another. Surely Locarno and the League of Nations would see to that, and perhaps at last recovery might really be in sight.

V

Depression and the Dictators
1929-1939

24

The Second Labour
Administration 1929–1931

1. The onset of the slump

Recovery might seem in sight, but the process of change had been too gradual for this to do the Conservatives any great good and the continuing existence of more than a million unemployed was a constant reproach to the apparent passivity of the government. For some time the leaders of the party organization watching the by-elections had been unhappily aware of indications of their declining popularity and many of them would have favoured a general election before the situation became worse.

Ironically, it was one of their own measures that made this impossible. 'The cabinet went mad yesterday,' wrote Lord Birkenhead in April 1927, 'and decided to give votes to women at the age of twenty-one.' This extension of the franchise did not become law until July 1928, after which the electoral registers had to be revised and the time required for this meant that there could be no general election before 1929. As a consequence the Conservatives had to linger on, while Parliament ran its full term of five years. With a snap election ruled out the only alternative course for the government would be to create a new sense of vitality with some radical changes in the cabinet. This, however, would certainly unleash the latent dissension over tariff reform and imperial preference, and emphasize the division between the left and the right of the party, which only Baldwin seemed able to bridge. Passivity appeared inescapable and when the election finally came, the Conservatives fell back on the slogan 'safety first', which was more appropriate to their own internal condition than to a party hoping to capture the support of the nation.

The Liberals at this time appeared to be in rather better shape. Asquith had resigned the leadership of the party in 1926 and this left Lloyd George free to establish a predominant influence before the next election, aided by the resources of his own political fund. The Liberal programme faced the country's problems with uninhibited zest (see p.

215). A series of publications outlined a system of close governmental participation in the running of the economy, and the most famous of these, entitled *We Can Conquer Unemployment*, proposed vast public works, principally in road-building, to be financed by a deficit in the budget. This last reflected the influence of J. M. Keynes, who commented somewhat characteristically at the time: 'The difference between me and some other people is that I oppose Mr Lloyd George when he is wrong and support him when he is right.'[1]

Labour's preparations had been less specific. An official document, *Labour and the Nation*, was largely a statement of general principle and at the party conference of 1928 it had been seriously criticized by the ILP for being far too moderate in its brand of Socialism. This debate between varieties of left-wing opinion allowed little time for devising a precise electoral programme and Labour eventually fell back on producing a replica of Lloyd George's proposals, merely maintaining that anything that Liberals could do, Labour could do better—an empty boast, as it turned out.

The general election was held in May 1929. The result was hardly conclusive, beyond suggesting that the voting system did not allow an accurate representation of the true balance of political opinion in the country. The Liberals gained a poll of over 5 million, but their support was so scattered that they won only fifty-nine seats. This justification of their earlier demand for proportional representation did little to remove the sting of disappointment and one of them wrote in despair: 'The future of the old party hardly bears thinking about.' The Conservative and Labour parties captured the bulk of the seats, each polling more than 8 million votes, although here too there was an anomaly in that the Conservatives polled 300,000 more than Labour, but owing to the distribution of the constituencies Labour won 288 seats against the Conservatives' 260.

At least this meant that the Liberals held the balance, but Baldwin had no intention of letting them demonstrate their power over the Conservatives in the House of Commons. He did not trust any proposal that Lloyd George might make for a Conservative–Liberal combination against Labour and he rejected Neville Chamberlain's advice that they should carry on until they met open defeat in the Commons. On 4 June Baldwin handed in the resignation of his government and Ramsay MacDonald became Prime Minister for the second time.

The Labour administration of 1929 was very similar in personalities to that of 1924; so too were the difficulties over satisfying some of the individuals involved. This time Arthur Henderson was determined to be

Foreign Secretary, and J. H. Thomas, whom MacDonald would have preferred for that position, was eventually made Lord Privy Seal, in which capacity he was to attempt to deal with the unemployment problem. Philip Snowden was again to be Chancellor of the Exchequer, J. R. Clynes took the Home Office and Sidney Webb became Colonial and Dominions Secretary, moving to the House of Lords with the title of Lord Passfield. Two parliamentary secretaries of the 1924 administration now took charge of their previous departments, Arthur Greenwood as Minister of Health and Miss Margaret Bondfield as Minister of Labour, the first woman to attain cabinet rank in British history. Of the newcomers who were eventually to play various parts on the political scene, Herbert Morrison, who had become Mayor of Hackney in 1920 and had built up Labour power in the London County Council, took over the Ministry of Transport; Sir Oswald Mosley, a brilliant young recruit to the Labour movement, became Chancellor of the Duchy of Lancaster, Hugh Dalton Under-Secretary for Foreign Affairs and, in 1930, Sir Stafford Cripps Solicitor-General. Clement Attlee, who was too occupied as a member of the Simon commission on India (see p. 290), held no post for the moment.

The most striking feature of the new government was the absence of any strong doctrinaire left-wing element. The older members represented a very cautious constitutional outlook and those who might have taken things at a faster pace, Mosley, Cripps and Dalton, were too junior to exercise any great influence—all of them, oddly enough, the products of a public school education. John Wheatley, James Maxton and F. W. Jowett, who had been spokesmen of the more radical ILP programme, were excluded, and George Lansbury, one of the few left-wingers to find a place in the government, was rendered harmless with the post of First Commissioner of Works. 'He would not have much opportunity for squandering money,' commented Philip Snowden, 'but would be able to do a great many small things which would improve the amenities of government buildings and the public parks.'[2] And so the most revolutionary achievement that was open to Lansbury was the building of an open-air swimming pool on the Serpentine in London.

Although Labour did not command a majority in the Commons, they were in a slightly stronger position than in 1924. Liberal abstention they could now withstand; a sizeable Liberal vote alongside the Conservative Opposition could bring them down. Nevertheless, Ramsay MacDonald clearly did not feel that he could act as if the government had a mandate from the country. 'I wonder how far it is possible without in any way abandoning our party positions,' he said in his opening speech as Prime Minister in the House of Commons, '. . . to consider ourselves as a Council of State and less as arrayed regiments facing each other in battle.'[3] This did not mean, as was later suggested, that he was already contemplating the formation of a National government, but it does underline the sense of insecurity with which he embarked upon his second administration, and one of his supporters suggested that the government's position restricted it to the task of 'keeping things going'—another version of 'safety first'.

In fact, his position was not at all as weak as it might appear, owing to the state of confusion in the other parties. The Liberals, their hopes dashed, had reverted to their normal condition of quarrelling factions. In the Commons Lloyd George's tactics led him first to oppose Labour and then to swing over to a policy of support, and this 'roving political eye', as a colleague described it, added greatly to the mistrust with which he was regarded within his own party—by as many as one-third, Sir Herbert Samuel stated in his *Memoirs*.

The Conservatives, too, were caught up in a struggle over their own leadership. To the younger men it seemed that Stanley Baldwin accepted the second electoral defeat under his management all too benignly. 'Everywhere', wrote Neville Chamberlain to his sister in July 1930, 'I hear that there is no confidence in his leadership or belief in his determination to carry any policy through.' Only the fierce differences that divided his critics saved him from eviction. Winston Churchill and Austen Chamberlain stood together in support of free trade and in the field of parliamentary tactics advocated an alliance with the Liberals to oust the Labour government—an echo of the battle over the continuation of the Coalition in 1922. Against them Leo Amery rejected the idea of a Liberal alliance and continued to preach the doctrine of an imperial economic system: free trade within the Empire protected by tariffs against foreign imports. Baldwin satisfied none of them. He refused to commit himself to a tariff on foreign foodstuffs which the Empire scheme would involve, and he agreed to support Labour's negotiations which would allow greater self-government for India, an issue which eventually led Winston Churchill to renounce any official position within the Conservative party (see p. 291).

The question of the tariff gained Baldwin a particularly dangerous enemy in the shape of the Beaverbrook–Rothermere press campaigning vigorously for imperial preference, but an episode in 1930 soon showed that he was equal to this challenge. Lord Rothermere had written a letter to a Conservative MP saying that his support of Baldwin would be dependent upon knowing what his policy was, together with the names of eight or ten of his prominent colleagues in the next Conservative administration; this gave Baldwin the opportunity to denounce such terms as 'a preposterous and insolent demand' before a meeting of Conservative MPs at Caxton Hall. In March 1931 the issue came to a head when the press lords sponsored their own anti-Baldwin candidate in a by-election at St George's, Westminster. The party rallied to the support of their leader by putting up Duff Cooper as the official Conservative candidate and two days before the polling Baldwin delivered his great onslaught: 'What the proprietorship of those papers is aiming at is power, and power without responsibility—the prerogative of the harlot through the ages.'[4] Duff Cooper won the election and Baldwin had established himself once again in the public eye as the quiet moderate man who would always stand for the defence of constitutional practice, whether the attack came from a general strike or from the press lords.

Despite its short life the MacDonald administration did achieve a little. The conditions under which the unemployed might qualify for benefit were eased. The Coal Mines Act of 1930 reduced the working day from eight hours to seven and a half without any lowering of wages, and in the same year a Housing Act launched a programme of slum clearance. There was less success with other domestic measures, and Bills raising the school-leaving age to fifteen, legalizing sympathetic strikes, and revising the electoral system with the abolition of plural voting and the introduction of the alternative vote were all rejected or wrecked by amendment in the House of Lords.

Abroad there was more to show. Henderson worked to restore diplomatic relations with Russia, broken off in 1927, and was able to complete this with a commercial treaty. At Geneva he became a leading figure in pressing on with the preparatory arrangements for the disarmament conference, of which he was eventually elected president when it met in 1932. Some of this goodwill was lost when Snowden at a conference at The Hague insisted that Great Britain's share of German reparations should not be reduced in a revised system of payment under the Young plan (see p. 255) and gained most of what he was demanding. Still, it could be hoped that relations with Germany might improve with the Allied evacuation of the Rhineland. Ramsay MacDonald, with his penchant for foreign affairs, also had his moment of triumph. A further round of talks over naval disarmament had failed in 1927 (see p. 254), but after a successful visit to the United States MacDonald was able to bring about a new conference at London in January 1930, where some of the gaps left by the Washington agreements of 1922 (see p. 199) were plugged. He offered to reduce the number of British cruisers to fifty and with this managed to secure agreement that the relative strength of the

British, American and Japanese navies should be of the ratio 5: 5: 3 in cruisers, destroyers and submarines, although the rivalry of France and Italy made it impossible to include them in the general settlement.

When all this is said, the entire history of the Labour administration is overshadowed by the world slump which began when a wild boom in the United States suddenly faltered and then collapsed in the Wall Street crash of October 1929. This was bound to affect the rest of the world in two ways. First, the growth of unemployment in America meant that she no longer supplied a great market for the exports of other countries, who in turn now found their own purchasing power reduced; thus trade everywhere declined. Second, the need to realize their capital caused many American concerns frantically to call in a large number of short-term loans. Germany in particular had depended on such loans; once deprived of them, there was no escape for her from rapidly mounting unemployment and the consequent shrinking of the German market meant a further descent down the economic spiral.

Between 1929 and 1931 the value of British exports dropped from £729 million to £391 million, and unemployment rose from just over a million in June 1929 to 2·5 million in December 1930 and had reached 3 million by 1933. Imports dropped correspondingly, but since they were still in excess of her exports, Great Britain remained dependent on her invisible earnings from investment income, shipping and insurance to close this gap. In the new world situation these earnings now fell away and by 1931 she had a deficit in her balance of payments, a factor which was to have a decisive influence on government reactions to the crisis.

None of this should have come as a surprise to orthodox Socialists, since they had always predicted the eventual collapse of capitalism. MacDonald himself said as much when he addressed the annual party conference in October 1930. 'My friends, *we* are not on trial, it is the system under which we live. It has broken down, not only on this little island; it has broken down in Europe, in Asia, in America; it has broken down everywhere, as it was bound to break down. And the cure, the new path, the new idea is Organization.'[5] This, then, should have been the great opportunity for Socialism to prove its worth and for a Labour government to establish a comprehensive governmental control of the economy in sharp contrast to the anarchy of *laissez-faire* amid the fluctuations of the trade cycle. The irony for Labour at this moment was that the senior members of the government could not cut loose from existing economic precepts and were thus condemned to policies which ran directly contrary to their ideological outlook.

No one could doubt the sincerity of Philip Snowden's belief in Socialism, but like so many of the earlier working-class leaders who had rejected the outright Marxism of the SDF (see p. 27), he saw it in moral terms rather than economic. 'Socialism to me', he wrote in his *Autobiography*, 'has been a principle, the principle of cooperation as opposed to competition.'[6] He wanted to bring about the regeneration of society, but although he was prepared to reduce the great inequalities of income through parliamentary processes of taxation, he was no advocate of radical change in the actual mechanism of the economy. Given the present situation, his mind was set in a nineteenth-century mould. For him there could be no abandonment of the gold standard, even though this might enable British exporters to sell their goods at lower prices in foreign currencies. He believed that Great Britain would be guilty of a breach of good faith if she reduced the value of the pound sterling in which others had invested, and, worst of all, he was convinced that uncontrollable inflation would ensue, once the anchor of gold had been lost—the great fear that explains so much of the economic attitudes of the time. Equally, he would not contemplate protection as a means of reducing British imports from abroad, as it had always been assumed in the Labour party that this would bring a rise in the cost of food.

Still more, any notion of stimulating the economy by more positive government intervention was totally abhorrent to Snowden. In this he was strongly supported by Treasury officials and here can be seen a clear instance of the great divide in economic thinking (see p. 214). Younger men of all parties believed that the government had a duty to reverse the prevailing trend by using its own credit to stimulate the domestic market. 'Government investment will break the vicious circle,' said Keynes in February 1930. 'If you can do that for a couple of years, it will have the effect, if my diagnosis is right, of restoring business profits more nearly to normal and if that can be achieved, then private enterprise will be revived.'[7] For Snowden any such tinkering with the economic processes had always seemed unsound. 'An expansion of the currency', he had said in 1927, 'must respond to a genuine demand arising out of real purchasing power and not be used to create a demand.' And now at a time of wide depression he could not contemplate the expenditure demanded by the vast schemes of public works which had formed part of Labour's electoral programme. It seemed to him unpardonable that the government of a country whose balance of payments figures were unfavourable should embark on domestic expenditure which would also entail a deficit.

Once his mind was made up, Snowden was a difficult man to shift.

'He had been crippled by an accident in youth,' wrote Amery of him, 'and his lean face, hollow cheeks and sunken eyes bespoke the pain from which he habitually suffered, while his rat-trap mouth told of a will, not only steeled to conquer pain, but intolerant of all concession or compromise.'[8] Debt he hated as fiercely as he hated drink and gambling. The budget must balance and a policy of retrenchment and economy must bring down the nation's expenditure in accordance with the world-wide fall in prices; as under the Conservatives, the trade cycle had to be allowed to call the tune.

Among the rank and file of the Labour party there was actually little enthusiasm for marshalling squads of unemployed to work on the roads. It all smacked too much of the municipal public works schemes of the nineteenth century, a disguised form of charity remote from the thought of a Socialist society. Yet the alternative seemed equally remote from it, as the Labour Chancellor held firm with puritanical zeal to his policy of curbing public expenditure. Certainly it appeared so to one Labour MP, W. J. Brown, secretary of the Civil Service Clerical Association, when he wrote: 'It seems that we have spent twenty years destroying the Liberal Party in order to get a government whose policy is less radical in relation to the needs of today than that of the Liberals was in relation to the needs of 1906–14.'

There was not total unanimity in the government over the action to be taken. J. H. Thomas, with his special responsibility for the problem of unemployment, set about his task with some vigour, aided by a team consisting of George Lansbury, Sir Oswald Mosley and Thomas Johnston, Under-Secretary for Scotland. During the early months of the administration they produced a host of ideas, including road-building, land reclamation and even a settlement in Western Australia. The outcome was always the same. The relevant departments, and behind them the Chancellor of the Exchequer, all declared such schemes to be prohibitively expensive. 'Jimmy,' Leo Amery had said to Thomas, 'you are starting your job with a noose round your neck and the other end of the rope in Snowden's hands',[9] and as Thomas learnt the truth of this, he eventually gave up the struggle.

This surrender by Thomas was too much for Mosley. Indeed, these two were hardly compatible personalities. Educated at an elementary school, Thomas had started life as an engine driver before rising rapidly in the world of railway trade unionism to become general secretary of the NUR in 1917. Good-humoured and irrepressible, he appeared to regard himself as a music-hall caricature of the working man, and while this may have endeared him to some Conservatives, it only irritated many of the left. For them he had too many friends in the City and they did not laugh when the cartoonist Low called him 'Right Hon. Dress Shirt' in the *Evening Standard*.

In contrast, Sir Oswald Mosley was a young man of wealthy upper-middle-class background. Educated at Winchester, he had served as an officer in the war and later married the daughter of Lord Curzon. In the 1920s he had steered an impetuous course from party to party, always impatient to achieve results, consumed with a desire to lead, temperamentally averse to the slow working of parliamentary constitutionalism. 'I doubt, indeed,' wrote Snowden afterwards, 'if anyone would be able to work with Mosley, unless he were prepared to meekly follow him.'[10] It was soon clear at least that Mosley could not work with Jimmy Thomas, for whom he had utter contempt, and early in 1930 he produced on his own initiative a memorandum for consideration by the cabinet after only the most desultory consultation with the Lord Privy Seal.

The Mosley memorandum, as it became known, was a remarkably imaginative and powerful document, an elaboration of the scheme that he had already put forward in *Revolution by Reason* in 1925 (see p. 215). It proposed the forming of a central executive committee under the Prime Minister, aided by a number of standing committees. This body would be responsible for implementing two sets of policies. First, a long-term plan would aim at insulating the British economy, reducing exports to a level sufficient merely to cover the cost of the importing of foodstuffs, and concentrating otherwise on internal development with government aid and the diverting of investment away from overseas back into the home market. Second, a short-term plan to deal with unemployment would establish a great programme of public works, and at the same time the amount of idle labour to be absorbed by this would be reduced by lowering the retirement age and raising the school-leaving age to fifteen. Most of this would have to be financed by loans, which Keynes had already assured him would not be impossible.

These proposals amounted to a revolution in the state management of finance and industry; they also struck at the root of the great controversy over economic policy, and it was not hard to predict Snowden's attitude towards them. He regarded Mosley's figures as absurd; furthermore, the scheme would mean the abandonment of the gold standard and of free trade, and in May 1930 the cabinet rejected it.

Mosley resigned, made two unsuccessful appeals to the parliamentary party, and then in October came close to defeating the executive at the party conference held at Llandudno. Had he been prepared to rally a group from within the Labour party, he might eventually have achieved success, and there are many who reckon that a man of his ability could eventually have become Prime Minister in a later Labour administration. As it was, the fatal flaw of impatience undermined him. In February 1931 he announced the formation of a New Party, and this resulted in his expulsion from the Labour party. The New Party failed to win any by-elections. The few parliamentary associates who had joined him began to move away, as they came to suspect Mosley's autocratic tendencies, and a year later their fears were confirmed when he founded the British Union of Fascists (see p. 288). In this way a brilliant young politician wrecked his career, and as one potential Prime Minister vanished from the scene, another moved forward to ministerial rank, when Clement Attlee was appointed Chancellor of the Duchy of Lancaster in his place.

The government had not wanted Mosley's policy; they were still a long way from discovering one of their own. Thomas, clearly unable to achieve anything, was made Secretary for the Dominions, and MacDonald himself became chairman of a panel of ministers to deal with unemployment. In February 1930 an economic advisory council had already been set up, including Keynes and Ernest Bevin, but its large membership inevitably reflected the continuing debate between the two schools of thought—deflationary versus expansionary policies— and by August 1931 its thirteen meetings had produced nothing very concrete.

In July 1931 a committee of finance and industry, which had been sitting since 1929 under the chairmanship of Lord Macmillan, did reach some conclusions which were a little more positive in that, while advocating the maintenance of the gold standard, they recommended the beginning of a reflationary policy on the basis of international loans organized in conjunction with France and the United States. The government, however, had scarcely had time to consider the findings in the Macmillan report, when the report of yet another committee, published at the end of July, was to bring the Labour administration to its supreme crisis.

2. Labour's dilemma

Since the early months of 1931 Philip Snowden had viewed the chances of balancing his April budget with profound gloom. The figures for unemployment were rising beyond 2·5 million; the consequent increase in the total payment of benefit was driving the unemployment insurance fund into debt to the extent of £90 million, and this would ultimately have to be financed by the Exchequer. Extra revenue could only come from further taxes, but he was sure that he ought not to add to the burden on industry already in serious difficulty. The only alternative was a reduction in government expenditure. This must almost certainly mean a cut in the amount of unemployment benefit, which had stood at 17 shillings (85p) since 1928, and the problem here was that such a policy would fly in the face of all the stated beliefs and pledges of the Labour party.

For the moment he tried to play for time in the hope that the trade figures would improve. In February, in response to a Liberal proposal, a new committee was appointed to explore means whereby government expenditure could be reduced, and this set to work at once under the chairmanship of Sir George May, the retiring chairman of the Prudential Insurance Company. Meanwhile, in April Snowden produced an interim budget, which outlined no new financial policy, but simply made temporary arrangements to avoid an immediate deficit, mainly through raids and anticipations, with a minimum of new taxes; he knew, however, that in all probability there could be no escape from a real austerity budget in the autumn.

The report of the May committee, which was published on 31 July 1931, could hardly have painted a more desperate picture. By including the Sinking Fund requirement and the whole of the debts of the unemployment insurance fund it declared that by April 1932 government finances would show a deficit of £120 million. Over the possible remedies the committee was divided, since the two Labour representatives stated in their minority report that the principal solution lay in additional taxation. The other five members, however, were only prepared to recommend the raising of £24 million by extra taxes; a further £97 million must be found by a reduction in government expenditure. They proposed that the salaries of teachers should be cut by 20 per cent, the police by 12·5 per cent and the fighting services by 10 per cent. The greatest saving was to come from the unemployment fund with a reduction of 20 per cent in the standard rate of benefit, a limitation of benefits to twenty-six weeks in any single year, a means test and an increase in weekly contribution. Thus the majority report was a firm statement of the orthodox deflationary view—'the most foolish document I have ever had the misfortune to read',[11] commented Keynes afterwards.

The significance of its publication lies in the fact that this coincided with a new phase of the international financial crisis in Europe. In June

1931 Kreditanstalt, the largest banking concern in Austria, declared virtual bankruptcy, and as securities in Austria and Hungary were frozen, there ensued a frantic race among European concerns to realize their foreign investments elsewhere in order to meet their immediate requirements. Withdrawals from German banks reached such a point that on 15 July the Reichsbank had to impose exchange control and the pressure shifted to London. The problem for the London bankers was that they had to face this demand by foreign creditors to withdraw their sterling investments at a time when many of their own assets were frozen in central Europe. With Great Britain still on the gold standard the run on the pound resulted in the Bank of England paying out £33 million in gold in the last two weeks of July, and as a consequence a loan of £50 million had hastily to be arranged with the Bank of France and the American Federal Bank.

Strictly this new turn of events had no economic connection with the difficulties that Snowden was anticipating in balancing his books. The publication of the May report, however, did draw the attention of the world's bankers to the likelihood of an unbalanced budget in Great Britain. Like Snowden and many others they believed that this was an unsound situation, if it was allowed to happen at a time of economic stress, and thus a lack of confidence was created just when the Bank of England was seriously in need of foreign credit. Furthermore, orthodox banking circles were highly suspicious of a Labour government; the possibility of a budget deficit raised the question of the type of government expenditure responsible for it, and from this moment it was not merely Snowden's rigidity of outlook, but also the attitude of the foreign bankers that placed the Labour administration in its dilemma.

There was no great sense of urgency in the government's immediate reactions. The May report was not published until a few hours after Parliament had adjourned for its summer recess on 31 July. Snowden had informed the Commons that the government would produce its proposals when they reassembled in October and a cabinet economy committee, including MacDonald, Snowden, Henderson, Thomas and Graham, President of the Board of Trade, was set up, with a first meeting arranged for 25 August. The response of the bankers to the May report soon altered this schedule. On 11 August Ramsay MacDonald hurried back from Lossiemouth and at a meeting of the cabinet economy committee Snowden informed his colleagues that the estimated deficit for April 1932 would be as much as £170 million rather than the £120 million suggested by the May committee; furthermore, the opinion of the bankers was that no further credits from abroad would be available unless the autumn budget wiped that out; and without these credits the gold standard could not be preserved.

The first part of the story revolves round MacDonald's attempts to retain cabinet unity in the face of this crisis. On the whole, the need for a balanced budget seems to have been accepted; it was the means whereby this was to be achieved that was the reason for the anguished controversy which ensued amid a welter of proposals for economic cuts and new taxes. On 18 August the cabinet economy committee put forward for consideration cuts in government expenditure of £78·5 million, which must mean a reduction of unemployment benefit, although Henderson and Graham insisted that they would not be bound by this proposal. On 19 August the cabinet debated this, but could not agree on a figure beyond £56 million. Even this would mean increasing unemployment insurance contributions and limiting the payment of benefit to twenty-six weeks, but it did at least avoid reducing the rate of benefit to be paid out. It still left a large gap to be bridged, and the only alternative solution discussed—a tariff for the purpose of raising revenue—was totally unacceptable to Snowden.

MacDonald's problem was not confined to reaching a formula which would satisfy his colleagues. He was caught between the fire of two uncompromising bodies outside the cabinet: the Opposition leaders and the TUC. Neither the Conservatives nor the Samuel Liberals would consider cuts of anything less than £78·5 million. The attitude of the general council of the TUC, dominated by its secretary Walter Citrine and Ernest Bevin, was that the City financiers had created their own difficulties by borrowing on short-term and lending on long-term and were now attempting to use the unbalanced budget as a scapegoat. Thus, when MacDonald appealed to them, they would hear nothing of reductions in salaries or in unemployment benefit.

Wearily during the next two days MacDonald attempted to manoeuvre the cabinet towards an acceptance of greater economies, but a sizeable section of his colleagues, now strengthened by the known attitude of the TUC, remained determined not to take them above £56 million, leaving the rest of the deficit to be covered by new taxation. The situation seemed hopeless. On the morning of 23 August Ramsay MacDonald went to Buckingham Palace to warn the King that the opposition of Henderson and Graham within the cabinet must probably mean the resignation of the Labour government, and the King decided with his consent to interview the leaders of the other two parties.

The events of the subsequent twenty-four hours make up the second part of the story. Sir Herbert Samuel, acting for Lloyd George who had been undergoing an operation, was the first to see the King. He suggested that ideally a reconstituted Labour cabinet should devise a scheme for drastic economies, but if that proved impossible, then in his own words 'a National government of members of the three parties would be the best alternative' under the continued leadership of Ramsay MacDonald. That afternoon the King, deeply impressed by this advice, interviewed Baldwin, who confirmed that he would be prepared to serve in such a government.

The idea of a combination of the three parties in a National government to deal with the crisis had been in the air for some time. It had been discussed in the press and had been a common talking point among politicians. Ideally it conjured up an attractive picture of the parties sinking their differences in an effort to work together for the good of the country. At the less idealistic level of party politics it had other attractions as well. MacDonald had certainly reflected upon it—although how seriously and at what stage has remained a matter of debate—reckoning that, as unpopular measures had to be introduced, it would be better for the image of the Labour party if the responsibility for these were shared by all parties. For precisely the same reason the leaders of the two Opposition parties had preferred that the Labour government should manage the task alone. Now, however, as the intransigence of the TUC had been made clear, they could also see advantages to be derived from the forming of a National government under MacDonald, since this might very well create a split in the Labour party.

Certainly the cabinet itself was already virtually split. On the evening of 23 August a vote was taken on a purely tentative proposal to the Opposition for a 10 per cent cut in unemployment benefit, making a total economy of £76 million. Nine out of twenty-one rejected this and MacDonald now decided that the Labour government could not carry on. It was agreed that he should go at once to Buckingham Palace to recommend to the King a meeting of the three party leaders for the next morning, and on his return none of the ministers seemed to be in any doubt that the resignation of the government would follow on the next day and that Labour would once again be in Opposition under MacDonald. This, too, was the impression of the leading members of the Conservative party with whom MacDonald conferred later that night.

They were all due for a surprise. On the morning of Monday 24 August at the meeting at the Palace the King asked that, since Labour was unable to continue, the three leaders should consider Samuel's proposal. In little more than an hour MacDonald had taken his decision.

He agreed that on the resignation of the Labour administration he would head a National government, not a coalition, but 'a co-operation of individuals', based on the understanding that economies of £70 million would be introduced, including a 10 per cent cut in unemployment benefit and increased insurance contributions.

It must have been a remarkable scene when MacDonald returned to his cabinet and announced what he had done. There was a silence of shocked horror. To his colleagues it seemed that he was deserting his party in order to continue in alliance with their political foes, and it was immediately clear that the great majority of the cabinet were opposed to following their Prime Minister in such a course. From the many accounts there seems to have been no anger and no recrimination; there was a little formal business, even a vote of thanks to MacDonald for his past services, carried unanimously. At the end of the meeting the Prime Minister asked J. H. Thomas, Lord Sankey and Snowden to remain behind and these three did agree to serve under him in a new administration. Thus amid an atmosphere of strained official decorum the second Labour administration came to a close and Ramsay MacDonald entered upon the twilight of his political career.

That afternoon he addressed a meeting of junior ministers and whips to tell them the reasons for his action, how he believed that the budget must be balanced in a way that would satisfy foreign creditors, that otherwise sterling would collapse and in the ensuing run on the banks individual savings would be destroyed. He did not ask them to follow him, because he realized that he was committing political suicide. 'It is as though a martyr was speaking, just before a cruel death,'[12] noted Hugh Dalton in his diary. Later that day MacDonald gave the King his resignation as Prime Minister of the Labour government and on 26 August the Labour cabinet surrendered their seals of office.

The new emergency cabinet was sworn in almost at once. MacDonald as Prime Minister and Lord Sankey, Snowden and Thomas in their former positions were all that was left of the previous government. Baldwin as Lord President of the Council, Neville Chamberlain as Minister of Health, Sir Samuel Hoare as Secretary of State for India and Sir Philip Cunliffe-Lister* as President of the Board of Trade represented the Conservative element, while of the Liberals Sir Herbert Samuel became Home Secretary and the Marquis of Reading Foreign Secretary.

There may have been few recriminations around the table at that last cabinet meeting, but a great many followed soon afterwards. There was

* He became Viscount Swinton in 1935 (see p. 300).

much talk of sinister unconstitutional forces undermining the unity of the government. The most common cry from the left was that the whole thing had been a 'bankers' ramp', placing Labour in an impossible situation. It was even said that the King had acted unconstitutionally in advocating a National administration, while from the right the TUC were accused of attempting to dictate to the government.

There seems little substance in any of these charges. The bankers, like the Treasury officials, held traditional views on finance and genuinely believed that the run on the pound, which had arisen out of recent economic events on the Continent, could only be checked by a restoration of confidence in sterling; their demand that the budget should be made to balance at the price of cuts in government expenditure may have reflected their natural suspicion of Labour extravagance, but prejudice and adherence to nineteenth-century economic principles do not amount to a conspiracy.

Nor is there any evidence that George V acted other than strictly in accordance with the constitution. He had summoned the two Opposition leaders on the Prime Minister's advice; it had been Samuel who had proposed a National government and the King had done no more than to suggest further discussion of this, after endeavouring unsuccessfully to persuade Ramsay MacDonald to carry on with his Labour government. At that time MacDonald had a bare majority of the cabinet with him and the King may have felt that this would also be reflected in the parliamentary party. Had he known how little Labour support MacDonald would have in forming a National government, he might have abandoned the project and asked Stanley Baldwin to take over instead.

The general council of the TUC had also been perfectly within their rights in stating their opposition to the proposed 10 per cent cut, when asked for their advice, and although they made alternative suggestions and were outspoken at a joint meeting with the national executive and the consultative committee of the Parliamentary Labour Party after the government had resigned, they do not seem to have exercised any pressure on Labour MPs and cabinet ministers beyond the expression of their disapproval.

The central enigma lies in the motives of Ramsay MacDonald. It was easy for his opponents to accuse him of ambition; he certainly enjoyed the social trimmings of high office and he loved his official country residence at Chequers. Equally, if he accepted the views of the established economists and financiers, as he clearly did, it could be said that he had preferred to put his country before his party, believing that the alternative of an insecure Conservative–Liberal combination in conflict with a large Labour Opposition in the Commons would be an undesirable situation at a time when a united national effort appeared vital. He had always been on the right wing of Labour and when the opposition of the general council of the TUC had been made apparent, he may well have felt that he alone could save the country from economic disaster amid political discord. Vanity confused with a genuine sense of responsibility probably lay at the heart of his decision rather than any more cold calculation. 'Any man in my position at the time knowing all that I did would have acted as I acted,' he said to Harold Nicolson long afterwards. 'However, I wish sometimes that someone else had been in my position at the time.'

His regret was understandable. Almost the entire Parliamentary Labour Party rejected MacDonald's manoeuvre. Only a handful stood by him in the Commons to form a National Labour group and on 28 August a combined meeting of the Parliamentary Labour Party and the general council of the TUC removed him from the leadership of the party. The rest moved into Opposition under Arthur Henderson, and Ramsay MacDonald now found himself at the head of a government dependent on Conservative and Liberal votes and harried by the party to which he had devoted his life.

25

The Domestic Record of the National Government 1931–1939

1. The consolidation of the National government

Once the new government had been formed the bankers kept their word, and on 28 August a credit of £80 million was raised from Paris and New York. Parliament reassembled on 8 September. The Commons passed a vote of confidence by a majority of sixty against the Labour Opposition under Arthur Henderson and two days later Snowden produced his balanced budget. He gained an extra £76 million with new taxes, raising income tax to 5 shillings (25p) in the pound, lowered the payment to the sinking fund by £17·5 million and introduced the stipulated economies of £70 million. The salaries of ministers, judges, civil servants and the armed forces were lowered by 10 per cent, while teachers were singled out for a cut of 15 per cent. Unemployment benefit was also reduced by 10 per cent, a means test imposed, contributions increased and the benefit period limited to twenty-six weeks in a year.

The immediate consequence of Snowden's budget was precisely the reverse of what had been anticipated. The House of Commons might be prepared to accept the projected cuts in pay; the sailors at Invergordon were not, and on 15 September they refused to fall in for duty. The episode was at once damped down with some tactful concessions, but the damage had been done. To foreign investors, their nerves already on edge, the thought of mutiny in the British Navy was like the crack of doom; there was a new rush to sell sterling. In three days the Bank of England paid out £33 million in gold and foreign exchange and by 19 September the country's holdings of gold were down to £130 million. Two days later, on the urgent advice of the Bank, Great Britain officially went off the gold standard.

Few naval operations have accomplished so much. In the eyes of the Treasury officials and of Philip Snowden the gold standard had until now been sacrosanct and the main object of the National government had been to preserve it. Yet within a few weeks of the forming of the new administration it had been abandoned after all. No disaster followed. London remained the principal money market and there was certainly no likelihood of inflation. The pound, no longer tied to a fixed rate, fell from $4·86 to about $3·80, which in more prosperous times would have helped the export trade greatly and even now had some effect. The average member of the public, somewhat bewildered by the fickleness of the experts, was not aware of any great difference in his pound note; he worried far more about keeping his job or, if he was in state employ, about coping with the reduction in his salary.

There followed in October 1931 a general election. It was obviously correct that after such a strange sequence of events the electorate should be able to express their feelings, although MacDonald did not relish the prospect, fearing rightly that an election coming so soon would probably confirm his own isolation. The great problem was to decide the programme on which the National government should campaign. The only feasible solution was to have none, to ask for a 'doctor's mandate', *carte blanche* to do whatever seemed best. 'The government must therefore be free,' said Ramsay MacDonald in an election broadcast, 'to consider every proposal likely to help, such as tariffs, expansion of exports and contraction of imports, commercial treaties and mutual economic arrangements with the Dominions.'

Carte blanche might certainly appeal to an electorate that had little idea of the correct economic remedy, but the separate election manifestoes which each party issued suggested that a doctor's mandate would end in a long squabble over the diagnosis. Baldwin emphasized the need for tariffs; the Liberals demanded the retention of free trade. The Liberals, however, were in their usual state of disarray; a group under Sir John Simon accepted protection, and Lloyd George, now convalescent, was so furious with Samuel for agreeing to an election that he refused to sign the official party manifesto. Instead, he issued his own in which he denounced the election as 'a mere Tory ramp to exploit a national emergency for Tory ends', and refused the party financial assistance from his own political fund. Outside the government, Labour under Arthur Henderson produced an orthodox statement criticizing the recent budget and advocating public control of the banking system and the basic industries, which after Labour's recent performance was not likely to carry much weight.

The election proved to be a remarkable vote of confidence for the National government, which was returned with 554 seats. This was a barely disguised victory for the Conservatives who won 473 of them, in comparison with thirteen National Labour, thirty-five Simonite Liberals and thirty-three Liberals. The Opposition amounted to no more than sixty-one, including forty-six Labour and six ILP. The extremes of political opinion were decisively rejected by the electorate; neither the Communists nor Mosley's New Party gained a single seat, and of Mosley's twenty-four candidates twenty-two forfeited their deposits.

These figures might suggest that the country as a whole strongly favoured the action MacDonald had taken. It does not seem likely, however, that they reflect any great support for him within the Labour party. His own National Labour group only polled 341,000 votes, although this is partly explained by the fact that he was unable to run more than twenty candidates. The main reason for the dramatic fall in Labour seats was that in many constituencies Labour was fighting a combination of the other main parties, who were careful to deploy their candidates in such a way as to avoid splitting the National vote. This strategy also meant that for once the Liberals did not suffer from the working of the electoral system and their representation on both sides of the new House rose from fifty-nine to seventy-two, despite a drop of 3 million in their popular vote. Of course, it is difficult to say whether this fall entirely accounts for a corresponding increase in the Conservative poll. In the circumstances the Liberals were running far fewer candidates; Labour also dropped 1·5 million in their popular vote and it could be that some Labour voters swung over to the National government. The total poll throughout the country, however, was a million less than in 1929 and it would seem probable that many of these abstentions came from Labour. If this is so, then the election of 1931 suggested disillusionment among Labour supporters rather than any positive split. Nevertheless, Labour had suffered an appalling setback and there had been a devastating casualty list among their leading personalities. Henderson, Clynes, Greenwood, Dalton, Morrison, Shinwell, Ellen Wilkinson and Wedgwood Benn all failed to regain their seats and George Lansbury, one of the few survivors, assumed the leadership of the parliamentary party with Attlee as deputy leader.

Not unnaturally the government had now to be reconstituted, since the balance of parties represented in the small emergency cabinet set up at the end of August bore little relation to the new situation in the House of Commons. It was hardly surprising that the full cabinet of twenty re-established in November should include eleven Conservatives; indeed, their numbers in the Commons entitled them to a still higher proportion, but the need to preserve the image of a truly National government ensured that the remnants of MacDonald's group should have four places and the Liberals five. MacDonald himself remained Prime Minister, a lonely anomaly. Stanley Baldwin, whose position at the head of the Conservatives had once again been put beyond doubt, was still Lord President of the Council, Sankey Lord Chancellor, Sir Herbert Samuel Home Secretary and J. H. Thomas Secretary of State for the Dominions. Sir John Simon became Foreign Secretary and Neville Chamberlain took over as Chancellor of the Exchequer from Snowden, who accepted a peerage but remained in the cabinet as Lord Privy Seal. And so with their dispositions made and with an impregnable position in the Commons the National government embarked upon the task of proving that they were worthy of the confidence that the electorate had so emphatically expressed.

2. The paradoxes of economic recovery

The appointment of Neville Chamberlain as Chancellor of the Exchequer left little doubt that the National government, having abandoned the gold standard, was now about to depart from that other principle of the nineteenth century, free trade. Almost at once an Abnormal Importations Act was passed in order to check a great influx of imports before Great Britain went protectionist and then on 4 February 1932 Neville Chamberlain introduced his Import Duties Bill. A general customs duty of 10 per cent was placed on all goods entering the country; an advisory committee was set up with powers to establish additional duties and by April had recommended considerable increases for manufactured articles. Certain commodities including wheat, maize and meat were to be exempt; so, too, were all goods imported from the Empire, prior to a conference to be held at Ottawa later that year.

A mixture of motives explains the decision to return to protection. It was a natural reaction to the tariff barriers to which all other countries were resorting at this time; it might rescue some home industries threatened with failure; it would provide revenue for a continued balancing of the budget. When he introduced the Bill, Chamberlain recalled with some emotion his father's great struggle over tariff reform (see p. 42). Yet, whatever else protection might achieve, it seemed unlikely to create the situation which Joseph Chamberlain's original scheme had envisaged. The notion of a self-contained economic unit, within which Great Britain would guarantee the purchase of imperial primary products in return for an unrestricted market for her industrial goods throughout the Empire, seemed by now a ludicrous echo of the eighteenth-century colonial system. It was utterly inappropriate in the present circumstances. The mother country wished to encourage her own agriculture; the Dominions hoped to foster their own growing industries, and this divergence of aim was soon made clear amid the vituperative negotiations at the Ottawa conference in the summer of 1932. The Dominions would allow no reduction of duties already operating against British imports within their own countries; imperial preference was to mean no more than the raising of these tariffs still higher against foreign imports, while in return Great Britain would establish a system of quotas which would encourage empire products without harming British farmers.

The proportion of British trade with the Empire did increase over subsequent years, but protection could hardly be said to have created a new atmosphere of imperial economic cooperation, and at home it widened the cracks which the doctor's mandate had been designed to paper over. Throughout the summer the situation had only been preserved by allowing Samuel in the Commons and Snowden in the Lords to proclaim their objections to Chamberlain's Bill, while remaining members of the government. Ultimately this could only make nonsense of the doctrine of cabinet responsibility and in any case by September the free traders could take no more. Snowden, Samuel and Sir Archibald Sinclair, the Liberal Secretary of State for Scotland, all resigned, and Samuel took with him some thirty followers, although these did not move into formal Opposition until the end of 1933. That left only a handful of Labour and Simonite Liberals alongside 473 Conservatives, and the isolation of Ramsay MacDonald, who continued to preside as Prime Minister until his retirement in June 1935, appeared to be complete.

Although the abandonment of the gold standard and the establishment of protection had come as a shock to some, these moves were largely an immediate response to what appeared to be the dictate of economic expediency. They did not point to a new adventurous radicalism in facing the crisis of the depression. Chamberlain's budget of April 1932 produced no innovations, merely reducing expenditure on armaments and depending upon the tariffs to overcome any deficit, which in fact they failed to do. Unemployment continued to mount, reaching almost 3 million by January 1933, but Chamberlain was adamant that the schemes for public works which had been canvassed by various groups were impractical and irrelevant to the needs of the nation.

Chamberlain may have intended no revolutionary change. Nevertheless, the subsequent years were to illustrate a remarkable break with the economic attitudes of the past, as the government began reluctantly to grope its way towards a controlled economy. Agriculture was to provide the most striking example of this. It has been seen (p. 21) how since the 1870s the doctrine of *laissez-faire* had left British farmers hopelessly exposed to foreign competition. Their plight had grown still worse in the 1920s, when food prices had been falling everywhere throughout the world, and even livestock, on which they had relied increasingly before the war, offered no security. Under free trade there could be little relief by government action. In 1920 an Act had guaranteed minimum prices for wheat and oats, but this had been repealed within a year; otherwise, the principal government intervention had been a subsidy in 1925 to encourage the cultivation of sugar beet. Now, however, *laissez-faire* was largely abandoned. In 1932 the Wheat Act gave home producers a guaranteed price. Two Agricultural Marketing Acts in 1931 and 1933 enabled farmers to organize prices and output through a variety of marketing boards for potatoes, milk, bacon and meat; home production was subsidized and foreign competition was restricted by quotas of imports from outside the Empire. The implications of all this were enormous, although the index of agricultural prices still failed to regain the 1927–29 level and farm labourers continued to give up work on the land at the rate of 10,000 a year.

At the same time a new closeness of cooperation was developing among major units in industry. The older concerns which had been in decline were pushed towards a ruthless policy of rationalization, operated mainly by boards of industrialists, such as the British Iron and Steel Federation established in 1934, or National Shipbuilders Security Ltd in 1930. Mergers were formed, prices were fixed and obsolete firms were bought up and closed. The destruction of shipyards blotted out over a million tons of building capacity and in the cotton industry six million spindles had been scrapped by 1939. A similar process in the coalmines was attempted by the Coalmines Reorganisation Commission, but here the resistance of the owners of the smaller pits proved more stubborn. In general, however, the underlying principle was that collective action should wipe out the weaker elements, so that the rest of the industry could survive with the reduced market.

A more positive form of government intervention arose out of the realization that unemployment was essentially a regional problem, and in 1934 a Special Areas Act established two commissioners, one for Scotland and one for England and Wales. It was soon seen, however, that little could be done to revive the moribund industries of South Wales or Cumberland and Durham, and subsequent Acts in 1936 and 1937 enabled the commissioners to offer financial and practical inducements to firms who were prepared to establish new factories in the depressed areas, although even this could soak up only a small fraction of the unemployed.

The sheer extent of this change might suggest that it was the depression rather than the First World War that finally sounded the knell of nineteenth-century assumptions. Even so, it is doubtful whether these measures had much to do with any immediate recovery from the depression itself. Protection may well have saved some concerns that would have been destroyed by foreign competition under a continuation of free trade; it could do little to help the export market, where difficulties might be increased by foreign retaliation. Essentially it provided a screen behind which the vital restructuring of industry could begin, but this was a long-term objective that did not immediately help the unemployed. Indeed, although the rigorous streamlining of the older industries was ultimately to be beneficial, its immediate effect was to make the position temporarily worse; the classic instance of this was the decision to close Palmers' shipyards at Jarrow, with the result that by 1935 nearly three-quarters of the insured work force in the town had been thrown into unemployment.

How, then, did Great Britain find her way to recovery? In the main, like the depression itself, the emergence from it was a worldwide phenomenon. This was largely haphazard. There is little evidence of international cooperation, although the cancellation of German reparations by general agreement and of war debts by unilateral action may have removed one unhelpful factor. Some believed that the old theory of the trade cycle still worked, that the low point had been reached and that the curve could begin to move upwards again with new investment and expansion. Others looked to the example of the United States, Nazi Germany and Socialist Sweden, where governments of utterly different political complexions launched attacks on unemployment with state-sponsored schemes. The debate over the possible reasons has continued to this day, but whatever they may have been, recovery did come, and took Great Britain along with it.

The slowness of the process may be measured in her figures for unemployment (see Appendix 5, p. 441) which dropped to 2 million in 1934, but only fell very gradually after that until they had come down to 1·5 million in 1937. For the employed section of the population, however, the change was more marked, and the index of production in Great Britain shows that the 1929 level had already been surpassed by 1934. Even so, by 1939 the proportion of goods for export was half what it had been before 1914, and although the balance of payments, including invisible exports, improved in the middle years of the decade, this never fully recovered and soon became unfavourable again.

Thus the principal outlet for this revived production was on the domestic market and the essential element here was the growth of a greater spending power among the public at large. This internal aspect of recovery, which had been stressed by J. M. Keynes, may have been assisted by two government measures, although their true impact has been a matter of controversy among economic historians, and in any case it is unlikely that the government could have foreseen their full consequences at the time.

First, in June 1932 the Bank rate was reduced to 2 per cent. The reason for this was partly to check an influx of foreign investment which might prove unreliable amid the uncertainties of circumstances abroad; principally, however, it was to allow the government to convert nearly £2,000 million of War Loan from an interest rate of 5 per cent to 3½ per cent, thereby enabling the Chancellor of the Exchequer to make a saving of £80 million. It does not appear that the government was aiming directly as providing 'cheap money', but the consequent general lowering of interest rates did help firms in need of capital. The building industry was particularly affected by this, the prospective purchaser of a house rather less so, since building societies, which grew enormously in the 1930s, did not significantly lower their mortgage rates.

The second government measure was motivated by a desire to move cautiously back to normality. In 1934 the cuts in unemployment benefit were ended; in 1935 salaries were restored to their former level and income tax was lowered from 5 shillings (25p) to 4 shillings and 6 pence (22½). By itself this increase in net income would only have added slightly to spending power. What really made the difference was the fact that world prices of primary products, particularly food, were continuing to fall, and for the man who was still in employment this created a far wider margin for expenditure outside the necessities of life. The paradox is that falling prices, which had been a main feature of the depression, were eventually to put Great Britain on the road to recovery and in this context the 1931 cuts which naturally reduced spending power seem nothing more than self-inflicted wounds.

The most remarkable boom was in housing. During the 1930s roughly 2·7 million houses were built in England and Wales, almost entirely by private enterprise, in contrast to the 1·5 million built in the 1920s, two-thirds of which were aided by government subsidy. These houses supplied in turn a growing opportunity for a large number of light industries producing consumer goods, such as furniture and household appliances, in the Midlands and in the region of London where they were close to their markets. The new factories depended largely on electric power and the geographical shift was facilitated by the Central Electricity Board which had been established in 1926 to standardize the previous confusion of voltages and frequencies and which by 1933 had completed a national grid at a cost of £27 million. In itself the growth of electric power, whose consumers rose in number from 730,000 in 1920 to 8,920,000 in 1938, was responsible for a variety of types of employment in electrical engineering. The car industry with its centres at Oxford, Coventry, Luton and Birmingham was the greatest single instance of expansion, output rising from 182,000 vehicles in 1929 to 511,000 in 1937, while the aircraft industry, which was employing 35,000 workers in 1933 was to grow in the late 1930s under the pressure of rearmament. All this naturally had a beneficial effect on the steel firms; chemical industries, too, developed considerably under Imperial Chemical Industries Ltd (ICI), created out of a merger of four companies in 1926; and textiles were assisted by the creation of man-made fibres, principally rayon.

This new expansion points to a further paradox in the image that these years have acquired. For long they were regarded as a bleak age of austerity, insecurity and human suffering, and the memory of them undoubtedly played a part in the overwhelming victory of the Labour party in 1945. More recently, a new view has been expressed by some economists that the interwar years form a highly significant period during which the British economy began to emerge from its earlier obsolescence. The fining down of the old export industries and the harnessing of modern technology to new requirements were part of an essential readjustment that was to be the basis of the prosperity of the 1950s and 1960s; it has been maintained by some that over the whole period the 1930s were the key decade in this process, and that far from being a bleak age, they created a new level of relative prosperity for many sections of the working class.

In human terms it is possible to find illustrations of either of these images and in 1934 J. B. Priestley published a study entitled *English Journey* in which he dwelt at length on both. In fact, he found that there were four Englands. The first was the world of ancient cathedral cities and historic remains, the playground of tourist whimsy. The second was the world of nineteenth-century industrialism, the ugly cities of factory, slum and slagheap throughout the north and the Midlands. Here men might still have work, but the background of their lives was squalid and dreary. In *The Road to Wigan Pier* George Orwell described how he had lived for a while in a mining community, sharing the same living conditions, and as the train took him to his destination, he looked out over a great area of slumland.

> At the back of one of the houses a young woman was kneeling on the stones, poking a stick up the leaden waste pipe which ran from the sink inside and which I suppose was blocked. I had time to see everything about her—her sacking apron, her clumsy clogs, her arms reddened with cold. She looked up as the train passed and I was almost near enough to catch her eye. She had a round pale face, the usual exhausted face of the slum girl who is twenty-five and looks forty, thanks to miscarriages and drudgery; and it wore, for the second in which I saw it, the most desolate hopeless expression that I have ever seen.[1]

At least the worker in employment had his pay and his self-respect, but there was too a third England represented by the unemployed man living in enforced idleness on 15 shillings and 3 pence (76p) a week, after the 1931 cuts, with 8 shillings (40p) for his wife and 2 shillings (10p) for each child. Even these benefits could only be drawn by right for twenty-six weeks. After this, by the ruling made in the autumn of 1931, the unemployed had to depend upon 'transitional payments' after undergoing a means test conducted by the local public assistance committee. This means test became the most hated feature of these years. The income of any member of an unemployed man's household—war widow's pension, old-age pensions or his own savings in the Post Office—could deprive him of benefit; officials could enter his house to assess the value of his furniture; neighbours could report that his child had a new pair of shoes. He had to become a pauper before the state would offer the little that might just keep him from outright starvation. Many of these were the long-term unemployed, the older man in the declining industries of South Wales and the north. Too unadaptable to move to a different region or to learn a new trade, he was likely to remain unemployed for ever, once his job was lost. Others, young skilled men, found themselves laid low by a sudden turn of the economic screw.

When it is remembered that, allowing for wives and children, a figure of 2 million unemployed could represent the condition of life of some 7 or 8 million people out of a total population of 47 million, it is hardly surprising that Sir John Boyd Orr, in a survey published in 1936, should reckon that 10 per cent of the population were suffering from malnutrition; or that 62 per cent of all recruits for the Army in 1935 should fail to reach the necessary physical standard. There is an Edwardian ring to this scene, although it may be that the destitution was not so utterly savage as it had been earlier. Rowntree's study of York in 1901 (see p. 5) had found 15 per cent of the wage-earners living below the poverty line; applying the same standard in a new survey of York in 1935, he brought this percentage down to 6·8, although a more generous definition of primary poverty suggested that 31 per cent came below the line.

It was natural that such times should give some encouragement to the political extremes of left and right. Young intellectuals began to look to Russia as an instance of the planned society that really offered hope for the future and the Communist party made some gains at the universities. There was a strong note of protest in the writings of the modern poets—W. H. Auden, Stephen Spender and C. Day Lewis; when the Left Book Club was founded by Victor Gollancz in 1936, it grew very rapidly to a membership of 50,000, and in the Conservative party itself young MPs, such as Harold Macmillan, increasingly advocated a policy of economic planning and nationalization. On the right Sir Oswald Mosley had formed the British Union of Fascists in 1932 and before long the physical violence with which hecklers were treated at his meetings and the open antisemitism of the movement appeared to make it indistinguishable from the Nazi party which came to power in Germany in 1933. There were street battles fought out in the East End of London, but Mosley never attracted a very large following and by 1937 the dangers from Fascism on the Continent made it less likely that he ever would.

In the main, however, except for the occasional hunger march the poor themselves endured these years in a spirit of glum acceptance, and the population as a whole still seemed wed to the notion of tranquillity which Bonar Law had preached in 1922. The reason for this probably lies in the existence of the fourth England which Priestley described in his book, the England of the housing boom and the new light industries, most apparent in the south. This was a world in which real wages were slowly rising, families were smaller and a house with indoor sanitation, electric light and a gas cooker could be bought on a mortgage by the skilled artisan or white-collar worker for as little as £300. He had to count his pennies, but if he did, they could buy a great deal. Bus services took him to work or his wife to the shops; sumptuous cinema palaces regaled them with the latest creation of the Hollywood dream factory. By 1939 well over half of the 18·5 million who earned £250 or less were enjoying an annual week's holiday with pay, and the salaried classes earning somewhat more could often afford a car and a resident maid. By the standards of the 1960s this may not sound very much;

nevertheless, it does suggest a considerable improvement on those of the Edwardian era.

Thus the social scene in Great Britain during the 1930s would seem to supply a justification for both optimistic and pessimistic views of the economy. The misery of the unemployed and certain types of worker is undeniable; and yet paradoxically this period also marks a new peak in the standard of living for many of the population, and for the lower middle classes it was a heyday of relative affluence on which they were to look back with some nostalgia in the years after the Second World War.

3. The Empire and the monarchy

The Ottawa conference of 1932 had hardly been a model of imperial harmony, but perhaps an outspoken independence was a natural and healthy expression of the relationship that had developed between the mother country and the Dominions. It had already long been assumed that those parts of the British Empire which had attained Dominion status were in effect sovereign states. The four Dominions had had separate representation at the peace settlement in 1919 and, together with India, were independent members of the League of Nations. It now seemed time to give legal recognition to what was already an accepted fact. At an imperial conference in 1926 a committee under Balfour's chairmanship had put forward a definition of the British Commonwealth as a free association of autonomous communities and after the Dominions had had time to debate this, the Statute of Westminster was passed in December 1931, removing the few restrictions that the United Kingdom had theoretically still been able to impose upon Dominion legislation.

In fact, even less was changed than had originally been proposed. Canada and Australia, conscious of the internal difficulties of their federal systems, and New Zealand, well content with her own arrangements, all requested that any constitutional amendments in the future should remain dependent on legislation passed by the Parliament of the United Kingdom. Later, New Zealand in 1947 and Canada in 1949 requested the removal of this safeguard, which was granted at once. The only anomaly at this time was Newfoundland who, after being reduced to a state of bankruptcy by the world slump, relinquished her Dominion status in 1934 and placed her affairs under a commission appointed by the British government, a situation which lasted until 1949, when after a protracted debate she decided to become the tenth province of Canada.

The principal change brought about by the Statute of Westminster was to be seen in the Irish Free State. Here de Valera, who became prime minister in 1932, decided to use the Statute to establish a far greater degree of independence than had previously been possible. As soon as he had taken office, he announced the withholding of the land annuities due to the British government from the Irish who had purchased their farms under the terms of the Act of 1903 (see p. 15). He abolished the oath of allegiance and the right of appeal to the judicial committee of the privy council and reduced the position of the governor-general to one of humiliating insignificance. In 1935 an Act passed by the Dail declared that Irish citizens were no longer British subjects, although de Valera was prepared to offer 'reciprocal citizenship' for British and Irish who were resident in each other's countries.

At home the National government was somewhat startled at this literal interpretation of the Statute of Westminster. In fact, since the Irish Free State enjoyed Dominion status under the treat of 1921, de Valera was simply taking the British at their word and they had no legal grounds for objection to his actions, except over the withholding of the annuities. On this no agreement could be reached and the two sides settled down to a tariff war. This at least enabled Great Britain to collect in duties slightly more than what was due to her in annuities, but it also clearly demonstrated the growing gulf between the two countries, and in May 1937 de Valera made this explicit when he published a constitution by which the Irish Free State was to enjoy sovereign independence under the new title of Eire.

Meanwhile in India, where the Montagu–Chelmsford reforms (see p. 196) were now taking effect, a commission appointed under Sir John Simon in 1927 had been exploring the possibility of a further extension of self-government. This should have been a good moment for Indian aspirations. Lord Irwin, later Lord Halifax, who was Viceroy from 1926 until 1931, was extremely sympathetic towards them and in October 1929 issued a declaration in favour of granting India Dominion status. The Simon commission, however, which produced its report in 1930 was not prepared to go so far. Their immediate recommendations merely included a wider franchise in the provinces, where Indian ministers responsible to their local legislatures should have greatly increased powers; the report went on to envisage the eventual creation of a federation of self-governing provinces throughout the whole of India, including the states of the princes. Gandhi, on the other hand, was demanding complete independence, and, resentful of the exclusion of Indians from the membership of the Simon commission, now embarked on a new campaign of civil disobedience. This took the form of a march to the sea, where he and his followers openly infringed the government's monopoly of salt and were accordingly all placed under arrest.

At home the Labour administration suggested a series of Round Table conferences to be held in London, representing all sections of Indian political life. Three of these duly took place between 1930 and 1933, but did not achieve very much. The Simon proposals were unlikely to give much satisfaction. There were outbreaks of violence in India, and Gandhi, now in prison, announced a boycott of the first conference by the Congress party. Irwin turned once more to conciliation, released Gandhi and opened a personal negotiation with him. As a consequence of the conversations between this incongruous pair Gandhi did attend the second conference, but the subsequent meetings only served to emphasize the irreconcilable divisions between the princes, the Muslims and the Congress party.

Among the British, too, the issue aroused a good deal of dissension. It was natural that Labour should support greater independence for India; more striking was the fact that Baldwin was also convinced that change must come, and he had somehow to take the Conservatives with him at a time when his leadership of the party had already been under attack. In this he succeeded, but there were to be several years of protracted campaigning before the Government of India Act was passed in 1935.

The most significant feature of this contest was the breach between Winston Churchill and Baldwin. For Churchill, who had served as a young subaltern in India in the 1890s, the question was one of profound emotional significance. He saw British rule in India as an essential bulwark against anarchy and bloodshed, and he fought passionately to prevent the passage of the Act. In January 1931 he finally broke with the official leadership of the party and resigned from the Opposition business committee. With this it seemed that he had sacrificed all future prospects, a lone rebel within his own party, which had always seen him as a brilliant but unstable political individualist. There was consequently no place for him in the National government formed later in 1931, and it was as a voice from the wilderness that he was later to harry the government over the question of rearming against Germany.

The terms of the Act itself were not very exciting, coming fairly close to the original proposals of the Simon commission. The eleven principal provinces of British India were given almost complete powers of self-government, and in subsequent elections seven of these were won by the Congress party, which continued to campaign for independence. Ultimate central control remained largely with the Viceroy and the projected scheme for federation came to nothing. Indeed, it was hardly likely that it could be otherwise, since the Muslim League representing some 80 million inhabitants, and the Indian princes who ruled nearly half the territory of the Indian continent were alike highly suspicious of the designs of the Hindu politicians of the Congress party.

Most of these imperial matters concerned regions too far away to be of great interest to the average citizen of Great Britain. Before long, however, events at home were to present him with a unique drama affecting the very heart of the Empire: the monarchy itself. King George V died on 20 January 1936, shortly after he had celebrated the silver jubilee of his reign in 1935. He was succeeded by his eldest son who assumed the title of Edward VIII. The new King had been extremely popular as Prince of Wales, but the more staid had feared the lack of respect for official decorum with which he occasionally treated his position, and almost at once it seemed that their fears were to be justified. Edward, still a bachelor, had fallen in love with an American lady, Mrs Wallis Simpson. It did not particularly matter that she was a commoner. The insuperable problem was that she had already divorced one husband and was now married to a second. The established Church, historically linked with the monarchy, would not recognize divorce and to the leaders of the nation it was inconceivable that Edward could hope to make her his Queen.

The crisis came to a head when Mrs Simpson obtained a decree *nisi* of divorce from her second husband at the end of October 1936. By now the American press had been full of the excitement for some time, but by common consent British newspapers had kept it from the public at home. Clearly this could not last long, and the editor of *The Times*, Geoffrey Dawson, persuaded Baldwin, who had taken over as Prime Minister from Ramsay MacDonald in June 1935, that he must make the matter clear to the King. Until now Edward had believed that once the decree of divorce became absolute, he would be able to marry Mrs Simpson before his coronation. Implacably Baldwin closed every door on these hopes. He maintained that in the eyes of the three political parties and of public opinion in general such a marriage would be impossible. He collected similar views from the prime ministers of the Dominions. He ruled out any chance of a morganatic marriage. He even gained a cabinet decision that it would be unconstitutional for the King to put his case to the people on the radio. Inexorably Edward was driven towards a single choice: to renounce Mrs Simpson or to abdicate. On that his mind was made up. 'I am going to marry Mrs Simpson and I am prepared to go,' he had told the Prime Minister, and on 10

December 1936 the short reign of Edward VIII came to a close with the signing of a document of abdication.

The episode has been the subject of some analysis. Baldwin, who at the time gained much credit for his felicitous handling of the affair, was accused later of having rushed the King into a hasty decision. It has been suggested that Edward's request for a morganatic marriage placed him at Baldwin's mercy, since this would depend on an Act of Parliament. Equally, it may be that Edward overestimated the effect that his threat of abdication would have on the government. In fact, assuming that his mind was set on marriage, the King had little to fight with and, given the attitudes prevalent in Great Britain at that time, it is hard to see what other outcome there could have been. In these circumstances both men were agreed at least that in the interests of the monarchy the matter must be settled as speedily as possible.

Thus Edward set sail for France, where eventually he was able to marry Mrs Simpson. It was a time of sadness for many who had looked forward to the accession of a young modern King, but the public memory was short. Edward's younger brother, the Duke of York, succeeded him as King George VI and there was a coronation in May 1937 after all. The alarm expressed by some that abdication would weaken the monarchy proved groundless, and the new King, a shy modest man supported by the personality of his wife, Queen Elizabeth, and by the surroundings of a happy family life, came to represent a combination of dignity and human appeal that was to take the British monarchy to a height of popular affection and esteem unknown in earlier centuries of its history.

26

The National Government and the Dictators 1931–1937

At home any optimism inspired by the slow recovery from economic depression was increasingly overshadowed throughout the 1930s by the growth of militarism on the Continent. In January 1933 Adolf Hitler, the leader of the Nazi party, was appointed German chancellor by President Hindenburg. Hitler's book *Mein Kampf*, written in 1924, and his subsequent speeches had openly advertised his passionate nationalism, his hatred of the Jews and of Bolshevism, his contempt for all democratic processes and his determination to free Germany from the terms of the Treaty of Versailles. Within a few months of his accession to power he had shown that these were not empty words. In March 1933 all parliamentary government was brought to an end in Germany; trade-union leaders and many of the left wing disappeared into concentration camps; Jews were harassed and dispossessed, and in June 1934 a massacre of the principal officers of Hitler's own private army, who now hampered his relations with the German general staff, pointed to a new order of gangsterism established as the government of the most powerful country in central Europe.

Hitler's attack on the terms of the Treaty of Versailles had to be rather more gradual, but he left no doubt over the direction of his aims. In October 1933 he withdrew Germany from the League of Nations, embarked at once upon a policy of rearmament and in March 1935 announced the introduction of conscription. This flouting of the west encouraged Mussolini in October 1935 to set out on the conquest of Abyssinia (now known as Ethiopia), and while Great Britain and France agonized over their different responses to this Italian aggression, Hitler seized his opportunity to reoccupy the demilitarized zone of the Rhineland in March 1936. Thus far, these acts of defiance had merely affected circumstances within the existing frontiers of Germany, but they did establish a situation of resurgent German power from which

Hitler was able to undertake his annexations in eastern Europe in 1938 and 1939.

Baldwin had retired in May 1937 and it was his successor Neville Chamberlain who had to cope with the later phase in the destruction of the Treaty of Versailles. Chamberlain has not been spared in the general recrimination that has been heaped on British foreign policy during the 1930s, but at least it may be argued that by the time he had taken office the greater strength of Germany did pose new problems. Critics have consequently looked further back and the charge that has been laid against the MacDonald–Baldwin administrations is that they failed to prevent Hitler from achieving this position during the years when he might still have been checked without a major war. Baldwin in particular has been bitterly attacked. Yet, while it is undeniable that Great Britain's attitude towards continental events up to 1937 was hazy and confused, it is too easy to write off the entire period as one of complacent folly and to ignore the peculiar difficulties that faced the men of these years.

1. The question of rearmament

The fundamental factor for the British government, when Hitler came to power, was the dangerously low point to which the country had run down its armed forces. The effect of the ten years rule (see p. 255), only cancelled as late as 1933, had been to reduce British expenditure on defence to 2·5 per cent of her budget. In numbers of first-line aircraft Great Britain stood fifth in the world. The manpower of her Navy had never been so small since the 1890s, and her Army was in an impoverished state, unmechanized and out of date, with only one infantry division and one cavalry brigade available for mobilization.

Hitler's first steps towards the rearming of Germany followed immediately on the collapse of the disarmament conference which had opened at Geneva in February 1932. As the months went by, proposal after proposal had been wrecked by the incompatibility of Germany's demand for equality of status and France's desire for security, and in July 1932 the German delegates had given notice of withdrawal. The debate was renewed for a short while after Hitler had become chancellor, but in October 1933 Hitler announced that Germany would leave both the conference and the League of Nations, and in the following year talks at Geneva about disarmament finally petered out.

The unsuccessful negotiations had already included a western offer of an army of 200,000 for Germany, twice the size allowed by the Treaty of

Versailles, so that there was every reason to suppose that Hitler would now set about establishing a far greater force than that. At first he had to be careful not to provoke the French into taking action, and in any case the German general staff reckoned that too rapid an expansion would be difficult to administer. In January 1934, however, Hitler's non-aggression pact with Poland, which undermined the French system of alliances in eastern Europe, gave him the confidence to ignore these objections, and in the spring of 1934 a memorandum envisaged the creation of an army of 300,000 within the next twelve months. On 9 March 1935 the existence of the German air force—the Luftwaffe—was officially announced, and on 16 March Hitler declared publicly that conscription would be introduced for the establishment of an army of thirty-six divisions, numbering 550,000 men.

For some time before this there had been clear evidence of Hitler's intentions and it was later argued that MacDonald and Baldwin should have embarked immediately on a corresponding programme of British rearmament. In the House of Commons one lone voice constantly urged them to do so, almost from the moment of Hitler's accession to power. In the midst of the controversy over the question of India Winston Churchill never ceased to point out the dangers of allowing Germany to overtake Great Britain in air power. MacDonald and Baldwin, however, were inhibited by two major factors: the mood of the country, and the expense that such a rearmament would entail.

It would be almost impossible to overestimate the sense of revulsion that the thought of war inspired in Great Britain at this time; for thousands of ex-servicemen who had survived the western front and whose families were now of military age a repetition of that experience was unthinkable. The early 1930s saw the publication of a number of anti-war novels (see p. 134); it was in February 1933 that the Oxford Union Society passed its celebrated motion that 'this House will in no circumstances fight for King and country', and some eighteen months later Dick Sheppard, the vicar of St Martin-in-the-Fields, founded the Peace Pledge Union, an outright pacifist movement. There was not only the memory of the past behind all this. The public imagination was by now obsessed with the vision of universal destruction through the aerial bombardment of cities and the use of poison gas. A film of H. G. Wells's *Shape of Things to Come*, produced in 1938, reflected this fear perfectly: the sudden air attack by night, the panic in the streets, the madly rushing feet and afterwards the cratered ruins in which all civilized life had broken down. The film was a remarkable glimpse of the later fate of Dresden and Hiroshima in 1945, but for the historian its significance lies not in the accuracy of the prophecy, but in the fact that people believed that this would be the *immediate* consequence of the outbreak of war, the old nightmare of the knock-out blow.

Faced with this public mood it is difficult to see how any government could have made the idea of rearmament acceptable except by the most gradual stages. To many people it seemed that the creation of two great armed camps before 1914 had helped to bring about the First World War, while those of left-wing persuasion were convinced of the sinister role of the international armaments industry. In any case, Hitler in his early years did not arouse any widespread antagonism in Great Britain. Many visitors came back from Germany impressed by the signs of economic recovery, just as Mussolini had been praised for making the trains run on time in Italy. Naturally there were some misgivings about dictatorship and the stories of the mistreatment of Jews, but few people believed that this should govern the course of foreign relations. In right-wing opinion Nazi Germany seemed a powerful bulwark against Bolshevik Russia, and the episode of the Zinoviev letter shows how strong an emotion this could be. 'If there is any fighting to be done,' wrote Baldwin to Winston Churchill in 1936, 'I should like to see the Nazis and the Bolsheviks doing it.'

Most significant of all was the sense of dislike and guilt with which many of the British regarded the Treaty of Versailles—the principal object of Hitler's vituperation. The long tangle over reparations and the difficulty of working in agreement with France had left a bitter taste. Already revision was on the way. The Rhineland had been evacuated five years ahead of schedule; reparations had ended in 1932, and as late as 1935 a Foreign Office memorandum had stated: 'From the earliest years following the war it was our policy to eliminate those parts of the Peace Settlement, which, as practical people, we knew to be untenable and indefensible.'[1] The strength of Hitler's position was that he was challenging a European settlement that the public did not believe to be worth the bones of a British grenadier.

The second factor was the natural concomitant of the first. Rearmament, which Baldwin judged would be unpopular in itself, was bound to be expensive, and the average citizen, coping with the early stages of recovery from the depression, would hardly welcome the consequent prospect of higher taxation. In fact, as Hitler was to show, an enormous expansion of the armaments industry could supply a Keynesian type of solution to the problem of unemployment, but this was hardly in tune with the economic philosophy of the British government of that time.

These considerations convinced Baldwin that it would be hopeless to go to the country immediately to ask for a mandate for rearmament. Certainly all the indications at the end of 1933 seemed to support this view. At a by-election at East Fulham in October the Labour candidate, making disarmament one of his main issues, turned the previous Conservative majority of 14,000 into a Labour one of 5,000. Before the end of the year there were five similar results at other by-elections and two more in February 1934. From this Baldwin, mindful of the consequences of his hasty personal conversion to protection in November 1923 (see p. 228), deduced that an election held at this time could mean a Labour landslide. 'And then', he said to Sir Robert Vansittart, the head of the Foreign Office, 'you will have the Socialists who will give you no rearmament at all, instead of me who gives you not enough.'[2] Vansittart, who was highly sensitive to the German threat, urged him to take the risk, but Baldwin and MacDonald were adamant.

It is always hard to be sure of the significance of this kind of electrocal reaction, but the public feeling about disarmament was certainly something more than a by-election quirk. And there was no doubt about a potential Labour government's attitude towards it. The Labour party conference in October 1933 had denounced rearmament; George Lansbury, the leader of the parliamentary party, was a convinced pacifist who had stated at the Fulham by-election: 'I would close every recruiting station, disband the army and disarm the air force',[3] and in March 1934 Attlee, who was eventually to succeed him, declared in the House of Commons, 'we on our side are out for total disarmament because we are realists'.[4]

Of course, it could be argued that MacDonald and Baldwin had no need of a mandate. The government was very strongly established in the House of Commons and a general election was unnecessary until the summer of 1936, by which time a programme of rapid rearmament could be well under way. The two leaders did decide to wait, but they were hardly the men to rouse the nation in the meantime with a powerful call to arms. Indeed, they viewed their role with the utmost abhorrence; MacDonald had been a pacifist in the First World War and Baldwin's comment that 'the bomber will always get through' sounded a note of defeatism that did little to steel the country to new dangers.

Nevertheless, in the period before the next general election Baldwin did press forward with the first slow steps towards rearmament. In October 1933 a Defence Requirements committee was set up under Sir Maurice Hankey and in the following February produced a report advising a programme that would cost £72 million, most of it over the next five years. Resistance from the Chancellor of the Exchequer, Neville Chamberlain, brought the proposed expenditure down to about £50 million. This meant that the defence of the Far East would have to depend largely on the fortifying of Singapore, but Baldwin held out for the expansion of the Air Force. In March 1934 he promised that the government 'will see to it that in air strength and air power this country shall no longer be in a position inferior to any country within striking distance of our shores', and in July he announced in the House of Commons the plans for an additional forty-one squadrons in the next five years. 'When you think of the defence of England, you no longer think of the white cliffs of Dover,' he said. 'You think of the Rhine. That is where our frontier lies.'[5]

For Winston Churchill this was still inadequate. In November 1934, armed with figures from a Foreign Office source, he attacked Baldwin's assertion that Great Britain would, for the moment, retain a 50 per cent lead over Germany in air power. In fact, Baldwin's figures were correct at the time of speaking, but the Air Ministry was already beginning to revise its estimate of Germany's potential rate of expansion, and these doubts seemed to be confirmed when in March 1935 Sir John Simon, the Foreign Secretary, and Anthony Eden on a visit to Berlin were informed by Hitler that Germany's air power already equalled Great Britain's. Hitler was bluffing, but Baldwin took him at his word. He was certainly right to assume that the publicized plans of 1934 had failed to act as a deterrent against further German rearmament, and in May 1935, declaring that he had been misled over his estimate for the future in the previous November, he announced a new scheme to expand the RAF to 123 squadrons of 1,512 first-line aircraft by March 1937.

This was not the only aspect of rearmament undertaken in these years. In January 1935 the first meeting of a scientific committee under Henry Tizard decided to explore an idea of R. A. Watson-Watt that approaching aircraft might be detected by the reflection of radio waves, and in February the first steps were taken for setting up a chain of radar stations along the east and south coasts. Then there was the question of how industry could respond to the possible demand of an enormous war effort. In 1935 plans were set in motion under the direction of Lord Weir for the building of 'shadow' factories which could be switched easily from civilian purposes to the production of aircraft and munitions on the outbreak of war. There was, too, a need for a greater and more flexible skilled labour force; here the trade unions, nervous of any return to the 'dilution' which they had accepted in the First World War (see p. 138), were to be one more obstacle for the planners, and it was not until

March 1938 that the TUC agreed to the removal of various restrictions within the engineering industry.

Nevertheless, the crux of the matter was reckoned to be air power. Over this Lord Swinton, Air Minister from June 1935 until May 1938, not only had to struggle with the difficulties imposed by too narrow a budget. He knew that expansion alone was not enough. It was vital to modernize as well; metal monoplanes had to replace wooden biplanes and their fire power be increased. With this policy Swinton avoided the mistake made by the French who had rushed into increased production after 1933 with the result that their air force was largely obsolete by 1939. It was, however, bound to be a slower process, even though Swinton took the risk of ordering the production of new models straight from the drawing-board. In the spring of 1935 the plans for two new fighters—the Spitfire and the Hurricane, each carrying eight machine-guns—were approved. By the time of the Sudetenland crisis in September 1938 there were only five squadrons of these planes available and their guns had not yet been modified to fire at a height above 15,000 feet, but by September 1939 there were five hundred of them in the first line and in the summer of 1940 they saved Great Britain.

Slowly the mood of the public was changing. The result of a peace ballot, announced in June 1935, showed that although there was an overwhelming hankering for disarmament, nearly 7 million out of a poll of 11 million were prepared to accept military measures in a collective action against aggression. In October 1935 Mussolini's invasion of Abyssinia aroused a general hostility, and that autumn the Labour party conference at Brighton demanded sanctions against Italy, rejecting the pacifism of George Lansbury who resigned the leadership to Clement Attlee after a ferocious attack from Ernest Bevin. With these indications Baldwin, who had taken over from MacDonald as Prime Minister in June, now judged that the time for an appeal to the electorate had come. On 14 November 1935 the country went to the polls and the National government was returned with 432 seats against 154 Labour and 21 Samuel Liberals, after Baldwin had campaigned on a mandate for re-armament in support of the League of Nations.

Thus far, Baldwin's record is not entirely indefensible. Certainly more money could have been allocated to rearmament and his statements to the country more urgent. Nevertheless, in an unpropitious season he had turned to a deliberate policy of rearmament and most of the signifi-cant decisions—radar and the new fighters—had been taken in these years. The actions of the dictators had done more to initiate a gradual swing in public opinion than any statement of his, but it is arguable that more belligerent utterances might have been counterproductive with the mood that had prevailed in the country.

The months after the election of November 1935 are more open to criticism. Baldwin now had his mandate, but it does not seem that the government thrust on with much greater urgency. There is a sense of lethargy about his last premiership. Money remained in short supply and the service departments struggled among themselves for what they needed. It is true that in February 1936 a new target for 124 squadrons of 1,736 first-line aircraft was established for March 1939, but the general tenor of thought was merely to maintain parity with the German air force, when it was clear that Great Britain was falling behind. Memories of the naval armaments race before 1914 may have played some part in this reluctance. It may, too, have been prompted by a desire to leave the way clear for an eventual agreement with Germany, but in the subsequent years it appeared increasingly that without some measure of British superiority the only agreements possible would be at the dictate of Hitler.

2. The diplomacy of collective insecurity

Lack of armaments was not the only problem hampering the government in this period. British foreign policy was also inhibited by the fact that Germany did not at first represent the principal danger. The immediate evidence of aggression lay elsewhere, for at the time when Hitler became chancellor, Japan had already embarked on a new policy of expansion on the mainland of China, where considerable British interests were at stake.

At the beginning of the century Russia had seemed the major threat in this area, hence the Anglo-Japanese Treaty of 1902 (see p. 49). In the 1920s, however, China herself was showing signs of resisting foreign intrusion, when the Kuomintang, a Chinese nationalist movement under the leadership of Chiang-kai-shek, acting with Russian support, seemed likely to oust the official government at Peking. The British, who had shifted to a policy of working on the basis of naval agreements with the United States and Japan (see p. 198), were held back from any firm reaction to this by American determination to preserve good relations with China. The Japanese thought differently. They regarded Manchuria as their sphere of influence and when a new ruler there began to adopt the anti-foreigner policy of Chiang-kai-shek, who was now finally established in power at Peking, they resolved to take action.

Consequently, in September 1931, the Japanese government launched an invasion of Manchuria which was overrun in a few months (map, p.

379). China appealed to the League of Nations, now confronted for the first time with a major act of aggression. For some months there was hesitant talks of applying sanctions against Japan. A commission under Lord Lytton eventually reported in October 1932 that the Japanese attack was unjustified, but by this time Japan had proclaimed Manchuria as the new independent state of Manchukuo. The League passed a motion condemning Japan, upon which Japan, whose government was now virtually under the control of the military, announced her intention of leaving the League. And there the matter ended.

The Manchurian incident was the first outstanding illustration of the inadequacy of the League of Nations. It also revealed a depressing lack of harmony between Great Britain and the United States over the Far East. The Americans had been pressing the British to apply economic sanctions against Japan but were not prepared to do so themselves, without which such a policy would be ineffectual, and they were unlikely to contemplate any other form of involvement with a presidential election approaching in November 1932.

Worst of all, the incident had brought the British face to face with the utter weakness of their own position in the Far East. In January 1932 a Japanese attack on the Chinese at Shanghai, where Great Britain had assets of some £64 million, and in 1933 a renewed advance from Manchuria into the border province of Jehol made it clear that Japanese expansion on the mainland of China was a continuing reality. Yet if the British did adopt a policy of sanctions against Japan, this would almost certainly be followed by a Japanese blockade of the China coast which British naval forces, seriously depleted since the agreements of the 1920s, would not be strong enough to break—with profound consequences for British trade at a time of economic crisis. 'If there is trouble in the Far East,' said Baldwin in March 1934, 'I simply do not know how we could deal with it.'[6] This meant that for the moment Great Britain could only try to parry the challenge from Japan by reaching some kind of understanding with her, although bargaining from a position of weakness could only mean appeasement at the expense of China.

The implications of the tension in the Far East went further than that. Eventually Great Britain might be strong enough to cope with Japan. What was absolutely clear, however, was that she could not allow herself to be drawn into two disputes at the same time in different parts of the world. Involvement in one theatre of operations would automatically preclude any action elsewhere and this is one reason why the government was so reluctant to become locked irretrievably in either a Japanese or a European commitment as long as there was any chance of avoiding such a step.

The dilemma reveals another difficulty which was to have a bearing on Great Britain's policy in Europe: the attitude of the Commonwealth countries. In the latter part of the 1930s the attention of the British was drawn more and more towards Germany, but at the same time Canada, Australia and New Zealand were becoming increasingly conscious of the possible advance of Japan across the Pacific—a matter of greater consequence for them than the fate of eastern Europe. Thus, while the British government reckoned that they might have to condone aggression in the Far East in order to be free to check it on the Continent, the Dominions favoured a reverse order of priorities. There was consequently strong support within the Commonwealth for the policy of appeasement in Europe, an attitude which did not change until a few months before the outbreak of war in 1939.

Within Europe the Powers were equally at loggerheads over their priorities. The British government's attitude was particularly confused since, like Sir Edward Grey before 1914, they hoped that the need to present a firm front to Germany would not rule out the possibility of improved relations with her. Hitler's speeches, combining demands for German rights with pleas for a general European harmony, helped to encourage these divided aims and the British continued to hover unhappily between the two.

The same ambivalence of attitude was to be seen in Great Britain's relations with Italy. In the public imagination the bombastic militarism of Mussolini's regime was almost indistinguishable from that of German Nazism, and the eventual Italian invasion of Abyssinia in October 1935 appeared to suggest that he was the more aggressive of the two. This emotional reaction, however, did not square with the hard diplomatic realities. If Hitler's position was not to be strengthened, it was vital that Mussolini should be persuaded to work in conjunction with Great Britain and France and this could only mean condoning his actions in the same way as the British were practising delaying tactics with Japan in China. There were just too many aggressors in the 1930s to make it feasible to resist them all. The fundamental question was not whether to appease, but rather whom to appease.

The French never had much doubt about this. Their eyes were on Germany and they subordinated all other considerations to building up a diplomatic bloc against her. An early episode soon showed how significant Italian participation in this could be. In 1934 the activities of the Austrian Nazi party indicated that a coup might be imminent in Vienna and on 17 February Great Britain, France and Italy published a statement that they would maintain the independence of Austria. The inclusion of Italy in this was vital, since of the three she alone had a common frontier with Austria, across which immediate intervention would be possible. Thus, when the coup was attempted on 25 July and the Austrian chancellor Dollfuss was murdered, Mussolini moved divisions up to the Austrian border and Hitler hurriedly disowned the entire affair.

The determination of the French to strengthen their position was further illustrated when, in 1934, Louis Barthou, the French foreign minister, anxious to repair the damage done to France's eastern European system of treaties by a German-Polish pact, harked back to that earlier French policy of alliance with Russia and, as a preliminary, managed to engineer her acceptance as a member of the League of Nations. In this he had the support of Anthony Eden, but older members of the British government looked askance at any closer relations with Soviet Russia. The other countries of eastern Europe were similarly nervous and with this Hitler could always make considerable play. Before any treaty had been signed, however, Barthou had been killed at the time of the assassination of King Alexander of Yugoslavia on a state visit to France in October 1934. His successor, Pierre Laval, preferred to concentrate on Italy and in January 1935 signed a treaty with Mussolini which guaranteed the independence of Austria and confirmed the existing agreements over German armaments, as well as settling various colonial disputes in North Africa.

At the beginning of 1935 Hitler made his only orthodox acquisition when a plebiscite under the terms of the Treaty of Versailles gave the Saar territory back to Germany with an overwhelming vote. In March his announcement that he would introduce conscription was a flagrant violation of that treaty and created the heightened sense of alarm that helped Baldwin to bring in his further expansion of the RAF in May. 'It must not be assumed that the present demand for conscription and a large army is the end of the list,' wrote Sir John Simon. 'On the contrary, the demilitarized zone, the navy, Memel, Danzig and the former German colonies may be expected to be within the ultimate German programme.' Others thought so too. In the middle of April Simon and MacDonald attended a conference with France and Italy at Stresa, where they all agreed to combine against the unilateral repudiation of treaties; and on 2 May a Franco-Soviet pact of mutual assistance was finally signed.

Thus the late spring of 1935 might seem the high watermark of the

Powers' determination to present a united front to Hitler. In truth, it was a very flimsy front. There was still no general community of aim among the three western governments. Laval had not informed the British of the terms of his treaty with Italy in January; Mussolini was largely concerned with preparing the ground for his attack on Abyssinia, with whom he had been carefully provoking a quarrel over the past year, and assumed that the absence of any reference to this at Stresa meant that there would be no objection from Great Britain. As for Russia, now under the rule of Stalin, she remained an enigma and the attitude of the western Powers towards her was understandably cautious.

Within a few months two events had destroyed the entire basis of the Stresa conversations. First, the conciliatory aspect of Great Britain's policy towards Germany once more came to the fore and in June 1935 an Anglo-German naval agreement was signed in London whereby it was established that the German navy would not go beyond 35 per cent of British strength, although there was a higher percentage for submarines. Viewed in isolation, this agreement could be seen as something of a *détente*; it suggested a slowing down of the arms race in an area where Great Britain was particularly sensitive, and since it would be difficult for Germany to carry on naval expansion in secret, Baldwin reckoned that it might prove a useful gauge of Hitler's good faith. Politically, however, the agreement was utterly destructive of the Stresa front, since it meant that almost immediately after adhering to France and Italy against any attempt by Germany to ride roughshod over existing treaties, Great Britain was making a bilateral agreement with Hitler to repudiate that part of the Treaty of Versailles which allowed Germany virtually no navy at all.

Whatever may have been left of the Stresa front after this finally disintegrated in October 1935 when Mussolini invaded Abyssinia. His pretext was a quarrel over a disputed border territory, his aim the acquisition of empire in a region where Italy's economic influence had recently been weakened by the independent policy of the emperor of Abyssinia, Haile Selassie.

This at once placed the British government in a cleft stick. Haile Selassie's appeal to the League of Nations put the concept of collective security to the test, and a public outcry in Great Britain, heightened by romantic notions of fair play for weaker countries, demanded resistance to Italian aggression. The government certainly did not relish seeing Italy gain control of the headwaters of the Nile and inaction now might be an encouragement to Hitler for the future. They were, however, convinced that war with Italy was out of the question; they doubted whether they would be strong enough to hold the Suez Canal against Italian attack and loss of control there would render the situation in the Far East still more precarious. The impact on the German question was the most significant aspect of all; if Mussolini found himself actively opposed by Great Britain, he might turn to Germany, and that could mean the end of the independence of Austria. For those who, like Vansittart at the Foreign Office, took the French view that Germany was the greater threat, the tragedy of the general awakening of British public opinion to the dangers of militant Fascism was that it was aimed at the wrong country and might deprive the west of an important ally. For the British government it was to result, as in their attitude towards Germany, in wavering between a conciliatory and a resolute policy.

Resoluteness took the form of acting through the League of Nations—perhaps a good way of ensuring that nothing much would happen. At Geneva on 12 September 1935 Sir Samuel Hoare, who had succeeded Simon as Foreign Secretary in June, had declared that Great Britain would stand by the maintenance of the Covenant, and in the autumn, after Mussolini had invaded, a scheme was drafted by a committee of eighteen member states for the application of economic sanctions—fairly innocuous, as they did not include oil.

At the same time appeasement, strongly encouraged by the French, was in the air. Already in June 1935, before the outbreak of hostilities, Eden had gone to Rome to persuade Mussolini to be content with the province of Ogaden (map, p. 203) in southern Abyssinia, if Haile Selassie would accept the use of a port, Zeila, in British Somaliland by way of compensation. Mussolini refused and thereafter Eden became an advocate of collective resistance to him.

In December 1935 Sir Samuel Hoare, together with Vansittart, conferred with Laval in Paris where they reached agreement on a pact which would have offered Mussolini some two-thirds of Abyssinia. The object of this was to try to restore the shattered Stresa front, but when the terms of the Hoare–Laval pact leaked out to the press, the British government was suddenly faced with an outcry from public opinion, and after some hesitation the cabinet decided to disown Hoare who resigned and was replaced by Anthony Eden.

The new Foreign Secretary was soon presented with the consequences of the vacillations of the previous twelve months. Hitler could not fail to note the disarray of his opponents and on 7 March 1936, arguing that the recent French ratification of the Franco-Soviet pact nullified the Locarno agreements, he sent a token military force across the Rhine to reoccupy the Rhineland.

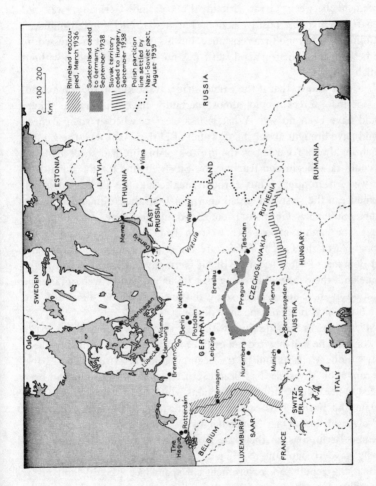

Rhineland reoccu-
pied, March 1936

Sudetenland ceded
to Germany,
September 1938

Slovak territory
ceded to Hungary,
September 1938

Polish partition
line settled by
Nazi-Soviet pact,
August 1939

0 100 200
Km

5 CENTRAL EUROPE 1933-39

Once again the contravention of existing treaties aroused different responses on the two sides of the Channel. British public opinion, still incensed with Mussolini, was relatively unmoved by the Rhineland which in the contemporary phrase they saw merely as 'Germany's own back garden'. Eden, far more concerned to build up a new working agreement between Great Britain, France and Germany, was not prepared to take any positive action. The new French foreign minister, Flandin, pressed for a firm resistance, but his government, impressed by the pessimism of their general staff, was not prepared to move without British support.

It is now known that if the French had advanced into the Rhineland, the German forces would almost certainly have withdrawn. There would have been no war. What is less clear is whether such a check would have brought about the downfall of Hitler. As it was, the gamble which he always regarded as the greatest of his life had succeeded and he could now begin constructing the Siegfried line for the defence of his western frontier. Thus through neglecting the earlier advice of Clemenceau the west had added enormously to their difficulties for the future. 'So long as Germany is contained on the Rhine,' he had said in 1925, 'she cannot expose her western front by a move against the stronghold of the Czechs. These are the critical points, the Rhineland and Bohemia. That is security. But if Germany is allowed to fortify the Rhineland, then she will move against Bohemia, will be free to raise the question of the Sudetenland, settle the question of the *Anschluss** and take off in any direction she may decide.'

Meanwhile, in their dealings with Italy the west had had the worst of all worlds. The half-hearted policy of economic sanctions failed to check Italy's military efforts and by the beginning of May 1936 Addis Ababa, the capital of Abyssinia, had been captured and Haile Selassie had been forced to flee. Worse still, the objections which had been raised by Great Britain and France now caused Mussolini to take the step which they had always feared. On 1 November 1936 he announced the existence of a Rome–Berlin axis; in the same month Germany and Italy simultaneously gave recognition to General Franco's right-wing insurrection against the republican government in Spain (see p. 313), and on 21 November Germany signed the anti-Comintern pact with Japan, to be joined a year later by Italy. Collective security had proved to be a vain illusion and the military weakness and divided counsels of the west had at last brought the dictators together.

*The incorporation of Austria within Germany.

27

The Foreign Policy of
Neville Chamberlain 1937–1939

In May 1937 on Baldwin's retirement Neville Chamberlain finally
attained the position of Prime Minister which had eluded his father
and his half-brother Austen. It was an unhappy moment for any
man to assume responsibility for the country's affairs. From the early
months of 1938 the history of Europe was to be dominated by Hitler's
expansion eastwards (map, p. 307). In March 1938 Germany absorbed
Austria, and in September annexed the Sudetenland from
Czechoslovakia; in March 1939 the rest of Czechoslovakia was dismantled and placed under her control, and in the summer Hitler followed this up with a demand for the return of Danzig. Amid this
depressing series of crises the principal concern in the west was whether
the peace of Europe could still be preserved in the face of this incessant
German advance. On 1 September 1939 Germany's invasion of Poland
finally established that it could not, and Great Britain found herself
committed to her second great war with Germany in the twentieth
century.

At the time when he became premier Neville Chamberlain was sixty-
eight. The bushy eyebrows, small moustache and alert posture of the
head, together with the wing-collar and the rolled umbrella, enabled
cartoonists to present him as a figure of prim respectability in strange
contrast to the military style of the dictators. One thing was clear,
however, as soon as he had taken office. Whereas Baldwin had been
content to allow his ministers a free hand, Chamberlain emphatically
took over the direction of the country's foreign policy. With his precise
businesslike mind he abhorred the earlier tendency towards drift. He
could be ruthless in his practical approach to a problem and impatient of
those who disagreed with him. His indefatigable determination was
based on an unshakable self-confidence. 'My method is to try and make
up my own mind first as to the proper course,' he wrote during his first

year as Prime Minister, 'and then try and put others through the same course of reasoning.'[1]

He had little faith in the efficacy of the League of Nations. He mistrusted the French and, still more, the Russians. He had no liking for the Axis Powers, but he believed that the formation of a bloc against them would only make matters worse. Consequently it seemed to him that the situation in Europe demanded an active and calculated policy of appeasement, and at the beginning of his administration he set down in writing the course that he intended to follow. 'I believe the double policy of rearmament and better relations with Germany and Italy will carry us safely through the danger period, if only the Foreign Office will play up.'[2]

There were consequently two strands in his policy of appeasement. It never stood for pacifism. He knew that it was vital to be able to argue eventually from a position of greater strength, and the programme of rearmament continued to develop along the lines of the plans made in the mid-1930s, although it was not until after the Sudetenland crisis in September 1938 that this began to move with a slightly greater sense of urgency. In the last analysis Chamberlain was prepared to contemplate war. 'If I were convinced that any nation had made up its mind to dominate the world by fear of its force,' he said in a broadcast in September 1938, 'I should feel that it must be resisted.'[3]

Nevertheless, he maintained passionately that this could only be a last resort. He hated the thought of the suffering that war would entail. Furthermore, it seemed to him unlikely that military intervention by Great Britain and France could save any eastern European country from being overrun by Germany. All that they could do would be to embark on a war of their own in the west and here the French general staff were profoundly pessimistic about the strength of the Siegfried line that confronted them. Nor did there seem much hope of effective resistance from further east. Until Hitler took up the question of Danzig, Poland preferred to rely on her non-aggression pact with Germany, and Russia, even if she were prepared to act, was geographically shut off by Poland and Romania, neither of whom would countenance the passage of the Red Army through their territories; equally, conservatives in the west had no wish to facilitate a Russian advance, which was only too probable if the war became general and prolonged.

Chamberlain's main hope of avoiding the necessity for such a war lay in the second strand of his policy. This was based on the assumption that Hitler was fundamentally a reasonable man, that he had legitimate grievances over the German minorities left outside the frontiers of

Germany by the Treaty of Versailles (see p. 165), and that if these could be redressed, it would be possible to re-establish friendly relations with him. The essence of the policy of appeasement was summed up by Nevile Henderson, the British Ambassador at Berlin, when he wrote after the outbreak of the war: 'I never had a shadow of doubt that his [Hitler's] aims were the incorporation of Austria, Sudetenland, Memel and Danzig. His claims in these respects were based on the principle of self-determination and a negotiated settlement in regard to them should not, therefore, have been impossible.'[4]

The trouble was that the appeasers in their pursuit of reasonableness had made it all too clear to Hitler that they had no objection to the substance of the changes that he wanted. In November 1937 Lord Halifax, then Lord President of the Council, assured Hitler during a visit to Germany that peaceful evolution could resolve the issues of Austria, Czechoslovakia and Danzig, and in September 1938 Chamberlain remarked somewhat unwisely at Berchtesgaden that he did not care two hoots whether the Sudeten Germans were in the Reich or out of it according to their own wishes. Thus, when German demands were presented with the plain threat of military action, it was only the method to which the appeasers could object, and Hitler simply did not believe that the west would embark on a major war over such a distinction. Until September 1939 he guessed correctly and in each crisis the appeasers were reduced to seeking a form of words which would give the Germans what they would otherwise apparently take by force.

After the outbreak of war, followed by the desperate days of the summer of 1940 when France had fallen, it was perhaps natural that men should look back on the period of appeasement with resentment. It was denounced as a policy of weakness and a betrayal of small countries, and it seemed inexplicable that there could have been such an obstinate blindness to the upsurge of a new German attempt to dominate the Continent.

At the time, however, there were only a few who strongly criticized the policy of appeasement and this opposition never took any organized political shape. The Labour party's attitude remained negative throughout. The extreme left, such as Sir Stafford Cripps, regarded all war as a manifestation of a capitalist society, and the majority under Attlee pursued the contradictory aims of support for the League of Nations and demands for disarmament, although after July 1937 they did agree to abstain rather than to vote against the armaments estimates. Within the House of Commons the objections came mostly from a few Conservatives. Winston Churchill never ceased to give dire warnings of the consequences of not presenting a firm front to Hitler; Leo Amery and, later, Anthony Eden were each leaders of other small anti-appeasement groups, but none of these really achieved any degree of unity. The head of the Foreign Office, Sir Robert Vansittart, was utterly outspoken in his dislike of Nazi Germany, but as an official he was more vulnerable and found himself side-tracked in 1937 into the post of chief diplomatic adviser to the Foreign Secretary, which meant in effect that he need not give advice.

In the main, Chamberlain had pretty full support for his policy of appeasement in the cabinet, in the Commons and in the country as a whole. Among senior ministers the only resignations were those of the Foreign Secretary, Anthony Eden, in February 1938 and the First Lord of the Admiralty, Duff Cooper, in October 1938; and only some thirty-five Conservatives abstained from voting in the debate after the set-tlement of the Sudetenland. Otherwise, Chamberlain was secure. He could work in close harmony with an inner group of the cabinet—Sir John Simon who became Chancellor of the Exchequer in 1937, Sir Samuel Hoare, the Home Secretary, and Lord Halifax who succeeded Eden as Foreign Secretary after his resignation. Among the officials there was pre-eminently Sir Horace Wilson, an outstanding civil servant, who since 1935 had had his own room at No. 10 Downing Street after being seconded from the Treasury for service with the Prime Minister. Chamberlain had, too, the support of the press. Lord Rothermere had earlier advocated the return of some of Germany's ex-colonies and in May 1938 announced in the *Daily Mail* that 'Czechoslovakia is not of the remotest concern to us'. *The Times* under the editorship of Geoffrey Dawson was fiercely on the side of the appeasers. 'There is little sym-pathy here with the view which has sometimes seemed to prevail on the Continent,' wrote Dawson in October 1937, 'that the proper way to treat Germany is to ring her about with vigilant allied states, sometimes masquerading as the League of Nations, like trained elephants round a tiger in the jungle, to prevent her expansion in any direction beyond the limits imposed twenty years ago.'[5]

Chamberlain's determination to concentrate on a settlement with Germany meant that problems in other parts of the world had largely to be subordinated to that end. In the Far East the continuing threat from Japan had brought British policy round to giving positive economic support to Chiang-kai-shek's regime in China, but when in July 1937 Japan resumed open hostilities on the Chinese mainland and began to push slowly down the eastern coastline, Chamberlain knew that any effective stand against her must depend on the cooperation of the United States. When this was not forthcoming, he fell back on the old mixture of diplomatic protest and conciliatory approaches which might prevent too close a consolidation of the German–Japanese alignment.

At the same time in Palestine the tension between the Jews and the Arabs was a growing source of embarrassment for the government, torn, as ever, between the promises of the Balfour declaration (see p. 191) and the need to remain on good terms with the Arab world. The antisemitic policy of Nazi Germany had naturally built up the pressure of Jewish immigration into Palestine and in the autumn of 1937 the Palestinian Arabs, always resentful of this intrusion, broke out in a revolt which had to be put down by British forces from the Suez Canal zone. Plans for partition between Arabs and Jews were aired and then discarded as impractical, and eventually a White Paper in May 1939 established a severe restriction on the number of Jewish immigrants—the inescapable price of restoring order in a region which Great Britain dared not leave in a state of unrest.

Ireland, too, gained from the government's need to resolve peripheral disputes. In May 1937 de Valera had proclaimed the constitution of Eire (see p. 290), and Chamberlain decided that if she was to be independent, she must at least be kept friendly. The British government accordingly accepted the new situation, maintaining that this still left Eire within the Commonwealth. There followed in April 1938 a series of agreements whereby the tariff war between the two countries was ended and the question of the land annuities was written off with a single payment of £10 million to Great Britain. The three naval bases in the south were also handed back—a concession constantly deplored by Winston Churchill, although in the view of the Chiefs of Staff they would be of little use in the event of Irish neutrality in a future war.

All these difficulties could to some extent be treated in isolation. The implications of the Spanish civil war, however, were to prove more intricate. General Franco's right-wing rising against the Republican government in Madrid had begun in the summer of 1936 and the subsequent years of war, which only ended with Franco's victory in January 1939, had a marked impact on the attitudes of most other European countries. In the west public opinion saw the conflict as a final polarization of right and left amid the growing tensions of world politics. For this very reason most governments were ostensibly opposed to taking sides for fear of a general escalation, and by August 1936 nearly thirty of them had signed declarations of non-intervention. The dictatorships, however, had little intention of honouring this agreement

and throughout most of the war Russia supplied the Republican government, while Germany and Italy sent massive support in the form of
troops and war material to Franco.

The Italian contribution was particularly great and this involvement
was to be a serious obstacle for Neville Chamberlain. He was convinced
of the need to re-establish better relations with Mussolini and in July
1937 he had written a personal letter to him in terms of general friendship. His efforts, however, were constantly undermined by the struggle
over non-intervention, involving an endless wrangle to persuade
Mussolini to withdraw the forces of Italian 'volunteers' who were aiding
Franco. Also in 1937 unknown submarines, correctly suspected of being
Italian, had been attacking merchant ships of all nationalities delivering
supplies to the Republican government, and at a conference at Nyon in
September 1937 Great Britain, France and Russia agreed to establish
naval patrols in the Mediterranean. This highly significant and historic
combination of Powers proved effective, but one consequence was to
tighten the links between Germany and Italy and it was in November
that Mussolini joined the German-Japanese anti-Comintern pact.

Chamberlain was nevertheless absolutely determined to pursue the
question of opening conversations with the Italian government and
before long this had brought about a rift between the Prime Minister
and his Foreign Secretary Anthony Eden. Both men were agreed that
there must be some kind of *rapprochement* with Italy and that a British
recognition of Italian possession of Abyssinia would be a useful bargaining counter to achieve this. Eden, however, was profoundly mistrustful
of Mussolini and believed that there should be no conversations until he
had withdrawn his forces from Spain as a token of good faith. Chamberlain, on the other hand, was convinced of the need to act with speed and
wished to dispense with that preliminary condition. By this time relations between Chamberlain and Eden had greatly deteriorated. Eden
resented Chamberlain's use of his own private lines of communication,
as for example with Sir Austen Chamberlain's widow who was living in
Rome, and he had been furious at Chamberlain's rejection of an
American proposal in January 1938 for an international conference. The
climax came at a meeting on 19 February 1938 between the Italian
ambassador Grandi and Chamberlain. Eden insisted on attending and
the divergence of view between the Prime Minister and his own Foreign
Secretary was so great that on the next day, after the cabinet had
supported Chamberlain's view, Eden gave in his resignation. His place
was taken by Lord Halifax and in April 1938 an agreement was signed
between Great Britain and Italy defining each other's interests in the

Mediterranean and including British recognition of Italy's conquest of Abyssinia and a meaningless Italian promise to observe non-intervention in Spain.

The reason for Chamberlain's sense of urgency in February had been the indications that Hitler was now on the verge of absorbing Austria into the German Reich and, as in 1934, Mussolini's attitude towards this would be crucial. On 12 February 1938, a week before Eden's resignation, the Austrian chancellor, von Schuschnigg, had gone to Berchtesgaden for an interview with Hitler, who had forced him to agree to a close coordination of the foreign and economic policies of the two countries and to the appointment of an Austrian Nazi, Seyss-Inquart, as minister of the interior, a post which would give him control of the police. It seems probable that Hitler would have been content to leave matters like that for the moment, but on 9 March von Schuschnigg, back in Vienna, resolved to challenge Hitler with a plebiscite on continued Austrian independence. It was a fatal decision. Hitler knew that he must strike at once before the plebiscite was held. He addressed a personal appeal to Mussolini, who duly gave his consent, since at this stage the Anglo-Italian conversations were far too tentative to persuade him to abandon his friendship with Hitler. German pressure on Vienna forced the cancelling of the plebiscite, the resignation of von Schuschnigg and the appointment of Seyss-Inquart as chancellor who under instructions from Berlin asked for German aid. On the night of 11 March the German army, leaving behind a trail of broken-down vehicles that indicated the haste of the whole operation, advanced over the frontier, and on 13 March Austria was declared incorporated within the Reich.

Protest and condemnation were heard everywhere, but no action followed. The French government had just fallen and Chamberlain was convinced that the west was in no position to resist. 'Nothing could have arrested what actually has happened,' he said in the House of Commons, 'unless this country and other countries had been prepared to use force.'[6]

Indeed, far from contemplating aid for Austria, the west was already thinking apprehensively of the next step. 'I give you my word of honour,' said Goering to the Czech minister in the middle of the Austrian crisis, 'that Czechoslovakia has not the least reason to feel any anxiety.' This sounded ominous, and yet here too Chamberlain could see little prospect of effective military resistance to Hitler. Two years earlier his half-brother Austen had said, 'if Austria perishes, Czechoslovakia becomes indefensible', and on 20 March the Prime Minister wrote in his diary: 'I have abandoned any idea of giving guarantees to

Czechoslovakia or the French in connection with her obligations to that country.[7] It is true that on 24 March he did utter a warning that there were circumstances in which Great Britain would be compelled to fight, but his personal hope was that if changes were to come in the Sudetenland, they could be contained within a peaceful framework. After that, he wrote, 'it may be possible for Europe to settle down again and some day for us to start peace talks again with the Germans'.[8]

It was not long before all these anticipations were realized. Inevitably the Austrian *Anschluss* gave an immediate stimulus to the demands of the Sudeten Germans, numbering 3 million under Czech rule. Between February and May 1938 the membership of Konrad Henlein's Sudeten party rose from 550,000 to 1,310,000 and on 24 April, after earlier consultations with Hitler, Henlein addressed the annual meeting of the party at Karlsbad, where he laid down an eight-point programme demanding autonomy for the predominantly German regions of Czechoslovakia.

The problem for the Czechs was that such an arrangement would threaten their highly composite state with disintegration; more particularly, the Sudeten Germans resided mostly in the extreme western area which included the mountain fortifications on which Czech defence depended, and for this reason Hodza, the Czech prime minister, believed that autonomy would be 'tantamount to suicide'.

A very different view prevailed in the minds of the British government and of their representatives, Nevile Henderson at Berlin and Basil Newton at Prague. To them it did not seem that autonomy was an unreasonable plea and it was vital to press the Czechs to make concessions before the quarrel had developed into a confrontation with Hitler. The French could not afford to be so dispassionate. Unlike the British they already had a treaty of mutual guarantee with Czechoslovakia which they had reaffirmed on 14 March and they regarded the possible extension of German power eastwards with gloom. Their military leaders, however, were obsessed with the idea of defence and had not changed their exaggerated view of German strength along the Rhineland frontier. Thus when Daladier, the French prime minister, and Bonnet, his foreign minister, conferring in London on 28 March, were unable to get Chamberlain to agree to a firm military alliance, they were increasingly inclined to surrender the initiative to the British government whose more uncommitted position might enable them to push the Czech President Beneš into submission.

Towards the end of May these mild attitudes suddenly changed when there were rumours of German troop movements in the frontier regions.

The Czechs partially mobilized and British and French statements made it clear to Berlin that if Germany attacked, the Czechs would not stand alone. Although the rumours seem to have been unfounded, this at least was a positive front, but it was to do the Czechs little good. It roused Hitler to a state of fury and on 30 May he stated, 'it is my unalterable decision to smash Czechoslovakia by military force in the near future',[9] establishing 1 October as the date for this. At the same time the episode created a sense of urgency among the British and the French that a settlement must be negotiated before a further crisis should arise.

Indeed, throughout the summer of 1938 there was a reasonable degree of unanimity between the British government and its critics. Even Churchill wrote on 23 June: 'There is no doubt that Henlein, Hodza and President Beneš are working for a settlement and that a good settlement is possible between them on the basis of Home Rule for the Sudeten German regions within the Czechoslovakian state.'[10] The only issue that seriously divided them was the extent to which Hitler should be warned off direct interference. There was consequently reasonable support for the government's decision to send Lord Runciman to Prague at the beginning of August to act as a mediator between the Sudeten Germans and the Czech government, and on 4 September, as a result of pressure from Runciman and Newton, President Beneš finally granted the Sudeten Germans all the concessions that they needed for autonomy.

By now, however, after Germans and Czechs in the Sudetenland had clashed in a series of violent incidents throughout the summer, Sudeten enthusiasm had moved on to take up the cry of direct inclusion within Germany. This would seem to be in accord with Hitler's conversations with Henlein in March, when they had agreed that 'we must always demand so much that we can never be satisfied', although even they could hardly have anticipated a leading article in *The Times* on 7 September suggesting that the Sudetenland might be ceded to Germany. Then on 12 September in a speech at the Nuremberg party rally Hitler made a virulent attack on the Czech government on behalf of the Sudeten Germans, and although he did not explicitly state that he would invade Czechoslovakia in order to annex the Sudetenland, the likelihood of war appeared very great.

It was at this point that Neville Chamberlain took the dramatic decision to fly to Germany for a personal conversation with Hitler in an effort to preserve peace. They met at Hitler's residence at Berchtesgaden on 15 September. Here Hitler formulated his demand for the transfer of the Sudetenland wherever there was a bare majority of

German inhabitants, and maintained that this must be the preliminary to any future Anglo-German understanding. Chamberlain was careful to press him on whether he had any further designs on Czechoslovakia, and when Hitler gave him a contemptuous assurance, said that he personally would be prepared to accept such a transfer.

On his return to London Chamberlain persuaded the cabinet that this was the only possible solution; Daladier and Bonnet also agreed and in Prague President Beneš was forced to give way. With this Chamberlain was confident that he had brought the crisis to an end and on 22 September he had his second meeting with Hitler, this time at Godesberg on the Rhine, where he hoped that the final arrangements could be made fairly speedily.

He was to be disappointed. Hitler now raised his terms, demanding that Poland and Hungary should also receive concessions and that the areas which were to be ceded to Germany must be evacuated almost immediately by the Czechs without any plebiscite or compensation for loss of property. Chamberlain was utterly taken aback; he reckoned that he had gone to the absolute limit in accepting the Berchtesgaden proposals and there were several heated exchanges between the two of them before he returned again to London.

Thus the crisis had reached a new height. The Czechs refused to accept the Godesberg terms and ordered a general mobilization. The French called up 500,000 men and on 25 September in a statement to be presented to Hitler Chamberlain promised Daladier that if France were to go to the assistance of the Czechs, Great Britain would support her. On the next day the British fleet was mobilized and in London the appearance of anti-aircraft guns and the instructions for the evacuation of schoolchildren to the provinces left the British public in little doubt that war was imminent.

Nevertheless, the prospect of resistance looked bleak to Chamberlain. He was unconvinced and unattracted by recent Russian proposals to support the west. The United States would remain neutral and a report from the British Ambassador in Paris emphasized that feeling in France was generally against war. The British Chiefs of Staff were adamant that they were insufficiently prepared and the high commissioners of the Dominions were almost entirely unsympathetic towards the idea of a war fought over the distinction between the Berchtesgaden and the Godesberg proposals. This was also Chamberlain's view and in a broadcast on 27 September his voice, far from rallying the nation, only reflected the numbed despondency of British public opinion. 'How horrible, fantastic, incredible it is,' he said, 'that we should be digging trenches and trying on gas masks here, because of a quarrel in a far away country between people of whom we know nothing.'[11]

With all this in mind Chamberlain still hoped for an international conference and an attempt was made to enlist the support of Mussolini. This last did produce a response. On 28 September Chamberlain was in the middle of a speech in the House of Commons, when an invitation from Hitler for a meeting of the four Powers, Great Britain, France, Germany and Italy, was handed along the front bench to him, and his announcement of this brought almost the whole of the Commons to their feet in an unrestrained outburst of cheering.

The Munich conference, which, contrary to Chamberlain's original intention, did not include any Czech representation, lasted some fourteen hours and produced a settlement that only slightly modified the Godesberg demands. Evacuation of the Sudetenland was to take place in five stages over a period of ten days from 1 October. Doubtful areas were to be settled by plebiscites under an international commission, and Czechs wishing to move out were to be allowed to take their possessions with them.

Apart from that, Munich could be seen as a complete victory for Hitler and an outright desertion of the Czechs, who were only informed afterwards and decided to acquiesce rather than to fight a war with Germany without western support. 'We have sustained a total and unmitigated defeat,' declared Churchill in the Commons, and certainly there were many angry voices and uneasy consciences that autumn. Yet at home public opinion seemed largely to express an overwhelming sense of relief. Chamberlain was given a tumultuous reception by delighted crowds on his return and for weeks he was inundated with letters and gifts from every part of Europe, including Germany, thanking him for having averted war.

All this was forgotten within a year, when Munich had become a discredited term, a symbol of inglorious surrender, and then those who still supported Chamberlain were reduced to the argument that one of his motives had been to play for time in order to build up British armaments for the inevitable conflict. There is, however, little evidence of this. In the autumn of 1938 the rearmament programme was accelerated, but no new expenditure was authorized. Preparation concentrated on defence in the provision of fighter planes and the organization of air raid precautions (ARP); and proposals to enlarge the Army which might assist the French were firmly damped down. For Chamberlain Munich represented a total justification of the doctrine of appeasement. He reckoned that he had saved the peace of Europe; a dangerous corner had been turned and he attached enormous importance to the document which he and Hitler had signed on the morning after the conference, reaffirming the Anglo-German naval agreement, 'as symbolic of the desire of our two peoples never to go to war with one another again', and promising that all further difficulties would be resolved by the method of consultation. Not even the way in which the Germans rode roughshod over the details of implementing the Munich settlement in arbitrarily handing over the Czech territory to Poland and Hungary would shake that faith. He was determined to press on with his policy and in January 1939 he and Lord Halifax paid a personal visit to Rome, although this achieved very little in the way of detaching Mussolini from Hitler.

Disillusionment finally came in March 1939, when Hitler annexed the rest of Czechoslovakia. After Munich the earlier form of government centred on Prague had been replaced by a federal system for Bohemia, Slovakia and Ruthenia, and Nazi propaganda had continued to play on these separatist tendencies. On 14 March Slovakia was bullied by the German government into proclaiming independence, and on the next day President Hacha, who had succeeded Beneš, came to Berlin to see what could be salvaged from the wreck. Here he was forced under the threat of the immediate bombing of Prague to sign away Czech independence; Bohemia and Slovakia became German protectorates and Ruthenia was annexed by Hungary. A week later the same tactics compelled Lithuania to give back Memel, and at the same time Romania was coming under heavy economic pressure from Germany. Not even Italy had been consulted over these moves and now, to keep pace with his obstreperous ally, Mussolini embarked on the invasion of Albania on 7 April.

The hopes of appeasement lay in ruins. The official reaction of the west was that the dissolution of Czechoslovakia had come about with the consent of the governments concerned and that therefore no resistance was feasible. Nevertheless, Hitler's actions made nonsense of any claims based on the rights of German minorities and utterly discredited his earlier assertion that the Sudetenland was the limit of his demands on Czechoslovakia. In Great Britain government circles and public opinion alike responded to this with a startling change of mood. It was at last clear that there could be no peace or security based on continuing surrender to the threat of German military force. Chamberlain, who was at first inclined merely to express irritation, was nudged by Halifax into seeing the full implications of this further German advance eastwards and on 17 March in a speech at Birmingham he asked the question in everyone's mind: 'Is this in fact a step in the direction of an attempt to dominate the world by force?'[12]

There was little doubt where the next thrust would come. Hitler was already pressing the Poles for the incorporation of the Free City of Danzig within Germany and for a road and rail link under German control across the Polish corridor, and the Poles were determined to resist. Chamberlain still hoped for a negotiated settlement, but not in the manner of 1938. The population of Danzig was almost entirely German, and Poland, like Czechoslovakia, was a far away country, but these were no longer the issues. On 29 March Anglo-French staff talks began the planning of the dispatch of British divisions to France in the event of war and on 31 March Chamberlain announced in the House of Commons an assurance that Great Britain would come to the aid of Poland, if she were attacked by Germany. On 13 April he gave similar guarantees to Greece and Romania, and on 26 April, as a gesture to the French, he introduced conscription.

Hitler was unimpressed by all this. He never seemed to understand that with the destruction of Czechoslovakia he had also destroyed the hopes and illusions on which his success at Munich had depended. Despite the efforts of the German ambassador in London to convince him of the new mood which lay behind the recent volte-face in British policy, he believed that this was bluff. On 28 April he denounced the Anglo-German naval treaty and the German-Polish pact of 1934, and on 7 May his position seemed further strengthened when Mussolini signed a treaty of military alliance with him—the so-called pact of steel.

Indeed, Chamberlain's hastily devised system of guarantees was of little significance in military terms. It was hardly likely to be an effective deterrent as long as it lacked one essential partner—Soviet Russia. The British and the French were well aware of this, and Chamberlain's first reaction in March had been to suggest a pact between Great Britain, France, Poland and Russia. The Poles, however, rejected this, since they reckoned that the presence of the Red Army on their territory, nominally as an ally, would be as great a threat to their independence as that posed by Hitler. With this the British and the French were once again faced with the fundamental dilemma of eastern European politics, and since they fully understood these fears and were dubious about the quality of the Russian army, they gave their first allegiance to Poland.

They knew, however, that Russian support was essential and throughout the summer a series of Anglo-French delegations in Moscow attempted to discover a formula for enlisting Russian aid without opening the door to Communist expansion. This was an impossible task. The

Russians were deeply suspicious of the west. They mistrusted Great Britain's mildness towards Japan, Russia's potential enemy in the Far East; the rejection of their offer to form a bloc against Hitler at the time of the Sudetenland crisis only strengthened their conviction that the west wanted to do a deal with Hitler in anticipation of an eventual war between Germany and Russia far from western frontiers, an idea not entirely absent from the minds of some British and French politicians. For the Russians the obvious retaliation was an alliance with Germany. 'My poor friend, what have you done?' said the Soviety deputy commissioner for foreign affairs to the French ambassador at Moscow after Munich. 'For us I see no other way out except a fourth partition of Poland.'[13] On 3 May the pro-western foreign minister Litvinov was replaced by Molotov and all the time that the British and French delegations were wrangling endlessly at Moscow about the terms and circumstances of any Russian involvement in the defence of eastern Europe, Stalin was putting out cautious diplomatic feelers towards Berlin. The outcome was a Nazi-Soviet pact signed on 23 August allotting the two countries their respective spheres of influence in eastern Europe and sharing Poland between them.

For Hitler this seemed to put the matter beyond doubt. Already in April he had ordered his generals to prepare for an invasion of Poland beginning on 1 September. German demands for the return of Danzig had slowly mounted to a crescendo and Hitler was certain that the announcement of his agreement with Stalin would ensure that the west would not resort to war. A personal letter from Chamberlain, stating that the Nazi-Soviet pact would make no difference to Great Britain's determination to support Poland, had little effect on him and in the face of Polish intransigence he gave orders for the military invasion to begin on 26 August. On the day before this, however, the news of the signing of an Anglo-Polish pact in London coincided with a warning from Mussolini that Italy was not yet ready for war, and this did cause Hitler to cancel his orders. For the next few days he continued his hectoring demands, at the same time throwing out the odd remark that might reawaken hopes of appeasement in the west. Then, gambling on his intuition, he renewed his orders for attack, and in the early hours of the morning of 1 September German armies swept over the border into Poland.

The British and the French response to this was not immediate. Chamberlain had never given up hope that it might be possible to find a peaceful solution to the question of Danzig, but the real problem was that the French generals were pressing for delay until they had completed their mobilization. Thus, throughout 1 and 2 **September** there were frantic exchanges of notes and telephone calls merely requiring the Germans to withdraw their forces as a preliminary to further negotiation.

In the end it was the House of Commons who forced the issue. When on the evening of 2 September, in a chamber darkened by an approaching thunderstorm, they heard from the Prime Minister that no ultimatum with a time limit had yet been delivered to Berlin, a feeling of anger and frustration united members of all parties. They scented appeasement. The German *blitzkrieg* over the Polish plains had not been halted. There could be no further parley with military force. There was only one answer, however ill chosen the moment might be. As Arthur Greenwood, the Labour spokesman, rose to reply, a Conservative backbencher shouted in despair across to him: '*You* speak for Britain', and the cheers from both sides of the Commons, when Greenwood demanded immediate action, compelled Chamberlain to realize that he could no longer hold the House.

Later that evening a deputation from the cabinet came to No. 10 Downing Street to insist on an ultimatum and Chamberlain at last took the step that he had always dreaded. 'Right, gentlemen,' he said quietly, 'this means war,' and as he spoke there was suddenly a great clap of thunder and a flash of lightning lit up the cabinet room. The French were informed that there could be no more delay; an ultimatum was sent to Berlin giving Hitler until eleven o'clock on the morning of 3 September to withdraw from Poland, and when no reply had been received, the Prime Minister addressed the nation on the radio at 11.15 to tell them that Great Britain was now at war with Germany.

VI

The Second World War
1939–1945

28
The Débâcle

1. The phoney war: September 1939–May 1940

The fortunes of Great Britain in the Second World War have an emotional force almost unique in her history. Within a few months of its outbreak the British were to face the most hazardous and desperate year of their national existence, as one country after another fell before the blasting onrush of *blitzkrieg* and Germany came to command almost the entire Continent from the Pyrenees to the plains of eastern Poland. The British Isles lay under the threat of invasion which they had not known since the days of Napoleon, and the nightmare imaginings of the pre-1914 writers (see p. 51) now assumed an imminent reality. For a year the British stood alone and as a consequence, perhaps, imagined that they could continue to do so after peace had come. Then, as Russia and the United States were drawn in, the war ran its worldwide course and at the end, when in the summer of 1945 Germany had been overcome, there was revealed a regime more evil than even wartime propaganda had dared to suggest. This sense of high drama, the fight against appalling odds and the ultimate triumph of right, at least in the west, has coloured the whole memory of the Second World War in extraordinary contrast to the image of the first.

It would, however, be wrong to think that this was how the British saw themselves in September 1939. The embattled singleness of purpose was to be the product of the crisis of 1940; at the beginning the general mood of the British people was very different—merely one of glum resignation to an apparently inescapable conflict which was not going to be over by Christmas.

Neville Chamberlain himself set about the organization of his war administration with a brisk efficiency. The Liberal and Labour parties were invited to form a coalition, but both refused on the grounds that they could serve better in Opposition. But the coming of war did close the ranks of the Conservatives, with the return to ministerial posts of Winston Churchill as First Lord of the Admiralty and Anthony Eden as Dominions Secretary. A war cabinet was created at once, larger than

Lloyd George's and including the three service ministers; a Chiefs of Staff committee for interservice decisions had already been in operation for some years, and earlier planning now facilitated the immediate formation of war-time ministries for economic warfare, food and shipping. The machinery of conscription had been running since the spring of 1939 and now merely had to be expanded. Exchange control, food rationing and a blackout were all imposed from the outset, and 1·5 million schoolchildren, wearing labels on their coats and clutching civilian gas masks in cardboard containers, were evacuated from London and from the major urban areas of the south.

All this was in admirable contrast to the muddle of August 1914; it suggested a government settling down methodically to the problem of fighting a major war with Germany, which it declared might well last three years. What it did not do was to offer much help to the Poles who at this moment were fighting for their lives. Since 1 September one German army group under von Bock had thrust south from Pomerania and East Prussia, while another under von Rundstedt swept in east from Silesia. The tactics of *blitzkrieg*, relying on speed and the creation of confusion, enabled armoured Panzer columns with air support to drive through and behind the Polish forces, initially placed too far to the west, and by 8 September German tanks were outside Warsaw. The bulk of the Polish army, cut up and disorganized, was trapped to the west of the Vistula and on 10 September orders were given for a general retreat to the south-east. A week later Russia, in accordance with the recent Nazi–Soviet pact, advanced into eastern Poland, the Polish government fled to Romania and by the beginning of October all resistance had ended.

The spectacle of Poland struck down without military assistance from her Allies lends a little support to one argument of the appeasers: that it would be impossible to save any eastern European country over whose fate the west might go to war. The facts of geography were inexorable. Yet the moment when Germany's military effort was devoted to a major campaign in the east should have provided a splendid opportunity for an attack on her western frontier, where until the last week of September she had less than twenty-five divisions. Such an attack could only have come from the French, since the immediately available British force of four divisions would take a month to ferry across the Channel. But although the French had in theory an army of 110 divisions, of whom sixty-five were active, they had never prepared a mechanized assault force of regular soldiers ready for the instant action that this situation demanded; their whole policy had been based on defence behind the Maginot line; their large army depended on the mobilization of civilian conscripts and this could not be complete before 17 September, by which time it was too late to save Poland.

There was not even any air attack. This was because in March 1939 the British and the French had agreed that they would 'not initiate air action against any but purely "military" objectives in the narrowest sense of the word'. So far, although they had bombed Polish towns mercilessly, the Germans had carried out no bombing in the west. This was advantageous for the Allies at the present stage in their preparations and they were anxious not to take the first step. In any case, Allied bombing attacks on western Germany could do little to help Poland and the inevitable loss of civilian life would have been a gift for German propaganda in neutral countries.

During the rest of the year there was some activity at sea. Merchant shipping suffered heavily from the German U-boats and a new weapon, the magnetic mine. The aircraft carrier *Courageous* and the battleship *Royal Oak* were both sunk, the latter while actually in harbour at Scapa Flow, but in December the British gained a victory when the German pocket battleship *Graf Spee*, which had been sinking merchant ships in the Atlantic, was attacked by three British cruisers and driven to take refuge in Montevideo, where Hitler ordered her to be scuttled.

Apart from this, the first six months of the war were pervaded with a strange sense of anticlimax. All was so quiet on the western front that there seemed to be no front at all. A parliamentary delegation crossed to France to inspect the French troops manning the great underground ramifications of the Maginot line. 'They did not look like soldiers at all,' commented Harold Nicolson, 'but had the white faces of troglodytes and the nervous white hands of scientists.'[1] In the air the RAF continued to drop propaganda leaflets; no bombs fell on Great Britain, and many people who had been evacuated began to drift back to London. Hitler's peace offer to the west, made early in October after he had digested Poland, was rejected; yet the continuing state of hostility seemed to be largely nominal—the 'phoney' war as American commentators christened it.

The principal concern of the CIGS, General Sir Edmund Ironside, was to build up British forces in France. In September the British Expeditionary Force (BEF) under the command of Field-Marshal Lord Gort consisted of two corps, each of two divisions, one in reasonably good shape under General Sir John Dill, the other an extremely scratch force under General Alan Brooke. The ferrying process continued throughout the winter until in April 1940 394,000 British troops were established in France, the British government having already promised the French to provide thirty-two divisions by the end of the first year of the war.

Gort and the BEF were placed under the orders of General Gamelin, the French Commander-in-Chief, but Gort retained the right of appeal to his own government. On the whole, Allied cooperation worked well, although the French generals still regarded the British as incorrigible amateurs and Sir Edward Spears, a member of the parliamentary delegation, noted that they appeared to see Gort 'as a sort of jovial and friendly battalion commander'. [2] The winter was spent constructing defences on the Franco-Belgian border, and Gamelin's principal preparation was for a projected entry into Belgium in the event of Germany violating Belgian neutrality.

It was never Hitler's intention that there should be so long a lull in the west. Since the rejection of his peace offer he had been pressing hard for the immediate opening of an offensive into France through Belgium and the Netherlands, but had been constantly frustrated by bad weather reports and by the reluctance of his generals. Then in January 1940 the capture of the operational plan of attack, after a German staff officer flying to Bonn had had to make a forced landing in Belgium, imposed a further postponement while an entirely new plan was devised.

Hitler was not the only one who was impatient for action during these months. In London Winston Churchill at the Admiralty was looking further afield. He was particularly concerned over the supply of Swedish iron ore to Germany passing through the Norwegian port of Narvik and then down the coast within the shelter of Norway's territorial waters, but his proposals that these waters should be mined were resisted by the Foreign Office. At the end of November 1939 a new development in the north opened up another possibility. Russia, who had already established garrisons in Estonia, Latvia and Lithuania, embarked on a war with Finland, after the Finns had rejected Russian proposals for a readjustment of their eastern frontier. In Great Britain the news of the resistance put up by the Finns aroused enormous public sympathy, demanding that the Allies should send immediate assistance. For the government the attraction of such a policy was that the despatch of an expeditionary force across the top of Scandinavia to Finland would provide an excellent excuse for the holding of Narvik and the iron ore fields of northern Sweden. Both Sweden and Norway were adamant, however, that they would not accept this and it was not until March that the cabinet set plans in motion for landings on the Norwegian coast. By then the Finnish resistance had come to an end, thereby removing the principal justification, but in April some British forces were still in readiness to launch what was hoped would be a reasonably peaceful invasion of Norway.

The Allies had made their interest in Scandinavia too apparent and waited too long. Hitler, intent on his plans for attacking France, was now won over to the view that he must forestall any interference with the vital supply of Swedish iron ore and at the same time protect his northern flank. In the early hours of 9 April 1940 German forces were landed by sea at Narvik, Trondheim, Bergen and Oslo, all of which were captured without difficulty. At the same time Denmark was invaded and Copenhagen occupied. The Danes decided not to resist in a hopeless situation. The Norwegian army, caught unawares, had not even mobilized, but continued to fight back for the next two months.

From the British point of view the Norwegian campaign was a complete fiasco. The Navy knew that German cruisers had sailed, but awaited them in the open sea and thus failed to intercept the landings. British forces, already prepared for the invasion of Norway, landed near Narvik on 14 April, but failed to retake it. Other forces were then directed to landings north and south of Trondheim, but the nature of the terrain and German air attacks brought these to nothing and the troops were eventually taken off again on 2 May. This meant that southern and central Norway was now firmly in German hands, and only in the north the Allied besieging forces clung on in the hope of recapturing Narvik.

The echoes of these forlorn and ineffectual military clashes were soon to be heard at Westminster. On 7 May Neville Chamberlain made a statement of explanation before a crowded and critical House of Commons and it soon became very clear that many of his own Conservatives were no longer prepared to support him. The fate of Poland, the long winter of inactivity and now the German conquest of Norway were proving too much for party loyalty. Sir Roger Keyes, a naval veteran of the First World War, clad in the full uniform of Admiral of the Fleet, made a long denunciation of the Narvik episode and a little later Leo Amery rose to scourge the whole war administration of the government, ending with the words of Oliver Cromwell: 'You have sat too long here for any good you have been doing. Depart, I say—let us have done with you. In the name of God, go!'[3]

On the next day the debate opened with a speech from Herbert Morrison who declared that Labour would demand a vote on the adjournment—in effect, a vote of confidence. 'I accept the challenge,' declared Chamberlain and appealed to his friends in the House. This was a gross tactical error. The issue was greater than friendship, but amid the fury of speaking that ensued there was one delicate area round which the attackers had to steer. Most of them were convinced that Winston Churchill must be the man to succeed Chamberlain; yet Churchill as First Lord of the Admiralty was dangerously involved in the Norwegian affair. Nor did he avoid the fact. 'I take complete responsibility for everything that has been done by the Admiralty,' he growled from the front bench, when Lloyd George tried to exonerate him.

The division came. Thirty-three Conservatives went into the Opposition lobby; some sixty abstained. The government had won the vote, but their majority had dropped from about 230 to 81, and to Chamberlain such a disastrous fall in Conservative support could mean only one thing as he left the House that night. 'I, who had felt so bitterly opposed to his policy,' wrote Sir Edward Spears afterwards, 'felt intensely sorry for him as he walked out, solitary, following in the wake of all his dead hopes and fruitless efforts.'4

In negotiation on the next day the Conservative dissidents demanded a Coalition, but neither Labour nor Liberals would agree to form one unless Chamberlain gave up the premiership. The choice now lay between Lord Halifax and Churchill. Halifax was not keen; he admitted afterwards that the mere thought gave him a bad stomach-ache; in any case, as he pointed out, it would be wrong in these circumstances for the Prime Minister not to be in the House of Commons. And so on 10 May, after Labour leaders had consulted the party conference at Bournemouth, Winston Churchill assumed the position of Prime Minister at the head of a Coalition government.

That very morning the German army launched its attack on Belgium and Holland as a prelude to the assault on France and it was against the background of those first encounters that Churchill set about shaping the machinery of government with which he intended to organize the country's war effort. In one sense he was more fortunately placed than Lloyd George had been in 1916. No one could accuse him of having conspired for high office; at this moment of crisis the mood of the parties pointed only to unity of effort and he was careful to avoid any recriminations that might upset this. Neville Chamberlain set a superb example, consenting to serve under the new Prime Minister as Lord President of the Council, a vital decision since he was still leader of the Conservative party—in marked contrast to Asquith's sulky withdrawal in 1916. By the same token Lord Halifax and Sir John Simon remained in the government, to the resentment of some Labour members. Labour itself was strongly represented in the Coalition with Attlee and Arthur Greenwood both in the war cabinet, Ernest Bevin as Minister of Labour and National Service, A. V. Alexander as First Lord of the Admiralty and Hugh Dalton as Minister of Economic Warfare. Sir Archibald Sinclair, the leader of the Liberals, became Air Minister. The supply of aircraft was now withdrawn from the Air Ministry and entrusted to a new Ministry of Aircraft Production under the unorthodox and dynamic control of Lord Beaverbrook.

Churchill's plan was to return to a small war cabinet consisting of himself, Chamberlain, Attlee, Halifax and Greenwood, but the most striking innovation was his own assumption of a new post as Minister of Defence, in which capacity he presided over the Chiefs of Staff committee. Thus there was created at one stroke a central decision-making body for the direction of the war under the immediate and boisterous surveillance of the Prime Minister, whose presence bridged the gap between 'frocks' and 'brass hats' that had so bedevilled the government in the First World War. The service ministers did not belong to either the war cabinet or the Chiefs of Staff committee and were simply charged with the day-to-day running of their departments.

All this was promising enough, but the greatest factor in the new situation was the remarkable personality of the Prime Minister. At heart Winston Churchill was a romantic, steeped in the political history of his ancestry, delighting in great affairs of state which his ebullient imagination had always translated into terms that were slightly larger than life. Antwerp, the Dardanelles, his belligerence at the time of the general strike, which had made him so hated by the Labour movement, his resistance to self-government for India, all were evidence of a temperament that combined a dynamic will with deep emotional commitment. Until 1939 success in politics had seemed likely to elude him, but now at last there had come a time of national drama in total accord with that great spirit whose words appeared to take fire from the peril that faced the country.

'I have nothing to offer but blood, toil, tears and sweat,' he told the Commons on 13 May.

> 'You ask what is our policy? I will say: it is to wage war by sea, land and air with all our might and with all the strength that God can give us: to wage war against a monstrous tyranny never surpassed in the dark lamentable catalogue of human crime. That is our policy. You ask: what is our aim? I can answer in one word: victory—victory at all costs, victory in spite of all terror; victory, however long and hard the road may be. For without victory there is no survival.'[5]

The nation had found its man, and the man had found his hour.

2. The battle of France: May–June 1940

On 10 May Germany opened the battle for the west with three separate assaults. In the Netherlands bombing by the Luftwaffe and airborne landings at Rotterdam and The Hague paved the way for a break-through across the Dutch frontier by a single Panzer division, reaching Rotterdam by 13 May and forcing the Dutch to a cease fire on 15 May. On the Belgian frontier another airborne attack captured the bridges over the Albert canal and by 11 May two Panzer divisions had swept back the initial Belgian defence. And at the same time further south von Rundstedt's army group was finding its way through the forests of the Ardennes in Luxembourg moving towards the Meuse north of Sedan.

A German violation of Belgian neutrality had always been anticipated by the Allies and now, in answer to an appeal from Belgium, the BEF under Gort and the French First Army left the defence line which they had spent the winter preparing and moved east to take up a position on the river Dyle. In the view of the French Commander-in-Chief, Gamelin, this was the main direction of the German thrust—a repeti-tion of the Schlieffen plan of 1914—and accordingly he put most of his strength into this area, leaving the Ardennes only lightly guarded; the Maginot line did not extend so far north, but the French general staff regarded such country as impassable for tanks. The senior German generals, von Brauchitsch, the commander-in-chief, and Halder, the chief of the general staff, would have agreed with this appreciation, but since January 1940 their views had been overruled by Hitler who had become so enamoured of an idea of General von Manstein's that he soon adopted it as his own. The real thrust was now to be concentrated on the Ardennes in the belief that this could be penetrated by tanks, and here von Rundstedt's army group of six Panzer divisions was to strike for a crossing of the Meuse well to the south of the principal Allied forces.

By 13 May General Guderian commanding three of these divisions had reached the Meuse; with the aid of twelve squadrons of dive-bombers the crossing was accomplished and by the evening of 15 May the three Panzer divisions were over the river and had crushed French resistance. Within a further twenty-four hours they had pushed on fifty miles as far as the river Oise. By now it was clear that the Allied advance eastwards into Belgium, so far largely unopposed, had simply taken them into a trap, as the Panzers swept through to the south of them and then wheeling north, in contradistinction to the Schlieffen plan, threatened to reach the Channel ports and to cut them off completely.

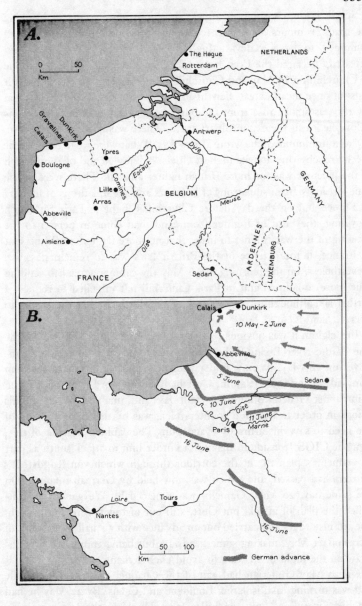

6   THE SECOND WORLD WAR
A. France and Belgium, May–June 1940
B. France, May–June 1940

Speed, noise, constant air attack, the confusion of refugees blocking the roads, rumours about fifth columnists and parachute landings, all combined to have a devastating effect on morale. 'We have been defeated,' declared the French premier Paul Reynaud on the telephone to Churchill on 15 May and Churchill, perplexed that an enemy assault must at once mean defeat, flew to Paris the next day. Here at the Quai d'Orsay, as smoke rose from the burning of documents in the gardens below, he learnt the extraordinary truth. There was no strategic reserve. 'I was dumbfounded,' he wrote afterwards. 'What were we to think of the great French army and its highest chiefs?'[6] The demand of the French at the meeting was for more British fighter aircraft. There were at the time already sixteen squadrons of bombers and six squadrons of fighters in France and on the day before Churchill's flight to Paris Sir Hugh Dowding, the head of Fighter Command, had come in person to the meeting of the war cabinet to insist that no more fighters could be sent to France, if the defence of the British Isles was to remain possible. Nevertheless, on the morning of 16 May the cabinet agreed to sending four more squadrons and in Paris Churchill felt impelled to request a further six, although owing to a lack of airfields in France these were to operate from Kent.

In Belgium it was obvious that the Allied forces must fall back to the line of the river Escaut, where they succeeded in establishing themselves on 19 May, by now under pressure from the northern German army advancing into Belgium. Gort had had no word from his French commander General Billotte for eight days and, unable to disengage his troops in order to launch a counterattack, was by this time thinking of the need to save his army by evacuation. The cabinet, hearing of this, sent the CIGS Ironside to Belgium to order him to attack south as part of Gamelin's plan to cut the corridor through which von Rundstedt's Panzers had passed, and which was now held by German infantry. On the same day, 20 May, Gamelin was replaced by Weygand who cancelled the plan of attack, but Gort, still out of touch with the French, obeyed his orders and carried out an advance with a small force south of Arras on 21 May, making some headway, but being compelled to withdraw on the night of 23 May to avoid encirclement.

On 20 May Guderian had gained the Channel coast near Abbeville and was turning east, isolating Boulogne and Calais. By 22 May he had reached Gravelines only ten miles from Dunkirk, the last remaining Allied port, but on the next day he received categorical orders to stop. The motives that prompted Hitler and von Rundstedt to take this decision have been debated ever since—nervousness over the state of the German armour, doubts about the security of the corridor after the Arras attack, or a desire to allow Goering's Luftwaffe to give the *coup de grâce*—but whatever they may have been, that decision saved the BEF.

Gort at this time was still being urged to make a fresh attack southwards in conjunction with a French thrust northwards against the far side of the corridor. This plan, which Weygand propounded on 21 May to Billotte at Ypres, was almost a replica of Gamelin's which he had just cancelled, and that delay coupled with the difficulties of communication made it hopelessly unrealistic. Billotte was killed almost immediately after the conference at Ypres, at which his successor Blanchard had not been present. In fact, Blanchard was not officially appointed until 24 May; by that time the projected French attack from the south had been called off and the Weygand plan was in ruins.

Gort was not informed of this, but at this point it was clear to him that the appallingly dangerous state of his east and west flanks made any further southern thrust on his part unthinkable. Ammunition was short and his troops were on half rations; there was the increasing likelihood that a collapse of the Belgians would leave a vast gap to the north-east and captured German documents revealed an impending two-corps attack in the area of Ypres. On the evening of 25 May he took his own decision to abandon the Weygand plan—already jettisoned, unknown to him—and pulled in the few forces that might have been available for it in order to plug a widening gap between the British and the Belgians along the line of the Ypres–Comines canal.

Justification arrived on the next day in the form of a telegram from the War Office ordering a retreat to the coast. It seemed that it might well be too late. 'I must not conceal from you,' reported Gort to London, 'that a great part of the BEF and its equipment will inevitably be lost.'[7] 'The House,' said Churchill to the Commons on 28 May, 'should prepare itself for hard and heavy tidings.'[8] In fact, throughout these tense savage days a remarkable deliverance was accomplished. On 26 May Guderian was told by Hitler to renew his advance on Dunkirk, but the British garrison at Calais, a vital enclave on the west flank, had orders to fight to the last and did not succumb until the evening of 27 May; the French fought a stubborn resistance around Lille and General Brooke successfully carried out the hazardous disengagement on the eastern flank. Early on 28 May the Belgians finally surrendered, but by the next day most of the BEF were within the perimeter of the Dunkirk beachhead.

The Navy had already made its preparations for taking the troops from the harbour and from the beaches under the incessant bombing of the German Luftwaffe. From the ports and coastal inlets of England there set out a motley array of some four hundred small craft, largely manned by volunteers—tugs, launches, yachts, fishing vessels, paddle-steamers and lifeboats from liners—which served to ferry the troops on the beaches out to the waiting destroyers. For seven days, while the sea remained utterly calm, the prodigious operation continued until by the end some 338,000 British troops had been saved. The French still had no orders to embark and on 31 May Churchill flew again to Paris to negotiate this. As a consequence 139,000 Allied soldiers, mostly French, were brought off by 2 June and on the last night of the evacuation, before the Germans finally closed in, a final 26,000 were got away.

For France the end was in sight. The Germans regrouped their forces which now amounted to ten Panzer divisions and 130 infantry divisions; against this Weygand could dispose of only forty-nine divisions to the south of the corridor, while leaving seventeen in the Maginot line. On 5 June the German assault began; on 9 June they achieved a breakthrough and by 11 June were on the Marne. The government moved from Paris to Tours and later to Bordeaux. On 10 June Mussolini finally threw in his lot with Hitler and declared war. The eventual Italian offensive was easily repulsed by the depleted French forces in the south-east, but by now the situation in metropolitan France seemed hopeless. Churchill had been constantly faced with pleas from Paul Reynaud that the major part of the RAF should be flung into the battle, but Sir Hugh Dowding was adamant that no more planes could be spared, if there was to be any hope of defending Great Britain; of those already operating in France, 250 Hurricanes had been lost in ten days fighting in the middle of May. Nevertheless, Churchill, deeply conscious of the French agony, did send across additional squadrons; a great many more were operating over France from British bases, and as a further token of good faith General Brooke, who had just returned from Dunkirk, was ordered back to France with two divisions.

None of this was enough for the French. The only question now was whether they would continue the fight from their territories in North Africa. Twice, on 11 and 13 June, Churchill flew to France to urge them to do so, but he found it difficult to stem the sense of despair and, despite the determination of Reynaud, the French government was talking openly of surrender. On 16 June Reynaud was outvoted in the French chamber and resigned. His successor, Marshal Pétain, asked for an armistice on the next day and on 22 June the new French government accepted the terms which placed the north and west of France under German occupation.

Thus in little more than a month Hitler's army had accomplished what the Kaiser had been unable to achieve in four years. Inevitably the last days saw some bitterness between the Allies. The French accused the British of running away at Dunkirk; the British harped on the low state of French morale among civilians and soldiers. The truth was that the Germans deserved their success in 1940. The Manstein plan was infinitely better than the Schlieffen plan; the German general staff had in the interwar years thought out a new technique of war which had already proved its worth in Poland, and in the actual handling of the campaign the German breakthrough in the Ardennes and the absence of any strategic reserve revealed an incompetence on the part of the French high command that not even the most patriotic Englishman would have conceived possible. Gort, a VC of the First World War, was not a particularly intellectual soldier, but no one could doubt his courage, and the decision which he took on his own initiative to desist from the thrust south of Arras, at a moment when his east and west flanks seemed likely to give way, probably saved the British Army. As Churchill pointed out to the Commons, wars are not won by evacuations, but without the evacuation from Dunkirk the war might have been lost in 1940.

29

The Long Retreat

1. Alone: June 1940–June 1941

Since the last week of May the British had known that soon they might have to stand alone against the inflated military might of a Germany in control of almost the entire Continent. Neither the French nor the Germans had seriously believed that Britain would remain at war long after the fall of France. In fact, the British, united by the immense simplification of issues that military disaster had brought, never contemplated any other course. The matter was not put to a vote. It was assumed without question. 'Of course, whatever happens at Dunkirk, we shall fight on,' Churchill remarked casually at a meeting of senior ministers on 28 May, and at once found himself surrounded by a surge of excited emotion. 'It fell to me in these coming days and months,' he wrote afterwards, 'to express their sentiments on suitable occasions. This I was able to do, because they were mine also.'[1]

The statement is over-modest, for the tensions of that summer inspired Churchill to a new height of oratory that voiced the less articulate defiance of the nation. 'We shall go on to the end,' he told the House on 4 June.

> We shall fight in France, we shall fight in the seas and oceans, we shall fight with growing confidence and growing strength in the air; we shall defend our Island, whatever the cost may be. We shall fight on the beaches, we shall fight on the landing grounds, we shall fight in the fields and in the streets, we shall fight in the hills; we shall never surrender; and even if, which I do not for a moment believe, this Island or a large part of it were subjugated and starving, then our Empire beyond the seas, armed and guarded by the British Fleet, would carry on the struggle, until in God's good time the New World with all its power and might steps forth to the rescue and the liberation of the Old.[2]

Behind the splendid phrases and indomitable will there lay one thought for the future: that eventually the United States would come to the aid of Great Britain. Shortly after the beginning of the war President Roosevelt had initiated an informal correspondence with Churchill who now made use of this channel of personal diplomacy to stress two facts with all his force: that his administration would fight on to the end, but that if the end came, the United States' position would have been considerably worsened. He was blunt. 'If members of the present administration were finished and others came in to parley amid the ruins, you must not be blind to the fact that the sole remaining bargaining counter with Germany would be the fleet.'[3]

Roosevelt needed little persuading, and early in June, despite the profound isolationism of public opinion in the United States, authorized the sale to Great Britain of a vast portion of the American army's reserve stock of rifles and machine-guns. This was followed at the beginning of September by the handing over of fifty old American destroyers in return for the lease of British bases in the West Indies and a promise that the British fleet would not be surrendered, if Hitler succeeded in overrunning the country. And by the end of the year Roosevelt had embarked upon his scheme of lend–lease whereby, when the British ran short of dollars, the USA would initially finance the acquisition of all war material that the British ordered. At this dark moment of the war the resounding eloquence of Churchill had convinced the American government that Great Britain was worth backing as a bulwark against Fascism.

If Roosevelt was concerned about the possible fate of the British fleet, Churchill had more reason to be worried over the position of the French. Admiral Darlan had earlier promised that their navy would never be surrendered to Germany, but at such a time Churchill felt that he could take no chances over the possibility of the Germans making such an increase in naval power. French warships in British ports, at Alexandria and in the West Indies were interned without great difficulty, but when in July French battleships at Oran and Dakar on the African coast refused either to sail for British-controlled ports or to scuttle themselves, ships of the British Navy were ordered to open fire and seriously damaged or sank most of them. It was a horrible episode that could well have had a dangerous effect on the attitudes of the new French government. To Churchill, however, it had seemed that the stakes were too high and his action had made it indisputably clear that his government would stop at nothing.

None of these moves of broader strategy could alter the fact that immediate survival depended on resistance to invasion. Already measures had been taken to place the country on a basis of total war. Shortly before the evacuation from Dunkirk an Emergency Powers Act, passed by Parliament in a single day, gave the government a revolutionary degree of control over property and every aspect of civilian life. 'I have to ask you,' said Ernest Bevin, the new Minister of Labour, at a conference of representatives of more than 150 trades unions, 'virtually to place yourselves at the disposal of the state.'4 He was determined, if possible, to avoid compulsion and, indeed, none was required at any level of the nation's war effort in that summer of 1940.

Perhaps the clearest indication of the new spirit at work was the response to an appeal in the middle of May for volunteers to guard bridges and crossroads and to deal with small bodies of German parachutists. Within a fortnight 300,000 had enrolled in the Local Defence Volunteers (LDV), known later as the Home Guard, parading in the evenings, drilling with broomsticks and scraping together a fantastic armament that ranged from shotguns to golf-clubs and sticks.

The will to resist was powerful and vital, but it had also to take practical matters into consideration. Towards the end of May the Chiefs of Staff had set out their assessment of Great Britain's chances of survival in the event of a French collapse. If the Air Force was intact, then the Navy and the Air Force together could hold off invasion; if Germany gained air superiority, then the Navy alone could hold off invasion for a time, but not indefinitely; and if the Germans were eventually able to make a substantial landing, the British troops available would be inadequate ultimately to prevent military defeat.

General Ironside, who had been replaced as CIGS by Sir John Dill, commanded Home forces, some fifteen divisions at half strength, composed mostly of the tattered army that had escaped from France; seriously lacking in tanks and guns, he struggled to devise a system of linear defence, until in June General Brooke took over from him and turned to a policy of mobile reserves. In the Thames estuary a force of four destroyer flotillas waited, supported by smaller groups along the east coast and in the Channel. On the airfields of southern England and the Midlands Fighter Command under Sir Hugh Dowding had made its dispositions; the chain of radar stations gave them an early warning system against the 900 bombers and 900 escorting fighters that Goering could soon unleash against them, but with 400 British fighters already lost in France the margin looked desperately thin.

'In the fierce light of the present emergency,' said Churchill, 'the fighter is the need,' and the first stage of the battle of Britain was fought and won in the aircraft factories. At the newly instituted Ministry of Aircraft Production the titanic energy of Lord Beaverbrook burst upon the existing organization, cannibalizing with spare parts and disrupting the plans for the building of bombers in order to fill that need. Public railings were uprooted for scrap metal; housewives, informed of the shortage of aluminium, voluntarily handed in their kitchen utensils, and on the factory floor men and women responded by working hours that made nonsense of any earlier trade-union regulations. In April the figure for the output of fighters had been 256; in May it was 325, in June 446, in July 496, in August 476 and in September 467. The result was better than Dowding had ever dared to dream. In June he had only 446 operationally serviceable aircraft with a reserve of 36; by 11 August he had 704 with a reserve of 289, most of them Spitfires and Hurricanes.

Meanwhile Hitler and his generals, having completed the conquest of France, were faced with their own problems. The continued resistance of Great Britain seemed to demand a German invasion of the island, but until July there had been little thought or preparation for such an operation. The French campaign had absorbed all energies. Now on 16 July Hitler issued orders for plans to be drawn up for an invasion, Operation Sea Lion, to take place by the middle of August. There followed a long interservice dispute, the German generals wishing to establish landings on a broad front from Ramsgate to Lyme Bay, the navy insisting that they could only manage a narrow corridor for the crossing, and even that must depend upon achieving German air superiority. These difficulties led to a postponement of the date of invasion until the middle of September, but the military preparations continued at great speed and Brauchitsch was confident that, once landed, his armies could gain their first main objective roughly along the line of the North Downs—an echo here of 'The Battle of Dorking' (see p. 51)—before thrusting north over the Thames to the west of London, which he intended to seal off. The thoroughness of German organization even included the arrangements for the military government of the country once under occupation and specified the internment of men between the ages of seventeen and forty-five, who were to be sent to the Continent for forced labour.

For the opposing forces on either side of the Channel the crux lay in the air. The battle began with a preliminary phase throughout July and the first week of August, when the Luftwaffe concentrated on convoys in the Channel and on coastal objectives. This was designed to wear down the British Fighter Command, a process of attrition in which the RAF lost considerably less than their opponents. Then came the next phase, a direct attack to destroy British Fighter Command, the vital preliminary to Operation Sea Lion. Thirteen German divisions were already deployed for invasion across the Channel and the defence of Great Britain now rested on the courage and skill of a few hundred young fighter pilots.

From 12 August waves of heavily escorted German bombers flew in day after day, intent on knocking out airfields, command posts and radar stations, as the Hurricanes and Spitfires came up to meet them. On 15 August the Germans launched nearly 1,800 planes; seventy-five were shot down at a cost of thirty-four British and the raiders had still failed to gain an ascendancy. 'Never in the field of human conflict,' declared Winston Churchill on 20 August in the House of Commons, 'was so much owed by so many to so few.'[5] By the end of August, as the murderous struggle went on, the British had lost 338 fighters with a further 104 badly damaged. The defence was unrelenting, but the losses in pilots were becoming greater than could be replaced. And meanwhile the concentration of German invasion barges was growing steadily in the ports of France and the Low Countries.

At this point, when Goering was closer to his objective than he imagined, the chance of war intervened. On 24 August some German bombs had been dropped by accident on London. Churchill at once ordered bombing raids to begin on Berlin. This should really have been irrelevant to the battle of Britain; in fact, it proved decisive. A furious Hitler ordered the German attack to switch from the airfields and radar stations to the bombing of London and on 7 September a great fire raid turned the East End and the docks into a raging inferno. The ordeal of London had begun, but for the RAF it was the turning-point in the battle, as the attack on their bases lifted. Hitler now postponed his decision on Sea Lion until 17 September, and two days before this a vast German air assault was launched on London; on that day every British reserve immediately available was flung into action and by the end, as they headed for home, the Germans had lost some sixty of their planes, although not 186 as the British jubilantly believed.

'Still no invasion,' wrote General Brooke on 16 September. 'Rumour has it that tonight is to be the night.'[6] It was not to be. The Channel was rough, the invasion barges in the French ports had been under constant bombing attack by the RAF, and the German High Command was convinced that the necessary air superiority had not been gained. Operation Sea Lion was postponed indefinitely, eventually to the following spring, by which time Hitler's thoughts had turned elsewhere.

As a postscript to this failure, Hitler now sought to break civilian morale. Throughout the autumn for fifty-seven nights in succession

London was bombed. The East End, the City, the House of Commons itself were all shattered, as well as hundreds of thousands of private houses. The underground tube stations became vast air-raid shelters, where the homeless spent the nights. The drainage systems were smashed and sewage had to be poured direct into the Thames. Delayed-action bombs added to the horror and had to be dismantled in a race against time by teams of volunteers. Civil Defence and the National Fire Service battled nightly with the devastation, and as incendiary bombs were increasingly used, a fire-watcher service was organized, whose members raced to the tops of buildings when the sirens sounded. Churchill, deeply conscious of the personal losses suffered by so many, introduced a system whereby all war damage would be made good by the state, and King George, who remained in residence at Buckingham Palace, instituted the George Cross for civilian gallantry. Then in November there came some relief for London, as the attack shifted to the provinces. Coventry was virtually destroyed; Birmingham, Bristol, Liverpool, Plymouth and Sheffield were among the other cities which endured the visitations of the Luftwaffe, but on 29 December the capital again suffered, when the City of London was laid waste in an appalling fire raid. With the New Year, however, the pressure began to diminish, by which time the Blitz, as Londoners had slightly inaccurately termed it, had caused the death of some 30,000 civilians.

The plan to invade Great Britain was not merely a failure; it was a mistake. The true weakness of the British lay elsewhere. If, as some of his generals advised, Hitler had used the defeat of France to occupy Algeria and from there in conjunction with Italy had launched his Panzers along the north coast of Africa, it is only too likely that he could have captured Egypt and the Suez Canal, and British control of the Middle East might have been lost.

But Hitler, the central European, did not think in these global terms. Instead, the desert of North Africa was left to the more dubious power of the Italian army. This on paper might seem serious enough. Mussolini had over 200,000 troops in Libya and another 200,000 in Italian East Africa. In Egypt General Wavell, whose two lines of communication across the Mediterranean and up the Red Sea were thus both threatened, had only 36,000 men with a further 27,000 in Palestine, apart from small detachments in the Sudan, Kenya, Aden and Cyprus; and these forces became still more dispersed when on 28 October Mussolini invaded Greece and Wavell was ordered to occupy Crete and to send two fighter squadrons to Greece.

In Libya, however, the Italian Marshall Graziani advanced very slowly. In September 1940 he moved over the Egyptian frontier as far as Sidi Barrani (map opposite), but in December General O'Connor, commanding a Western Desert force of two divisions, carried out a series of assaults sweeping out into the desert on the southern flank and attacking from the rear, until after an advance of 250 miles into Cyrenaica Benghazi fell on 7 February 1941 and the Italians surrendered. It was a remarkable campaign in which two divisions had destroyed an army of four corps with 130,000 prisoners taken, as well as 400 tanks and 1,200 guns. The news of all this, in addition to the destruction of three Italian battleships at Taranto by the Fleet Air Arm in the previous November, brought a great uplift for morale at home; almost immediately afterwards in another campaign launched from Kenya and the Sudan the Italians were routed in East Africa and, on 5 May 1941, Haile Selassie was able to enter his capital Addis Ababa once again.

Unfortunately the success in the desert could not be followed up; nor was it to last. This was because Hitler was now about to strike east. Romania and Bulgaria had been forced to join him, and at first it seemed that Yugoslavia would do so as well. Then on 27 March 1941 a *coup d'état* at Belgrade ensured a policy of resistance, and on 6 April the Germans launched an offensive against Yugoslavia and Greece. Churchill was determined that, if possible, any opponent of Hitler should have British aid, and although he had had some doubts over the final decision, it had been agreed by the cabinet in March that an Allied force of 57,000 troops, 24,000 of them British, should be dispatched to Greece in the event of a German attack.

The outcome was in every way disastrous. The Germans broke through the ferocious resistance of the Yugoslavs and towards the end of April cut off the Greek army, which capitulated. The British, compelled to withdraw by sea, fell back on Crete, where a massive German airborne operation launched on 20 May resulted in the capture of the island, and the British had to make one further evacuation after a loss of 13,000 men. All this meant more than the loss of Greece and Crete; the situation in the desert, too, had been reversed, since Wavell's forces there had had to be depleted in order to supply the troops for the Greek expedition. In March the German general Rommel had arrived in Tripoli and with a combination of tactical daring and bluff outmanoeuvred the British, who by 11 April found themselves back again on the Egyptian frontier.

It had been a season of catastrophe lightened only by one more naval victory over the Italians at Matapan in March and the crushing of two

347

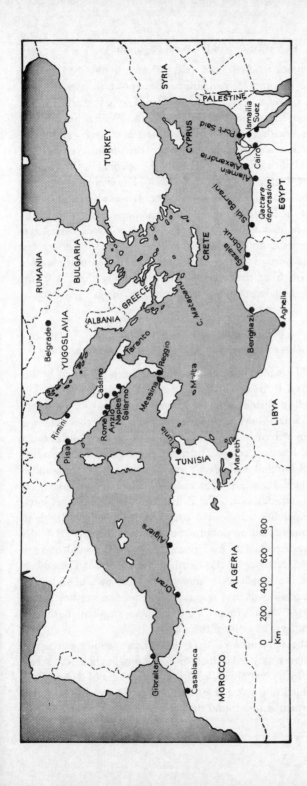

7 THE SECOND WORLD WAR
North Africa and Italy

pro-German regimes in Syria and Iraq. Churchill now had to face serious criticisms at home. He had always been known to favour Balkan projects and the decision to enter Greece seemed to have a whiff of the Dardanelles about it. In fact, Sir John Dill and Wavell himself had believed that the British landings in Greece were a necessary and viable operation. Later it was argued that although British intervention had been unsuccessful, it did retard significantly the opening of the German campaign against Russia. It seems more likely, however, that this was due largely to the sudden Yugoslav resistance. It was also claimed that the toughness of the fighting in Crete finally deflected Hitler from any passing thought he may have had of continuing the attack from Crete into Egypt; yet it is doubtful whether this was ever his intention. His mind was already firmly set in another direction. He was now about to deliver the British from their isolation by presenting them with the alliance which had eluded them in the summer of 1939.

2. The early days of the Grand Alliance: June 1941–August 1942

Since the fall of France Winston Churchill had been sustained by the hope that one day, if Great Britain could fight on long enough, she would find herself in alliance with the United States and Russia in her struggle against Hitler. Now, on 22 June 1941, one half of that hope was fulfilled when three German army groups thrust over the Polish border in an invasion of Russia. Perhaps Hitler did not believe that a government headed by Churchill could ever make an alliance with Communist Russia; perhaps he did not care. Whatever his reasoning may have been, it revealed a fatal misjudgment. The British, who had had secret intelligence of the impending attack, had attempted to warn the Russians, and Churchill himself had no doubt about his own attitude. 'If Hitler invaded Hell,' he remarked to his private secretary, 'I would make at least a favourable reference to the Devil in the House of Commons.' That same night in a broadcast he announced: 'Any man or state who fights against Nazidom will have our aid.'[7] The precise wording of any Anglo-Russian pact was still to take a lot of delicate negotiation, but the military alignment was clear from the start.

Throughout the remainder of 1941 the Russian armies put up an unrelenting resistance as 120 German divisions fought their way across the vast spaces which must always confront any invader of Russia. This time *blitzkrieg* failed to break a hole in the retreating line of the defenders and the German armies found themselves harassed in their rear by partisan forces. By the end of the first week of December their initial impetus was spent. They were thirty-five miles west of Moscow, Leningrad lay under siege, and to the south von Rundstedt had reached as far as Rostov, but the strategic objects of the campaign—Moscow and the Caucasus—were still unattained, when the onset of winter brought the advance to a halt.

From the day when the Germans launched their attack and Churchill announced the alignment of Great Britain with Russia, Stalin never ceased to demand an immediate invasion across the Channel to open a second front, and British Communists, who had now stopped their acts of sabotage in factories, took up the same cry. Churchill could only state emphatically that in military terms such an operation at that moment was utterly impossible, although the threat of it was keeping fifty German divisions in western Europe. 'They cut themselves off from an effective second front when they let the French Army be destroyed,' he commented to Sir Stafford Cripps, the extreme left-wing British Ambassador at Moscow. He knew, however, that this was no time for recrimination; the Russians spoke from desperate need and the British government, determined to give their new ally what aid they could, embarked on a long ferrying of supplies, which they could ill afford, around the north of Scandinavia to Murmansk and Archangel, a total of 481 tanks and 705 planes by the end of 1941, as well as quantities of other vehicles, ammunition and petrol.

Meanwhile, Churchill still nursed his other hope. The United States remained at peace with Germany, but the bombing of London had made a great emotional impact and throughout 1941 the British government continued to foster the growing sympathy and support of the Americans. By the summer of that year the United States had taken over the policing of a part of the Atlantic and had agreed to establish their own bases in Iceland for this purpose. Indeed, for the British the Atlantic was as significant as the Russian front. All their supplies from America must come that way and, with the Mediterranean virtually closed, all reinforcements for the North African campaigns had to take the Atlantic route round the Cape of Good Hope. German U-boats played constant havoc with the merchant convoys and in May the appearance of the battleship *Bismarck* allowed Churchill no rest until he knew she had been sunk. In August he crossed by sea to Newfoundland for personal conversations with President Roosevelt. Further lend–lease was to materialize, but the most striking feature of the meeting was a statement of general principles, known as the Atlantic Charter, demanding liberation for all states that had been deprived of self-government.

Considering that the United States was still not at war with Germany, it was remarkable how far the American President and the British Prime Minister between them had been able to coax her.

Then, at the beginning of December 1941, no further coaxing was necessary. On the other side of the world Japan suddenly solved Churchill's problem for him. Since 1937 the Japanese had been continuing their advance on the Chinese mainland (see p. 312) and by 1940 Chiang-kai-shek had been pushed back into the interior, where he was still able to obtain supplies from the USA and Great Britain along the Burma road. Japan, short of essential war materials and hoping to persuade the Americans to bring Chiang-kai-shek to terms, forced an agreement on France in July 1941, whereby Japan might establish bases in Indo-China. The immediate consequence of this was a total embargo by America on Japanese trade, somewhat reluctantly followed by the British and the Dutch in South-East Asia. In Tokyo the war party now gained the upper hand, insisting on a bid for power in the Pacific, which with the capture of British and Dutch colonies in Malaya and the East Indies would give them the oil, nickel, tin and rubber that they so badly needed.

Early on the morning of 7 December 1941, before any declaration of hostilities, Japanese planes from aircraft-carriers in the Pacific swept over the American fleet stationed at Pearl Harbor in Hawaii, and in an hour and a half put out of action six battleships, six cruisers and destroyers and some two hundred aircraft. It was a reincarnation of the knock-out blow and for the moment it gave Japan a free hand in the Pacific.

For Hitler, coping with the failure of his armies to reach Moscow, the attack came as a complete surprise and this perhaps led him to make his supreme mistake in the war. There was nothing in the Anti-Comintern pact that bound him to support Japan against America. Indeed, if he had remained neutral, the United States' war effort might have become concentrated on the Japanese theatre of operations to the detriment of the surreptitious aid that they had been giving to Great Britain. But Hitler, irritated by a succession of minor incidents during the past two years and convinced that American attitudes were part of a vast Jewish conspiracy, resolved not to hold back. On 11 December Germany and Italy declared war on the United States.

For Winston Churchill it meant that the lonely struggle since 1940 was now at an end: '. . . at this very moment,' he wrote afterwards, 'I knew the United States was in the war up to the neck and in to the death. So we had won after all!'[8] He lost no time in acting on the new situation. Within a week of the Japanese attack he had set sail for America accompanied by a team of service advisers. In the course of an impressive diplomatic visit his resolute, exuberant personality won the American public and delighted the two houses of Congress whom he was invited to address. At the same time conferences at Washington reached two decisions that were to be fundamental to the shaping of the war. The total military and economic resources of the two countries were to be placed under a common command, the Combined Chiefs of Staff, which proved to be the most remarkable example of joint planning in the history of all alliances. And it was also agreed that the Allies would first give their full attention to the defeat of Germany before turning to deal with Japan.

At the same time as Great Britain had gained a new ally, Churchill had acquired a new CIGS, General Brooke, who succeeded Dill that December. The relationship between Churchill and Brooke, who was to remain at this post until 1946, is one of the most fascinating aspects of the higher direction of the war. Immaculate, precise and staccato in utterance, Brooke was a man of first-class mind whose clear grasp of strategic planning brought him constantly into disagreement with the wide ranging and politically conscious brilliance of the Prime Minister. Night after night until the early hours of the morning Brooke would have to battle against some new brain child presented with all of Churchill's overwhelming persuasiveness; yet, when he had plumbed every line of argument, the Prime Minister would eventually yield, sometimes with bad temper, more often with an impish quip. For Brooke the exasperation was momentary; his admiration and respect for Churchill remained profound. 'He is the most difficult man I have ever served,' he wrote in his diary, 'but thank God for having given me the opportunity of trying to serve such a man in a crisis such as the one this country is going through.'[9]

The policy, for which Brooke argued and in the main achieved, was based on an assessment of strategic priorities and a determination to concentrate existing forces on the attainment of these objects. He saw the North African coast as the key to the situation. Once this had been cleared of enemy, then the Mediterranean would be relatively open, shipping could be released from the long sea route round the Cape, and with Italy as a target for invasion, Mussolini might be knocked out of the war and more German troops drawn south to check the new threat. He believed that these were the essential preliminaries, if an eventual cross-Channel invasion of France was to have any hope of success, but it was to cost him many months of weary argument to resist the demand for an immediate invasion of France which he knew would be premature and disastrous.

All this, however, lay far in the future. For the moment the newly formed Grand Alliance was powerless to prevent a succession of setbacks that brought the Allies to their lowest point in the war. On 10 December 1941 the battleship *Prince of Wales* and the battle-cruiser *Repulse*, which Churchill had rushed out unescorted for the protection of Singapore, were both sunk by Japanese aircraft. 'It means,' wrote Brooke, 'that from Africa eastwards to America through the Indian ocean we have lost command of the sea.'[10] On 25 December Hong Kong, held by only six battalions, fell to a Japanese attack. In January 1942 Japanese forces began a rapid infiltration of Malaya and on 15 February Singapore was compelled to surrender. Early in March Rangoon in Burma had to be evacuated and with the retreat of the British forces northwards across the Chindwin river the whole of the mainland of South-East Asia had come under Japanese control (map, p. 379).

In the Pacific the Japanese made use of their naval power to leapfrog across the islands—Borneo and the Celebes—and early in February they had landed in New Guinea. Resistance in the Philippine Islands under the American general MacArthur lasted longer, but in May the defence of the island fortress of Corregidor was finally overcome. At this point, the Japanese advance was checked by two naval encounters with the American fleet, in the Coral Sea in May and off Midway island in June.

In Russia a new German offensive opened in June 1942 consisting of two thrusts in the south, one into the Caucasus, the other towards Stalingrad on the Volga. By the end of August they had reached the Volga to the north and south of Stalingrad, where the Russians continued to fight a fanatical resistance, and early in September in the Caucasus they had come to within a hundred miles of the shore of the Caspian.

At the same time, the violent oscillations of the desert war had finally brought Rommel to a position only sixty miles from Alexandria. In November 1941 British forces, now known as the Eighth Army under the command of General Auchinleck, had become locked in a confused and fluctuating battle designed to smash Rommel's divisions on the Egyptian border. At one moment it looked as if the Germans might achieve a breakthrough, a situation only saved by the personal intervention of Auchinleck; then Rommel, conscious of his dwindling number of tanks and shortage of petrol, fell back as far as Agheila and by the New Year the British had again occupied Benghazi.

Supply was one key to the desert campaign, a problem that increased the further each army in turn advanced from its base. The maintenance of those bases themselves involved their own difficulties for each side— for the British the sheer length of the Cape route, for the Germans the constant harassing of their Mediterranean convoys under attack from Malta. In October 1941 Rommel lost 63 per cent of the supplies due to reach him in Africa and it was in belated recognition of this that the Germans and Italians now launched a furious air offensive on Malta, although an invasion would have served them better.

The other key was Rommel's superior handling of his tanks. This again became apparent in a new offensive that he launched on 21 January 1942. As an extremely mobile battle developed, Winston Churchill once more had to face a highly critical House of Commons. 'I cannot tell you what the position at the present moment is on the western front in Cyrenaica,' he announced to them. 'We have a very daring and skilful opponent against us, and may I say across the havoc of war, a great general.'[11] The romantic in him could not resist paying this tribute to Rommel, which the peculiar psychology of the British soldier would have echoed; and it did not seem unwarranted, when by the beginning of February the British had fallen back east of Benghazi to the Gazala line.

Both sides now struggled to build up their forces in preparation for a new assault, but it was Rommel who struck first on 26 May. For the next three weeks there was fought out a furious battle of manoeuvre in which the Germans and Italians numbered rather more in troops, while the British had significantly more tanks. At one stage a part of Rommel's forces were almost cut off behind the British line, but by 14 June the concentrated strength of his armour had broken the British resistance.

Once more the British had to retreat, but this time they did not stop at the Egyptian frontier. Auchinleck decided to move right back to Alamein, where the great quagmire of the Qattara depression to the south would be an effective guard against any wide flanking movement by the enemy. The hope was to leave Tobruk as a beleaguered fortress in the German rear, but Rommel's pursuit was so fast that the defence could not be organized in time and its surrender followed on 21 June. The main Alamein position, however, had been well chosen and in the first weeks of July Rommel's attempts to break it not merely failed, but almost led to the defeat of his forces. 'Although the British losses in this Alamein fighting had been higher than ours,' wrote Rommel, 'the price to Auchinleck had not been excessive, for the one thing that had mattered to him was to halt our advance and that unfortunately he had done.' The Eighth Army now stood at bay only two hundred miles from the Suez Canal.

The news of enemy advance on every front was to have several consequences. It meant that Churchill had to face a vote of censure early in July in the House of Commons, criticizing his administration of the war effort, an open debate which must have been a delight for German propaganda, although in the division the critics could muster no more than twenty-five votes. 'Good for you,' telegraphed Roosevelt to Churchill. A more fortunate consequence was that the strained circumstances of the Allied situation lent strength to the British objections to a cross-Channel invasion of France that year. In June, when Churchill and Brooke had flown to the United States, there had been strong pressure from the American chief of staff, General Marshall, for such an expedition, but in July the Americans accepted the British objections and agreed instead to Operation 'Torch', an American landing in French North Africa, which would be far more in accord with Brooke's fundamental strategy.

With this settled, Churchill was now eager for another epic journey. He wished to see for himself what was wrong at Cairo; he wanted also to have a meeting with Stalin in order to be able to tell him personally why there could be no second front in 1942. Early in August he and Brooke made a hazardous flight to Cairo via Gibraltar and Malta. Here they were both resolved to make a change. Auchinleck was a fine general, but morale had suffered, and after some debate it was agreed that General Alexander should become Commander-in-Chief, while General Montgomery took over command of the Eighth Army.

From Cairo they flew via Teheran to Moscow, and Churchill had his first encounter with Stalin at the Kremlin. On hearing that there was to be no second front that year, Stalin became abusive, accusing the British of not wanting to fight. At this Churchill lost his temper and embarked on an impassioned oration. Stalin, not waiting for its interpretation into Russian, said with a broad grin: 'I do not understand what you are saying, but by God I like your sentiment.'[12] After that the visit went better. Stalin grudgingly agreed that the North African landing would make sense, although he still hankered for a second front in France, and Churchill was able to satisfy himself that the Russian defence line was still unbroken. For Brooke the greatest ordeal was a banquet of nineteen courses at the Kremlin, laced with incessant toasts in vodka, an occasion that Churchill appeared to take in his stride.

Within a few days they had all flown back to Cairo. Here at his desert headquarters General Montgomery explained to the Prime Minister the manner in which he would defeat Rommel, all uttered with a grasp and a brisk assurance with which the British public was soon to become very familiar. 'I went to bed that night,' wrote Brooke, 'with a wonderful feeling of contentment.'[13] There was a new atmosphere in the desert army; the American landings in North Africa lay only a few weeks ahead; a reasonably cordial relationship had been established with the Russians. At that moment when the situation looked at its worst, it seemed at last as if the tide was about to turn for the Grand Alliance.

30

Great Britain under Siege

Naturally the vast majority of those who served in the war knew nothing of the excitement and tensions of strategic planning. As ever, the life of the serviceman was enclosed in a pattern of long periods of discomfort and boredom, far from home, punctuated by moments of extreme fear and confusion in battle. Yet although the emotions of the soldier—the desperate longing for survival—were the same, whether he fought on the Somme or in the African desert, his response to them this time was different. The shocked anger of the war poets of the First World War had already taught him what to expect. There was as well a more humane and intelligent attitude towards the rank and file. Most higher commanders had previously served as junior officers on the western front and as a result of that experience were determined to break down the great divorce between the staff at their headquarters and the soldier in his trench. They were concerned, too, to be as sparing of the lives of their troops as possible, and for them the great nightmare was the thought of the lines settling down into a war of attrition. This they were able to avoid, partly because Churchill and Brooke both shared their view, partly because the major killing ground was to be the Russian front; Great Britain's losses in all were to be roughly half what she had suffered in the First World War. As a consequence, perhaps, the reactions of the servicemen lacked the furious sense of revolt which characterized the writings of those who fought in the First World War; no clearly stamped school of war poets emerged in the Second, yet many wrote—wry, reflective, wistful, rather than angry.

'Long months of trial and tribulation lie ahead of us,' said Winston Churchill in the House of Commons in October 1940. '. . . Death and sorrow will be the companions of our journey; hardship our garment; constancy and valour our only shield.'[1] For the civilian hardship proved to be a very shabby garment. He lived those years in a besieged fortress. This meant physical danger from bombing—if not death, then possibly the loss of his home. Otherwise, the picture was one of tedium and increasing shortages. Before long almost every item of food was rationed; many simply disappeared. His clothes were rationed and were of a standardized utility design. He had little or no petrol for his car. When his ration of soap allowed him to bath, he was exhorted not to use more than five inches of water. It seemed that for everything he had to stand in a queue. He had few holidays and there was nowhere to go if he took one. At the end of his day's work he found his way home through unlit streets to rooms made stuffy by heavy blackout curtains, and his evenings might well be spent in the sandbagged quarters of the Home Guard, the ARP or the Observer Corps.

However, although life was drab, it was not cheerless. The bombing and the sense of emergency helped to create a camaraderie which optimists believed might do much to bring a permanent end to old class barriers. There was a rivalry over bomb stories; the blackout encouraged a revival of interest in long Victorian novels, and the radio became a vital weapon in maintaining morale, creating new features of entertainment whose names are always to be associated with wartime: the Brains Trust, Tommy Handley's Itma and the postscript talks of J. B. Priestley. There was, too, a remarkable flowering of popular interest in music and drama, and a new organization, the Council for the Encouragement of Music and the Arts (CEMA, the forerunner of the postwar Arts Council), sponsored the production of plays and concerts throughout the provinces. Despite the austerity diet there were no serious epidemics during the war. The government constantly took scientific advice on the calory content of the basic rations; free milk, orange juice and cod-liver oil were provided for children, as well as midday meals at school, and with food subsidies keeping the price of food low many of the poor found themselves better nourished than they had been in the 1930s.

The need to organize a total national effort under siege conditions created a situation that could be termed 'war Socialism'. Early in 1941 a Production Executive, consisting of the Ministers of Supply, Aircraft Production and Labour and the First Lord of the Admiralty, coordinated the broad pattern of the programme of supply, a task eventually assumed by a single Minister of Production. Almost all other aspects of home government came under the control of Sir John Anderson's Lord President's Committee. Agricultural policy, aided by the Women's Land Army, extended land under cultivation from 12 million to 18 million acres, and corn even grew on the grass verges between pavement and roadside. All railways were under the control of the Minister of War Transport; and after a coal crisis in 1942 the production and distribution of all fuel under the Minister of Fuel and Power.

The most revolutionary innovation lay in local government. It had always been a characteristic of British institutions that the link between the central government and the multiplicity of borough and county councils should remain fairly tenuous, but from the beginning of the war the government had established an independent system of twelve regional commissioners, initially to organize civil defence, later to exercise executive powers in the event of German invasion, and finally settling down to supervise and coordinate all aspects of administration.

If all this was Socialism, it was a very British form of it. It had no specific doctrine. It relied on cooperation, an ability to improvise and a readiness to leave the loose ends untidy. It did not concern itself with public ownership; it merely established public control, and even here there were some surprising anomalies in the way that control was exercised.

One instance of this was to be seen in the relationship between the Ministry of Information and the BBC. It might be imagined that in wartime, at least, the BBC would have to relinquish its cherished independence, yet although there were frequent clashes at the beginning, the BBC was able to retain a remarkable freedom in organizing its programmes, imposing its own censorship and mounting an extensive campaign of propaganda to enemy and neutral countries.

Another instance was the tact and caution with which Ernest Bevin handled the labour force of the country. His task was enormous. He was responsible for the drafting of conscripts into the forces; he had to channel millions of others into the essential factories and to ensure that once they were there, they could not leave. To achieve this he was armed with considerable powers, but for the first part of the war, conscious of the sensitivity of the trade unions, he took great pains to rely on persuasion and to ensure that necessary transfers did not entail personal financial loss. Thus, when the need for greater compulsion became apparent, the way was open for more drastic action entirely in accord with public opinion. In December 1941 compulsory national service was introduced for women between the ages of twenty and thirty; orders for the direction of labour multiplied and by the summer of 1943 the numbers of men and women in the armed services, civil defence and the munitions factories amounted to 46 per cent of the working population.

One factor fundamental to the life of the whole community was the possibility of inflation; this would be bound to lead to wage demands, complicate the problems of the Minister of Labour and encourage the profiteering that had flourished in the First World War. The danger lay in the gap between the diminished quantity of goods available and the increased effective demand due to the fuller employment of wartime. Thus one solution seemed to depend on making this demand less effective by curtailing spending power. To J. M. Keynes, whose services were eventually rewarded with a peerage in 1942, it seemed that higher taxation alone would not be sufficient to achieve this and he proposed a scheme whereby part of a man's income would be temporarily held back by the government as a form of compulsory saving. In fact, the government tried most ways. The 1941 budget put income tax up to 10 shillings (50p); Keynes's system, known later as postwar credits, was also introduced. Voluntary savings campaigns flourished, helped by the rationing or disappearance of goods, which meant that there was very little on which money could be spent. Price control, less to Keynes's liking, was established over a growing range of commodities, and government expenditure on subsidies rose from £72 million in 1940 to £215 million in 1944. In the main, the efforts to stabilize the cost of living were relatively successful. From an index figure of 100 in September 1939 it had only risen to 132 by June 1945. Most wage rates had risen considerably higher, and on average the working man was financially better off at the end of the war than at the beginning, although there was little by which he could measure this in practical terms.

On the international scene the situation was less cheerful. In order to beat Hitler, the British were forced to destroy the whole basis of their economic life. By the beginning of 1941 all their gold and dollar reserves had gone, although these were eventually to recover a little. By 1945 they had sold £1,000 million of their overseas investments, and the circumstances of war, coupled with the stipulations of the Lend–Lease Act and the need to avoid open competition with their American ally, had reduced their exports in 1945 to a point some 70 per cent lower than the figure for 1938. 'Victory at all costs', Winston Churchill had declared in May 1940; victory was to come, but the cost seemed likely to be economic ruin.

None of this was reckoned to matter in the struggle for national survival, but the strain of war did demand a belief in something more positive as an ultimate goal; it stimulated a determination that for the men and women who were fighting and working for the future, there must be something better than the conditions of prewar Britain. The most exciting blue-print for reconstruction emanated from a committee under the chairmanship of Sir William Beveridge. The main proposals of the Beveridge Report, published in December 1942, were concerned with a comprehensive system of insurance against old age, ill health and unemployment, covering all classes of society, who were to pay a uniform premium. Working on an actuarial basis, the scheme was a vast extension of Lloyd George's Act of 1911 (see p. 63), with many undertones of self-help and Victorian liberalism, but it was, too, very reminiscent of some aspects of Sidney Webb's *Labour and the New Social Order*, published in 1918 (see p. 148). There was a visionary note in its broader references to adequate housing, children's allowances and a free health service, and it was not surprising that the report should make an enormous impact. Government reaction was lukewarm; no legislation followed and a division in the House of Commons gave a glimpse of the attitudes that were to come to the surface after the war, when 121 MPs—mostly Labour, together with a few young Conservatives and Liberals—expressed their disapproval of the postponement of any immediate implementing of the Report.

Still, if the Beveridge Report remained only an aspiration, at least one major reform did become the subject of legislation. This was the Education Act of 1944, pushed through by R. A. Butler who had become President of the Board of Education in 1941. Throughout the interwar years state schooling had continued to lag behind in a condition deplorable by any continental standard. The aim of establishing a separate secondary system expressed in the Hadow Report of 1926 (see p. 235) had been largely unrealized and many children still completed their education in all-age elementary schools. Even the plan to raise the school-leaving age from fourteen to fifteen, projected in the Education Act of 1936 and due to take effect on 1 September 1939, had been nullified by the outbreak of the war.

The jealousy of the religious sects was still the greatest obstacle to an extension of the state secondary system. The Church of England schools feared that they might have to surrender their Anglican religious teaching; the nonconformists still resented the Act of 1902 (see p. 40) which had given Anglican schools financial support from the rates; indeed, it was his memory of the political harm done to the Conservatives by their passing of that Act that caused Churchill to be extremely nervous about tackling the question during the war. Butler, however, was determined to bring about reform. There were three factors that gave him some hope of resolving the problem. In 1924 Anglicans and nonconformists had managed to devise an agreed syllabus of religious instruction; secondly, the financial position of many of the Anglican schools was so bad that they had simply been unable to respond to earlier proposals for separate secondary institutions and, therefore, had less of a case for retaining their independence; and thirdly, William Temple, who had become Archbishop of Canterbury in 1942, was a man of markedly liberal views whose concern for education eventually overcame his misgivings about Butler's plans. 'I am putting this very crudely,' he said, 'but I believe that Our Lord is much more interested in raising the school-leaving age to sixteen than in acquiring an agreed religious syllabus.' [2]

The essence of Butler's solution to the religious problem was to offer the voluntary schools two possible courses. If they chose to be 'controlled', all their expenses and the appointment of almost all their teachers would be in the hands of the local education authority; religious instruction would be in accordance with the agreed syllabus and the majority of the governors would be appointed by public bodies. If, on the other hand, they chose merely to be 'aided', the local education authority would only pay the running costs including teachers' salaries; independent governing bodies would control the appointment of teachers and the form of religious instruction, and would be responsible for capital expenditure, for which the exchequer would supply a grant of 50 per cent. The nonconformists would clearly opt for the 'controlled' status; in Temple's view, many of the hard-pressed Anglican schools would do the same. The Roman Catholics, who maintained that the 50 per cent grant was not enough, seemed at first unlikely to accept the 'aided' status, but after two and a half years of patient negotiation with all these bodies, Butler was at last able to establish a workable basis for free secondary education.

The Act was passed in 1944. It raised the school-leaving age to fifteen with a transition from the primary school to the secondary at the age of eleven. It spoke also of voluntary nursery schools and provided for free milk and midday meals. True to the character of English educational legislation, it left the precise nature of the secondary system in the hands of the local authorities (see p. 393), but the general current of opinion at the time suggested that on leaving the primary school a child would pass on to one of three types of secondary school—grammar, technical or modern—according to whichever would suit his abilities best.

Thus, just as the military commanders of the Second World War had been determined to avoid the worst follies of the western front, so the doctrines of Beveridge and Butler were a token of a similar determination that the way ahead should not lead to a repetition of the interwar years. These plans had emerged at a time when civilian life had never been so drab and threadbare and when the national economy seemed utterly shattered. Edwardian radicals would have applauded such aspirations; they would hardly have recognized the country which was about to give them practical expression.

31

The Victory of the Grand Alliance

1. The advance of the Grand Alliance: August 1942–June 1944

On 23 August 1942 the Prime Minister and his companions flew back from Cairo to London. Events were soon to justify that new sense of contentment which General Brooke had felt during his last days in the Egyptian desert. In the autumn of that year three separate military operations, each launched within a few weeks of each other, brought not merely local victories for the Allies, but also opened a new stage of the war which was to mean constant withdrawal and ultimate defeat for Germany. In the desert the battle of Alamein drove Rommel's Afrika Korps finally westwards; in French North Africa American landings were safely accomplished with little resistance, and on the Russian front a vast pincer movement cut off the German army besieging Stalingrad. It was, as Churchill said, the end of the beginning.

At Alamein, despite pressure from Churchill, General Montgomery was determined to wait until he had completed his preparations. At the beginning of September an attack by Rommel at Alam Halfa was driven off, but Montgomery's armour had clear orders not to leave their positions for any pursuit, thereby depriving Rommel of the loose battle of manoeuvre at which he excelled. Three hundred American Sherman tanks were now arriving at Suez, giving the British a total of more than 1,300 tanks, while artillery and the desert air force were also being greatly increased; at the same time Rommel's supplies across the Mediterranean were under heavy air and submarine attack, one half of them being lost in October. Montgomery thus enjoyed an immense preponderance. On the other hand, since the Qattara depression allowed no flanking movement, he was faced with the task of making a frontal attack on a defensive position completely sealed off from north to south by a deep belt of minefields, and in the event he was to need every ounce of that preponderance in a battle that lasted thirteen days.

Montgomery's plan was for one corps to smash a hole in the defences in the northern part of the line and for a second corps to pass through this and to destroy the German armour. The attack opened on 23 October with an enormous artillery barrage in the style of the First World War. Rommel, away on sick leave in Austria, hurried back on orders from Hitler, but after three days of fierce fighting it seemed that the British had failed to penetrate sufficiently. Consequently, on 28 October Montgomery switched his point of attack, aiming to break out further north towards the coast, but when this too was held up by German artillery, a sense of anxiety began to grow in high places. Alexander came to see Montgomery at his headquarters and in London Churchill stormed at Brooke. ' "What," he asked, "was my Monty doing now",' Brooke recorded in his diary, ' "allowing the battle to peter out?" (Monty was always *my* Monty when he was out of favour)."[1] Brooke defended Montgomery fiercely, but he too was assailed by doubts. They need not have worried. 'I haven't much hope left', wrote Rommel to his wife on the same day, and on 2 November Montgomery, having regrouped his forces, swung back to his original line of attack. That night Rommel began to prepare his withdrawal and on 4 November three British armoured divisions had broken through and were behind the German line.

Churchill wept, as he read Alexander's telegram announcing the victory. At a cost of 13,500 British and Commonwealth casualties the Eighth Army had inflicted a loss of more than 10,000 German and Italian dead and wounded; 450 tanks and 1,000 guns were left on the battlefield and some 30,000 prisoners were captured. Only Montgomery's caution in following up and the onset of heavy rain enabled Rommel to escape with some part of his shattered Afrika Korps, but so depleted that he could not attempt another serious stand until he had fallen back 1,500 miles to the eastern front of Tunisia.

At home church bells, kept silent since 1940 when they were only to be used as a signal of German invasion, pealed out across the country and the British public, starved so long of any resounding triumph, took 'Monty' to their heart. It was a position that he clearly enjoyed, but he did himself an injustice, somewhat uncharacteristically, when he maintained that everything had gone entirely according to plan, for his true quality had been shown in the resolute and thoughtful flexibility with which he had countered the setbacks in the course of the battle, still keeping within the broad framework of his general plan.

Later critics, perhaps irritated by the mystique of Alamein, have maintained that in view of the imminent landings at the other end of the North African coast the battle was entirely unnecessary and was fought simply to give Churchill the political weapon of a military victory in his negotiations with the Americans. It would seem, however, that both from a political and military standpoint the battle was a vital feature in the whole North African operation. Politically, it was needed to convince the French in Morocco and Algeria that it would make better sense not to oppose the American landings. Militarily, if Rommel had been able to withdraw westwards without the serious losses inflicted on him in the battle, the eventual campaign in Tunisia would have been a far more prolonged and doubtful affair. The hard fact was that somewhere along that African coast the Afrika Korps had to be defeated, and Alamein, where Rommel's supply line was stretched to its extreme, was the place where the matter could be put beyond doubt.

Even as the battle raged, American assault forces were already at sea, after embarking from their bases in Great Britain and the United States for the long debated invasion of French North Africa, and on 8 November simultaneous landings under the command of General Eisenhower took place at Casablanca, Oran and Algiers (map, p. 347). The potential hazards of this operation were enormous. Spain might throw in her lot with Germany and sever the Allied communications through the Straits of Gibraltar. French troops, who numbered 120,000 in North Africa, might resist on orders from their government. To counter the second of these, the Allies had already conducted secret negotiations with French commanders in North Africa, and although the French did at first resist, a heated confrontation after the landings between the American general Mark Clark and Admiral Darlan, the French minister of marine, who happened to be in Algiers, soon led to a cease-fire. In Spain Franco did not wish to commit himself at this stage, and Hitler who believed that he could still hold out in Tunisia made no attempt to persuade him, contenting himself with an occupation of the rest of France.

All these political risks had imposed a caution on the planning of the American landings which consequently did not extend sufficiently far to the east. Thus the Axis Powers won the immediate race for control of Tunisia, where at the end of the year some 50,000 German and Italian troops had assembled, and by February 1943 the outnumbered Americans were only holding with difficulty the western half of the region. The major Allied thrust was to come from the east, where Montgomery's Eighth Army after a pursuit along the African coast now faced Rommel on the Mareth line. Here Montgomery warded off an attack by Rommel, and on 20 March launched his own, which succeeded in outflanking the Germans. By April, as the Americans pressed in from the west, the German forces were slowly bottled up in the north-east corner of Tunisia and in the middle of May the fighting ended with the surrender of a quarter of a million Axis troops.

Only eleven days after the landings in North Africa, on 19 November 1942, the Russians had opened an immense counter-offensive, a pincer movement to the north and south of Stalingrad, which by 23 November had completed the encirclement of General Paulus's Sixth German Army, engaged to the west of the city. At the same time another wider thrust from the north held back any relieving attack and in December a further assault was launched beyond this. The frantic German efforts to relieve Paulus's army at Stalingrad only added to the cost. By the end of the year the Russians had taken 60,000 prisoners and when on 31 January 1943 Paulus finally surrendered, the Germans had lost virtually a quarter of a million men. This time there was to be no effective German counter-offensive when the winter ended, and by September 1943 Russian forces had reached the line of the Dnieper.

All this while, another kind of battle was being waged in the Atlantic. By the end of 1942 Admiral Doenitz had more than a hundred U-boats at sea at a time, hunting in wolf-packs and shifting their killing grounds from one part of the ocean to another. In March 1943 alone a tonnage of 538,000 of Allied shipping was sunk at a cost of only twelve U-boats and the British naval staff reckoned that Doenitz was 'very near to disrupting communications between the New World and the Old'. To meet this crescendo of attack a new offensive was opened in the spring of that year. A very-short-wave radar device, unknown to the Germans, enabled rocket-firing aircraft of coastal command to attack U-boats before they could submerge; and destroyers in a new organization of support groups, distinct from the naval escorts of convoys, now went out actively to hunt the wolf-packs. The effect was surprisingly swift. In May 1943 the Germans lost forty-one U-boats; the sinking of Allied shipping dropped to 205,000 tons, and for the moment the situation in the Atlantic had been stabilized.

This dramatic change in the Allies' fortunes since the autumn of 1942 marks the turning-point of the war. It also meant new problems; the Allies now had the initiative, and a conference held at Casablanca in January 1943 between Roosevelt and Churchill with their staffs revealed a highly significant divergence of view between the Americans and the British over the choice of plan for exploiting their advantage. On one thing they were agreed. Stalin was calling emphatically for the opening of the second front in France in the spring of 1943, but although the Americans had originally favoured this, it was clear by now that the Tunisian campaign was unlikely to be over before May; this meant that the necessary shipping and concentration of forces in England would not be ready until September, too late for an effective operation that year, and that consequently no second front could be opened until the spring of 1944.

The issue which divided them was the use to which they should put their forces in the intervening months. The Americans, who had from the first been dubious about the value of the landings in North Africa, had no wish to push on from there across the Mediterranean and in view of the postponement of the cross-Channel operation, known as Overlord, proposed that the Allies should shift their offensive effort to the Pacific for the later part of 1943. Churchill and Brooke argued energetically for an attack on Sicily, to be followed by an invasion of Italy, on the grounds that Mussolini might fall and more German troops would be drawn away from the eventual second front. It was also vital that Stalin, imagining that the Allies were losing interest, should not be tempted to make his own terms with Hitler. Eventually the British got their way over the Sicily operation, although at a subsequent conference at Washington in May there was still a strong American suspicion that Churchill was using their forces to foster British ambitions in the Mediterranean and the Balkans.

These divided views over the Mediterranean campaign were to have an unfortunate consequence. On 10 July American and British forces landed in Sicily and overran the island in a few weeks with Generals Patton and Montgomery racing each other for Messina. This brought more than conquest. On 25 July news came from Rome that Mussolini had fallen from power and a new government under Marshal Badoglio secretly let it be known that Italy was willing to sue for peace. If at that moment landing-craft had been available for an immediate invasion of Italy, General Eisenhower might have been able with Italian connivance to seize a large part of the mainland. As it was, the landing-craft were not there; many had been withdrawn for the Pacific or for the build-up of invasion forces in England. It was not until the beginning of September, after terms had been reached with the Italians, that the Allies were able to carry out landings at Taranto, Reggio and Salerno and by this time the Germans, suspicious of the new Italian government's intentions, had massed eight divisions in north Italy and a further eleven in the centre and the south. When the Italian armistice was announced at the moment of the Allied landings, the German Field-Marshal Kesselring managed to persuade the five Italian divisions near Rome to lay down their arms on the understanding that the troops should be allowed to go home, and then embarked on a defensive campaign which by the end of the year had brought the Allied armies to a halt a hundred miles south of Rome. (See map, p. 347.)

Although the Allied forces were now condemned to a long struggle up Italy in country ideally suited to defence, one aim at least was being achieved. The campaign drew more than twenty German divisions into Italy, and another eighteen were kept in the Balkans, where some 150,000 Communist Yugoslav partisans under their leader Tito were receiving supplies from the Allies by sea and air and already held parts of the country under their control.

None of this eased the framing of the later strategy of the war throughout the last months of 1943. In August Churchill and Roosevelt met at Quebec, and then in November at Cairo as a preliminary to a full conference with Stalin at Teheran. The air was full of plan and counter-plan, all largely incompatible with each other. Chiang-kai-shek was present at Cairo, accompanied by his wife, who was not above putting a very considerable gloss on her husband's statements. The Pacific lobby was now active again, demanding a major amphibious operation into Burma across the Bay of Bengal, while in the Mediterranean theatre the Americans were keen to start thinning out on the Italian front in prepar-ation for the cross-Channel Overlord operation, which they wished to supplement with a landing in the south of France. At the same time, Churchill, with a premonition of later Russian power in the Balkans, talked of 'the soft underbelly of the Axis' in the hope of striking up towards the Danube from Yugoslavia. Against all this, Brooke continu-ally struggled to keep the Allied forces concentrated to hold as many German divisions as possible in Italy.

By the end the British largely got their way. The debate over the Burma operation had been particularly violent, with the Americans General Stilwell and Admiral King strongly in favour of it. 'Brooke got nasty,' wrote Stilwell, 'and King got good and sore. King almost climbed over the table at Brooke. God, he was mad! I wish he had socked him.'[2] The landing-craft statistics were incontrovertible, how-ever, and eventually the Americans agreed to drop the Burma scheme, after Stalin at Teheran had promised to join the Allies against Japan as soon as Germany had been defeated. Churchill, too, had by now been convinced that a major invasion of the Balkans was not viable and operations here were to be restricted to Commando attacks in conjunc-tion with Tito's partisans. It was also agreed that General Alexander's offensive in Italy should continue, aiming at the Pisa–Rimini line, so that the Germans might not be able to release their forces in that area, even though this must mean a postponing of the cross-Channel operation in 1944 until the beginning of June. This last consequence does point to the most debatable factor in Brooke's strategy, since at times the Italian campaign seemed to come close to pinning the Allies down as much as it did the Germans. Still, all calculations were bound to be marginal and the twenty-eight German divisions that now confronted Alexander in Italy might well have made the decisive difference, if they had been available in France when the Allies launched their invasion in 1944.

There were two other factors noticeable at Teheran which were to be of particular significance in the final stages of the war. The first was a determination on the part of President Roosevelt to establish a personal relationship with Stalin. He was confident that he alone could do so. 'Stalin hates the guts of all your top people',[3] he had written to Churchill eighteen months before, and at Teheran he believed that he had laid the foundation of a new Russo-American understanding. The second factor was the enthusiasm with which Stalin welcomed the proposal for a landing in the south of France. By now with the Germans in retreat in Russia he could afford to give more weight to the political implications of Allied activity. He had no wish to see American and British forces working their way into the Balkans and on to the Danube, before the Red Army had established itself there, and it suited him perfectly if they gave their attention instead to an operation so far to the west. Churchill's abandoned dreams of a Balkan offensive may have misjudged the softness of the underbelly of the Axis, but Stalin was well aware of their political realism.

During the early months of 1944 military effort remained reasonably concentrated. On the Russian front Leningrad was relieved in January, German forces on the Dnieper were encircled in February and by the spring the Red Army had thrust past Odessa and over the Dniester, while the German Seventeenth Army was cut off in the Crimea from where it had to make a costly evacuation by sea. On the Italian front in January Alexander opened a new offensive on the Garigliano river. This was designed to draw in German reserves, so that the way might be open for a seaborne landing at Anzio behind the German lines, aimed at the rapid capture of Rome only twenty-five miles away. The Allied forces at Anzio, however, failed to exploit their initial advantage and were soon fighting desperately to avoid being pushed into the sea. Meanwhile, the rugged countryside around Monte Cassino made the general advance from the south hard going and it was not until May that Alexander was able to break through. On 4 June the Allies at last entered Rome, and two days later the news of this event was overshadowed by the launching of the long-planned invasion of northern France.

2. *The invasion of France and Germany: June 1944–May 1945*

The staff work for the invasion of France had been in progress since early in 1943, but it was not until December of that year that a supreme commander was selected for the operation. Brooke had dearly hoped for this appointment, but the eventual size of the United States forces involved demanded that it should be an American, and General Eisenhower was chosen for the task by President Roosevelt. Eisenhower's experience of command in wartime had been limited to the Mediterranean campaigns, but his great strength lay in his ability to win the loyalty of subordinate commanders of both countries and to foster a remarkable cooperation between the Allies at all levels on the staff and in the field. Everyone liked Ike. The deputy commander was to be British, Air Chief Marshal Tedder, and for the initial stages of the campaign in France General Montgomery was to exercise command over all land forces.

If the invasion was to have any hope of success, the first essential was to gain complete command of the air, as the Germans had realized in 1940. During the years since the Battle of Britain the determination of the air staff to preserve the independent role of the RAF had resulted in great emphasis being placed on a strategic bombing campaign over Germany. As the number and size of bombers and the destructive force of the bombs all grew, policy shifted in 1943 from attacks on selected industrial targets to area bombing in which whole towns in the Ruhr and, later, Hamburg and Berlin were devastated. None of these efforts seem to have broken German morale and the output of German industry was less seriously affected than had been hoped, but by 1944 this long campaign, strongly supported by the American air force, had established an undoubted mastery in the air for the Allies.

Command of the air alone, however, was not enough. In any invasion of a well guarded coastline the odds are always heavily in favour of the defenders, since once the main area of attack has become defined, forces on the landward side can be massed against it far more quickly than the build-up of the invaders, lacking a port and utterly at the mercy of the weather at sea. Despite Brooke's efforts to keep twenty-eight German divisions involved in Italy, there were still fifty-eight enemy divisions in France and the Low Countries, ten of them Panzers; and even with a revision of their plans early in 1944 the Allies could not hope to land more than six divisions by sea and three by air in the first twenty-four hours of the assault. Thus in the initial stages an overwhelming German preponderance could be rapidly assembled and might drive them back into the sea; or, if they escaped that, the Germans could effectively seal off the invasion area and the lines might settle down into a war of attrition.

To lessen these dangers the Allies used two separate methods. From the beginning of March RAF Bomber Command and the Eighth US Air Force opened an immense attack on the whole railway system of northern France and Belgium to derange German supply and the movement of reinforcements. Secondly, they devised a remarkable deception plan whereby through a series of subterfuges they convinced the German general staff that their main attack was to come in the Pas de Calais area. This scheme was so successful that even weeks after the landings Hitler, who had correctly guessed that the Allies would strike at the Normandy coast, but for once had allowed himself to be advised by his generals, was still keeping much of his reserve east of the Seine in the belief that the main assault was yet to come in that region.

For the landings themselves the Allies had to rely on tactical surprise, which in the event they were able to achieve. They also had air supremacy over the invasion beaches and an effective naval command of the Channel whose western end was blockaded against U-boat infiltration. Their earlier experience in the Mediterranean had given them great experience in the handling of amphibious operations, and this was now complemented by an extraordinary range of technical devices, such as tanks that would swim out of the sea on to the beaches and armoured flails for breaking a path quickly through minefields. By the late spring the southern districts of England were packed tight with troops and vehicles, and all now rested on the state of the weather at the moment when the tide and the moon would be right. The sea was rough, but there was a glimmer of hope in the forecast and on 5 June, after one twenty-four-hour postponement, General Eisenhower gave the order for attack.

That night British and American parachute forces captured the extreme flanks of the invasion area on the river Orne and at the bottom of the Cotentin peninsula (map opposite). An armada of shipping crossed from south of the Isle of Wight and early on the morning of 6 June, British, Canadian and American forces fought their way ashore on five different beachheads. At the western end the Americans encountered fierce German resistance; in the east the British failed to capture Caen, contrary to a BBC newsflash that afternoon, and in the evening part of a Panzer division pushed through momentarily to the coast. By nightfall

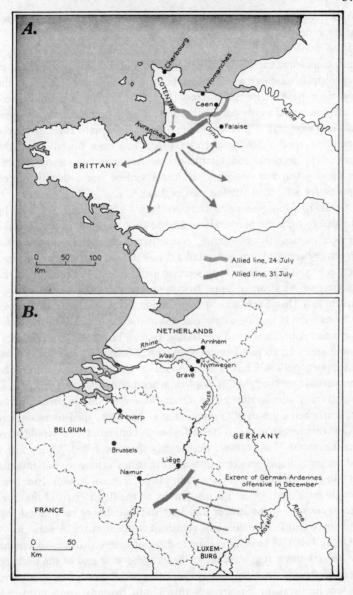

8   THE SECOND WORLD WAR
A. Normandy, June–July 1944
B. The Low Countries, September–December 1944

the footholds had been established at a cost of 11,000 casualties including 2,500 dead.

By 8 June the separate beachheads had been linked up to form a continuous front and in the subsequent weeks the fighting continued to deepen the invasion area to allow room for the build-up of forces. At the same time the Americans cut across the Cotentin peninsula from where an advance northwards led to the capture of Cherbourg on 26 June. This last was vital to give the Allies a port, since until then they were dependent upon a floating harbour which had been towed across the Channel in sections and established at Arromanches, a remarkable engineering feat but not proof against a violent storm that disrupted supplies for a week in the last part of June.

As usual, Montgomery had always had a clear picture of how he intended to fight the battle. He wished to keep the bulk of the German defence, particularly its armour, concentrated on the British sector in the east, where the Germans feared a thrust towards Paris; after this had been achieved, the Americans were to make the real breakout at the western end. As a consequence, British progress was slow and it was not until 9 July that Caen was in their hands. By now, however, Panzer divisions were beginning to move across to the western half of the front, where the Americans were expanding faster. To check this tendency, Montgomery on 18 July launched a heavy armoured assault with strong air support south of Caen. Two days of heavy rain and the depth of the German defence brought this to a halt, whereupon a storm of criticism of Montgomery's leadership broke out at Supreme Headquarters. At the moment when a group of German officers had just failed to assassinate Hitler, there were many in the Allied high command who would have liked to unseat Montgomery. Fortunately they too failed. Montgomery had certainly hoped to get a little further in his offensive, but this did not alter the general pattern of his plan. German armour had been brought back east to meet the new threat; on the British part of the front there were now seven Panzer divisions and four heavy tank battalions, while only two Panzer divisions remained in front of the Americans.

On 25 July the Americans launched the offensive that was to achieve the breakthrough at Avranches at the extreme west end of the invasion area and through that gap six days later General Patton's forces followed up for the breakout. Spearheads thrust into Brittany and southwards and then turned east, aiming to reach the British pushing south from their sector. It seemed as if the bulk of the German forces, forbidden by Hitler to withdraw, would be caught in the pocket as the Allied forces strove from the north and the south to close the gap at Falaise, while wider arcs swung south and east towards the Seine. Amidst weeks of appalling carnage the battle of Normandy ended in a rout in which the Germans lost 300,000 men and over 600 tanks.

The east of France was now wide open; in the south the projected landings had begun on 15 August and as the Allies raced eastwards, there seemed a prospect that the war might be over that autumn. Montgomery believed that this could be achieved with a concentrated Allied thrust along the extreme north, outflanking the Siegfried line and striking across the Meuse, the Waal and the Rhine into the Ruhr (map, p. 371). Eisenhower who had now assumed practical command in the field preferred to continue the advance on a broad front. He was less optimistic about the inability of the Germans to resist and with Le Havre, Boulogne, Calais and Antwerp still holding out, reckoned that the problem of supply militated against Montgomery's scheme. The most that Montgomery was allowed was a purely British operation whereby the bridges over the three rivers were seized in a series of daring airborne operations on 17 September. This, however, was only to be part of a general advance along the whole front, and although British forces following up were able to reach Grave on the Meuse and Nymwegen on the Waal, they were not strong enough to reach the last obstacle at Arnhem, from where the survivors of the airborne drop had eventually to be withdrawn after heavy losses.

Antwerp itself had been reached early in September, but it was not until 6 November that the islands commanding the estuary had been cleared of German forces and the first Allied convoy did not enter Antwerp before the end of that month. At the same time the American advance in the Saar and south of Aachen had been checked and in Italy Alexander's September offensive against the German Gothic line had developed into a slogging match in which his forces, depleted by the requirements of the landings in the south of France, were inadequate to avoid an eventual deadlock.

Thus there was to be a further winter of war and critics of Eisenhower's strategy maintained that the Allies had lost momentum through too great a dispersal of their forces. Nevertheless, the continuing strength of German resistance does lend support to Eisenhower's objections to Montgomery's plan, and before long this was emphasized when on 16 December the Germans launched a counter-offensive through the Ardennes, aiming at the recapture of Antwerp. Despite stubborn American resistance German spearheads penetrated some fifty miles towards the Meuse. To deal with this bulge, Eisenhower concentrated command of all forces to the north of the attack under

Montgomery, who assumed this new position with an air of superiority that brought his relationship with American generals to its lowest point. Montgomery grouped his forces to defend the sector of the Meuse between Liège and Namur, which he correctly believed to be the German objective, and took steps to organize a reserve for a counter-attack, but even before this was launched at the beginning of January 1945, the Americans had begun to push the Germans back.

With the Ardennes offensive the Germans had shot their bolt. Since the Normandy landing an immense programme of bombing by the combined air forces had devastated the cities, oil plants, roads and railways of Germany, and although Hitler's secret weapons—V1 pilotless flying bombs and, later, V2 rockets—offered some retaliation, he could manage little effective resistance in the air. Meanwhile, in the east the pattern of postwar Europe was in the making. In the autumn the Red Army had overrun Romania, thrust into Hungary and reached the outskirts of Warsaw. The concentration of German forces needed for the Ardennes counter-attack in the west now gave the Russians an admirable opportunity to launch a new offensive on 12 January 1945, which by the end of the month had driven the Germans as far back as Breslau and Kuestrin some fifty miles from Berlin (map, p. 307). This had been the real cost of the Ardennes venture, although it also strengthened the one hope left to Hitler that the Russian advance must undermine their alliance with the west. 'Do you think,' he asked, 'the English can be really enthusiastic about all the Russian developments?' 'If this goes on,' commented Goering, 'we will get a telegram (from the west) in a few days.'[4]

Indeed, Churchill was not very enthusiastic, but was largely unable to share his fears with President Roosevelt, who wished to cement his friendship with Stalin and seemed more concerned to speed the dismantling of the old European colonial empires than to check the growth of a new Russian one. The American government had not approved of a preliminary proposal that Churchill had made to Stalin in October 1944 for a rough division of interests in the various Balkan countries between Russia and the west. That transatlantic mistrust of European diplomacy was still strong and there was more than an echo of President Wilson's voice, when Roosevelt later predicted to Congress 'the end of the system of unilateral action, exclusive alliances and spheres of influence and balances of power and all the other expedients which have been tried for centuries and have always failed'.

Thus, when they met in conference with Stalin at Yalta in the Crimea in February 1945, the relationship between Churchill and Roosevelt was not an entirely happy one. When it came to ensuring Russian participation in the war against Japan, Roosevelt was prepared to agree that Russia should have the Kurile islands and southern Sakhalin as well as a considerable sphere of interest in Manchuria. In discussion over the future of Poland Stalin agreed that the provisional government should include non-Communists and that there should be free elections as soon as possible, but the Americans would not support the British demand that these elections should be supervised by the Allies. Otherwise, there were no great difficulties. Zones of occupation in Germany were agreed and Stalin accepted the inclusion of the French in this organization. In the last analysis, given the military situation in eastern Europe, any arrangement had to rest on Soviet good faith and Churchill did his best to put aside his undoubted qualms. At least, if Yalta was a victory for Stalin, it was also a defeat for Hitler. 'What would have happened,' wrote Churchill afterwards, 'if we had quarelled with Russia, while the Germans still had two or three hundred divisions on the fighting front?'[5]

On 8 February, the day before the end of the Yalta conference, Eisenhower had opened an offensive which aimed at clearing the region between the Meuse and the Rhine. British and Canadian forces pushed south from Nymwegen in a battle into which the Germans flung the main part of their reserves. The Americans moved up from the south to join them and on 7 March discovered an undemolished bridge over the Rhine at Remagen (map, p. 307) across which Eisenhower moved an entire American army in the space of a fortnight. By this time two further crossings had been established: the Americans in the south at Oppenheim, and Montgomery with another Army group in the north. From this position the Americans cut off the German forces in the Ruhr, where in April over 300,000 surrendered, while the British pushed eastwards towards the Elbe.

By the end of March on the Russian front the Red Army had captured Danzig and further south had reached the Austrian frontier. In April a new offensive took them across the Oder and by the last week of that month Berlin was surrounded. Eisenhower's southern army had now almost reached Leipzig, while in the north the British had rushed on to take Bremen and Hamburg and to reach Lübeck and Wismar on the Baltic a few hours ahead of the Russians on 2 May. Meanwhile, a major offensive launched by Alexander in the valley of the Po had resulted by the end of April in the surrender of all German forces in north Italy.

On 30 April Hitler committed suicide in his underground headquarters in Berlin. He had named as his successor Admiral Doenitz, who at once hastened the process of piecemeal surrender which had already begun. On 4 May Montgomery accepted the surrender of enemy forces in north-west Europe, and on 7 May there took place a formal surrender of all German forces before representatives of the United States, Great Britain, France and Russia at Eisenhower's headquarters at Rheims.

Thus, amid the ruin of Europe the war that Neville Chamberlain had so dreaded had come to an end at last. During more than five and a half years it had cost Great Britain 400,000 lives; her economic strength was all but exhausted and in the world she now stood dwarfed by the mighty allies that she had been able to enlist. But at least the nightmare was over; Great Britain had survived, and on the day of the German surrender an excited and grateful populace gathered outside No. 10 Downing Street to give their thanks to the man whose courage had brought them through.

3. The defeat of Japan

All this time a long ferocious war had been raging on the far side of the world. Japan had reached the full extent of her advance by the middle of 1942 (see p. 352) but the commitments of the Allies in Europe precluded them from opening any serious counter-offensive until July 1943, when the Americans began to push back in New Guinea. The fanaticism of the Japanese soldiers was such, however, that future campaigning looked as if it might become very costly in lives, and accordingly General MacArthur devised a strategy whereby American forces were to leapfrog across the Pacific, leaving many islands still in Japanese hands in their rear, until a position had been reached from where assaults could be made on the mainland of Japan. In November 1943 the Gilbert Islands were taken, in February 1944 the Marshalls and in June the Marianas. The campaign to regain the Philippines was longer, lasting from October 1944 until March 1945; finally, with the capture of Iwo Jima in March 1945 and of Okinawa in April the Americans were at last within striking distance of Japan.

In India a new South-East Asia Command had been set up under Admiral Lord Louis Mountbatten and when in March 1944 the Japanese launched a new offensive in north Burma aiming at Imphal and Kohima, General Slim was able to check this and to push back in a counter-offensive that reached the river Chindwin in July. In the following December a new British assault, thrusting down through the jungle and cutting off Japanese forces behind them, reached Rangoon by May 1945.

Then, on 16 July, the whole story of the Japanese campaign was transformed by an event far from the field of battle. On that day the first atom bomb was successfully exploded in a test from the top of a pylon in the desert of New Mexico, and the Americans knew that they now had a weapon of greater destructive power than anything previously know to mankind.

Pure scientific research before the war had long been concerned with attempting to harness the energy of the atom, but it was not until 1938 that Dr Hahn, a German scientist in Berlin, had discovered that by bombarding an atom of uranium with neutrons an immense energy could be released. As soon as the war began, British scientists feared that Hitler might eventually have at his disposal a bomb of appalling power and it seemed vital that Great Britain should be able to counter this threat by producing one of her own. The knowledge gained was made available to the United States and after 1942, in view of the enormous expense, the research was mainly in the hands of American teams including a large number of British and continental scientists. It was of course by no means certain that they would succeed in making one, and amid the excitements of the immediate decisions for winning the war no general agreement had been reached about the future control of the bomb beyond an understanding between the two countries that neither would use it without the other's consent.

This was the position when, in July 1945, Churchill and Attlee were informed of the successful test in New Mexico, while they were at Potsdam in conference with Stalin and President Truman, who had assumed office on the death of Roosevelt the previous April. British consent for the use of the bomb against Japan had already been given. A demand for unconditional surrender was rejected by the Japanese government and after eleven Japanese cities had been warned by leaflets from the air, one atomic bomb was dropped on Hiroshima on 6 August, and a second on Nagasaki on 9 August. The Japanese government now accepted the Allies' demands, only holding out for the retention of the Emperor as their sovereign ruler. On 14 August this was agreed, and on 2 September the formal surrender of Japan took place on an American battleship in Tokyo bay.

The devastation brought about by the two bombs was infinitely greater than had been expected. At Hiroshima 70,000 were killed, at Nagasaki 39,000, with a total of almost 100,000 injured. Square miles of territory were laid waste by the blast and the effects of radiation were still to bring death to thousands of survivors months and years after the explosions. Inevitably so horrible an event was bound to lead to considerable shock and recrimination in the west. It was claimed by some that there had been no need to drop the bombs, since the Japanese were already thinking of making terms, and that the real motive had been to justify the enormous expense of their production and to enable the military heads to see the full effects of this new weapon.

It is hard to say how close the Japanese had been to surrender. Although their air force and navy had virtually been destroyed, they had an army of 4·5 million men; they still held large areas of Malaya, Indo-China and parts of China as well as many Pacific islands, and the personal loyalty of the Japanese soldiers to the Emperor, maintained to a suicidal degree, suggested to the war party in Tokyo that they could continue to fight a defence ultimately so costly to the Allies that a compromise peace might result. It is true that since April a peace party in the Japanese cabinet had secretly put out cautious feelers through Russia, but the war party controlled the real centre of power in the supreme war council. Indeed, even after the bombs had been dropped and the Emperor had decided on surrender, the army still wished to go on and attempted a *coup d'état* in Tokyo.

Thus it seems likely that if the bombs had not been dropped, the war would have continued. In that event the comparative statistics of slaughter are difficult to calculate. The Americans certainly reckoned that the Japanese would fight to the last on the mainland islands and that the Allies' casualties might amount to one million. Not even the intervention of Russia, who in accordance with her promise declared war on 8 August, was likely to have made much difference, since she would probably have concentrated on her own sphere of interests, Manchuria and southern Sakhalin. There was also an additional consideration in the thousands of British and Commonwealth prisoners, already at the last extreme of malnutrition, who might have been massacred by their guards. And on the Japanese side there would have been enormous losses and most of their cities would have been devastated by conventional bombing.

On this assessment the dropping of the atom bombs may actually have saved lives. There is another factor. An appalling degree of destruction could now be wrought by a single bomb, and as the nuclear race between America and Russia developed after 1945, public imagination became riveted on the spectre of total annihilation. After the First World War it had been feared that the next war would be like the last; after the Second the prevailing fear was that the next might be something quite different. The thought was general, however, and a balance of terror was for many years to preserve the world from a nuclear war.

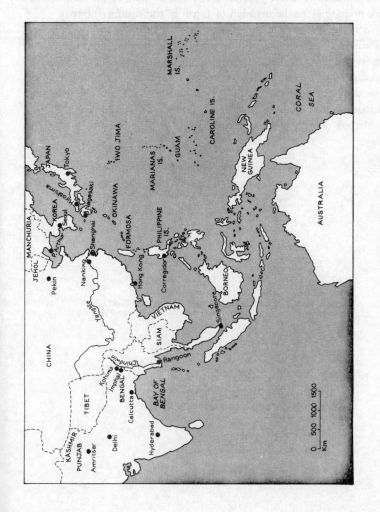

9 INDIA AND THE FAR EAST

Yet the destructive power of those first two bombs had taken even the experts by surprise, and if they had not been dropped the subsequent terror might not have been sufficiently effective to hold their later use in check. If that is so, then the dead of Hiroshima and Nagasaki may have saved the lives of future generations as well as those of the soldiers who were preparing for the invasion of Japan in the summer of 1945.

All these are terrible arguments. It may be possible to give some rational justification for the dropping of the bombs, but that cannot remove the thought that as a result of a carefully planned operation the populations of two large cities were wiped out, each at a single stroke. How does one measure death against death? Such are the gruesome calculations that the men in supreme command have to make in the vile murderous context of modern war, and we still live on those terms today.

VII

The Emergence of
Contemporary
Britain

32
Labour in Control 1945–1951

The Coalition government, formed at the onset of disaster in 1940, did not long survive the defeat of Germany. With the present House of Commons almost ten years old, a general election had soon to be held and it was clear that it would have to be fought out on the normal basis of party politics; the differences of opinion over the shaping of postwar Britain were too acute to allow of any other course. The only issue was the date. In contrast to Lloyd George's position in 1918, Churchill's acceptance of the leadership of the Conservative party shortly before the death of Neville Chamberlain in 1940 had freed him from depending on the continuance of the Coalition government into peacetime, but he did express the hope that the present government might be maintained until the end of the Japanese war. Attlee, however, after debate at the Labour party conference, proposed an election in October, whereupon Churchill decided, as he wrote later, that 'if there must be an election in 1945, the sooner it came the better'.[1]

Accordingly the Coalition ended on 23 May, and while Churchill headed a caretaker government, Parliament was dissolved in the middle of June. Polling day was 5 July, but the result was not to be declared until 26 July to allow time for the return of votes from servicemen overseas. Thus there was an unusual interlude of three weeks during which the nation had spoken, but its voice had not yet been heard. This anomaly meant that Churchill and Attlee both had to attend the Allied conference at Potsdam on 17 July, since the future government of Great Britain was still a secret locked up in the ballot boxes, a situation which Stalin must have found rather amusing.

On 26 July the secret came out with the force of a bombshell. Labour had gained an overwhelming victory in an electoral landslide comparable to the Liberal gains in 1906. They had won 393 seats against 213 for the Conservatives; the Liberals numbered twelve and the Communists two. The popular vote of the two principal parties was considerably closer than these figures would suggest, but in parliamentary terms Labour held an absolute majority and could legitimately claim a mandate from the country. By seven o'clock that evening Churchill had resigned and Clement Attlee kissed hands as the new Prime Minister.

To Churchill the outcome appeared an almost inconceivable act of ingratitude. 'All our enemies having surrendered unconditionally or being about to do so,' he wrote in his memoirs, 'I was immediately dismissed by the British electorate from all further conduct of their affairs.'[2] It was perhaps understandable that he should feel a bitterness at this, yet the general election had had nothing to do with a profound thankfulness and veneration for Churchill's leadership during the war. This had merely ceased to be relevant. The electors had voted for parties, not personalities. Millions of them were too young ever to have voted before, but old enough to remember the depressing image of the interwar years, a period of predominantly Conservative administrations. It seemed to be time for a change and in the new pattern of the two-party system that had been shaping since 1918 this was bound to open the way to Labour.

It was true that the Conservatives had produced a plan of social reform which was to include the Butler Education Act of 1944; a Ministry of National Insurance had been set up and the Bill for family allowances had become law during the few weeks of the caretaker government. Yet none of this could quieten an uneasy feeling that Conservative response to the publication of the Beveridge Report (see p. 360) had seemed slow and somewhat grudging, whereas Labour had unreservedly accepted it. Another more emotional factor may have been the attitude of the conscript rank and file of the armed forces, who still regarded their officers as an embodiment of the upper class and who saw a vote for Labour as a blow at the frustrations of military discipline.

Against all this the aura of Churchill's wartime leadership was of no avail. Indeed, that romantic imagination which had fired the spirit of the nation amid the awful simplicity of military crisis in 1940 was now something of a liability for his colleagues. He spoke of 'the cottage home to which the warrior will return'. He conjured up visions of a Socialist tyranny imposed by a secret police. He seemed unaware that the majority of warriors would return to bomb-racked slums in drab industrial towns and that the restraint of earlier Labour administrations and the obvious integrity and constitutional orthodoxy of Clement Attlee made nonsense of such charges of red revolution. In short, he had failed to achieve credibility and the outcome was a Labour majority so large that it could hardly be accommodated on the government benches of the House of Commons.

1. The fight for economic survival

Not even the most enthusiastic supporter of the new Prime Minister could have described him as a colourful personality. Clement Attlee eschewed flamboyance to an extent that was almost spectacular, and his public appearances could be guaranteed to reduce the most momentous issues to a flat banality. 'A sheep in sheep's clothing', Churchill called him, but he was wrong. Those who had served on committees under Attlee's chairmanship during the war had great respect for his power of swift incisive decision and the laconic comment with which he could defuse a situation or cut through any irrelevance. He listened, doodled and brought the meeting to a positive conclusion.

From the first he showed that he could act quickly. He was due to return almost immediately to Potsdam and within twenty-four hours the principal appointments to the cabinet had been made. Herbert Morrison as Lord President of the Council was to be deputy Prime Minister. Hugh Dalton, originally hoping for the Foreign Office, was made Chancellor of the Exchequer, and it was Ernest Bevin who became Foreign Secretary, a position from which he was less likely to have a chance of quarrelling with Morrison. Sir Stafford Cripps was to be President of the Board of Trade and Arthur Greenwood Lord Privy Seal.

In some respects, quite apart from its formidable position in the Commons, the Labour administration seemed well placed for the implementing of its electoral programme. Many of the leaders had behind them five years' experience of ministerial responsibility during the Coalition; a vast apparatus of government controls created in the course of the war lay at their disposal, and there was an added stroke of fortune when the surrender of Japan in the middle of August 1945 freed them from the burden of the war in the Far East.

None of this could offset the fact that their chance had come at a time when the state of the British economy presented the most appalling problems (see p. 359). While the quantity of Great Britain's imports was largely unchanged, her exports had dropped to a third of the prewar figure; her other earnings were now utterly inadequate to close this gap, since by the end of the war she had been forced to sell more than a quarter of her overseas investments and she had incurred a debt of £3,500 million. In this situation the only solution lay in a marked increase in exports, and the government declared that 150 per cent of the 1938 figure must be their aim—a brave cry, when the country's merchant shipping tonnage had fallen by 28 per cent and the potential market of a devastated continent of Europe was largely non-existent. Thus the Socialist experiment was to be carried out under the shadow of impending bankruptcy, forcing the Labour government to accept the terms of international capitalism and to utter constant exhortations for harder work and wage restraint, so that British export prices might remain competitive—demands which to some of their supporters seemed to have a strangely Conservative tone.

The full impact of the crisis was almost immediate. On 21 August 1945 President Truman announced an end forthwith to lend–lease and the new Labour government had at once to find an alternative supply of dollars to tide the country over the initial stages of its recovery. Lord Keynes set off for Washington in the hope that, since Great Britain's difficulties sprang from her unstinted efforts to win the war, she might have a moral claim to a gift or at least an interest-free loan of 6,000 million dollars from the United States. In this he was disappointed. The most that he could get was a loan of 4,400 million dollars. Of this 650 million was to be used to settle existing debts under lend–lease, and there was to be an interest charge of 2 per cent, although this payment was not to begin until 1951. More significant, it was stipulated, despite Keynes's protests, that sterling should be fully convertible into other currencies a year after the signing of the agreement. With this, as well as a Canadian loan of £1,250 million dollars, the government had to be content. The vital need for the moment was to have dollars at whatever cost, and with that accomplished, the target for exports was now raised to 175 per cent of the 1938 figure.

At first the outlook was promising. Government allocation of materials stimulated exporters who began to concentrate at last on the greatest areas of growth, and for the first half of 1946 exports were reaching £70 million a month. The subsequent twelve months gave less cause for optimism. The American loan was being used up at a far faster rate than anticipated. An appalling winter, in which deep snow made it impossible to transport the barely adequate supplies of coal to the power stations, virtually brought industry to a standstill throughout February 1947; 4·5 million workers had temporarily to be laid off and Sir Stafford Cripps calculated that the weather had cost the country £200 million in exports. Then on 15 July 1947, in accordance with the terms of the loan, sterling became fully convertible and all over the world Britain's creditors rushed to turn their pounds into dollars or Swiss francs. The consequent drain on Britain's gold and dollar reserves was so dramatic that within four weeks, on 10 August, the government had had to suspend sterling convertibility.

The late summer of 1947 marked the most desperate point in the fortunes of the Labour government. Attlee with characteristic economy of effort fought off a ministerial intrigue to remove him from the leadership and turned to Sir Stafford Cripps who, passing on the Board of Trade to Harold Wilson, assumed a general responsibility as Minister of Economic Affairs; a few weeks later he added to this the Chancellorship of the Exchequer after an innocent indiscretion by Hugh Dalton before the announcement of the proposals in an autumn budget.

Austere, patrician, with a puritan indifference to material pleasures, Cripps was like some Socialist counterpart of the Victorian ideal of high-mindedness, thrift and hard work. He always knew best. 'There, but for the grace of God, goes God,'[3] commented Churchill, but Cripps was undoubtedly the man to face this crisis. He attempted to redevise the whole shape of British trading; he restricted imports drastically and switched as many as possible to non-dollar areas; he launched a new export drive, appealed successfully to the trade unions to keep down their wage demands, prohibited all foreign exchange for personal travel and in the budget of 1948 imposed a capital levy.

It is hard to know how far these measures alone would have succeeded. There was certainly a prospect of lean years ahead and although Cripps himself might be unconcerned with personal popularity, the Labour party managers could not escape the thought that the world economic situation was giving to the Labour administration the image of an austerity even more dismal than the conditions of wartime. The Opposition naturally seized on the shortages as the natural concomitant of Socialism and deplored the waste of public money on the army of civil servants that rationing entailed. On the whole, it seems likely that a continuation of rationing would have been inevitable under any government, in view of the need to correct the country's balance of trade, and in any case the situation had been made far worse by the failure of some of the world's major food-producing regions at the end of the war. In July 1946 bread had had to be rationed; so, too, had potatoes late in 1947, and in 1948 the new stringency imposed by Sir Stafford Cripps produced the lowest level of drabness.

By now the average weekly ration for a single person in Great Britain was thirteen ounces of meat, one and a half ounces of cheese, six ounces of butter and margarine, one ounce of cooking fat, eight ounces of sugar, two pints of milk and one egg, while sweets, clothing, furniture, coal, petrol and soap were all seriously restricted. 'Fish and Cripps', groaned Harold Macmillan from the Opposition benches, but the government did what they could to keep cheerful. They stressed the reappearance of the banana, unknown since 1939; they discovered a new delight in tinned whalemeat and a new fish in the form of the snoek. The hunting of the snoek, however, did not appeal to the public and even the Minister of Food, John Strachey, confessed that he found it rather dull.

Fortunately economic recovery was not to depend on Cripps's measures alone. This was largely facilitated by a change of attitude in the United States. In 1945 the Americans had hoped for a rapid return to normal international trading relations. The provisions of lend–lease had avoided the worst aspects of accumulated war debts which had complicated the scene after 1918, and now with the world at peace again they had believed that the most salutary course would be the abandonment of the abnormal arrangements of wartime: hence the immediate ending of lend–lease, the terms of the American loan and the rapid restoration of convertibility. By 1947, however, the continuing weakness of Europe made it clear that they had underestimated the damage which the war had done to the international economy and they were driven to accept the truth of Keynes's argument that it was far too early for a return to 'normality'.

Their response to this, prompted by political as well as economic considerations (see p. 399), was a unique and startling proposal put forward in June 1947 by General Marshall, now the American Secretary of State. Marshall aid was nothing less than a plan to pump 17 thousand million dollars into the European economy, a fantastically generous effort to set the world on its feet again. For Great Britain this would not only mean more dollars; it would mean an economic recovery in Europe, where a growing purchasing power would open new markets for exports in a general spiral of returning prosperity.

The impact was almost immediate. Cripps's measures now coincided with a situation in which the western world was financially equipped to move towards a boom. In 1948 and 1949 the British balance of payments showed a small surplus. In November 1948 a large number of controls on internal trade could be removed and rationing became more relaxed. Nevertheless, the situation was still precarious and when a mild recession in the United States in the summer of 1949 reduced the size of the dollar markets, the British dollar deficit grew so alarmingly that in September the government decided on devaluation. The value of the pound was brought down from $4·03 to $2·80. This naturally made exports cheaper and therefore easier to sell, but it also meant dearer imports, and a rise in the cost of living was bound to bring higher wage demands. In the main, however, although there was debate over the extent of the devaluation, the manoeuvre succeeded. Wages rose relatively slowly whereas gold and dollar reserves went up from 1,425 million dollars in September 1949 to 2,422 million in the middle of 1950. National output was continuing to increase by nearly 4 per cent every year; between 1946 and 1950 exports increased by 77 per cent, and the surplus on the balance of payments in 1950 reached £300 million.

Inevitably the immediate postwar period had been shot through with a continuing sense of crisis, financial juggling and a frantic concern with exports. Labour had probably made mistakes; Cripps himself reckoned that they had been too optimistic in 1945, but at least they had governed with some strength at the risk of unpopularity and by 1950, although new problems were soon to appear with the outbreak of the Korean war (see p. 409) in the June of that year, there were reasonable indications that the country was emerging from its ordeal.

2. Nationalization and the welfare state

According to the Labour party constitution (see p. 147) the central aim of the government should have been 'to secure for the producers by hand and by brain the full fruits of their industry and the most equitable distribution thereof that may be possible, upon the basis of the common ownership of the means of production and the best obtainable system of popular administration and control of each industry and service'. Thus to the despair of the Conservatives it seemed that a Labour majority must mean a massive nationalization of all the principal industries of the country.

In fact, the most remarkable feature of the Attlee administration is the extent to which they did *not* nationalize. The bulk of industry producing consumer goods remained in private ownership; the City emerged unscathed. Even the process of allocations and controls on which the government relied to correct the balance of payments had presented innumerable problems, and in February 1947 an *Economic Survey* had admitted that 'the task of directing by democratic methods an economic system as large and as complex as ours is far beyond the power of any government'. This was not the language of a ruthless determination to create a Socialist society at a single stroke.

There was, nevertheless, a considerable programme of nationalization. In 1946 the Bank of England and civil aviation, in 1947 coal and electricity, in 1948 all forms of public transport and the gas industry were taken over. Except for coal, these all represented types of public service; some, such as gas and electricity, had previously worked in close conjunction with local authorities; others, such as the London Passenger

Transport Board, were already public corporations. In this respect the change meant little more than an extension of the collectivist process which in the nineteenth century had established the Post Office or the public health and main drainage services at a municipal level. The nationalizing of the mines might seem a more revolutionary step; yet the coal industry had been in such a weak state since the First World War that it could be argued that nationalization was now the only logical step, even if this implied that a takeover by the state was a rescue operation for industries in decay.

The methods of nationalization, too, were very moderate, largely at the insistence of Herbert Morrison. Shareholders were paid full compensation. There was no question of workers' control. Nor were the concerns placed under the management of the Civil Service. They became public corporations, each one run by a board whose chairman and members were appointed by the appropriate minister. This method had already been pioneered before the war with the BBC in 1926 and BOAC (the British Overseas Airways Corporation) in 1939, a compromise which provided a guise of public ownership, while avoiding the apparatus of a monolithic state control.

In only one respect did the Labour government attempt a major assault on the commanding heights of capitalism. This was the Bill for the nationalization of iron and steel, and their nervousness over this was such that it was not introduced in the Commons until October 1948. Anticipating that the House of Lords would use their two-year veto, established by the Parliament Act of 1911, the government had prepared the way with a new Bill in October 1947 reducing the length of that veto to twelve months, provided that any Bill in question should be passed twice by the Commons during that year. The Lords held up this further restriction of their powers for the statutory period of two years. This left the government so little time to get the Iron and Steel Bill through that the Conservative Opposition's delaying tactics forced them to accept an amendment whereby it would only become operative after the next general election, and ultimately when the Conservatives got back into power in 1951, they were able to reverse the process and to restore iron and steel to private ownership, although the Iron and Steel Board was to retain a certain degree of supervision.

Thus far, a doctrinaire Socialist might well complain that the Attlee administration was more concerned to tidy up a capitalist society rather than to create a Socialist one. In the field of social welfare, however, the Labour government did follow a highly radical policy, using its fiscal machinery not merely to improve the lot of the poor, but positively to bring about a redistribution of income which would narrow the gap between the standard of living of the working class and that of the rest of the population.

Subsidies rising from £265 million in 1946 to £465 million in 1949 kept the price of food low. The Minister of Health, Aneurin Bevan, a Welsh miner whose eloquence combined persuasiveness with invective, organized a housing programme which by 1950 had produced three-quarters of a million houses, and government controls ensured that only a small percentage of these were built for private ownership; the vast majority were on council estates to be let at very low rents. National Insurance and the National Health Service, both the fruits of the Beveridge plan, had been established by legislation in 1946 and were soon to form an immense charge on the budget, while the Butler Education Act of 1944 (see p. 361) involved its own programme of school building.

It was no wonder that income tax remained at 9 shillings (45p) in the pound; the higher income groups, beset by regulations, living on a monotonous diet, unable to repair or decorate their homes, were undoubtedly paying out a great deal and getting remarkably little for it, and Attlee, with his memories as a social worker in the East End of London, had every intention that this should be so. Anger mounted among the Conservatives, hardly mollified by Aneurin Bevan's reference to them as 'lower than vermin'. It was declared that the five-day week agreement of 1947 with the trade unions was utterly inappropriate and that with unemployment at less than 2 per cent the workers were not making the fullest possible effort, a fact of which the Coal Board was uneasily aware. It was argued that the government was being utterly extravagant at a time of appalling economic crisis, and although it could be said in reply that low food prices and low rents were keeping wage demands down and were thus helping the export drive, Cripps himself felt by 1949 that redistribution of income had gone far enough. In the main, however, Attlee stood firm. He was determined not to repeat the failure of 1931 and refused to allow the pressure of external difficulties to dictate the government's social programme.

The essence of the National Insurance Act was its comprehensiveness. As the Beveridge Report had suggested, it covered sickness and unemployment benefit, retirement pensions and maternity and death grants. The entire adult population was compulsorily included within it and paid a flat rate of contribution as employed, self-employed or non-employed persons. To this would be added contributions from the employer and the Exchequer. The hope was that since it applied to everyone without any kind of means test, the benefits received would not suffer from the stigma of earlier schemes which had been regarded as a form of state charity for the poor. However, in case its provisions were inadequate for those at the lowest level of poverty, a National Assistance Act was passed in 1948, establishing supplementary benefits for those who could prove extreme need. By the end of 1950 these allowances were being paid to 1,350,000 people, half of them old age pensioners, and with this reappearance of the means test it seemed that the government had come closer to the prewar systems than they would have wished.

The most sweeping and idealistic reform carried out in the sphere of social welfare was the National Health Service, established by Act of Parliament in 1946. Here again the government was determined to abolish the previous two-tier system, whereby those who could afford it paid privately for medical treatment, while the poor had to make do with an inferior system of panel patients. In future all forms of medical and dental service were to be available free for every individual in the country, ranging from hospital treatment to the supply of medicine, spectacles and false teeth. Hospitals were to be nationalized and run by hospital management committees set up by regional boards. Everyone was entitled to choose their own general practitioner from lists organized by local medical executive councils, and the entire cost would be met out of national revenue, apart from a small portion of the national insurance contributions.

The aim of the scheme was admirable, but many doctors resented the thought of becoming salaried civil servants and feared the loss of a professional relationship with their patients. For two years Aneurin Bevan found himself locked in a struggle with the British Medical Association, who at one point in December 1947 seemed to have the support of 90 per cent of their members for boycotting the whole scheme. The consultants and specialists, however, favoured it, and Bevan exploited this divide by conceding that there should be a number of beds in state hospitals for fee-paying patients, whose specialists could make their own charges, and that the teaching hospitals should not come under the regional boards. Later he won over the rank and file of general practitioners by agreeing that instead of being salaried they should receive a flat rate for every patient on their list; there would be no powers of direction over doctors, and compensation would be paid for private practices which were no longer to be bought and sold. Early in 1948 thousands of doctors were already signing on for the National Health Service. The council of the BMA, after having put up a fight of which any trade union would be proud, decided to accept the situation and on 5 July 1948 the National Health Service came into operation.

In one field the Labour government did not have to introduce its own legislation. The Education Act of 1944 had effectively resolved the problem of the voluntary schools and the way was now open for local authorities to develop their schemes for free secondary education for all children. What is interesting is that Labour was content to leave it at that. At a time when the sense of class friction was strong, they might well have been expected to move on from there to an attack upon the public schools. Instead, they left these strictly alone, possibly because they had too much to do in other spheres, possibly because they believed that the state system could be so improved that the public schools would become inferior and fall away into bankruptcy. But although the public schools escaped, the local grammar schools could hardly hope to do so. They were needed to implement the plan for free secondary education, and parents of the lower middle class, who had long regarded these schools as their own preserve for a modest fee beyond the reach of the working class, found that they would now only be available if their children were selected at the age of eleven plus. A hundred and sixty-five of the older grammar schools did retain a degree of freedom, drawing direct grants from the Exchequer on the understanding that half of their places would be free. Apart from this, the only fee-paying secondary education now available was at the independent public schools, which were much more expensive. Thus it seemed that, in education at least, Labour was not only prepared to countenance the two-tier situation, but had also ensured that the upper tier would become still more exclusive.

Furthermore, as local authorities, many of them under Labour control, went ahead with organizing the three streams of secondary education, it soon became clear that selection at the age of eleven plus had incorporated another aspect of the two-tier system within the structure of state education itself. The theory, reinforced by a great faith in the infallibility of intelligence tests, was based on a belief that children should have the type of education for which they were best suited. In effect, the eleven plus selection became a competition for the limited number of grammar school places, the only road to higher academic qualifications. Since there were virtually no secondary technical schools, those who were not selected (often as many as 80 per cent) were left with the prospect of a secondary modern and an end of schooling at fifteen. Thus it appeared that the whole course of a lifetime might be settled at the age of eleven. In the main, Labour did not see anything wrong with this at first. This may have been because, before the war, the truly tragic figure had been the clever boy who, owing to poverty at home, had been unable to take up the scholarships that he had won, and the eleven plus, opening the way to a free grammar school education and thence to a university by means of a county grant, appeared at least to establish equality of opportunity. It was only later that this assumption came to be questioned (see p. 417).

There were many other measures apart from these major areas of reform. In 1946 the Trade Disputes Act repealed the Act of 1927 (see p. 251), so that general strikes were now no longer illegal, and trade unionists, if they wished, had actively to opt *out* of making a financial contribution to the political fund. In the same year an Act was passed for the designing of entirely new towns in order to syphon off the agglomerations of population in larger cities, and fourteen of these were planned during the Labour administration. In 1947 the Town and Country Planning Act gave local authorities wide powers to control the development of whole areas. In 1948 the Representation of the People Act finally rounded off a democratic uniformity by ending the system whereby more affluent members of the community had been able to enjoy two or three parliamentary votes. The university seats and the business premises vote were abolished; the six months residential qualification was swept away, and in future the local government franchise was to be the same as that for parliamentary elections.

In the main, the inspiration behind much of this welter of legislation would seem to have come more from the memory of the past than from any rigid doctrine for the future. In their deep concern for social welfare Labour's measures had largely been a demonstration that a democratic and constitutional government could avert the harsher inequalities of the interwar period. They had not established a Socialist society, and a later Labour minister, Richard Crossman, commented: 'The nationalization of half a dozen major industries, the construction of an all-in system of social security and a free health service, and the tentative application of planning to the national economy—the achievement of these reforms seemed to have exhausted the content of British Socialism.' Still, however much the left-wing might deplore this moderation, these years do mark a point of fundamental change, and the economic impact of the war and the constructive work of the Attlee administration had together established a new pattern of British life that went far beyond the dreams of the more radical members of the Liberal government before 1914.

33

The New Shape of Foreign Policy 1945-1951

1. The cold war

In the summer of 1945 the British could reflect with weary relief that they had won their second great war against Germany. The long chapter that had opened with the challenge to their naval power at the beginning of the century was now closed, but the cost had been appalling and the economic difficulties that had so hampered Labour's domestic rule had also brought a radical alteration in Great Britain's position in the world.

The scene on the Continent was still worse. The path of war had spread devastation across the plains of Russia and Poland, up the entire length of Italy and throughout Normandy and the Low Countries. Newly established governments struggled everywhere against the likelihood of famine. Germany, devoid of any form of civil administration, her great cities transformed by air bombardment into mountains of rubble, her roads and railways smashed, lay at the mercy of the two vast military machines that had met over her dead body. In Asia the colonial empires of Great Britain, France and the Netherlands were now freed of the Japanese armies that had overrun them, but it remained to be seen whether those countries would have the strength to reclaim them. The old assumptions of world power were no longer valid; sheer exhaustion had created a great vacuum, and the new assumptions, still to be shaped, rested on the attitudes of America and Russia, whose wartime partnership would now have to stand a different kind of strain.

Despite all this the British and American governments do not seem to have been apprehensive of any immediate clash. In London the Labour administration was highly optimistic about maintaining friendly relations with Russia. At the Foreign Office the robust bluntness of Ernest Bevin, schooled in the rough world of industrial dispute, might be in odd contrast to the style of earlier foreign secretaries, but he was convinced that this was to his advantage in that 'left could speak to left'. In Washington the American administration under President Truman had great hopes of developing an idealistic sense of kinship with Russia, and would hear nothing of spheres of influence in Europe which Churchill had considered to be the only workable basis for an arrangement with Stalin (see p. 374). The Americans hoped for a rapid withdrawal from the Continent, after which the European states would put their own affairs in order without interference from outside. UNRRA (the United Nations Relief and Rehabilitation Administration), largely financed by the United States, would supply immediate aid in food and raw materials to the countries which had been overrun by Germany, and for the future the settlement of disputes was to be in the hands of the Security Council of the United Nations Organization (UNO) inaugurated at San Francisco in April 1945 as a more effective successor, it was hoped, to the League of Nations.

It was not long before these illusions were dispelled. At the meeting at Potsdam in July 1945 the victors could agree that Germany should be disarmed and remain for the moment under four areas of military occupation, with four corresponding sectors in Berlin. Beyond this there was only dissension. Russia intended to retain that eastern region of Poland that she had gained by the Nazi-Soviet pact of August 1939, and Poland was to be compensated with east German territory up to the line of the western Neisse river, not the eastern Neisse as the British and the Americans had thought. In addition, Stalin was determined that Germany should pay reparations of twenty billion dollars, half of which would be Russia's share. The western Allies, with unhappy memories of the reparations demanded at the time of the Versailles settlement, held back, but eventually agreed that the Russians should at least begin to help themselves in the form of food and capital equipment. Meanwhile, the acquisition of Bessarabia from Romania had extended the Russian frontier on the Black Sea down to the delta of the Danube, and Stalin was now bringing pressure to bear on Turkey, so that Russia might have greater control over the Straits.

In the autumn further conferences of the foreign ministers at London and Moscow brought greater discord, which culminated in an open clash at the first meeting of the Security Council of the United Nations at London in January 1946. The western Powers, already suspicious of a Russian claim to trusteeship of Libya and the Dodecanese islands, demanded why Russian troops had not been evacuated from Azerbaijan in northern Iran; the Russians demanded why British troops were still in Greece and Indonesia, and French and British troops in Syria and the Lebanon.

These were the opening stages of what was later to be known as the

10 EUROPE AFTER 1945

cold war. The alliance between Russia and the west, only brought about by Hitler's invasion in 1941, was already falling apart. To the west it appeared that Stalin was making use of the defeat of Germany to promote the advance of international Communism into the heart of Europe. By 1947 the governments of most of the countries of eastern Europe—Poland, Hungary, Romania, Albania and Bulgaria—had succumbed to Communist control. The Baltic states, Estonia, Latvia and Lithuania, and a part of east Prussia had been absorbed directly into Soviet territory. In Yugoslavia the Communist partisan leader, Tito, had never relinquished the power which victory had given him, while in Greece Communist guerrillas, who had originally been fought off by British troops, resumed a civil war in 1946 from bases in the north. To a student of nineteenth-century Europe there was nothing very new in this resurgence of the Eastern Question; what was new was the way in which Soviet Russia seemed to be coming close to its solution, thereby justifying the fears that had led the Czechs and the Poles before the war to refuse any Russian assistance against Hitler.

Ideology was not the only factor that prompted the attitude of the Russian government. They knew that Communism was anathema to the capitalist world. At the end of the war the western Allies had enormous forces spread halfway across Europe, and they were in possession of an atom bomb to which the Russians had no conceivable answer at this time. The acquisition of territorial space on their western frontier had always been the principal hope of Russian defence; it had been the motive for their pact with Hitler in 1939 and now the establishment of Soviet control over eastern Europe enabled them to widen that *cordon sanitaire* against future attack. Mutual mistrust is the simplest explanation of the cold war, and it was ironical that the speed with which Stalin took advantage of the situation in 1945 was to encourage the west to hasten the revival of Germany, the very hope to which Hitler's propagandists had clung in the last stages of the war.

There was another irony in the impact of all this on the Labour government's foreign policy. Left was certainly speaking to left, but mainly in terms of abuse. At the beginning the Americans were still inclined to view the Russians through the rose-tinted spectacles of the wartime alliance and to be more concerned about the colonial aspirations of western European Powers. It was the British who bore the main burden of resistance to Russian claims, and Bevin who had to listen to charges of warmongering and imperialism, to which he replied with a vividness not often associated with the Foreign Office. Thus, when Churchill in a speech in the United States in March 1946 spoke of an iron curtain that had descended across the Continent, there did not appear to be very much difference between Conservative and Labour foreign policy—not a very comforting thought for some Labour MPs. 'Hasn't Anthony Eden grown fat?' commented one of them.

But if British foreign policy seemed to be reverting to an earlier pattern, one fundamental element had changed for ever. The economic weakness of Great Britain and the emergence of vastly stronger Powers meant that she could never again hold a commanding position in the councils of the world. In February 1947, that bleak winter during which snow had brought British industry to a halt, she made the final admission of the changed state of her fortunes. The American government was informed that she could not afford to give aid to Greece and Turkey against Communist pressure for more than another month. It was this that brought the United States openly into the cold war. On 12 March the President outlined to Congress what became known as the Truman doctrine, and there followed a grant of 400 million dollars for the support of the existing Greek and Turkish regimes.

This was only the beginning. In June 1947 the American Secretary of State, General Marshall, in a famous speech at Harvard made his offer of an immense programme of financial assistance to bring about a revival of the European economy. In economic terms it certainly did not make sense for one industrial country to be rich while all the others remained poor. In political terms the economic morass in which Europe was still wallowing was bound to mean governmental instability and the likelihood of Communist gains still further west. The proposal was actually made to the whole of Europe but, as the Americans had foreseen, Russia rejected it and those countries within her sphere of influence reluctantly had to do likewise.

The nations of western Europe responded at once. In July a committee of European Economic Cooperation met at Paris. By September it had presented its report to Washington and in April 1948 Congress accepted the scheme which would provide Europe with 17 thousand million dollars over the next four years. It is, of course, possible to regard Marshall Aid cynically as an attempt to stop France and Italy going Communist, but even if that was one of its aims, it was nevertheless an extraordinarily farsighted and generous measure, remote from the narrow competitive manner in which the world had faced the great depression after 1929, and it was to form the basis of the remarkable recovery of western Europe in the 1950s.

From now on there was a steady escalation of the cold war. In

February 1948 a coup in Prague established a Communist government in Czechoslovakia. In the following month Great Britain, France, Belgium, the Netherlands and Luxembourg signed the Treaty of Brussels, setting up a consultative council of foreign ministers for a combined system of military defence. And then in the summer of 1948 things took a more serious turn over the question of Germany.

At Potsdam Russia's claim to some reparations from the western zones of occupation had only been granted in return for her accepting the western Powers' demand that Germany should be treated as a single economic unit. The British and American zones, heavily industrial and with a population swollen with refugees from the east, depended vitally on food from the agricultural regions of Germany now largely under Russian occupation. The Russians, however, had no intention of letting food cross their lines into the western zones and the British found themselves paying out heavily from their limited fund of dollars in order to ward off German starvation in their zone. Accordingly, in May 1946, reparations to Russia from the western half of Germany were stopped and the American and British zones were combined. For the next eighteen months the deadlock continued, the Russians demanding a renewal of reparations, the British and the Americans demanding that east German agricultural produce should be available in the western areas. Finally, it seemed that no agreement would ever be reached over the question of a united Germany and in June 1948 a preliminary plan was drawn up in London for the organizing of a western German Federal Republic out of the British, American and French zones of occupation. This was accompanied by a currency reform throughout the whole region, without which no German economic recovery would be possible.

This decision by the west to go their own way in a settlement with that part of Germany under their control awoke a furious response from the Russians. They had already denounced Marshall Aid as a piece of American economic imperialism and they now regarded the merging of the three western zones of occupation as a first step towards bringing West Germany into an anti-Russian bloc of Powers. They declared that this was a unilateral termination of the Potsdam agreements and decided to make their point by putting pressure on the western Allies' sectors of occupation in Berlin. Accordingly, on 19 June 1948, they stopped all land traffic from the west to Berlin.

This was a natural line of retaliation. With the deterioration of east–west relations these sectors had become little more than a hostage, a tiny island of territory a hundred miles within the Russian zone of occupation, offering a simple means whereby Russia could create difficulties for the west. They were by now a useless relic of an earlier situation, but it was politically out of the question to abandon West Berlin, since this would represent to the world another advance for Communism, and the Allies had consequently to improvise a vastly expensive system of supply by air. The blockade lasted nearly a year, during which some 200,000 flights kept West Berlin alive with 1·5 million tons of supplies, until eventually Stalin decided to call it off in May 1949.

The significance of the Berlin blockade was that it had brought relations between Russia and the west to a point just short of open conflict, and it was against this background early in 1949 that a new alliance between the United States and the signatories of the Treaty of Brussels was formulated. In addition to these Powers the North Atlantic Treaty, signed on 4 April 1949, included Canada, Iceland, Denmark, Norway, Italy and Portugal. It was essentially a military alliance for mutual defence and the North Atlantic Treaty Organization (NATO) set up a permanent international staff and headquarters, known as SHAPE (Supreme Headquarters, Allied Powers Europe) at Paris. The military forces under its command did not number much more than a dozen divisions and a few hundred planes in Europe, and this would mean little against the immense forces that Soviet Russia could deploy. The creation of NATO marked, nevertheless, a decisive step in the cold war; it had committed the United States and Great Britain to a continental alliance in peacetime, a unique development in the history of both countries, and with that the great divide in Europe had finally been consolidated.

2. *The transformation of empire*

While the two Power blocs had been tightening their grip on the areas under their control in Europe, the Labour government had been busy dismantling much of the British Empire in Asia. The principal feature of this policy was the British withdrawal from India. The Government of India Act of 1935 had implied eventual Dominion status at some unspecified future date, but by 1942 the Congress party had still been holding out for immediate independence and would not consider a mere promise of Dominion status after the war. 'I prefer Indian chaos to British order,' Gandhi had said, but with the approach of the Japanese army through Burma the British dared not risk Indian chaos and the uncompromising leaders of the Congress party, including Gandhi and his disciple Nehru, had been imprisoned until the end of the war. By then it was clear that the continuation of British rule could only be maintained with a considerable military force in India, equally clear that they could afford neither the economic cost of this, nor the antagonism which it would arouse in the United States.

This created no problem for the Labour government. They had always wanted independence for India and now practical necessity lent force to the political ideal. The only difficulty was how to accomplish it. The Muslim League, led by Mohammed Ali Jinnah, representing a minority of 80 million, wanted partition, so that they could establish their own state of Pakistan; the Congress party, dominated by the Hindus, insisted that India should remain undivided. For months the deadlock continued, while Muslims and Hindus slaughtered each other in riots in various parts of India, and it began to look as if it was as difficult to shed an empire as it was to acquire one. At this point Attlee and his cabinet made a ruthless decision. To force the two Indian parties to reach agreement, they imposed a time limit. On 20 February 1947 the Prime Minister announced publicly that Great Britain would in any case withdraw from India by June 1948 and Lord Mountbatten was sent out to replace Wavell as Viceroy to organize the evacuation.

Mountbatten's rule as the last Viceroy was a *tour de force* of energy and diplomacy. Immediately after his arrival in March 1947 he recognized that Jinnah's aim of an independent state of Pakistan was the only hope for a lasting settlement. His greatest achievement was to persuade Gandhi and Nehru to accept partition, but he had also to win over the Indian princes, who eventually agreed to join one or other of the two states. He was convinced that speed was essential and the British cabinet concurred with his view that the date of withdrawal should be brought forward to 15 August 1947.

The incidence of Muslim majorities was such that Pakistan had to consist of two separate regions on each side of India—eastern Bengal and the western Punjab, to which would be attached Baluchistan and Sind—and the frontiers were rapidly defined by a boundaries commission consisting of Muslims and Hindus and headed by a British barrister, whose casting vote was often the only means of reaching a decision in areas where the populations were inextricably mixed. In July the Indian Independence Bill establishing India and Pakistan as self-governing Dominions was swept through all its stages at Westminster in the space of a week, and on 15 August 1947 the British Raj was no more.

To Gandhi the division of India into 80 million Pakistani and 320 million Indians seemed an utter tragedy; yet the apparent inability of Muslims and Hindus to live at peace in one community was at once emphasized by appalling weeks of bloodshed in the summer of 1947. Hundreds of thousands of Muslims and Hindus died in a vicious succession of massacre and counter-massacre, as they attempted to move across the new frontiers into whichever state was appropriate to their religion. The supreme irony was when Gandhi, who throughout his struggle for independence had always set his face against violence, was assassinated in January 1948 by a Hindu extremist who objected to his tolerance of Muslims.

The Indian princes in the main presented no lasting difficulty. Consoled with the retention of their private fortunes, they faded from the political scene, as their states were absorbed into India or Pakistan. Only two gave any trouble. Hyderabad, with a Hindu population and surrounded by Indian territory, was occupied by Indian forces, when its Muslim ruler attempted to remain independent. There was no such simple solution in the north in Kashmir, whose territory adjoined both India and West Pakistan. The Hindu ruler opted for India; Nehru accepted this, but the bulk of the population were Muslim and looked to Pakistan whose subsequent resistance to India's claim was to bring the two countries to a lasting confrontation.

Anyway, the deed was done. Immense efforts were made to build up civil administrations for the two new countries, aided by Mountbatten, who with Nehru's agreement became the first Governor-General of India. Both countries decided to remain within the Commonwealth, although Nehru set the constitutional lawyers a problem by insisting that India should be a republic, with the result that the British monarch, who had formerly been Emperor of India, had eventually to acquire a new all-purpose title as Head of the Commonwealth. In 1948 all these developments were inevitably followed by the independence of Ceylon (now Sri Lanka), who chose to retain Dominion status, and of Burma, who moved out of the Commonwealth entirely. Thus, in less than three years the Attlee administration had succeeded in liquidating a large part of the British Empire, while retaining a peculiar but friendly association with much of it. The loss caused a good deal of bitter heartburning among some Conservatives, but the savage fighting in Indo-China and the East Indies, where the French and the Dutch were trying to regain their former colonial possessions, only served to show the wisdom of it, and it would be possible to reverse an earlier witticism and to say that the British lost their Empire in a fit of presence of mind.

The granting of independence in Asia had been made feasible and was partly necessitated by the earlier encouragement of representative and consultative bodies and the gradual assimilating of educated members of the local population into the civil administrations. Not even a Labour government imagined that such a situation existed in Africa.

What the government intended to do here was to send out a vastly increased number of experts in forestry and agriculture to lay the foundations of an eventual independence which at that time seemed many years away. For the British tax-payer the cost of this colonial administration rose from £5·5 million in 1939 to £41·5 million in 1950. Inevitably some mistakes were made; a groundnuts scheme in Tanganyika and an attempt to produce eggs in Gambia proved to be expensive failures. Some modification in direct colonial rule was made in 1946 in Nigeria and on the Gold Coast (later Ghana), when legislative councils with African majorities were set up, and although a new sense of impatience among local leaders was to take events through the predictable course of riots and imprisonments, the Labour government could reckon to have added a fairly powerful gust to what a later Conservative Prime Minister, Harold Macmillan, called the wind of change.

All this transformation of Empire might claim a certain aura of idealism, combined with a shrewd common sense in coming to terms with new circumstances. No such happy coincidence was possible in the Middle East. Here Great Britain was condemned to wrestle with the old dilemma; the national home for the Jews in Palestine, which lay under the protection of the British mandate from the League of Nations, had continued to be a source of resentment among the Arab states whose friendship was vital to Great Britain on account of the oilfields and the proximity of the Russian frontier in Asia. For a long time the Arabs had watched with concern the growth of the Jewish population in Palestine, but by exercising a strict control over immigration (see p. 313) during the war the British had been able to prevent the tension reaching fever pitch and by 1945 there were only about 600,000 Jews alongside a million Arabs living in Palestine.

Now, however, this proportion seemed likely to be completely upset by an influx of the hundreds of thousands of European Jews who were all that had survived the Nazi regime and who with the strong support of the Zionist movement were clamouring to be allowed to settle in Palestine. Already in 1944 the Labour party had advocated a greatly increased immigration, which would eventually create a Jewish majority, but shortly after taking office Ernest Bevin became convinced of the fierce Arab reaction which this would arouse throughout the Middle East; it would also threaten the sensitive negotiations with the Muslims in India, and almost certainly lead to a Palestinian war which Russia might hope to turn to her advantage. The British government accordingly held back on any change of policy for the moment.

This at once led to a wrangle with President Truman, who, conscious of the Jewish vote in subsequent American elections, urged the British to allow an immediate entry of 100,000 Jews. Early in 1946 an Anglo-American committee of inquiry endorsed this view, but the commission of experts appointed to explore the implementing of the plan virtually nullified it by stipulating that the Arabs must give their consent, a stipulation that Truman promptly set aside. In July 1946 the British, still looking for some means of preserving peace in Palestine, proposed a form of partition with a Jewish and an Arab province under a federal government. At the same time they suggested that the immediate plight of the European Jews might be resolved if the United States and Great Britain would open their doors to them, but neither of these schemes was acceptable at Washington.

Meanwhile, the Jews in Palestine had decided to seek their own salvation and had mounted a highly effective resistance movement, organizing illegal immigration and carrying out a series of attacks on British forces, including the destruction of the army headquarters in the King David Hotel in Jerusalem in July 1946, with the loss of ninety-one lives. Inevitably the Arabs too began to retaliate with their own underground forces. It was hardly surprising that Bevin's references to the Americans and the Jews became less and less diplomatic, and that a war-weary British public soon sickened at the thought of further military commitment. All the efforts of the British to handle an electric situation responsibly were being ignored by the Jews, the Arabs and the United States alike; their soldiers were dying in a hideous tripartite struggle, while Zionist propaganda branded them as the successors of Hitler. Finally, patience was exhausted. In April 1947 the whole matter was put to the United Nations, and while it was under discussion there, the British government announced that they intended to resign their mandate and to leave Palestine by August 1948. As Bonar Law had said in 1922 (see p. 205), the circumstances were not appropriate for them to continue to act as the policeman of the world.

Nor apparently were they for anyone else. The General Assembly of the United Nations produced their own plan for partitioning Palestine into a Jewish state and an Arab state, with Jerusalem under international control. Once again Jews and Arabs both rejected this, and if the plan was to take effect, a neutral peace-keeping force would be needed to impose it. The British were clearly precluded from this role, since the Jewish guerrilla movement regarded them as the enemy; none of the United Nations, however, was prepared to contribute to such a force and accordingly, on the departure of the British, the matter was left to the sword.

In June 1948 the Jews proclaimed the new state of Israel with Chaim Weizmann as president and David Ben-Gurion as prime minister. The surrounding Arab countries at once seized their chance to wipe out the intruders, but invading forces from Egypt and Transjordan were flung back by the more efficient Israeli army. The war lasted for a year, while the United Nations made unavailing attempts to mediate, and eventually in the summer of 1949 a series of military truces gave Israel a rather greater area than she would have gained from the original partition plan.

There could be no greater indication of the weakened position of Great Britain after 1945 than the drastic modification of her control of the Middle East. At the same time as she withdrew from Palestine, conversations with Egypt were anticipating her eventual evacuation of the Nile valley and the Suez Canal zone. In these new circumstances it was vital that she should retain the friendship of the Arab states, but that friendship was sorely tried when in 1950 a tripartite declaration by the United States, Great Britain and France recognized the existing frontiers of Israel. There seemed no escape from this recurring dilemma and the opportunity that it might offer to Russia. For the moment, however, Russia made no move beyond the formal recognition of Israel, and before long the attention of the world was to be drawn to a much more remote area of Asia.

3. The Korean war and the fall of the Labour government

In 1949 the whole context of the cold war was suddenly transformed when China became a Communist state. During the war with Japan Chinese Communists under Mao-tse-tung and Nationalists under Chiang-kai-shek had temporarily shelved their long quarrel, but after 1945 this uneasy truce had soon broken down. The evident corruption of the Nationalist regime aided Mao in gaining the allegiance of the peasantry; Stalin provided him with war material captured from the Japanese in Manchuria, and soon Chiang-kai-shek's forces found themselves thrust back towards the coast, as popular dissatisfaction with the Nationalist government cut the ground from under their feet. By September 1949 they had been driven to take refuge on the island of Formosa, and on the mainland Mao proclaimed the People's Republic of China.

Russia gave formal recognition to the new government straight away and there followed a treaty of friendship and mutual assistance between the two in February 1950. In fact, Stalin may have had some misgivings over the speed with which Mao had gained total victory and future relations between Russia and China might not necessarily be smooth. In the emotional atmosphere of the cold war, however, these more subtle considerations were obscured by the simple thought that the Communist world had made an enormous acquisition of territory, and among the Americans there was a particularly bitter resentment that China, with whom they had always fostered a special relationship, should have joined the enemy camp. Great Britain, reckoning that the facts of the situation must be accepted and anxious about Hong Kong, recognized the new government, but the United States adamantly refused to do so, establishing a trade embargo and opposing the admission of Communist China to the United Nations.

At the same time this new sense of alarm was further strengthened by the knowledge that in 1949 the Russians had succeeded in exploding their first atomic bomb. In this they had been greatly aided by certain leading atomic physicists in Great Britain, who had managed to pass a good deal of secret information to Moscow before they were caught or had made their escape to the other side of the iron curtain. In the United States, where public opinion was still reeling from the shock of a Communist China, these revelations led to a witch hunt, stirred up by the Republican Senator McCarthy, implying that any senior figure in American public or professional life with the slightest liberal inclinations was almost certainly a Communist agent. There was a note of hysteria in the mounting panic, and if any open clash were now to occur somewhere along the border between Communist and non-Communist states, the cold war could suddenly cease to be cold and might well become atomic. It was at this terrible moment in the world's affairs that hostilities broke out between North and South Korea (map, p. 379).

The position in Korea, which had belonged to Japan since 1910, derived from the circumstances of the Japanese surrender in 1945. The Americans had only had sufficient troops to handle this in the southern half of the peninsula and the Russians had accordingly received the surrender of Japanese forces in the north. As in Germany, the line dividing the two zones, the 38th parallel, rapidly became another frontier. In the south Syngman Rhee set up a right-wing government with its capital at Seoul; in the north a Communist government was established. Unlike the situation in Germany, however, the armies of the great Powers then withdrew, the Russians in December 1948 and the Americans in June 1949.

The crisis came on 25 June 1950, when the North Korean army launched a major invasion across the 38th parallel and marched on

Seoul. The Americans were clearly determined to resist this with the dispatch of forces to South Korea from Japan. The trend of opinion in the west at this time was bound to produce such a response to a Communist incursion, but there was obviously grave danger that the war might not remain limited to Korea. The risk was substantially reduced, however, by two factors. On the day of the invasion an emergency meeting of the Security Council of the United Nations called on the North Koreans to withdraw and two days later appealed to all members to send aid to South Korea. The absence of the Russian delegate from the Security Council in protest at the exclusion of Communist China meant that there had been no likelihood of this being vetoed, and the Americans could now act under the guise of giving support to the United Nations. In addition to that, before actually sending their troops across to Korea on 28 June, the United States did gain some reasonable indication from Moscow that Russia would not actively interfere.

Even so, the subsequent oscillations of the Korean war could at any time have led to a more general conflict. By September 1950 General MacArthur had stopped the retreat in the south and had pushed back to the 38th parallel. The question now was whether to carry the war into North Korean territory. The General Assembly of the United Nations gave their blessing for a continued advance which might lead to a reunited Korea, and by November MacArthur had swept up through North Korea as far as the Yalu river, which marked the northern boundary adjoining Manchuria. This brought things to a new peak of danger. China, faced with a victorious American army so close to her own frontier, sent 300,000 troops to the aid of the North Koreans. Technically they were 'volunteers', but this fiction would not have prevented a considerable extension of the area of the war if MacArthur had had his way and been allowed to bomb their bases in Manchuria. By January 1951 the overwhelming weight of the Chinese reinforcements had turned the tide of battle. Before long the United Nations troops had been pushed back well to the south of Seoul, and it was not until the spring that they were able to regain the line of the 38th parallel.

The British part in all this had been reluctant and minimal. In the Commons there had been unanimous agreement that Great Britain must support the United Nations front, but her total effort never amounted to much more than two infantry brigades, an armoured regiment and a few planes. There was less unanimity over the crossing of the 38th parallel in September 1950, and by December American talk of attacking Manchuria and of the possible use of the atom bomb caused such alarm that Attlee flew to Washington for conversations with President Truman.

Here he did gain some reassurance, but it was clear that British and American attitudes towards the Far East were still very much at variance. The United States had no intention of following Great Britain's example in recognizing Communist China; their Seventh Fleet was now protecting Chiang-kai-shek's forces on Formosa from invasion and they still clung to the hope of establishing a united and independent Korea, whereas Attlee was thinking more in terms of the *status quo ante bellum*. To many Americans the British view smacked of appeasement, and in any case Attlee could not press too hard for an American disengagement in Asia, since the corollary of this might be a similar abandonment of Europe. Still, Truman was aware of the dangers. Manchuria remained untouched, and in April 1951 he finally dismissed General MacArthur who had issued a policy statement from his headquarters, in which he envisaged a new advance into North Korea as the first step in an expanding war to smash Asian Communism. After this the lines settled down around the 38th parallel and there seemed some hope of negotiating a peace settlement.

The Korean war did great harm to the Labour government. The fighting was too far away to arouse a sense of national excitement and Great Britain's involvement seemed only to suggest that she was tied to the apron-strings of American foreign policy, a thought equally abhorrent to right-wing patriots and left-wing pacifists. Furthermore, it coincided with pressure in two other spheres which heightened the impression of British powerlessness. In 1951 a new prime minister in Iran, Dr Musaddiq, announced the expropriation of the Anglo-Iranian Oil Company with a policy of nationalization. American opinion and the pessimistic views of the service chiefs ruled out any military action to prevent this and the Company's staff had to quit Iran, leaving their installations in Iranian possession. Ultimately the lack of an oil-tanker fleet was to bring Musaddiq's scheme to nothing and the Company was restored to its former position. At the time, however, it looked like just one more instance of British decline, and in October 1951 the Egyptians were encouraged by this to repudiate an existing treaty with Great Britain and to lay claim to the Sudan.

A more serious consequence of the Korean war was that the new world demand for war materials created a boom which sent up British import prices by 41 per cent between April 1950 and May 1951. There was no comparable increase in exports, since British industry had been gearing itself to a peacetime market, and the surplus of £300 million in the balance of payments in 1950 changed to a deficit of £400 million in 1951. Furthermore, a new arms programme in January 1951, involving an expenditure of £4,700 million over the next three years, diverted national revenue away from investment in the long-term projects of Labour domestic policy.

These economic consequences had the effect of emphasizing the latent divisions within the Labour party. The left-wing element were determined that the new measures should not mean any tampering with the welfare services, and when in the spring of 1951 it was decided that small charges should be made for spectacles and false teeth, Aneurin Bevan, Harold Wilson and John Freeman resigned from the government. All this came at a time when ill health had already caused other losses. Sir Stafford Cripps, who had virtually worked himself to death, had had to retire in October 1950 and died in 1952; Ernest Bevin, suffering from heart trouble, held on at the Foreign Office until March 1951 and died a few weeks later. Indeed, most of the leading ministers in the government were by now utterly worn out, and Attlee himself was in hospital with a duodenal ulcer when he had to cope with the Aneurin Bevan revolt.

Meanwhile, through the period of the Labour administration the Conservatives had been busy reconstructing a political platform for their party. The leaders of the interwar years had now mostly gone and a new generation of Conservative MPs was in a position to formulate more progressive policies which they had previously been too junior to put through. The principal architect in this was R. A. Butler. Under him the party set about devising a new Conservative philosophy as significant as Peel's Tamworth Manifesto in 1834. He collected able young recruits for the party, as they emerged from the services—Iain McLeod, Enoch Powell and Reginald Maudling—and in 1947 an industrial policy committee outlined a programme which accepted the bulk of Labour legislation and went on to advocate a mixed economy in which private enterprise would operate under the aegis of governmental stimulus and control. In other words, the alternative to Labour was not to be *laissez-faire*, but a Keynesian type of loose state supervision, not unlike the course advocated by Harold Macmillan in his book *The Middle Way* in 1938. Perhaps this was not altogether surprising as Macmillan was a member of the committee, and he was to be a most exuberant exponent of the Industrial Charter that it produced. 'The Socialists are afraid of it,' he said on its publication. 'Lord Beaverbrook dislikes it. And the Liberals say it is too liberal to be fair. What more can one want? Was ever a child born under such a lucky star? It is, of course, a challenge as well as a charter. It is the true doctrine of the middle way.'¹ It was certainly a powerful bid by the Conservatives to recapture that central section of the electoral vote which was the crucial area in the struggles of the two-party system.

Even so, it was to take two general elections to get rid of Labour, who actually increased their total popular vote in each of them. The decisive factors were to be the marked growth of the Conservative vote in two abnormally high polls, and the peculiar working of the electoral system. In the general election of February 1950 Labour came back with 315 seats and a popular vote which had risen by more than a million to 13·25 million; the Conservatives gained 298 seats with a popular vote of 12·5 million, an increase of 2·5 million on 1945. With the margin so narrow in the House of Commons the Conservative Opposition pressed home the attack on an exhausted government, torn with internal conflict, until eighteen months later Attlee decided on a further dissolution. In the election of October 1951 the Labour popular vote rose to nearly 14 million, a quarter of a million more than that of the Conservatives, but the distribution of the votes was such that the balance of seats in the House of Commons was almost exactly reversed. The Conservatives came back with 321, while Labour had 295. It must have been almost with a sense of relief that on this result Attlee resigned, and Winston Churchill embarked on forming his first peacetime administration.

34
The Problems of the Middle
Way 1951–1965

The political pattern of the two decades following the Attlee administration is very simple. Victory in three general elections was to give the Conservatives thirteen years of continuous rule, to be followed by six years of Labour. Under the Conservatives Winston Churchill remained Prime Minister until his retirement in April 1955, when he was succeeded by Sir Anthony Eden. The strain of the Suez crisis and the breakdown of his health led to Eden's departure in January 1957, when his place was taken by Harold Macmillan. Then in October 1963 ill health forced Macmillan to retire, and Sir Alec Douglas Home succeeded him after an anguished period of lobbying over the party leadership. The Conservative reign was now nearly at an end. The general election of October 1964 gave Labour a narrow majority. With this Harold Wilson formed a Labour administration and after a further election in March 1966 had strengthened his position in the Commons, remained in office until 1970.

This pattern of government since 1945 might seem to imply the swing of the pendulum between two sharply defined party philosophies, alternating in accordance with the vagaries of the uncommitted voter. Certainly there were many Labour MPs who, after their defeat in 1951, believed that Conservative rule would mean a return to prewar policies, a dismantling of Attlee's work and a considerable rise in unemployment. In fact, the reshaping of their programme, outlined in the Industrial Charter, meant that the Conservative governments repealed very little of the basic legislation introduced by the Attlee administration. They were merely determined to show that they could manage it better. Both parties accepted the mixed economy and although the old war cries were kept up, they only differed over the precise detail of the mixture. Thus governmental practice and legislation in these years suggested some great transvestite charade in which both sides appeared to be stealing each other's clothes, ending up in a vaguely Liberal guise, while the real Liberals were left with very little to cover their nakedness.

This air of broad similarity between the two parties was largely due to the universal influence that the theories of Keynes had had on modes of economic thought in the west, establishing a new framework of assumptions and methods which were common to Conservative and Labour Chancellors of the Exchequer alike. Throughout the world the economic nationalism of the 1930s had been modified on the basis of a new interdependence with such institutions as the International Monetary Fund, the World Bank and the General Agreement on Tariffs and Trade (GATT). And at home the economic techniques of wartime (see p. 359) continued to be used in the subsequent years of peace. The budget had ceased to be merely a balance sheet; it had become an instrument of fiscal policy with which a government could attempt to guide the economic life of the country by means of the manipulation of income tax and purchase tax and the control of credit.

Both parties worked along the lines of this revolutionary change. Each aimed to use these methods to establish economic expansion and full employment; each was sometimes forced to modify those aims temporarily in the light of existing circumstances. Thus in 1951 Butler, who became Chancellor of the Exchequer in Churchill's government, responded to the pressure of the Korean war (see p. 409) in a way that was so close to the work of Hugh Gaitskell, the last of Attlee's Chancellors (import quotas, the halving of the tourist foreign exchange allowance and restrictions on building) that *The Economist* coined a new concept, 'Butskellism'. The ending of the Korean war and the recovery of world trade soon allowed the Conservatives to move on to their principal policy of showing that 'Conservative freedom works' with the gradual removal of controls and the final disappearance of food rationing in 1954, but the fact remained that Conservative freedom was working in a mould very different from before the war.

Under Churchill, Harold Macmillan at the Ministry of Housing and Local Government was made responsible for a new target of 300,000 houses a year, a programme which was maintained throughout the whole period of Conservative rule. The new towns envisaged in the Act of 1946 were completed and further plans were developed for enlarging existing small towns in order to cope with the overspill populations of large urban areas. In agriculture the heavy subsidies with which the Act of 1947 had given farmers a guaranteed price for their produce were continued. In education the expansion of secondary schooling had by 1955 doubled the prewar figure for children remaining at school until the age of seventeen. Central grants to the universities were increased, as were county grants to students who gained admission. By 1960 eight new universities had been set up and in 1963 the Robbins Report called for a further expansion which would create a total of 390,000 student places by 1973. Between 1958 and 1965 345 miles of motorway had been constructed, and, in all, national and local government expenditure, which at the beginning of the century had been about 15 per cent of the gross national product, amounted to 40 per cent by 1960.

This acceptance by the Conservatives of a far greater degree of planning and control was bound to mean a continuing expansion of the whole apparatus of government that many of them would certainly have deplored in the past. In 1937 an Act of Parliament had declared that there should be a maximum of eighteen senior ministers and twenty junior ministers serving in the House of Commons at any one time, but the present requirements of administration demanded a revision of these figures. In 1957 a new maximum was established at seventy and this was only adequate until 1964 when it was extended again to ninety-one. The cabinet, numbering between sixteen and twenty-three, now operated at the head of a mass of non-cabinet ministers, and this in turn brought new complications in the overlapping of responsibilities. As early as 1951 Churchill had been aware of this problem and attempted a solution by creating a small number of overlords, senior ministers who would supervise the activities of a group of departments, but the scheme did not prove satisfactory and was eventually abandoned.

The most striking change lay in the growth of the power of the executive. By 1964 the number of civil servants had reached approximately half a million. The sheer quantity of statutory measures meant that governments had to rely more and more on processes of delegated legislation, whereby the detailed implementing of Acts of Parliament rested on the devising of regulations at departmental level. This naturally gave rise to fears for the rights of the individual, who might feel himself to be at the mercy of a vast anonymous machine, and a number of administrative tribunals were set up, to which the citizen might appeal against action by the state in matters of land, property, social services and transport. This was rather a dubious safeguard, since the tribunals were merely executive courts in which the department was acting as its own judge, but although a commission under Sir Oliver Franks reported on the question in 1957, the subsequent legislation went no further than establishing a council on tribunals to keep an eye on the whole system.

Equally, at the county and borough level, officialdom was becoming far more widespread and local governments seemed increasingly to be acting as the agents of the central authority. This was due partly to the nature of the new legislation, partly to the fact that local government income from rates was now insufficient to meet their expenditure— largely on education and council houses—so that they were far more dependent on grants from the Exchequer. Obviously the multiplicity of small units, based on the reorganization at the end of the nineteenth century (see p. 13), was not ideal for this new closeness of control, and a series of commissions during these years explored possible ways of simplifying the structure of local government, but very little had been effected before the Redcliffe-Maud commission was set up in 1965. In London, however, there was a radical change, when in 1963 the London County Council was replaced by the Greater London Council, which included within its sphere Middlesex and parts of Surrey, Kent and Hertfordshire.

These were not the only features that marked the break with the past. A new sense of humanity was at work, reflected particularly in a proliferation of social services for the benefit of children, the elderly and the infirm. During the Attlee administration an attempt to abolish capital punishment had failed, but in 1957 the Homicide Act did define much more narrowly the instances of murder for which the death penalty would be imposed. Corporal punishment in prison had been abolished in 1948, and a number of penal reforms included the establishment of open prisons for first offenders. All this was in sharp contrast to the earlier harshness which had lingered on since the Victorian era, but although the reformers had hoped that punishment would now mean rehabilitation rather than retribution, it was a sad fact that the crime rate continued to mount.

Further evidence of change was to be seen in a greater social mobility. The possibility of a university education was now open to sections of society who could never have afforded this before. At the same time promotion within professions was becoming less dependent on formal qualifications; by 1966, for example, 40 per cent of the administrative class of the Civil Service, which before 1939 had been almost exclusively the preserve of Oxford and Cambridge graduates, had been recruited from the executive class. There were, however, some exceptions to this and in the Foreign Service, the City, various fashionable regiments and the highest posts in the Civil Service the background of public school and Oxford and Cambridge still tended to predominate.

For the population as a whole the most remarkable aspect of these years was an atmosphere of affluence beyond the dreams of the 1930s.

In the home, washing-machines, refrigerators, television sets and record-players became articles of everyday life. Plastic goods and man-made fibres regaled the domestic consumer, and by the end of the 1950s supermarkets were supplying a wider range of foodstuffs than the average housewife had ever known before. Between 1950 and 1967 the number of cars on the roads rose from 2·5 to 9·5 million; package tours, inaugurated in the early 1950s, took millions of people for holidays in the sun of the Mediterranean.

It was the working class for whom this represented the most remarkable transformation of life, largely made possible by a general rise in wages and the existence of easy credit facilities. The most striking feature was a narrowing of differentials. The unskilled worker was soon earning between 70 and 85 per cent of the skilled worker's wage, and the older types of white-collar worker, who had enjoyed a distinct superiority in the 1930s, now found themselves materially on a par with the majority of the working class. The rich were still rich, but they paid heavily in taxation; the poor were still poor, but there were fewer of them, and in a survey of York in 1950 Seebohm Rowntree, returning once again to his old field of research, reckoned that only 3 per cent of the working-class population were living in primary poverty, in contrast to 31 per cent in 1935 (see p. 288).

In the light of all this it is perhaps surprising that the literature of the 1950s should have been one of protest. The hero became an anti-hero. In John Osborne's play *Look Back in Anger* and in Kingsley Amis's *Lucky Jim* he railed against a shallow social snobbery; in John Wain's *Hurry on Down* he drifted in a world that seemed to have no lasting values; in John Braine's *Room at the Top* he made material success his goal and became corrupted in the process. The authors were the angry young men of the decade and their work was directly in the tradition of English writing, rich in social comedy and imbued with a serious moral purpose; yet to the unemployed standing in the dole queues of the 1930s it would have seemed a strange response to the new affluence. Later, anger turned into mockery, and in the 1960s the wider audiences of television were treated to programmes in which most aspects of social and political life were held up to ridicule, known currently as 'satire', although far closer to the old-fashioned lampoon.

Meanwhile, young people were reacting in their own way to the changed circumstances in which they were growing up. The first manifestation of this in the early 1950s was the drainpipe trousers, velvet collar and bootlace tie of the Teddy Boy; soon rival gangs of 'mods' and 'rockers' were indulging in pitched battles at seaside resorts. The general characteristics of the teenage culture, however, were less violent, although highly disconcerting for older generations. The wages of the young unmarried worker now gave him a spending power unknown to previous generations; this was to create a market for a new form of musical entertainment, steeped in adolescent fantasy, as glittering pop stars performed before their screaming audiences, and by 1959 teenagers accounted for 40 per cent of the sale of records. Eventually the movement reached all classes of the young, often at odds with their elders, whom they did not regard as their betters and whose warnings and admonitions they condemned as hypocritical. They inhabited a world of coffee-bars and established their group identity with new fashions in clothes, long hair styles and a special vocabulary. Some dropped out; some espoused extreme political causes; some took to drugs; some made love, not war. For most, perhaps, it was simply a fling before the waters of later responsibilities closed over them, but for their parents it was a perplexing phenomenon which they watched with anger, with bewilderment and sometimes with a touch of envy.

In the political field the new affluence also had its consequences, since it appeared to rob the Labour Opposition of any attractive alternative to put before the electorate. The principal difficulty confronting Labour at this time, however, was the widening gap between the left- and right-wings of the party. The left-wing, led by Aneurin Bevan, saw the work of the 1945–51 administration merely as a first step on the road to outright Socialism. They wanted a far more extensive programme of nationalization and social services; in education selection at the age of eleven plus was seen to operate to the advantage of children of the middle class, and accordingly they demanded the development of comprehensive schools which would include all forms of secondary education without selection. Abroad, they hoped for better relations with Russia, strongly disliked the rearmament of West Germany (see p. 425) and mistrusted the various defence pacts which were being created by the United States around the world. The right-wing, led by Attlee, Morrison and Dalton, were far less doctrinaire in their assumptions; they were sure that the left-wing programme would be electorally disastrous, and in the prevailing economic climate they had the support of the larger trade unions. The struggle between the two sides went on throughout the early 1950s at the party conferences and within the PLP, and came to a climax in March 1955 when Bevan was supported by sixty-two Labour MPs in objecting to a British development of the hydrogen bomb, against Attlee who was prepared to accept it. In the circumstances it was only to be expected that the Conservatives should win the general election of May 1955 with an increased majority, gaining 344 seats against Labour's 277.

In December of that year Attlee finally decided to retire. In the subsequent ballot in the PLP Hugh Gaitskell, the nominee of the moderates, defeated Bevan by 157 votes to 70, and at first it seemed that the Labour party might be prepared to close their ranks behind the new leader. The Suez crisis of 1956 (see p. 427) helped to draw them together and by 1957 Bevan had dropped his demand that Great Britain should disarm unilaterally. At the same time, however, the trade unions, who had originally strongly supported Gaitskell, started to shift to the left, and Frank Cousins, who had become head of the Transport and General Workers' Union in 1956, began openly campaigning for unilateral disarmament. This was not the only issue. Gaitskell was closely associated with groups of moderates who wished to revise the party strategy. They wanted to move away from the cloth-cap image of the Labour voter, many of whom now owned their own homes and were employed in technological and white-collar occupations, and they were increasingly convinced that the general aim of total nationalization stated in Clause 4* of the 1918 constitution was now outmoded by the new notion of the mixed economy.

In 1959 the Conservatives won their third general election, again with an increased majority. On this Gaitskell concluded that the retention of the clause was doing positive harm to the electoral prospects of the party and was determined that it should be explicitly expunged at the Labour party conference that was held immediately afterwards. Many who sympathized with him in principle regarded this, nevertheless, as an unnecessary and tactically dangerous move. As Harold Wilson commented later, there was no need to remove the Book of Genesis from the Bible. To tamper with the mythology at this moment was bound to bring about a collision between the two wings of the party, but Gaitskell, who behind a bland impassive exterior was a man of intense emotional conviction, was determined to clarify the issue. The result was disastrous. At the conference the left-wing revealed their new strength by outvoting him, and Labour now appeared openly in disarray. A year later, at the 1960 conference, he was defeated again when he unsuccessfully opposed a motion that Great Britain should unilaterally abandon her nuclear weapons. Fortunately for him his retention of the leadership depended upon the support of the Parliamentary Labour Party who did not desert him. He was even able to get the nuclear decision reversed at the 1961 conference, but, as the time for the next general election approached, it did not seem that Labour was any nearer to resolving their differences.

* This was Clause 3(d) of the Labour party constitution and was accordingly referred to as Clause 4 (see p. 147).

All this while, however, the Conservative administrations had been encountering problems of their own. They had succeeded in encouraging full employment with a policy of expansion, but the resultant prosperity, although gratifying to the public, was bound to depend ultimately upon the economic position of Great Britain in the world. Viewed internally, her performance showed a remarkable improvement on the years before 1939. In agriculture government aid and a considerable investment in mechanization helped to raise output from an index figure of 88 in 1950 to 129 in 1966. British production of steel doubled during the same years, and the rationalizing of the cotton industry, which had already been in progress before the war, resulted in an increase of 10 per cent in output by 1961. The most rapidly growing industries were cars, oil-refining and chemicals, and in the export field there had been a definite switch to the commodities for which there was the greatest market. Much of this reflected an improved technology and it is significant that government expenditure on scientific research rose from £6·6 million in the first year of peace to £295 million in 1968.

All this might seem an adequate basis for the new era of affluence, remote from the backward-looking state of the British economy at the beginning of the twentieth century. Unfortunately, although Great Britain could shed her past, she could not shed her competitors overseas. In the years immediately after 1945 many of these had been hampered by the far greater destruction that they had suffered during the war, but by 1960 it was clear that most countries of western Europe, the United States and Japan were fast outstripping Great Britain in their growth of output in the major industries. The principal reason for this was that her competitors had invested much more heavily in the re-equipping of their industrial plant during the 1950s. This now enabled them to produce more extensively and economically and as a result the British found themselves lagging behind in growth rate and export performance.

This weakened position in the world market made the British economy particularly vulnerable to a steady inflation which seemed to be the concomitant of a general prosperity. The consequent rise in the price of British exports naturally made them harder to sell and with a similar rise in the price of imports the balance of payments soon turned from a surplus to a deficit. Foreign holders of sterling became fearful at times that Great Britain might try to put her accounts in order by devaluing the pound, thus making her exports cheaper, and consequently rushed to convert their sterling into other currencies, thereby causing a considerable drain on British gold and dollar reserves.

At moments like this, the government, anxious to avoid the dramatic and only temporary alleviation afforded by devaluing the pound, would try to check the inflation at home by artificially depressing the economy. There were two periods, in 1955–58 and in 1961–62, when Chancellors of the Exchequer had to resort to this Keynesian rule of thumb. The raising of the Bank rate and restrictions on various forms of hire purchase made borrowing more expensive and more difficult. This 'credit squeeze' was bound to bring with it greater unemployment, which rose on each occasion to half a million, until the balance of payments had recovered and it was judged safe to embark upon a new period of expansion. Thus, whereas governments before the war had not known how to get rid of unemployment, governments after the war did know how to do so, but sometimes felt themselves forced purposely to create it. The Conservatives became rather adept at timing their reflation of the economy just before a general election, but they seemed to have no answer to the fundamental problem that, as soon as the economy was allowed to expand again, the previous inflationary tendencies returned and each time the effect on the balance of payments was worse than before.

The inadequacy of this policy of stop–go, as it was called, was due to the fact that it was based on only one aspect of Keynes's writings. Keynes had been concerned primarily with the circumstances of his own time—the long depression and high unemployment of the interwar years—and had concentrated on the way in which a government could end this by increasing purchasing power, and hence effective demand, through an expansion of credit. The operating of stop–go after the war simply assumed as a natural converse that rising prices and the consequent deficit in the balance of payments were the result of this demand becoming excessive. The economy, it was said, was becoming overheated and it was the duty of the government to cool it down.

The expansion of the economy, however, was not the only reason for inflation. There were other factors which lay in areas that stop–go did not touch. Some of these were beyond the immediate control of the government. For example, in contrast to the first half of the century there had been since 1945 a steady increase in the world prices of foodstuffs, a significant item in British imports. But there was one factor which was purely domestic—the continual rise in incomes, particularly the round of wage settlements which the Conservative governments, determined to preserve good industrial relations, at first did nothing to resist. In fact, this danger had been foreseen long before in a government White Paper published in May 1944.

'If we are to operate with success a policy for maintaining a high and stable level of employment, it will be essential that employers and workers should exercise moderation on wage matters. .... The principle of stability does mean . . . that increase in the general level of wage rates must be related to increased productivity due to increased efficiency and effort.'

The warning went unheeded; incomes rose every year on average 7 per cent, but this was far in excess of the increase in national output, which only averaged 3 per cent, and the gap between the two meant an annual rise of 4 per cent in prices.

Thus the policy of stop–go was only a palliative, not a cure. Indeed, it may have been positively harmful, since during the artificially created periods of depression there was a likelihood that investment in industry would actually be reduced, while the effect on consumption was only minimal. Consequently it was necessary to look elsewhere for a fundamental solution and to many it seemed that an essential feature of this must be some kind of machinery for ensuring that increases in incomes and output remained in step.

These economic difficulties for the Conservatives did offer the Labour Opposition a constructive line of criticism, but the competing theories of economists seldom fall neatly into the categories of party politics. When a new sterling crisis arose in 1961, the Conservatives, too, realized that they would have to grasp this nettle. In July the Chancellor of the Exchequer, Selwyn Lloyd, put the Bank rate up to 7 per cent and raised import duties by 10 per cent. The most drastic move, however, was to impose a pay-pause on all government employees, clearly in the hope that the private sector would follow the government's example. At the same time a National Economic Development Council ('Neddy') was created as a first step towards devising an economic strategy for the whole country.

From now on disaster seemed to dog the Conservatives. The trade unions, highly suspicious of the NEDC, only agreed to join it in January 1962. Attempts to continue wage restraint after March, when the pay-pause officially ended, led to difficulties with the Post Office workers and the railwaymen, and when a National Incomes Commission was set up for the examination of all wage claims, the trade unions resolved to boycott this. Throughout the summer a series of by-elections were lost by the government and in July Macmillan attempted to stop the rot with a wholesale reconstruction of his cabinet, in which seven ministers were dismissed. This, however, was not proof against a couple of incidents which, although virtually irrelevant, continued to undermine public confidence. In a recent spy case unsubstantiated press reports pointed to the involvement of a minister of the crown, who was later completely cleared by a judicial tribunal; and in the summer of 1963, after the Conservatives had lost heavily in the local government elections, a sordid sex scandal led to the resignation of the Secretary of State for War.

By now Conservative backbenchers were openly attacking Macmillan's leadership and in October, when ill health had taken him to hospital, he decided that it was time to look for his successor. The two principal contenders were Lord Hailsham, who declared that he intended to renounce his peerage and return to the House of Commons, and R. A. Butler, who had been defeated by Macmillan in the previous contest in 1957. Conservative methods of selection were based on taking informal soundings of opinion and these revealed a fair body of support for both men. Meanwhile, Macmillan had decided to run his own candidate, and when Queen Elizabeth, who had succeeded her father in 1952, came to see him in hospital, he advised her to send for Lord Home, the Foreign Secretary. This meant a further renunciation of a peerage and it was as Sir Alec Douglas-Home that the new Prime Minister presided over the last year of the Conservative administration before the general election of 1964.

By this time the Labour party had lost two of their chief personalities. Aneurin Bevan had died of cancer in 1960. Hugh Gaitskell had survived the challenge to his leadership, but not the strain which the struggle had imposed; in January 1963 he died of a virus infection and Harold Wilson succeeded him as leader of the party. Wilson had been closely associated with the Bevanite group in the 1950s; yet the campaign with which he fought the 1964 election seemed merely to sum up the metamorphosis of party politics. Labour's cry was for an efficient management of the country's affairs. The aristocratic background of Sir Alec Douglas-Home was not depicted as a symbol of class tyranny; it was simply declared to be out of date, and Wilson, the professional economist, revelling in depreciatory references to the grouse moors, put forward a new image of Labour as the party whose expertise would really make capitalism work.

Against the background of recent years a sweeping Labour victory might have been expected. In fact, Labour only managed to displace the Conservatives with an overall majority of four, although they were able to increase this at a subsequent election in 1966. The new government under Harold Wilson set about its task with freshness and enthusiasm. There was talk of a national plan with an imposing array of new **minis-**

terial posts. The National Income Commission became the National Board for Prices and Incomes. A selective employment tax attempted to divert employment into more productive channels, particularly in the export trades, and a capital gains tax was introduced as an answer to the criticism that it was wrong to curb wages while untaxed profits could be made on the stock market.

Everything, however, was overshadowed by a mounting deficit in the balance of payments and the consequent drain on sterling. Wilson fought hard against being driven back to the old temporary expedients; yet in the end he was unable to avoid any of them and it seemed that the economic difficulties had only served to emphasize the continuing closeness of the two parties in the 1960s.

35
The Suez Crisis and its Consequences

I n 1962 a former American Secretary of State, Dean Acheson, commented: 'Great Britain has lost an empire and not yet found a role!'
In fact, throughout the years immediately after the war Great
Britain saw herself in three different roles simultaneously. She claimed a
special relationship with the United States; she hoped to shape a new
entity out of a multi-racial Commonwealth, and she was more closely
associated with the Continent of western Europe than ever before in her
history. The problem was that these three roles were not always compatible, and her weakened position in the world did not allow her to act
with total assurance in any of them.

In Europe the continuing confrontation between the west and Soviet
Russia was to make the iron curtain a permanent feature, and on either
side of it the newly established governments of East and West Germany
were soon to be drawn into full membership of their respective blocs.
The British had participated actively in this form of western defence.
They were, however, much more cautious about other ideas at work for
the political and economic integration of western Europe. The first
practical step towards this dream of a new unity was the establishment
of the Council of Europe at Strasbourg in 1949, but although a British
delegation attended the consultative assembly, the Labour government's
attitude was lukewarm and even those who welcomed the scheme with
enthusiasm were hesitant over its implications for the Commonwealth.
'The Empire must always have first preference for us,' wrote Harold
Macmillan in the *Manchester Dispatch*. 'Europe must come second in a
specially favoured position.'[1]

These doubts became explicit when, in 1950, France put forward a
plan for merging the coal and steel industries of France, West Germany,
Italy, the Netherlands, Belgium and Luxembourg. The Labour gover-
ment would not associate themselves with these proposals and in 1951
the European Coal and Steel Community was set up without Great

Britain. The absence of the British was a source of great disappointment to the smaller countries in the Community. 'Why do you refuse, after having been Europe's leader in war, to be her leader in peace?' asked the Belgian Henri Spaak. It had been a Labour decision, but the return of the Conservatives to power in 1951 made no difference. In that year a more startling plan was put forward for the forming of a European Defence Community with a western European army under unified command, to which West Germany would contribute twelve divisions; this time it was Churchill and Eden who declared that Great Britain could play no part in it.

The Russians were naturally convinced that these manoeuvres were designed purely to attach West Germany more firmly to the western bloc. Nevertheless, the death of Stalin in March 1953, followed by a formal armistice in Korea in July, did encourage hopes that a new settlement of Europe might now be possible, based on the reunification of Germany. Unfortunately an anti-Communist rising in East Germany in June made it clear to the Russians that reunification would almost certainly bring the whole of Germany into the western camp; accordingly they stalled and a conference of foreign ministers at Berlin in January 1954 predictably failed to reach agreement. It did, however, pave the way for a more fruitful meeting at Geneva in the following April, where Vietnam, the long eastern coastal region of Indo-China, was partitioned in an effort to end the fighting between the French and the Communist forces there.

Meanwhile, the collapse of hopes for a *détente* in Europe had done little to help the prospects of the European Defence Community. In August 1954 the French National Assembly, nervous at the possible revival of German military power, refused to ratify French participation. There were also some general doubts over the prospect of a surrender of sovereignty to a supranational authority, as the supporters of the European plan wanted. All this was extremely irritating for John Foster Dulles, the American Secretary of State, who had been sponsoring the idea of a European army, and in the autumn Eden, fearful lest the United States might retaliate by withdrawing from Europe, arranged a compromise which offered greater British involvement as a means of quietening the fears of the French. He proposed that Great Britain would maintain four divisions and a tactical air force on the Continent, and in return for this it was agreed that West Germany should now be included in the Treaty of Brussels of 1948 (see p. 400); she would cease to be under formal occupation and as a member of NATO would contribute the twelve divisions originally suggested.

Thus far, it seemed that the British might be able to sustain the various roles that they wished to adopt. They were continuing to develop their nuclear armament and with a two-year system of conscription had considerable forces scattered around the world. Much of Africa still lay under their control. They were involved in the European military system and yet sufficiently detached to be able to act as a mediator between the United States and the Continent. It seemed to be a situation in which, despite their weakened position, they could still maintain some kind of independent initiative. Within two years, however, the Suez crisis had revealed that these hopes were based on an illusion.

The story of that highly significant episode begins in July 1952, when the rule of King Farouk in Egypt was overthrown by an army officers' coup. The new government of General Neguib continued the negotiations on two current problems: the future of the Sudan, which eventually became independent in 1953; and the question of the Suez Canal zone, which was by now the only area of Egypt under British occupation. Egyptian feeling ran high over this last and eventually in the summer of 1954, by which time Colonel Nasser had replaced Neguib as head of the Egyptian government, the British agreed that their forces would be withdrawn to the island of Cyprus; the Canal would remain in the possession of the Company in which Great Britain was the largest shareholder, and it was understood that they should be allowed to return to protect their interests there in the event of any attack on the Arab states or Turkey.

In the House of Commons a group of Conservative backbenchers objected furiously to this decision, claiming that the earlier withdrawals from India and Palestine had only been acceptable on condition that Great Britain would continue to maintain a direct control over the region of the Suez Canal. Labour spokesmen, too, pointed out the danger of creating a vacuum in the Middle East. The truth of the matter was that the retention of the isolated canal base amidst a hostile population would be virtually impossible without re-establishing British rule over the whole of Egypt. Withdrawal may have been inevitable. The choice of Cyprus as the reserve position, from which the canal zone could be reoccupied, was more debatable; the lack of adequate harbours for a major amphibious operation was a serious disadvantage, and the island was in a state of unrest fomented by Greek Cypriots demanding reunion with Greece.

The thought of a possible vacuum on the periphery of the Communist world outside Europe had already occurred to the American

government. Accordingly, in September 1954 they created an organiza-
tion of South-East Asian states, the South-East Asia Treaty
Organization (SEATO), and it was their encouragement that led in
February 1955 to the signing of the Baghdad Pact between Turkey and
Iraq, to which Great Britain, Pakistan and Iran acceded in the following
October.

Although the Baghdad Pact might seem nominally to provide a
defence against Russia along the southern border in the Middle East, it
had the unfortunate effect of opening up a new danger. Nasser regarded
it as a move fostered by the west, whereby Iraq might challenge the
leadership that Egypt claimed to exercise over the Arab states. His
reaction was to turn to the Communist world and in the summer of
1955, after a fierce attack by Israel on the region of Gaza had demonstrated Egypt's military weakness, he was able to negotiate a trade treaty
with Russia and the purchase of arms from Czechoslovakia. Thus the
Baghdad Pact, far from filling the vacuum with a united Middle East,
had only succeeded in exacerbating the divisions among the Arab states
and in giving Russia a chance to gain a foothold of influence.

In fact, Nasser had no intention of becoming a member of the
Communist bloc. He was vitally in need of a loan sponsored by the
United States in order to build the Aswan dam on the Upper Nile, a
project which would revolutionize the Egyptian economy. By flirting
with the Communists he hoped merely to emphasize Egypt's importance and thus make an American loan more likely. This, however, was
a risky game, since there was no alternative offer from Russia, and he
finally overreached himself in May 1956, when he gave formal recognition to Communist China. On 19 July the Americans withdrew their
proposals for a loan. On this Nasser announced the nationalization of
the Suez Canal company, whose revenue would offer an alternative
source of income to finance the building of the dam, and the fears of the
Conservative backbenchers now seemed to have been fully realized.

Sir Anthony Eden, Prime Minister since the previous year, was determined that Nasser must be stopped, if necessary by force. He had full
support for this from the French who believed that Egypt was giving aid
to a resistance movement in Algeria, but he gained very little from the
United States who was simply concerned that the Canal should remain
open. Throughout August and September a series of diplomatic moves
produced no result. Eighteen nations at a conference in London asked
Nasser to agree to internationalize the Canal. Later, a hastily formed
canal-users' association, the brain-child of John Foster Dulles, was
unable to make much progress, and Nasser, by now convinced rightly

that the American President, General Eisenhower, did not intend to take active measures, rejected all proposals. In October the question was put before the Security Council of the United Nations, but when a demand for the terms of the London conference was blocked by a veto from Russia, Great Britain and France resolved to go ahead with an armed intervention, regardless of American disapproval.

The shaping of this joint operation was complicated by a new factor. Israel's shipping had been excluded from the Canal and was now coming under Egyptian attack on the alternative route up the Gulf of Akaba. Thus to Israel the crisis over the Canal seemed a suitable opportunity to launch an offensive against Egypt which would clear the Akaba route and forestall a possible attack by Egypt, Syria and Jordan, encouraged by Nasser's recent defiance of the Powers.

Long afterwards debate raged over the extent to which Great Britain and France acted in collusion with Israel, but the full truth is bound to be a matter of speculation until the official documents are published. It would seem that the French, who had already been supplying the Israelis with aircraft, were keen to work in secret alliance with them, but Eden could not accept this. Such a scheme would certainly jeopardize Great Britain's delicate relations with the Arab states of the Middle East; more particularly, it would weaken that moral justification which Eden was anxious to maintain: the sanctity of existing treaties. His knowledge that the Israelis were likely to attack did, however, convince him that there was a considerable probability of a major war in the Middle East, and this caused him to change the ostensible reason for the Anglo-French landing. Once the Israelis had begun their advance westwards into Sinai, the proclaimed purpose of the British and the French would be to separate the combatants in order to prevent a general war and to safeguard the Canal in the interests of world commerce.

On 29 October Israel attacked across Sinai. On 30 October the British and the French issued ultimatums demanding that Egypt should withdraw to a point ten miles west of the canal, and Israel remain ten miles to the east of it, thereby creating a neutral zone along the Canal which would be occupied by an Anglo-French force. Since this would entail a considerable retreat by Egypt through her own territory, it was not unnatural that she should refuse. On the same day the British and French delegates at the Security Council in New York vetoed a resolution demanding the withdrawal of Israeli forces from Egypt, and on 31 October the Egyptian air force was virtually destroyed by British and French bombers.

The essential now was speed. Unfortunately Eden's scruples over avoiding collusion had meant that the main invasion force could not sail until Israel had opened her attack. Furthermore, since the harbours in Cyprus were unsuitable for such an operation, there was to be an interval of six days, while a vast armada of 150 warships, 7 aircraft-carriers, hundreds of landing-craft and 80,000 troops made the twelve hundred mile journey from Malta to Port Said. As the days passed, wild demonstrations mounted in Great Britain, the General Assembly of the United Nations demanded a cease-fire, and Russia, having eventually realized that Anglo-American relations had broken down, threatened London, Paris and Tel Aviv with rocket attack. By the time the Anglo-French landings at Port Said had begun on the morning of 6 November, both Egypt and Israel had at last accepted the cease-fire, and there were consequently no combatants to separate. The long delay had deprived Eden of the justification which he had been so keen to establish. Throughout that day the invading forces did clear Port Said and began to push down south towards Ismailia (map, p. 347), but in the evening the British cabinet agreed to a cease-fire and the French, unwilling to go on alone, reluctantly did the same.

There is little doubt that the whole of the Canal zone could have been theirs within a few hours. It was Dulles, of all people, who asked afterwards: 'Why on earth didn't you go through with it?' Eden himself maintained that their purpose had been achieved, although not before the Egyptians had blocked the Canal with sunken ships. There were, however, many other reasons for stopping. The sheer weight of world opinion, particularly of the United States, and the frenzy of attack from the Opposition in the House of Commons had been too much for Eden at a time when his health was completely undermined by an abdominal complaint. In Egypt Nasser had not fallen, and the Canal zone could not be held alone without occupying the whole country. In the British government there seemed the likelihood of several resignations; worst of all, a run on sterling had caused the gold reserves to fall by £100 million in a single week and the United States would not sanction a loan from the International Monetary Fund unless the British ordered a cease-fire.

There are so many historical echoes in this final demonstration of the shrinking of British power. It had been concern over the Canal which had originally brought the British into Egypt in 1882—a chapter that had opened with the bombardment of Alexandria and had now closed with the bombardment of Port Said; both episodes had been originally conceived as combined Anglo-French operations, but in 1882 it was the French who held back, and in 1956 the British who pulled the French out. To the world the Suez affair seemed like just one more imperial adventure—an elaborate piece of gunboat diplomacy—and in the autumn the Labour Opposition levelled this charge incessantly at the government. In the country at large, however, the debate never ran on party lines. Demands for the rule of international law wrestled with thoughts of Britain's past greatness and resentment at her diminished stature. The resignation of two ministers symbolized the extent to which the Conservatives were disturbed and divided; equally, Labour MPs were aware that many of the working class could respond to the excitements of imperialism, as they had done during the Boer War. The memory of the inglorious past played its part as well. Certainly his experience of the years of appeasement was a powerful factor in Eden's mind. At the beginning of August the British press had almost universally compared Nasser's actions to those of Hitler and Mussolini in the 1930s, as did Hugh Gaitskell at this point in the House of Commons. There must not be another Munich. Amid this maze of historical allusion no one, not even the Chancellor of the Exchequer, remembered the pound sterling and ultimately Eden's government gave way to the same pressure that had brought down the second Labour administration of Ramsay MacDonald in 1931, although this time there was no mention of a bankers' ramp, only anger at American opposition.

In Egypt the Anglo-French troops had been removed by December and their place was taken by a United Nations peace-keeping force of seventeen countries. Israel withdrew behind her own frontiers and Nasser, whose political life had probably been saved by the American attitude throughout the crisis, retained possession of the Canal on the understanding that all nations should have unrestricted use of it. This was not to include Israel, and in any case it was some time before the Canal could be cleared of sunken shipping. In January 1957 Sir Anthony Eden's health forced him to resign and Harold Macmillan took over as Prime Minister.

There were many more far-reaching consequences than this. The Suez episode was the final moment of truth for Great Britain. It had demonstrated to the world that she could no longer act independently of the United States in defence of her own imperial interests, and it appeared to have brought an unhappy end to the chequered history of the *entente cordiale* with France. Early in 1957 the American government extended financial protection to the states of the Middle East against Communist aggression, and in 1958 the fall of the French Fourth Republic, undermined by the Algerian war, led to the presidency of General de Gaulle, who set out on a new policy for France in which

Great Britain would play no part. It seemed that the three roles which the British had earlier conceived for themselves were all in dissolution.

Harold Macmillan's great achievement was to bring the country to terms with this realization and at the same time to restore the national confidence. He embarked upon his task with a flamboyance which his supporters described as Edwardian, though there was nothing very Edwardian about the situation with which he had to cope. Although he himself had been in favour of the expedition, he conducted a long diplomatic retreat from Suez in a manner which enabled the Conservative party to regain its unity. In conversations in Bermuda he re-established good relations with President Eisenhower, with whom he had worked in Algeria during the Second World War. In 1958 he carried out a great tour of the Commonwealth—India, Pakistan, Ceylon, Australia and New Zealand—the first time that any British Prime Minister had made such a visit. In 1959 he flew to Moscow for talks with the Russian premier Khrushchev, whom he hoped to persuade to attend a summit meeting with Eisenhower, and although the eventual meeting in Paris in May 1960 was a fiasco, his efforts had at least done something to re-establish the significance of Great Britain in the diplomatic field.

Much of this was simply rehabilitation, but the more profound consequences of Suez were also to become apparent during the Macmillan administration. If Great Britain was no longer free to defend the remaining parts of her Empire, then it would be better to shed them and to reduce the size of conventional military forces that had previously been thought necessary. Accordingly, conscription was ended in 1960. Ghana and Malaya in 1957 and Cyprus in 1959 became independent territories within the Commonwealth, but the full onslaught of independence came after Macmillan had virtually served notice of his intentions in a speech before the South African parliament at Capetown in 1960, when he spoke of the wind of change blowing across the African continent. In that year Nigeria and Somaliland, in 1961 Sierra Leone and Tanganyika, in 1962 Uganda, and in 1963 Gambia and Kenya became self-governing, although all except Somaliland remained within the Commonwealth. In 1963 the attempt to create a Central African Federation was finally abandoned and its component parts, Nyasaland and Northern and Southern Rhodesia, became separate states of the Commonwealth. At the same time another federation in the West Indies had fallen apart and the islands had become self-governing.

These radical changes called for delicate negotiation amid the rising force of black nationalism, the hopes for multi-racialism, and the fears felt by Asian minorities and the white populations, mostly in East Africa. Inevitably there were some casualties. In 1961 South Africa withdrew from the Commonwealth and in 1965 Southern Rhodesia issued a unilateral declaration of independence. Fear and antagonism had also been aroused at home by an influx of coloured immigrants whose British citizenship gave them the right of entry into the United Kingdom. For a long time Butler at the Home Office fought off the demands for restrictions on entry, but eventually the growing numbers, coupled with the pressure of public opinion and the evidence of race riots, forced him to give way with the Commonwealth Immigrants Act of 1962. The Act was hotly opposed by the Labour party at the time; yet they too had to listen to their own supporters and in 1968 the Wilson administration was to pass an additional Act which tightened up the existing legislation.

This was not all. Suez had compelled the British to realize that in the last analysis there was nothing very special about the special relationship with the United States; it had speeded up the emergence of a new form of Commonwealth too diverse to be likely to follow a concerted policy, and now a growing sense of isolation was bound to turn Great Britain back to reconsidering the question of the Continent.

Here the protagonists of a western Europe community had pushed ahead with their idea and in 1957 the Treaty of Rome had laid the foundations of a Common Market including France, Italy, West Germany, the Netherlands, Belgium and Luxembourg. Great Britain had stayed out, setting up instead in 1959 an organization of her own with Austria, Denmark, Norway, Sweden, Portugal and Switzerland, far more limited in its aims and known as the European Free Trade Area. By 1961, however, the Conservative government had become converted to the idea of joining the Common Market. Considerable economic ties with the Commonwealth made this highly problematical and negotiations led by Edward Heath continued at Brussels for more than a year. Public opinion was torn over the full political implications of entry, but as over so many other issues in these years, these doubts were not reflected in the division of the political parties. The only consistency seemed to lie in the attitude of the French. In 1963 the Conservative application to enter was hotly attacked by Labour Opposition before it was rejected by a French veto, and yet in 1967 the Labour administration of Harold Wilson was to make a second application to join, again defeated by the French. Many of the rank and file of both parties were still nervous over the implications of committing Great Britain to Europe; the leaders of both had accepted the idea and the only issue between them was the terms of entry. Of the two, however, it was Labour who was the more cautious. This was a strange gloss upon left-wing ideals of internationalism—nearly as strange as the dismantling of the British Empire under the auspices of the Conservative government. The Edwardians would have found it all most confusing.

The country had come through a good deal since Edward, Prince of Wales, had stood at the bedside of his mother Queen Victoria, as she lay dying at Osborne House. The land of hope and glory was by now a little battered; the sun had set on the British Empire and the rulership of the waves had largely passed into other hands. Yet the years which had seen the bulk of this transformation had also given her a healthier population, better fed and housed than ever before in her history. The social conscience of a few Edwardians had been translated into the legislation of the welfare state and for a time, at least, this had been accompanied by a period of unprecedented general affluence. And with all this change in the span of a single lifetime Great Britain had retained a degree of political freedom and a sense of fairness and tolerance that still marked her out from most other countries in an age when violence, instability and dictatorship appeared to predominate. This was one aspect of hope and glory that had so far survived the strains of the twentieth century and it mattered more than all the rest.

Appendixes

APPENDIX I

ROYAL GENEALOGICAL TABLE

The family tree has been very much simplified. The dates beneath the sovereigns refer to their reigns

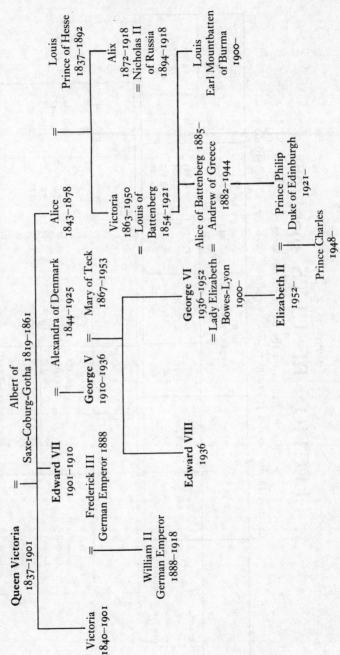

APPENDIX 2

ELECTION RESULTS 1900–1965

Only the figures for the major parties are given

Source: D. Butler and J. Freeman: *British Political Facts 1900–1968* (1969)

	1900 28 Sept.–24 Oct.		1906 12 Jan.–7 Feb.		1910 14 Jan.–9 Feb.		1910 2–19 Dec.	
	Seats	Pop. vote	Seats	Pop. vote	Seats	Pop. vote	Seats	Pop. vote
Conservatives	402	1,797,444	157	2,451,454	273	3,127,887	272	2,420,566
Liberals	184	1,568,141	377	2,757,883	275	2,880,581	272	2,295,888
Labour	2	63,304	30	329,748	40	505,657	42	371,772
Irish Nationalists	82	90,076	83	35,031	82	124,586	84	131,375

	1918 14 Dec.	
	Seats	Pop. vote
Coalition:		
Conservatives	335	3,504,198
Liberal	133	1,455,640
Labour	10	161,521
Total	478	5,121,359
Conservatives	23	370,375
Irish Unionists	25	292,722
Liberal	28	1,298,808
Labour	63	2,385,472
Irish Nationalists	7	238,477
Sinn Fein	73	486,867

	1922 15 Nov.	
	Seats	Pop. vote
Conservatives	345	5,500,382
National Liberal	62	1,673,240
Liberal	54	2,516,287
Labour	142	4,241,383

6 Dec.	Seats	Pop. vote
Conservative	258	5,538,824
Liberal	159	4,311,147
Labour	191	4,438,508

29 Oct.	Seats	Pop. vote
Conservative	419	8,039,598
Liberal	40	2,928,747
Labour	151	5,489,077

30 May	Seats	Pop. vote
Conservative	260	8,656,473
Liberal	59	5,308,510
Labour	288	8,389,512

1931 27 Oct.	Seats	Pop. vote
National govt.:		
Conservative	473	11,978,745
National Labour	13	341,370
Liberal National	35	809,302
Liberal	33	1,493,102
Total	554	14,553,519
Independent Liberal	4	106,106
Labour	52	6,649,630

1935 14 Nov.	Seats	Pop. vote
National	432	11,810,158
Liberal	21	1,422,116
Labour	154	8,325,491
I.L.P.	4	139,577

1945 5 July	Seats	Pop. vote
Conservatives	213	9,988,306
Liberal	12	2,248,226
Labour	393	11,995,152

1950 23 Feb.	Seats	Pop. vote
Conservatives	298	12,502,567
Liberal	9	2,621,548
Labour	315	13,266,592

1951 25 Oct.	Seats	Pop. vote
Conservatives	321	13,717,538
Liberal	6	730,556
Labour	295	13,948,605

1955 26 May	Seats	Pop. vote
Conservatives	344	13,286,569
Liberal	6	722,405
Labour	277	12,404,970

1959 8 Oct.	Seats	Pop. vote
Conservatives	365	13,749,830
Liberal	6	1,638,571
Labour	258	12,215,538

1964 15 Oct.	Seats	Pop. vote
Conservatives	304	12,001,396
Liberal	9	3,092,878
Labour	317	12,205,814

APPENDIX 3

MINISTRIES 1900–1965

	Government	Prime Minister	Foreign Secretary	Chancellor of the Exchequer
1900	Conservative	Lord Salisbury A. Balfour, July 1902	Lord Lansdowne	Sir M. Hicks Beach C. Ritchie, July 1902 A. Chamberlain, Oct. 1903
Dec. 1905	Liberal	Sir H. Campbell-Bannerman H. Asquith, April 1908	Sir E. Grey	H. Asquith D. Lloyd George, April 1908
May 1915	Coalition	H. Asquith	Sir E. Grey	R. McKenna
Dec. 1916	Coalition	D. Lloyd George	A. Balfour Lord Curzon, Oct. 1919	A. Bonar Law A. Chamberlain, Jan. 1919 Sir R. Horne, April 1921
Oct. 1922	Conservative	A. Bonar Law S. Baldwin, May 1923	Lord Curzon	S. Baldwin N. Chamberlain, Aug. 1923
Jan. 1924	Labour	R. MacDonald	R. MacDonald	P. Snowden
Nov. 1924	Conservative	S. Baldwin	A. Chamberlain	W. S. Churchill
June 1929	Labour	R. MacDonald	A. Henderson	P. Snowden

		Prime Minister	Foreign Secretary	Chancellor of the Exchequer
Aug. 1931	National	R. Macdonald S. Baldwin, June 1935 N. Chamberlain, May 1937	Lord Reading Sir J. Simon, Nov. 1931 Sir S. Hoare, June 1935 A. Eden, Dec. 1935 Lord Halifax, Feb. 1938	P. Snowden N. Chamberlain, Nov. 1931 Sir J. Simon, May 1937
May 1940	Coalition	W. S. Churchill	A. Eden, Dec. 1940	Sir K. Wood, Oct. 1940 Sir J. Anderson, Sept. 1943
May 1945	Caretaker	W. S. Churchill	A. Eden	Sir J. Anderson
July 1945	Labour	C. Attlee	E. Bevin H. Morrison, March 1951	H. Dalton Sir S. Cripps, Nov. 1947 H. Gaitskell, Oct. 1950
Oct. 1951	Conservative	W. S. Churchill Sir A. Eden, April 1955 H. Macmillan, Jan. 1957 Sir A. Douglas Home, Oct. 1963 (formerly Earl of Home)	A. Eden H. Macmillan, April 1955 S. Lloyd, Dec. 1955 Earl of Home, July 1960 R. Butler, Oct. 1963	R. Butler H. Macmillan, Dec. 1955 P. Thorneycroft, Jan. 1957 D. Heathcoat Amory, Jan. 1958 S. Lloyd, July 1960 R. Maudling, July 1962
Oct. 1964	Labour	H. Wilson	P. Gordon Walker M. Stewart, Jan. 1965	J. Callaghan

POPULATION OF THE UNITED KINGDOM

Figures are given in thousands. There was no census in 1941.

Sources:
B. R. Mitchell and P. Deane,
Abstract of British Historical Statistics (1962)
B. R. Mitchell and H. G. Jones,
Second Abstract of British Historical Statistics (1971)

	1901	1911
England and Wales	32,528	36,070
Scotland	4,472	4,761
Ireland	4,459	4,390
Total	41,459	45,221

	1921	1931	1951	1961
England and Wales	37,887	39,952	43,758	46,105
Scotland	4,882	4,843	5,096	5,179
Northern Ireland	1,257*	1,280†	1,371	1,425
Total	44,026	46,075	50,225	52,709

* Figure for 1926 after the establishment of the boundary (see p. 189).
† Figure for 1937.

UNEMPLOYMENT 1900–1965

Source: As for Appendix 4

A: 1900–1926

There are no general statistics for unemployment before 1922. The figures in this section are *percentages* of unemployment based on monthly returns from trade unions of engineers, shipbuilders, carpenters and printers.

1900	2·5	1909	7·7	1918	0·8
01	3·3	10	4·7	19	2·4
02	4·0	11	3·0	20	2·4
03	4·7	12	3·2	21	14·8
04	6·0	13	2·1	22	15·2
05	5·0	14	3·3	23	11·3
06	3·6	15	1·1	24	8·1
07	3·7	16	0·4	25	10·5
08	7·8	17	0·7	26	12·2

B: 1922–1965 (in thousands)

These figures are derived from labour exchange records. They include insured and uninsured, but not salaried workers, and are the average for the whole year.

1922	1,543	1937	1,484	1952	414
23	1,275	38	1,791	53	342
24	1,130	39	1,514	54	285
25	1,226	40	963	55	232
26	1,385	41	350	56	257
27	1,088	42	123	57	312
28	1,217	43	82	58	457
29	1,216	44	74	59	475
30	1,917	45	137	60	360
31	2,630	46	374	61	341
32	2,745	47	480	62	463
33	2,521	48	310	63	573
34	2,159	49	308	64	381
35	2,036	50	314	65	329
36	1,755	51	252		

NUMBERS AND MEMBERSHIP OF TRADE UNIONS 1900–1965

With headquarters in Great Britain or Northern Ireland
Source: As for Appendix 4

	No.	Membership (000)		No.	Membership (000)		No.	Membership (000)
1900	1,323	2,022	1923	1,186	5,429	1946	757	8,803
01	1,322	2,025	24	1,188	5,544	47	734	9,145
02	1,297	2,013	25	1,170	5,506	48	749	9,362
03	1,285	1,994	26	1,158	5,219	49	742	9,318
04	1,256	1,967	27	1,153	4,919	50	732	9,289
05	1,244	1,997	28	1,136	4,806	51	735	9,535
06	1,282	2,210	29	1,128	4,858	52	723	9,588
07	1,283	2,513	30	1,114	4,841	53	720	9,527
08	1,268	2,485	31	1,101	4,624	54	711	9,566
09	1,260	2,477	32	1,074	4,443	55	704	9,741
10	1,269	2,565	33	1,074	4,389	56	685	9,778
11	1,290	3,139	34	1,056	4,570	57	685	9,829
12	1,252	3,416	35	1,049	4,867	58	675	9,639
13	1,269	4,135	36	1,036	5,295	59	668	9,623
14	1,260	4,145	37	1,032	5,842	60	664	9,835
15	1,229	4,359	38	1,024	6,053	61	646	9,897
16	1,225	4,644	39	1,019	6,298	62	626	9,887
17	1,241	5,499	40	1,004	6,613	63	607	9,934
18	1,264	6,533	41	996	7,165	64	598	10,079
19	1,360	7,926	42	991	7,867	65	583	10,181
20	1,379	8,347	43	987	8,174			
21	1,269	6,632	44	963	8,087			
22	1,226	5,625	45	781	7,875			

REFERENCES

CHAPTER 1. THE EDWARDIAN SCENE

1. R. Roberts, *The Classic Slum*, Penguin 1973, p. 19.
2. *Ibid.*, p. 75.
3. D. H. Lawrence, in *Selected Essays*, Penguin.
4. H. Rider Haggard, quoted in R. W. Breach and R. M. Hartwell, eds., *British Economy and Society 1870–1970*, Oxford U.P. 1972, p. 74.

CHAPTER 2. ASPECTS OF GOVERNMENT

1. W. Somerset Maugham, *The Summing Up*, Heinemann 1940, p. 2.
2. Hilaire Belloc, *Essays on Liberalism*, quoted in H. J. Hanham, *The Nineteenth-Century Constitution*, Cambridge U.P. 1969, p. 23.
3. Roberts, *The Classic Slum*, p. 142.

CHAPTER 3. NEW CHALLENGES AT HOME

1. *The Times*, 15 May 1867.
2. H. G. Wells, *Anticipations*, Chapman & Hall 1902, p. 212.
3. Charles Booth, quoted in introduction to A. Fried and R. M. Elman, eds., *Charles Booth's London*, Penguin 1969, p. 39.
4. Beatrice Potter, quoted in *ibid.*, p. 39.
5. Herbert Samuel, *Liberalism*, Grant Richards 1902, p. 30.
6. G. B. Shaw, *Sixteen Self Sketches*, Constable 1949, p. 65.

CHAPTER 4. THE FORTUNES OF THE PARTIES

1. *The Times*, 17 January 1899, quoted in J. Wilson, *C.B.: a life of Sir Henry Campbell-Bannerman*, Constable 1973.
2. Quoted in H. Pelling, *The Origins of the Labour Party*, Oxford U.P. 1965, p. 87.
3. Miss Katharine Conway at Bradford. Quoted in *ibid.*, p. 39.
4. *The Times*, 15 January 1897, quoted in H. A. Clegg, A. Fox and A. F. Thompson, *A History of British Trade Unionism*, Oxford U.P. 1964, p. 312.

CHAPTER 5. CONSERVATIVE DECLINE, 1902–1905

1. Quoted in K. Young, *Balfour*, Bell 1963, p. 171.
2. Winston S. Churchill, *Great Contemporaries*, Thornton Butterworth 1937, p. 242.
3. Quoted in Young, *Balfour*, p. xvii.
4. Quoted in J. Amery, *Joseph Chamberlain*, Macmillan 1969, Vol. V, pp. 186, 191
5. Quoted in R. Jenkins, *Asquith*, Collins 1964, p. 137.
6. Quoted in Amery, *Joseph Chamberlain*, VI, p. 471.

CHAPTER 6. NEW CHALLENGES ABROAD

1. *Hansard*, quoted in A. J. Marder, *British Naval Policy 1880–1905*, Putnam 1940, p. 105.
2. Quoted in P. Magnus, *King Edward VII*, Penguin 1967, p. 418.
3. Erskine Childers, *The Riddle of the Sands* (1903), repr. Sidgwick & Jackson 1972, p. 289.
4. William Le Queux, quoted in I. F. Clarke, *Voices Prophesying War*, Oxford U.P. 1966, p. 64.
5. *Ibid.*, p. 7.
6. F. T. Jane, quoted in A. J. Marder, *From Dreadnought to Scapa Flow*, Oxford U.P. 1961, Vol. I, p. 10.
7. *Ibid.*, I, p. 348.

CHAPTER 7. LIBERAL HEYDAY 1906–1911

1. Quoted in Jenkins, *Asquith*, Collins 1964, p. 174.
2. Sir John Walton, quoted in Clegg, Fox and Thompson, *A History of British Trade Unionism*, p. 394.

CHAPTER 8. LIBERAL TRIBULATIONS 1911–1914

1. Quoted in R. Blake, *Bonar Law*, Eyre & Spottiswoode 1955, p. 85.
2. Quoted in Jenkins, *Asquith*, p. 276.
3. Quoted in G. Dangerfield, *The Strange Death of Liberal England*, MacGibbon & Kee 1966, p. 80.
4. Quoted in Blake, *Bonar Law*, p. 130.
5. Quoted in Harold Nicolson, *King George V* (Constable 1952), Pan Books 1967, p. 304.
6. Quoted in Dangerfield, *The Strange Death of Liberal England*, p. 120.
7. Quoted in Jenkins, *Asquith*, p. 315.

CHAPTER 9. SIR EDWARD GREY AND THE APPROACH OF WAR

1. Lord Selborne, in K. Bourne, ed., *Foreign Policy of Victorian England*, Oxford U.P. 1970, p. 479.
2. Sir Edward Grey, in *ibid.*, p. 480.
3. Quoted in E. L. Woodward, *Great Britain and the German Navy*, Oxford U.P. 1935, p. 262.
4. Quoted in *ibid.*, p. 263.
5. Quoted in G. M. Trevelyan, *Grey of Fallodon*, Longmans 1937, p. 162.
6. Quoted in Z. Steiner, *The Foreign Office and Foreign Policy 1898–1914*, Cambridge U.P. 1969, p. 130.
7. Quoted in K. Robbins, *Sir Edward Grey*, Cassell 1971, p. 262.
8. Quoted in Steiner, *The Foreign Office and Foreign Policy*, p. 131.

CHAPTER 10. ASQUITH'S WAR ADMINISTRATION,
AUGUST 1914–MAY 1915

1. Rupert Brooke, *Complete Poems*, Sidgwick & Jackson 1934, p. 145.
2. Quoted in E. L. Woodward, *Great Britain and the War of 1914–18*, Methuen 1967, p. 54.
3. Quoted in Jenkins, *Asquith*, p. 348.
4. Quoted in Violet Bonham-Carter, *Winston Churchill As I Knew Him*, Eyre & Spottiswoode 1965, p. 337.
5. Quoted in Philip Magnus, *Lord Kitchener* (Murray 1958), Grey Arrow 1961, p. 298.

CHAPTER 11. COALITION UNDER ASQUITH
MAY 1915–DECEMBER 1916

1. Quoted in T. Jones, *Lloyd George*, Oxford U.P. 1951, p. 67.
2. *Ibid.*, p. 65.
3. Brig.-Gen. John Charteris, quoted in J. Terraine, *Douglas Haig*, Hutchinson 1963, p. 161.
4. There are full accounts of the negotiations during these weeks in Jenkins, *Asquith*, R. Blake, *The Unknown Prime Minister: Bonar Law*, Eyre & Spottiswoode 1955, and Lord Beaverbrook (Max Aitken), *Politicians and the War*, Hutchinson 1968.

CHAPTER 13. THE IMPACT OF WAR

1. Wilfred Owen, *Complete Poems*, ed. C. Day Lewis, Chatto & Windus 1963, p. 22.

2. Siegfried Sassoon, quoted in I. M. Parsons, ed., *Men Who March Away*, Chatto & Windus 1966, p. 79.
3. Owen, *Complete Poems*, p. 40.
4. H. G. Wells, *Experiment in Autobiography*, Gollancz 1934, Vol. 2, p. 687.

CHAPTER 14. PARTY PROSPECTS AND THE GENERAL ELECTION OF 1918

1. M. McDonagh, *In London during the Great War*, Eyre and Spottiswoode 1935.
2. W. S. Churchill, *The Aftermath*, Macmillan 1941, p. 20.
3. Quoted in Blake, *Bonar Law*, p. 388.
4. Quoted in G. D. H. Cole, *History of the Labour Party since 1914*, Routledge 1948, p. 44.
5. Quoted in *ibid.*, p. 71.
6. Quoted in *Ibid.*, p. 72.
7. *Beatrice Webb's Diaries 1912–24*, Longmans 1952, p. 139.

CHAPTER 15. PEACE-MAKING AND ITS IMPLICATIONS

1. J. M. Keynes, *Essays in Biography*, Hart-Davis 1951, p. 21.
2. J. M. Keynes, *Economic Consequences of the Peace*, Macmillan (1919), repr. 1971, p. 188.
3. J. M. Keynes, *Two Memoirs*, Hart-Davis 1949, p. 56.
4. Harold Nicolson, *Peacemaking*, Methuen 1964, p. 369.
5. P. Birdsall, in I. J. Lederer, ed., *The Versailles Settlement*, D. C. Heath, p. 26.
6. H. G. Wells, *The Shape of Things to Come*, Hutchinson 1933, p. 98.
7. J. M. Keynes, in *The Versailles Settlement*, p. 43.

CHAPTER 16. INDUSTRIAL UNREST AND THE DREAM OF WORKING-CLASS SOLIDARITY

1. Keynes, *Economic Consequences of the Peace* (1971 edn), p. 188.
2. Cynthia Asquith, *Diary 1915–1918*, Hutchinson 1968, p. 480.
3. Tom Jones, *Whitehall Diary*, Oxford U.P. 1969, Vol. I, p. 103.
4. Quoted in Nicolson, *King George V*, p. 443.
5. Quoted in L. J. Macfarlane, 'Hands Off Russia in 1920', *Past and Present*, December 1967, p. 127.

6. *Ibid.*, p. 130.
7. Quoted in Cole, *History of the Labour Party*, p. 99.
8. Quoted in Macfarlane, 'Hands Off Russia in 1920', p. 126.
9. *Beatrice Webb's Diaries 1912–24*, p. 208.

CHAPTER 17. THE IRISH QUESTION

1. Quoted in Blake, *Bonar Law*, p. 417.
2. Quoted in H. Montgomery Hyde, *Carson*, Heinemann 1953, p. 448.
3. Quoted in Nicolson, *King George V*, p. 452.
4. Quoted in Lord Birkenhead, *F. E. Smith*, Eyre & Spottiswoode 1965, p. 387.

CHAPTER 18. THE AFTERMATH OF PEACE-MAKING

1. Quoted in Harold Nicolson, *Curzon: the last phase*, Constable 1934, p. 177.
2. J. Gore, quoted in Nicolson, *King George V*, p. 129. (The name of the Indian was Gopal Gokhale.)
3. Quoted in K. Young, *Balfour*, p. 420.
4. Lord Beaverbrook, *The Decline and Fall of Lloyd George*, Collins 1963, p. 144.
5. Quoted in F. Owen, *Tempestuous Journey*, Hutchinson 1954, p. 614.
6. *Ibid.*, p. 615.
7. Quoted in Nicolson, *Curzon: the last phase*, p. 80.
8. W. S. Churchill, *The Aftermath*, Macmillan 1941, p. 423.
9. Quoted in Blake, *Bonar Law*, p. 448.

CHAPTER 20. THE PARTIES IN FLUX, 1922–1924

1. L. S. Amery, *My Political Life*, Hutchinson 1952, Vol. II, p. 225.
2. Austen Chamberlain, quoted in R. T. McKenzie, *British Political Parties*, Heinemann 1963, p. 89.
3. The Marquis of Salisbury, quoted in *ibid.*, p. 84.
4. Amery, *My Political Life*, II, p. 233.
5. A. Chamberlain, quoted in McKenzie, *British Political Parties*, p. 102.
6. Bonar Law, quoted in Blake, *Bonar Law*, p. 461.
7. Asquith, quoted in *ibid.*, p. 13.
8. Quoted in Blake, *Bonar Law*, p. 455.

9. Winston S. Churchill, *The Second World War*, Vol. I, Cassell 1948, p. 17.
10. Violet Asquith, quoted in Jenkins, *Asquith*, p. 495.
11. Curzon, quoted in Blake, *Bonar Law*, p. 486.
12. Quoted in *ibid.*, p. 481.
13. Quoted in K. Middlemas and J. Barnes, *Baldwin*, Weidenfeld & Nicolson 1969, p. 212.
14. Quoted in Jenkins, *Asquith*, p. 500.

CHAPTER 21. THE TRIALS OF LABOUR, I. THE FIRST LABOUR ADMINISTRATION JANUARY–OCTOBER 1924

1. Quoted in Nicolson, *King George V*, p. 503.
2. Quoted in K. Feiling, *Neville Chamberlain*, Macmillan 1946, p. 111.
3. Quoted in Jenkins, *Asquith*, p. 500.
4. Beatrice Webb, *Diaries 1924–32*, p. 2.
5. *Ibid.*, p. 2.
6. R. H. Tawney, *Secondary Education for All*, 1923.
7. Quoted in A. Bullock, *Ernest Bevin*, Heinemann 1960, Vol. I, p. 244.
8. Quoted in Chester, Fay and Young, *The Zinoviev Letter*, Heinemann 1967, p. 118.

CHAPTER 22. THE TRIALS OF LABOUR, II. THE GENERAL STRIKE OF 1926

1. Quoted in R. R. James, *Churchill: a study in Failure*, Penguin 1973, p. 204.
2. Middlemas and Barnes, *Baldwin*, p. 387.
3. Quoted in Bullock, *Ernest Bevin*, I, p. 291.
4. Quoted in *ibid.*, p. 311.
5. Quoted in *ibid.*, p. 334.
6. *Ibid.*, p. 337.

CHAPTER 24. THE SECOND LABOUR ADMINISTRATION 1929–1931

1. Quoted in R. F. Harrod, *John Maynard Keynes*, Macmillan 1951, p. 396.
2. P. Snowden, *Autobiography*, Nicolson & Watson 1934, p. 760.
3. Quoted in R. Skidelsky, *Politicians and the Slump*, Macmillan 1967, p. 83.

4. Quoted in Middlemas and Barnes, *Baldwin*, p. 600.
5. Quoted in Skidelsky, *Politicians and the Slump*, p. 241.
6. Snowden, *Autobiography*, p. 362.
7. Quoted in Roy Harrod, *J. M. Keynes*, Macmillan 1963, p. 47.
8. Amery, *My Political Life*, Hutchinson 1955, III, p. 29.
9. Amery, *My Political Life*, II, p. 502.
10. Snowden, *Autobiography*, p. 875.
11. Quoted in Harrod, *J. M. Keynes*, p. 438.
12. H. Dalton, *Call Back Yesterday*, F. Muller 1953, p. 272.

CHAPTER 25. THE DOMESTIC RECORD OF THE NATIONAL GOVERNMENT 1931–1939

1. George Orwell, *The Road to Wigan Pier* (Gollancz 1937), Penguin edn. 1962, p. 16.

CHAPTER 26. THE NATIONAL GOVERNMENTS AND THE DICTATORS, 1931–1937

1. Quoted in K. Middlemas, *Diplomacy of Illusion*, Weidenfeld & Nicolson 1972, p. 11.
2. Quoted in Middlemas and Barnes, *Baldwin*, p. 600.
3. *Ibid.*, p. 745.
4. *Ibid.*, p. 754.
5. *Ibid.*, p. 775.
6. *Ibid.*, p. 760.

CHAPTER 27. THE FOREIGN POLICY OF NEVILLE CHAMBERLAIN 1937–1939

1. Quoted in Feiling, *Neville Chamberlain*, p. 311.
2. *Ibid.*, p. 319.
3. Quoted in Churchill, *The Second World War*, I, p. 247.
4. Neville Henderson, *Failure of a Mission*, Hodder & Stoughton 1940, p. 102.
5. Geoffrey Dawson, quoted in M. Gilbert and R. Gott, *The Appeasers*, Weidenfeld & Nicolson 1963, p. 100.
6. Quoted in A. Bullock, *Hitler*, Penguin 1962, p. 436.
7. Quoted in Feiling, *Neville Chamberlain*, p. 348.
8. *Ibid.*, p. 342.
9. Quoted in Bullock, *Hitler*, p. 447.
10. Winston S. Churchill, *Step by Step*, Butterworth 1939, p. 255.

11. Quoted in Churchill, *The Second World War*, I, p. 246.
12. *Ibid.*, p. 270.
13. Quoted in C. Thorne, *The Approach of War 1938–39*, Macmillan 1967, p. 136.

CHAPTER 28. THE DÉBÂCLE

1. H. Nicolson, *Diaries*, Collins 1967, Vol. II, p. 42.
2. E. Spears, *Assignment to Catastrophe*, Heinemann 1954, Vol. I, p. 47.
3. Quoted in *ibid.*, p. 47.
4. *Ibid.*, p. 130.
5. Churchill, *Second World War*, II, p. 24.
6. *Ibid.*, p. 42.
7. Quoted in A. Bryant, ed., *The Turn of the Tide*, Collins 1957, p. 133.
8. Churchill, *Second World War*, II, p. 87.

CHAPTER 29. THE LONG RETREAT

1. Churchill, *Second World War*, II, p. 88.
2. Winston S. Churchill, *Speeches: Into Battle*, Cassell 1941, p. 223.
3. Churchill, *Second World War*, II, p. 51.
4. Quoted in Bullock, *Ernest Bevin*, II, p. 20.
5. Churchill, *Speeches: Into Battle*, p. 259.
6. Quoted in Bryant, *The Turn of the Tide*, p. 219.
7. Churchill, *Second World War*, Cassell 1950, II, pp. 331, 332.
8. *Ibid.*, III, p. 539.
9. Quoted in Bryant, *The Turn of the Tide*, p. 514.
10. *Ibid.*, p. 479.
11. Churchill, *Second World War*, Cassell 1951, IV, p. 59.
12. Quoted in Bryant, *The Turn of the Tide*, p. 461.
13. *Ibid.*, p. 479.

CHAPTER 30. GREAT BRITAIN UNDER SIEGE

1. Churchill, *Speeches: Into Battle*, p. 291.
2. Quoted in R. A. Butler, *The Art of the Possible*, Hamish Hamilton 1971, p. 103.

CHAPTER 31. THE VICTORY OF THE GRAND ALLIANCE

1. Quoted in Bryant, *The Turn of the Tide*, p. 312.
2. Quoted in A. Brynt, ed., *Triumph in the West*, Collins 1959, p. 512.
3. Quoted in Winston S. Churchill, *Second World War*, IV, p. 177.
4. Quoted in C. Wilmot, *The Struggle for Europe*, Collins 1952, pp. 626–7.
5. Churchill, *Second World War*, Cassell 1954, VI, p. 352.

CHAPTER 32. LABOUR IN CONTROL 1945–1951

1. Churchill, *Second World War*, VI, p. 512.
2. *Ibid.*, I, p. 526.
3. Quoted in M. Sissons and P. French, *The Age of Austerity*, Penguin 1964, p. 185.

CHAPTER 33. THE NEW SHAPE OF FOREIGN POLICY, 1945–1951

1. Quoted in Anthony Sampson, *Macmillan*, Allen Lane 1967, p. 81.

CHAPTER 35. THE SUEZ CRISIS AND ITS CONSEQUENCES

1. Quoted in Sampson, *Macmillan*, p. 87.

FURTHER READING

POLITICAL AND GENERAL HISTORIES

OUTLINES

MARWICK, A. *Britain in the Century of Total War*, Bodley Head, Penguin 1968

MEDLICOTT, W. N. *Contemporary England 1914–1964*, Longman 1967

MOWAT, C. L. *Britain between the Wars 1918–1940*, Methuen 1955

MURPHY, J. A. *Ireland in the twentieth century*, Gill and Macmillan 1975

TAYLOR, A. J. P. *English History 1914–1945* (Oxford History of England, vol. xv), Oxford University Press 1965; Penguin 1970

POLITICAL SURVEYS

BLAKE, R. *The Conservative Party from Peel to Churchill*, Eyre & Spottiswoode 1970

COLE, G. D. H. *History of the Labour Party from 1914*, Routledge 1948

MORGAN, K. O. *The Age of Lloyd George 1890–1929: The Liberal Party and British Politics*, Allen & Unwin 1971

SOURCES, STATISTICS, ETC.

BUTLER, D. and FREEMAN, J. *British Political Facts 1900–1968*, 3rd edn., Macmillan 1969

LE MAY, G. H. ed. *British Government 1914–1963: Select Documents*, Methuen 1964

BREACH, R. W. and HARTWELL, R. M. eds. *British Economy and Society 1870–1970*, Oxford University Press 1972

MITCHELL, B. R. and DEANE, P. eds. *Abstract of British Historical Statistics*, Cambridge University Press 1962

MITCHELL, B. R. and JONES, H. G. eds. *Second Abstract of British Historical Statistics*, Cambridge University Press 1971

ECONOMIC HISTORY

ASHWORTH, W. *Economic History of England 1870–1939*, Methuen 1960

POLLARD, S. *The Development of the British Economy 1914–1967*, E. Arnold 1969

SAYERS, R. S. *History of Economic Change in England 1880–1939*, Oxford University Press 1967

STEWART, M. *Keynes and After*, Penguin 1970

YOUNGSON, A. J. *Britain's Economic Growth 1920–1966*, Allen & Unwin 1967

IMPERIAL HISTORY

BELOFF, M. *Imperial Sunset*, vol. I: *Britain's Liberal Empire 1897–1921*, Methuen 1969

MARLOWE, J. *Anglo-Egyptian Relations 1800–1953* (1954); 2nd edn., *1800–1956*, F. Cass 1965 ·

MONROE, E. *Britain's Moment in the Middle East 1914–1956*, Chatto and Windus 1963

WALKER, E. *The British Empire 1497–1953* (1953), 2nd edn., Cambridge, Bowes 1954

BIOGRAPHY

(Listed alphabetically by subject. Personal memoirs appear under the relevant periods.)

JENKINS, R. *Asquith*, Collins 1964

MIDDLEMAS, K. and BARNES, J. *Baldwin*, Weidenfeld and Nicolson 1969

YOUNG, K. *Arthur James Balfour*, G. Bell 1963

BULLOCK, A. *Life and Times of Ernest Bevin*, vol. I: *1881–1940*; vol. II: *1940–1945*, Heinemann 1960, 1967

BLAKE, R. *The Unknown Prime Minister: Bonar Law*, Eyre & Spottiswoode 1955

FEILING, K. *Neville Chamberlain*, Macmillan 1946

PELLING, H. *Winston Churchill*, Macmillan 1974

JAMES, R. R. *Churchill: a Study in Failure 1900–1939*, Penguin 1973

NICOLSON, H. *King George V*, Constable 1952

ROBBINS, K. *Sir Edward Grey*, Cassell 1971

ROSKILL, S. W. *Hankey: Man of Secrets*, 3 vols, Collins 1970–74

HARROD, R. F. *The Life of John Maynard Keynes*, Macmillan 1951; Penguin 1972

ROWLAND, P. *Lloyd George*, Bame and Jenkin 1975

MARQUAND, D. *Ramsay MacDonald*, Cape 1977

HISTORICAL PERIODS

1. *Before 1914*

DOCUMENTS AND ORIGINAL WRITINGS

READ, D. ed. *Documents from Edwardian England 1901–1915*, Harrap 1974

BOOTH, CHARLES *Charles Booth's London* (selection from *The Life and Labour of the People of London*, ed. A. Fried and R. M. Elman), Penguin 1969

JONES, L. E. *An Edwardian Youth*, Macmillan 1956
LONDON, J. *People of the Abyss*, (1903) repr. Arco 1962
MASTERMAN, C. F. G. *The Condition of England* (1909); reset, ed. J. T. Boulton, Methuen 1960

NOVELS
CHILDERS, E. *The Riddle of the Sands*, (1903) repr. Sidgwick and Jackson 1972
GALSWORTHY, J. *The Forsyte Saga*, Heinemann 1922
GROSSMITH, G. and GROSSMITH, W. *The Diary of a Nobody*, (1894) J. M. Dent, Everymans Library 1940
SACKVILLE-WEST, V. *The Edwardians*, Hogarth Press 1930
TRESSELL, R. *The Ragged Trousered Philanthropists*, (1914) Lawrence & Wishart 1955
WELLS, H. G. *Kipps*, (1905) Collins 1952

SECONDARY SOURCES
ENSOR, R. C. K. *England 1870–1914*, Oxford History of England, vol. 14, Oxford University Press 1936
HALÉVY, E. *History of the English People in the Nineteenth Century:* vol. V: *Imperialism and the Rise of Labour 1895–1905*; vol. VI: *The Rule of Democracy 1905–1914*, Benn 1926, 1932
PELLING, H. *The Origins of the Labour Party 1880–1900* (1954), rev. edn. Oxford University Press 1966
CLEGG, H. A., FOX, A. and THOMPSON, A. F. *A History of British Trade Unionism since 1889*, vol. I, Oxford University Press 1964
BROWN, K. D. *Labour and Unemployment 1900–1914*, David & Charles 1971
WOODWARD, E. L. *Great Britain and the German Navy*, Oxford University Press 1935
MARDER, A. J. *From Dreadnought to Scapa Flow*, vol. I: *1904–1914*, Oxford University Press 1961
BOURNE, K. *The Foreign Policy of Victorian England 1830–1902*, Oxford University Press 1970
STEINER, Z. S. *The Foreign Office and Foreign Policy 1898–1914*, Cambridge University Press 1969

2. *First World War*

MEMOIRS AND DIARIES

GRAVES, R. *Goodbye to All That*, Cape 1929
RICHARDS, F. *Old Soldiers Never Die*, Faber 1933
SASSOON, S. *Memoirs of an Infantry Officer*, Faber 1930

SPEARS, E. L. *Liaison 1914*, Heinemann 1930

HAIG, D., 1st EARL HAIG, *The Private Papers of Douglas Haig 1914–19*, ed. R. Blake, Eyre & Spottiswoode 1953

AITKEN, WILLIAM MAXWELL (LORD BEAVERBROOK) *Politicians and the War*, Hutchinson 1928

AITKEN, WILLIAM MAXWELL (LORD BEAVERBROOK) *Men and Power 1917–21*, Hutchinson 1956

ASQUITH, LADY CYNTHIA *Diaries 1915–1918*, Hutchinson 1968

BRITTAIN, V. *Testament of Youth*, Gollancz 1933; repr. Chivers, New Portway Books 1971

LAWRENCE, T. E. *The Seven Pillars of Wisdom*, Cape 1926

NOVELS

HERBERT, A. P. *The Secret Battle*, Methuen 1919

MANNING, F. *Her Privates We* (1930), repr. P. Davies 1964

MOTTRAM, R. H. *The Spanish Farm*, Chatto 1924

WELLS, H. G. *Mr. Britling Sees It Through* (1916), repr. Baker 1970

SECONDARY SOURCES

CHURCHILL, W. S. *The World Crisis 1911–1918*, 3 vols. Thornton Butterworth 1923–27; repr. Mentor 1968

CRUTWELL *History of the Great War 1914–1918*, Oxford Clarendon Press 1934

FALLS, C. B. *The First World War*, Longmans 1960

BARNETT, C. *The Swordbearers*, Eyre & Spottiswoode 1963

WOLFF, L. *In Flanders Fields*, Longmans 1959

MOOREHEAD, A. *Gallipoli*, Hamish Hamilton 1956

MARWICK, A. *The Deluge: British Society and the First World War*, Bodley Head 1964; paperback Macmillan 1973

3. 1919–1939

POLITICAL MEMOIRS: DOMESTIC

AMERY, L. S. *My Political Life*, 3 vols., Hutchinson 1952–55

COOPER, A. DUFF *Old Men Forget*, Hart-Davis 1953

DALTON, H. *Call Back Yesterday 1924–31*, Muller 1953

DALTON, H. *The Fateful Years 1931–45*, Muller 1957

JONES, T. *Whitehall Diary 1916–30*, ed. K. Middlemas, 3 vols., Oxford University Press 1969–71

NICOLSON, H. *Diaries and Letters*, ed. N. Nicolson, vol. I: *1930–39*, Collins 1966

SNOWDEN, P. *Autobiography*, Nicolson and Watson 1934

WEBB, B. *Diaries 1912–24* and *1924–32*, Longmans 1952, 1956

POLITICAL MEMOIRS: FOREIGN POLICY

KEYNES, J. M. *The Economic Consequences of the Peace* (1919), vol. II: *Collected Writings*, Macmillan 1971

NICOLSON, H. *Peace-making 1919*, Constable 1933, Methuen 1964

EDEN, A. *Memoirs*, Part 1, *Facing the Dictators*, Cassell 1962

HOARE, S. *Nine Troubled Years*, Collins 1954

VANSITTART, R. *The Mist Procession*, Hutchinson 1958

HENDERSON, N. *Failure of a Mission*, Hodder and Stoughton 1940

PERSONAL MEMOIRS

HOGGAT, R. *The Uses of Literacy*, Chatto and Windus 1957; Penguin 1969

MARTIN, K. *Father Figures*, Hutchinson 1966

ORWELL, G. *The Road to Wigan Pier*, Gollancz 1937; repr. Penguin 1962

PRIESTLEY, J. B. *English Journey*, Heinemann 1934

GREENWOOD, W. *There was a Time*, Cape 1967

Men without Work, a report made to the Pilgrim Trust, 1938

NOVELS

GREENWOOD, W. *Love on the Dole* (1933), repr. Cape 1966; Penguin 1969

HUXLEY, A. *Eyeless in Gaza* (1936), repr. Chatto and Windus 1969

PRIESTLEY, J. B. *Angel Pavement* (1930), repr. Heinemann 1967

WAUGH, E. *Vile Bodies* (1930), repr. Chapman & Hall 1965; Penguin 1970

SECONDARY SOURCES

DOMESTIC

COWLING, M. *The Impact of Labour 1920–1924*, Cambridge University Press 1971

SYMONS, J. *The General Strike*, Cresset Press 1957

SKIDELSKY, R. *Politicians and the Slump: the Labour Government of 1929–31*, Macmillan 1967

BASSETT, R. *Nineteen Thirty-One: Political Crisis*, Macmillan 1958

ADDISON, P. *The Road to 1945*, Cape 1975

GRAVES, R. and HODGE, A. *The Long Weekend*, Faber 1940; repr. Penguin 1971

ABRAMS, M. *The Condition of the British People 1911–45*, Gollancz 1946; repr. Bath, Chivers, 1970

FOREIGN POLICY

REYNOLD, P. A. *British Foreign Policy in the Interwar Years*, Longmans 1954

ROSKILL, S. W. *Naval Policy between the Wars*, vol. 1: *1919–29*; vol. 2: *1930–39*, Collins 1968, 1976

TAYLOR, A. J. P. *The Origins of the Second World War*, Hamish Hamilton 1961; rev. edn. 1963

MIDDLEMAS, K. *The Diplomacy of Illusion; the British Government and Germany 1937–39*, Weidenfeld and Nicolson 1972

ROBBINS, K. *Munich 1938*, Cassell 1968

4. Second World War

MEMOIRS

CHURCHILL, W. S. *The Second World War*, 6 vols., Cassell 1948–54

ALANBROOKE, LORD *The Turn of the Tide* and *Triumph in the West*, ed. A. Bryant, Collins 1957, 1959

SPEARS, E. L. *Assignment to Catastrophe*, 2 vols., Heinemann 1954

MACLEAN, F. *Eastern Approaches*, Cape 1949

SLIM, W. *Defeat into Victory*, Cassell 1956

NICOLSON, H. *Diaries and Letters 1939–45*, ed. N. Nicolson, Collins 1967

NOVELS

MONSARRAT, N. *The Cruel Sea*, Cassell 1951; Penguin 1970

SHAW, I. *The Young Lions*, Cape 1949; Pan 1970

WAUGH, E. *Sword of Honour* (trilogy), Chapman & Hall 1965

SECONDARY SOURCES

LIDDELL HART, B. H. *History of the Second World War*, Cassell 1970

ROSKILL, S. W. *The War at Sea*, 3 vols., HMSO 1954–61

RICHARDS, D. and SANDERS, H. ST. G. *Royal Air Force 1939–45*, 3 vols., HMSO 1953–54

PARKINSON, R. *Peace for our Time: Munich to Dunkirk—the inside story*, Hart-Davis 1972

PARKINSON, R. *Blood, Tears, Toil and Sweat: War History from Dunkirk to Alamein, based on War Cabinet Papers of 1940–42*, Hart-Davis 1973

PARKINSON, R. *A Day's March Nearer Home: War History from Alamein to VE Day, based on War Cabinet Papers of 1942–45*, Hart-Davis 1974

WILMOT, C. *The Struggle for Europe* (1952), Collins 1965

COLLIER, B. *The Defence of the United Kingdom (History of the Second World War)*, HMSO 1957

GOWING, M. M. *Britain and Atomic Energy 1939–45*, Macmillan 1965

5. *Since 1945*

MEMOIRS

ATTLEE, C. R. *As It Happened*, Heinemann 1954

BUTLER, R. A. *The Art of the Possible*, Hamish Hamilton 1971

CROSSMAN, R. *The Diaries of a Cabinet Minister, 1964–66*, Hamilton & Cape 1975

DALTON, H. *High Tide and After 1945–1960*, Muller 1963

EDEN, A. *Memoirs*, Part 2, *Full Circle*, Cassell 1960

MACMILLAN, H. *Memoirs*, 5 vols., Macmillan 1966–72

NICOLSON, H. *Diaries and Letters 1945–1962*, ed. N. Nicolson, Collins 1968

WILSON, H. *The Labour Government 1964–1970: a personal record*, Michael Joseph 1971

SECONDARY SOURCES

COLE, G. D. H. *The Post-war Condition of Britain*, Routledge 1956

SHONFIELD, A. *British Economic Policy since the War*, Penguin 1958

WORSWICK, G. D. N. and ADY, P. H. *The British Economy 1945–50*, Oxford University Press 1952

WORSWICK, G. D. N. and ADY, P. H. *The British Economy in the 1950s*, Oxford University Press 1962

GREGG, P. *The Welfare State*, Harrap 1967

HOPKINS, H. *The New Look*, Secker and Warburg 1963

SAMPSON, A. *Anatomy of Britain*, Hodder and Stoughton 1962

PROUDFOOT, M. *British Politics and Government 1951–1970*, Faber 1974

SISSONS, M. and FRENCH, P. eds. *Age of Austerity 1945–1951*, Hodder and Stoughton 1963; Penguin 1964

BOGDANOV, V. and SKIDELSKY, R. eds. *The Age of Affluence 1951–1964*, Macmillan 1970

WOODHOUSE, C. M. *British Foreign Policy since the Second World War*, Hutchinson 1961

THOMAS, H. *The Suez Affair*, Weidenfeld and Nicolson 1967; Penguin 1970

INDEX

Dates after sovereigns refer to their reigns. Acts of Parliament, parliamentary elections, trade unions and treaties are listed together alphabetically.